HOW NOT TO SUMMON A
DEMON LORD

7

Story
YUKIYA MURASAKI

Art
NAOTO FUKUDA

Character Design
TAKAHIRO TSURUSAKI

HOW NOT TO SUMMON A DEMON LORD

CHARACTERS

INTRODUCTIONS

Race: Demon
Level: 150

A self-proclaimed Demon Lord from another world.

Thanks to "Magic Deflection," an effect of the Demon Lord's Ring that he received in-game, Rem and Shera were stuck with Enslavement Collars instead of him when they attempted an Enslavement Ritual. In the real world, Diablo was unpopular, didn't have a way with words, and couldn't interact with other people to save his life. But in this world, he's tall, handsome, and practically invincible! He still doesn't have a way with words, but he manages to make it through tough situations by acting like a Demon Lord.

Diablo (Sakamoto Takuma)

STORY

Takuma Sakamoto is an elite gamer in the fantasy MMORPG *Cross Reverie*. He is so overwhelmingly strong that he is known as the "Demon Lord." One day, he is summoned to another world practically identical to the game by two girls: Shera, an Elf, and Rem, a Pantherian. Thanks to a pair of Enslavement Collars, Takuma Sakamoto—now Diablo—has control over the girls…but he really sucks at talking to other people!! To hide this, Diablo begins behaving like his Demon Lord persona from the game. While demonstrating his power, built up through skills he acquired by playing *Cross Reverie*, Diablo sets out on an adventure with Shera and Rem.

After the Fallen, Edelgard, told them about a ritual to release the Demon Lord living inside Rem, the strong-willed Pantherian decided to face her destiny. Diablo poured his magic energy into her, completing the ritual, and the Demon Lord was resurrected—but it turns out she's a biscuit-loving little girl!

Apparently, she has no desire to destroy the races, so Diablo decides to take her to Faltra with them…

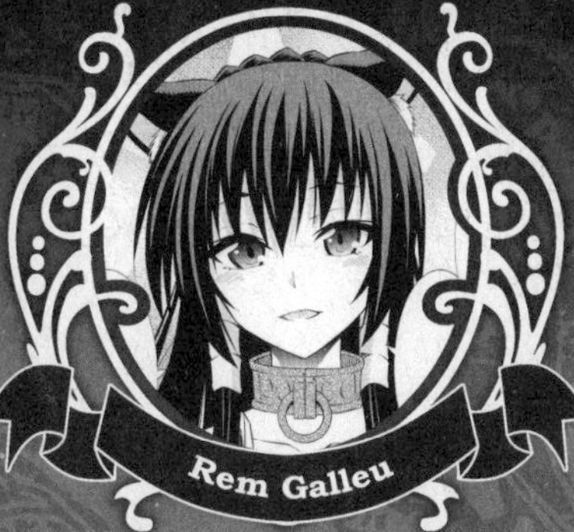
Rem Galleu

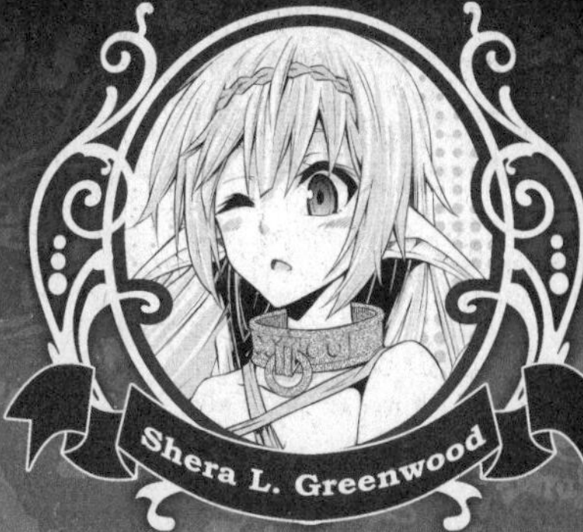
Shera L. Greenwood

Race: Pantherian Level: 40
A Summoner and an Adventurer. She has a small, catlike body with fluffy ears and a tail. She's also flat as a board. When Diablo poured his magic into her, the soul of the Demon Lord Krebskulm sealed within her was finally released. She's at a loss about what to do with Klem, the strange Demon Lord who appeared as a result of the ritual.

Race: Elf Level: 30
A Summoner, she is an expert archer, as one would expect of an Elf. She is slender and elegant, but also has an impressively large bosom that is at odds with the rest of her body. Her innocent and naive personality calms everyone around her. She's actually the princess of the Kingdom of Greenwood, but has left home in order to live freely.

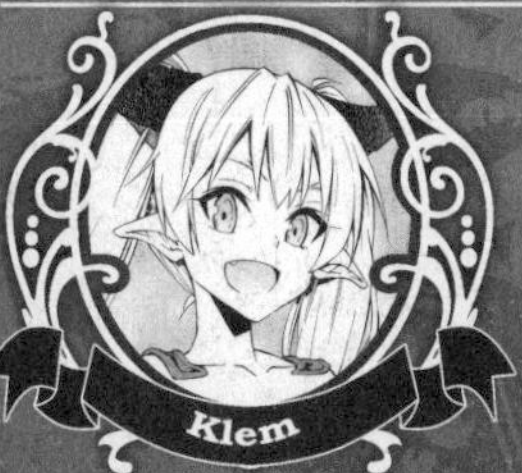
Klem

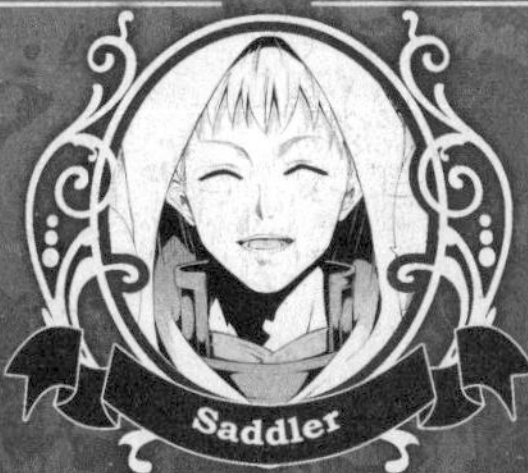
Saddler

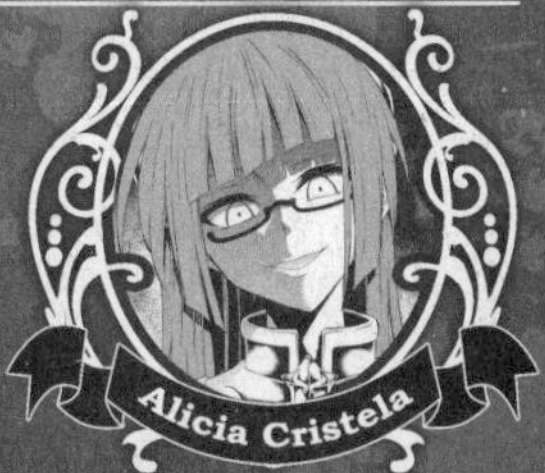
Alicia Cristela

A being in the shape of a little girl, who appeared after the Demon Lord's soul inside Rem was released during a less-than-perfect resurrection. Doesn't seem to want to destroy the races. Passionately loves biscuits.

Race: Human.
A Paladin working under the Church, a powerful organization in this world. Paladins are said to enact the will of the gods through force, but they brutally torture and murder suspected Demon Lord worshippers under the pretense of "salvation."

Race: Human.
An Imperial Knight, she is under the direct control of the King himself. Dispatched from the Royal Capital to assist in solving the problems with the Kingdom of Greenwood. Extremely good with communication. In reality, she's lost faith in the races, and seeks to resurrect the Demon Lord.

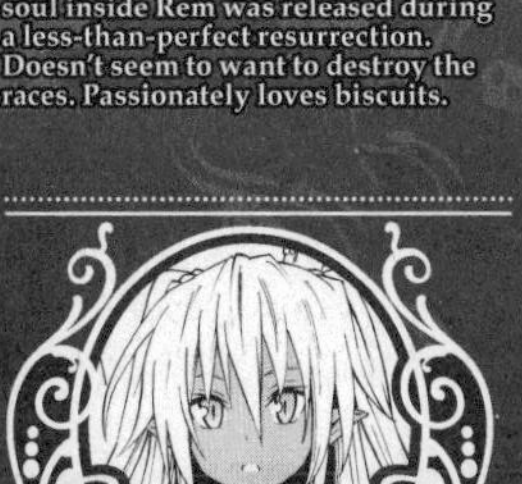
Edelgard

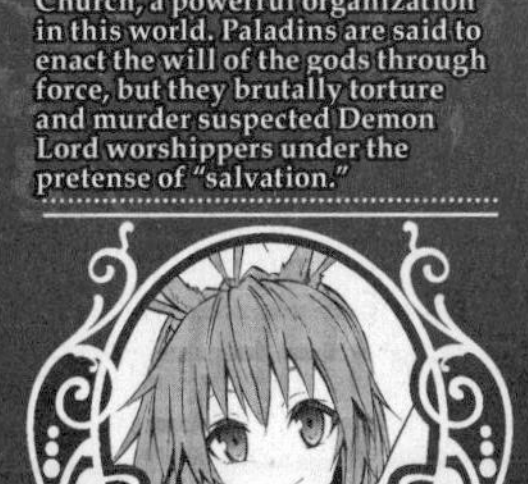
Sylvie

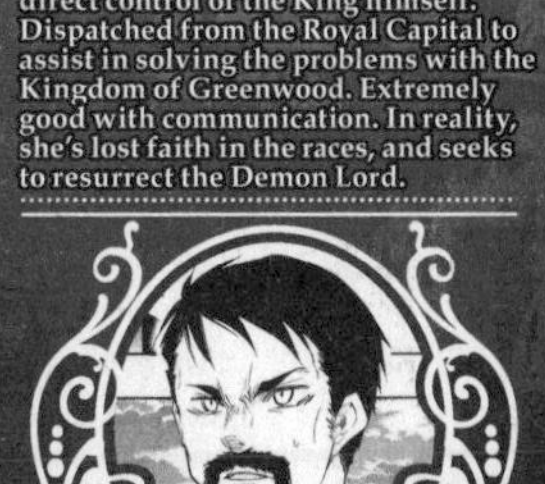
Chester Ray Galford

The Fallen who fought Diablo in the battle on the Bridge of Ulug. She is strong enough to withstand a direct hit from Diablo's ultimate spell and survive. She is an acquaintance of Alicia, a Demon Lord worshipper.

Race: Grasswalker

Guildmaster of the Adventurer's Guild in Faltra. Assists Diablo and the others, but finds dealing with them tricky at times.

Race: Human Level: Over 100

The governor of the Stronghold City of Faltra. Faced off against Diablo during the Kingdom of Greenwood incident.

HOW NOT TO SUMMON A DEMON LORD

7

CONTENTS

30 GOING TO A CAFÉ I

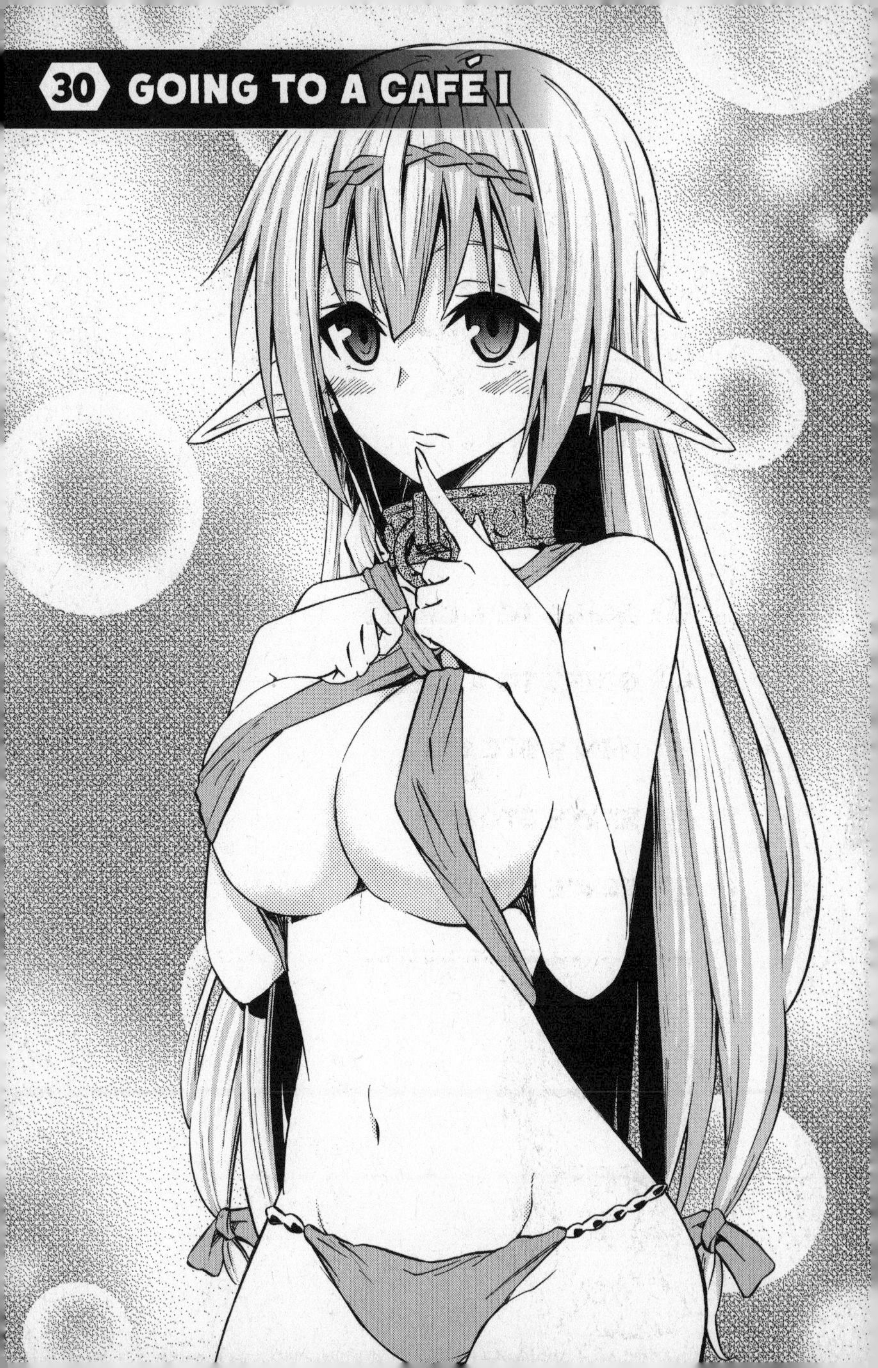

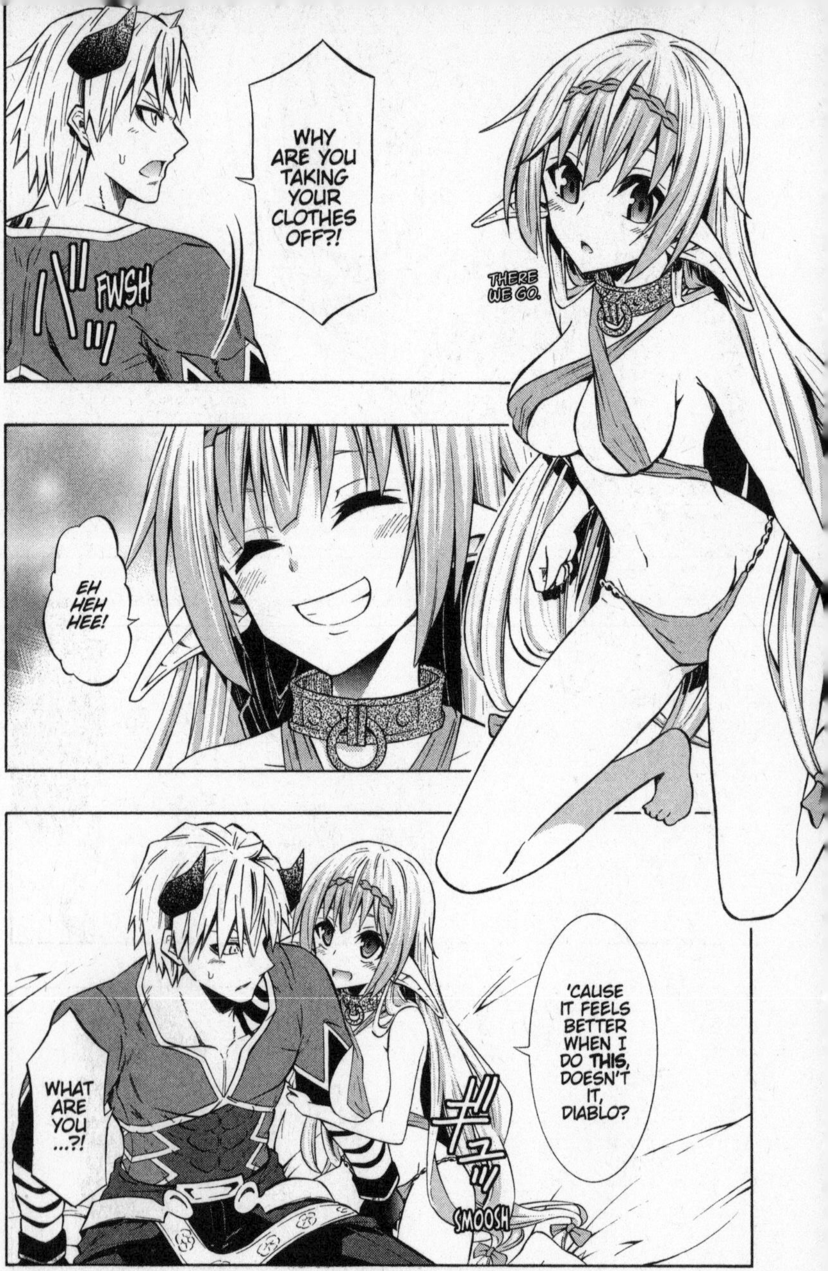
THERE WE GO.
WHY ARE YOU TAKING YOUR CLOTHES OFF?!
FWSH
EH HEH HEE!
'CAUSE IT FEELS BETTER WHEN I DO THIS, DOESN'T IT, DIABLO?
SMOOSH
WHAT ARE YOU ...?!

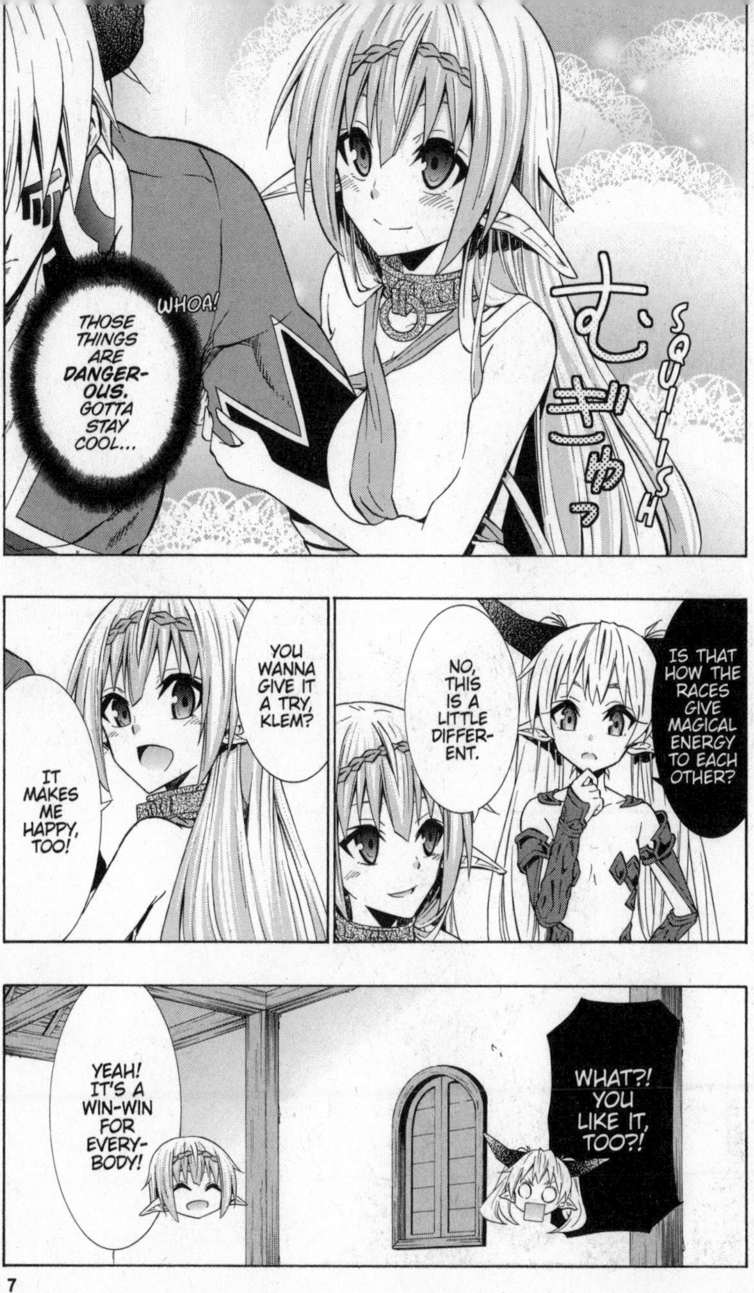
むぎゅっ
SQUIISH
WHOA!
THOSE THINGS ARE DANGEROUS. GOTTA STAY COOL...
IS THAT HOW THE RACES GIVE MAGICAL ENERGY TO EACH OTHER?
NO, THIS IS A LITTLE DIFFERENT.
YOU WANNA GIVE IT A TRY, KLEM?
IT MAKES ME HAPPY, TOO!
WHAT?! YOU LIKE IT, TOO?!
YEAH! IT'S A WIN-WIN FOR EVERYBODY!

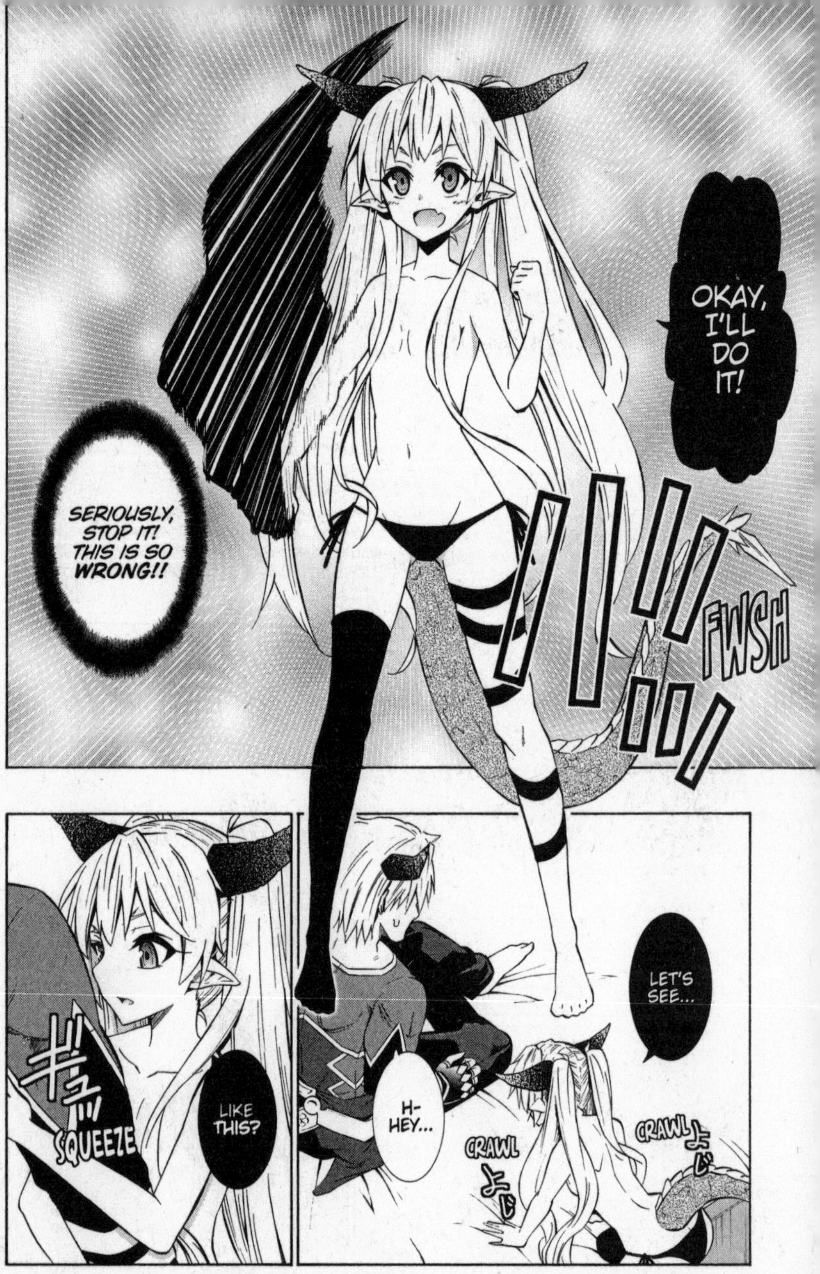
OKAY, I'LL DO IT!
SERIOUSLY, STOP IT! THIS IS SO WRONG!!
FWSH
LET'S SEE...
CRAWL
CRAWL
H-HEY...
LIKE THIS?
SQUEEZE

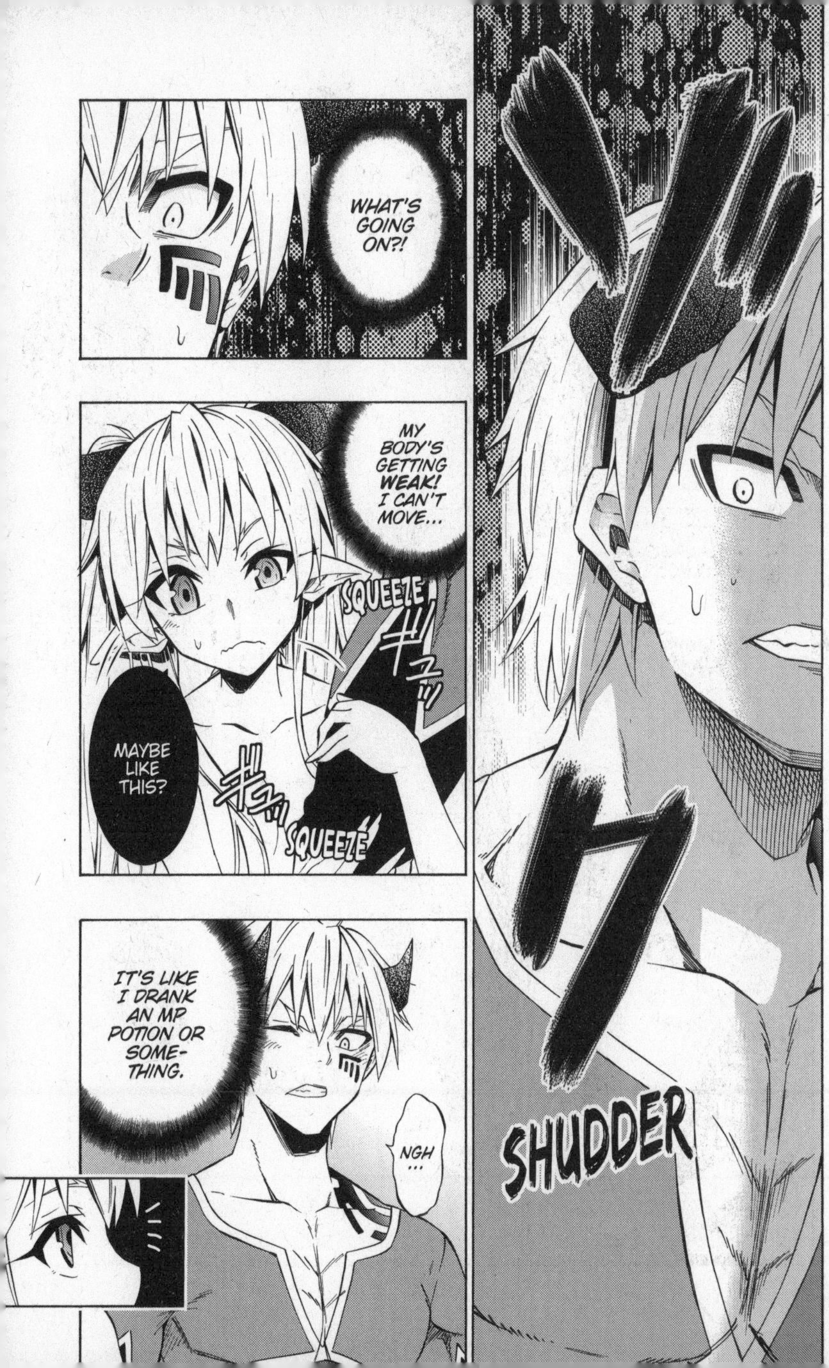
SHUDDER
WHAT'S GOING ON?!
MY BODY'S GETTING WEAK! I CAN'T MOVE...
SQUEEZE
MAYBE LIKE THIS?
SQUEEZE
IT'S LIKE I DRANK AN MP POTION OR SOME-THING.
NGH...

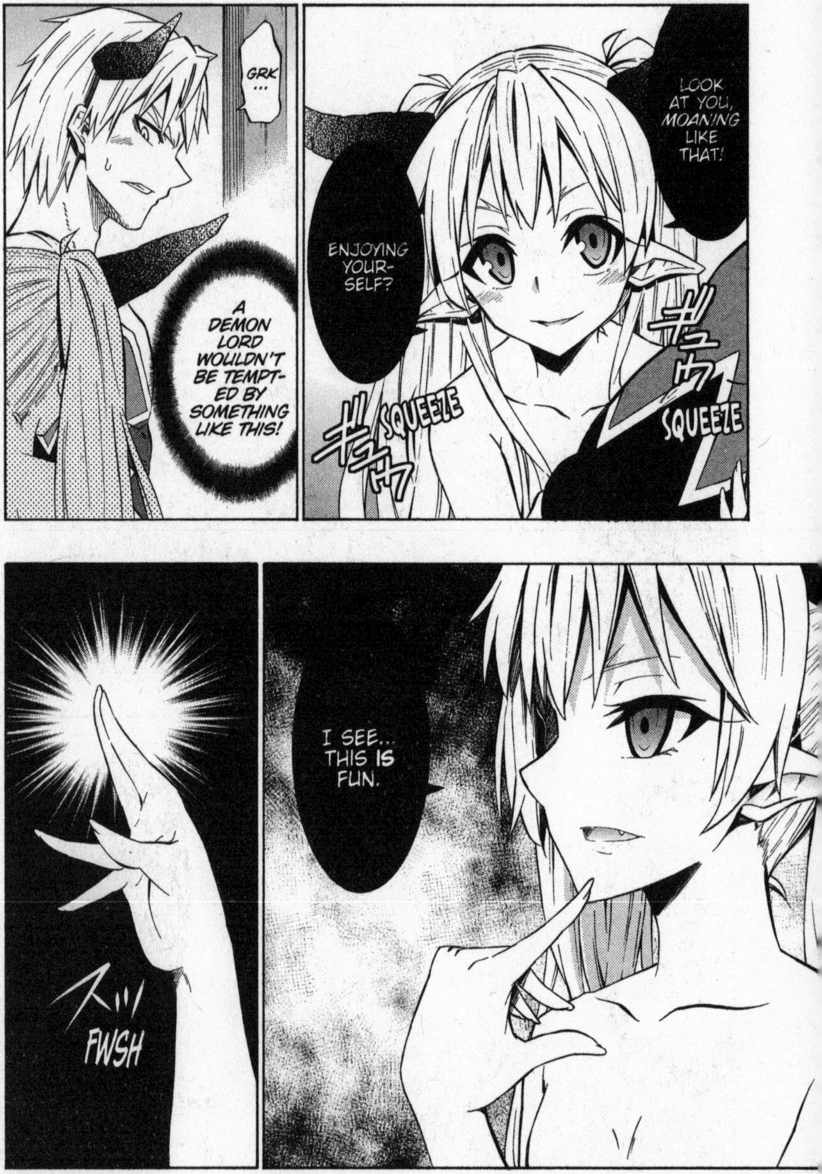
LOOK AT YOU, MOANING LIKE THAT!
ENJOYING YOUR-SELF?
ギュウ
SQUEEZE
ギュウ
SQUEEZE
GRK ...
A DEMON LORD WOULDN'T BE TEMPT-ED BY SOMETHING LIKE THIS!
I SEE... THIS IS FUN.
スッ
FWSH

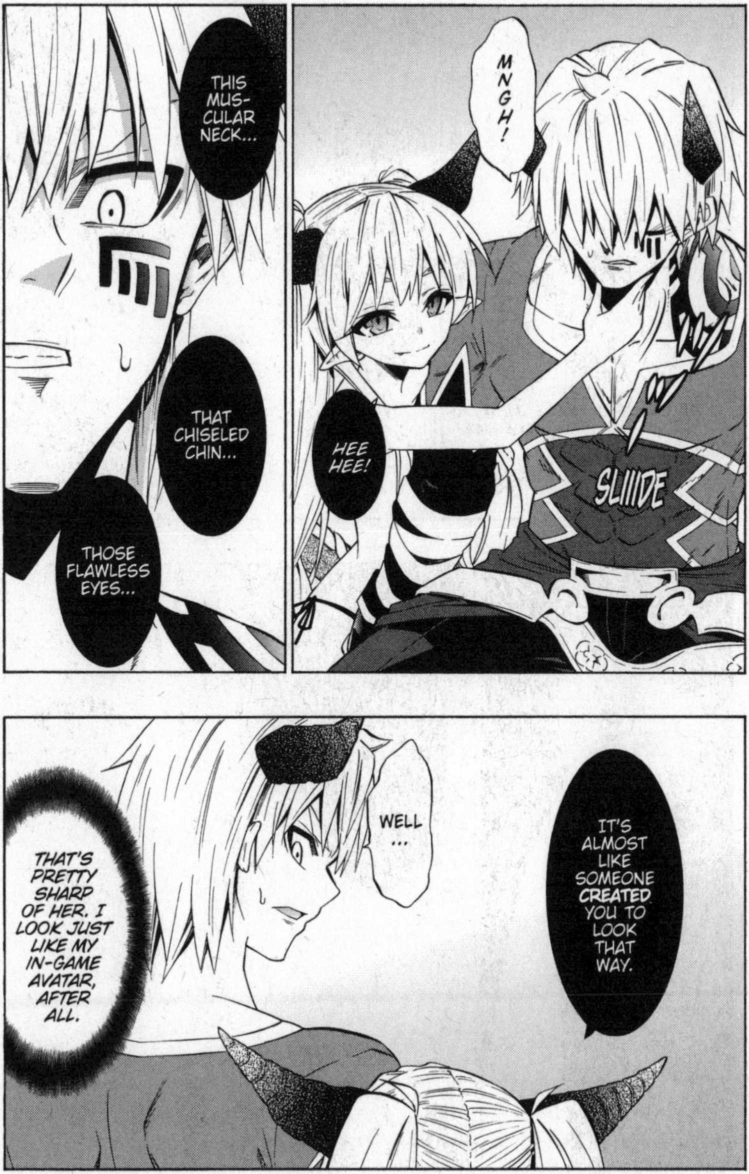
MNGH!
HEE HEE!
SLIIIDE
THIS MUS-CULAR NECK...
THAT CHISELED CHIN...
THOSE FLAWLESS EYES...
IT'S ALMOST LIKE SOMEONE **CREATED** YOU TO LOOK THAT WAY.
WELL ...
THAT'S PRETTY SHARP OF HER. I LOOK JUST LIKE MY IN-GAME AVATAR, AFTER ALL.

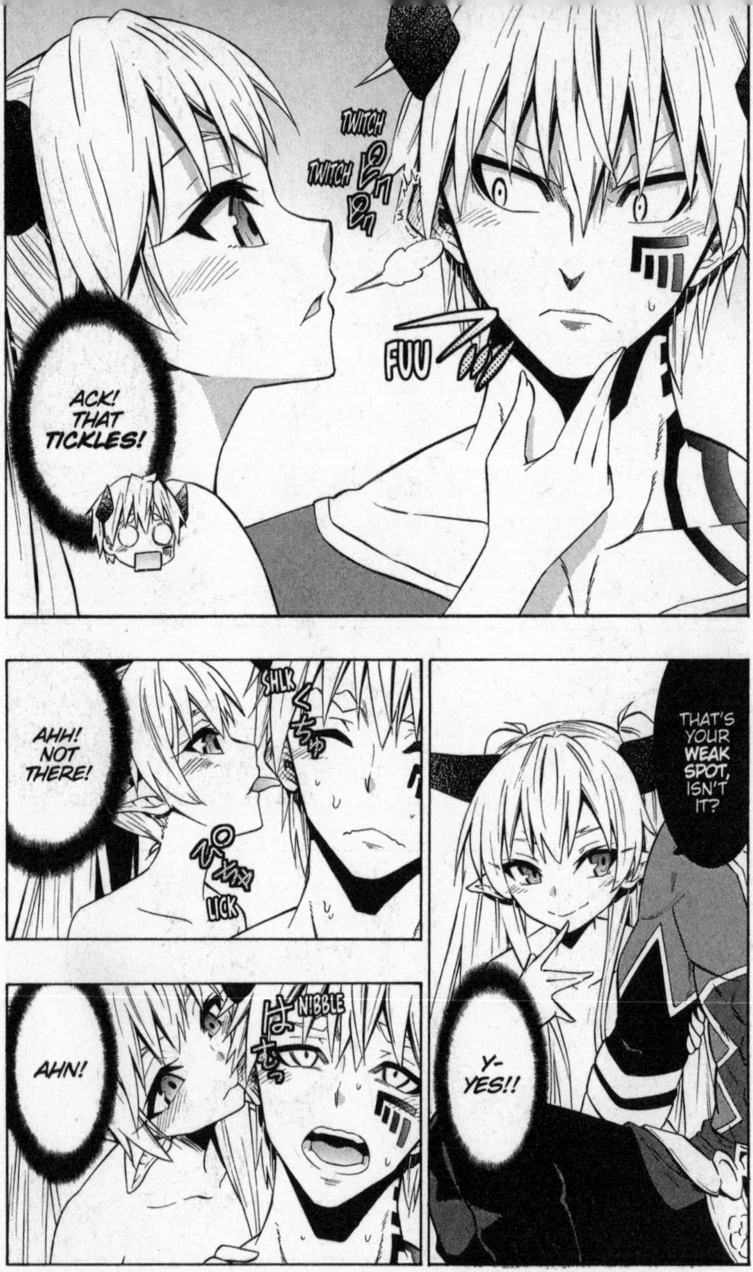
TWITCH
TWITCH
FUU
ACK! THAT TICKLES!
THAT'S YOUR WEAK SPOT, ISN'T IT?
Y-YES!!
SHLK
AHH! NOT THERE!
LICK
NIBBLE
AHN!

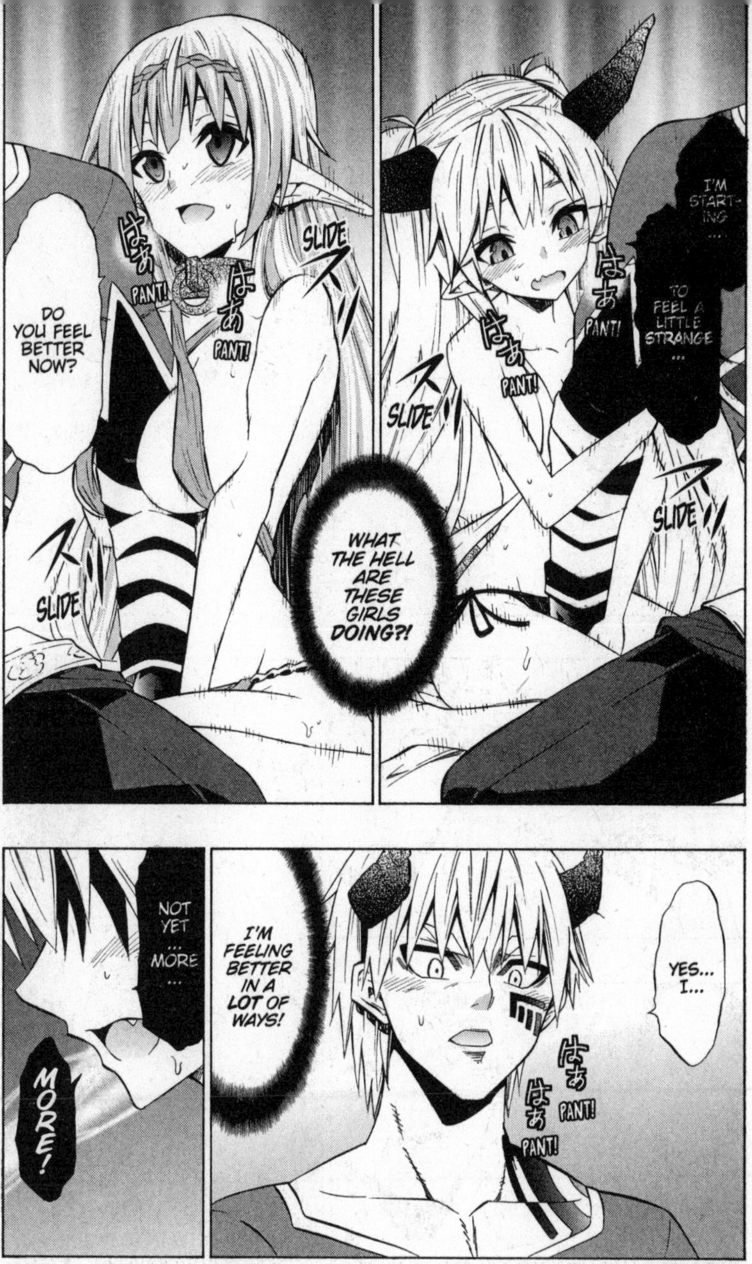
I'M STARTING... TO FEEL A LITTLE STRANGE...
はぁ PANT!
はぁ PANT!
ス SLIDE
ス SLIDE
DO YOU FEEL BETTER NOW?
はぁ PANT!
はぁ PANT!
ス SLIDE
ス SLIDE
WHAT THE HELL ARE THESE GIRLS DOING?!
YES... I...
はぁ PANT!
はぁ PANT!
I'M FEELING BETTER IN A LOT OF WAYS!
NOT YET... MORE...
MORE!

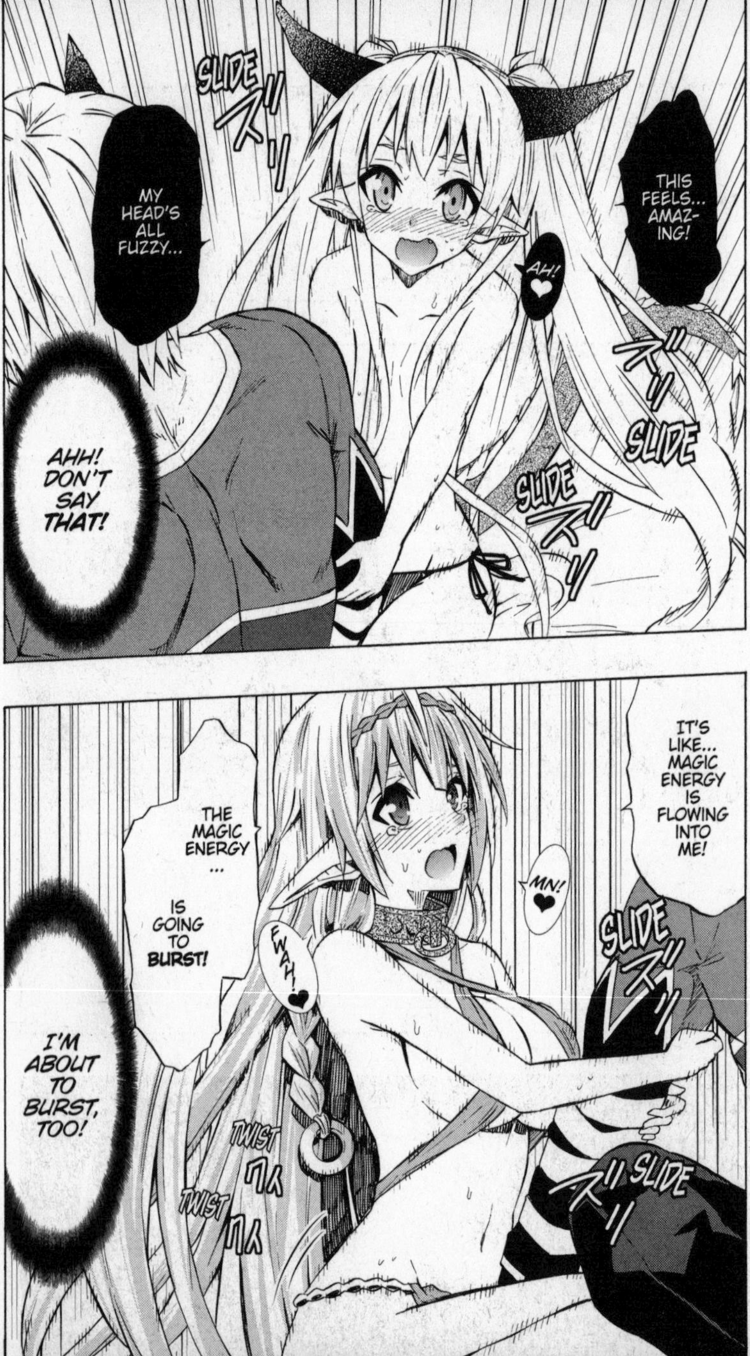
SLIDE
THIS FEELS... AMAZ-ING!
AH! ♥
MY HEAD'S ALL FUZZY...
SLIDE
SLIDE
AHH! DON'T SAY THAT!
IT'S LIKE... MAGIC ENERGY IS FLOWING INTO ME!
MN! ♥
THE MAGIC ENERGY ...
IS GOING TO BURST!
FWAH! ♥
SLIDE
I'M ABOUT TO BURST, TOO!
TWIST
TWIST
SLIDE

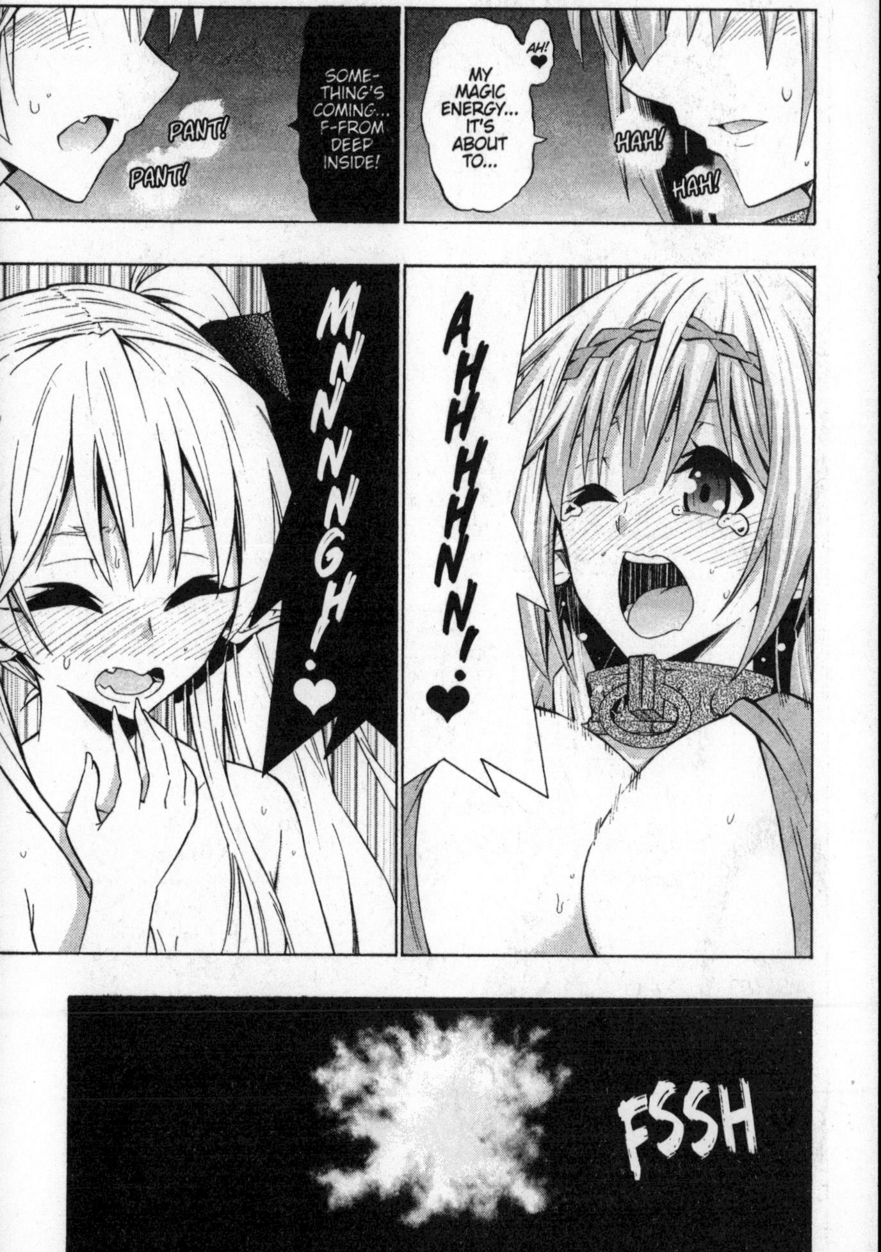
AH! ♥
MY MAGIC ENERGY... IT'S ABOUT TO...
HAH! HAH!
SOME-THING'S COMING... F-FROM DEEP INSIDE!
PANT! PANT!
AHHHHHNN! ♥
MNNNNGH! ♥
FSSH

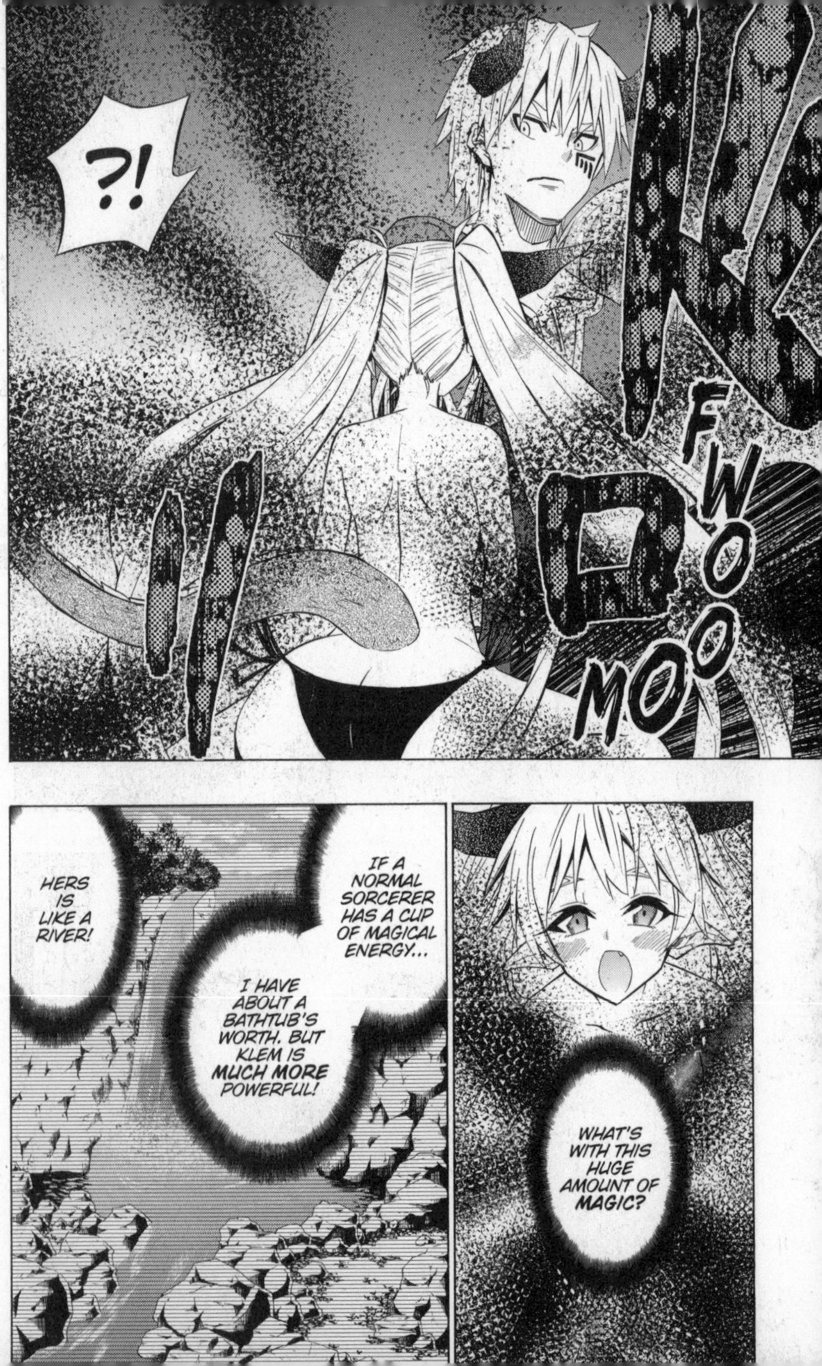
?!
FWOOOM
WHAT'S WITH THIS HUGE AMOUNT OF MAGIC?
IF A NORMAL SORCERER HAS A CUP OF MAGICAL ENERGY...
I HAVE ABOUT A BATHTUB'S WORTH. BUT KLEM IS **MUCH MORE** POWERFUL!
HERS IS LIKE A RIVER!

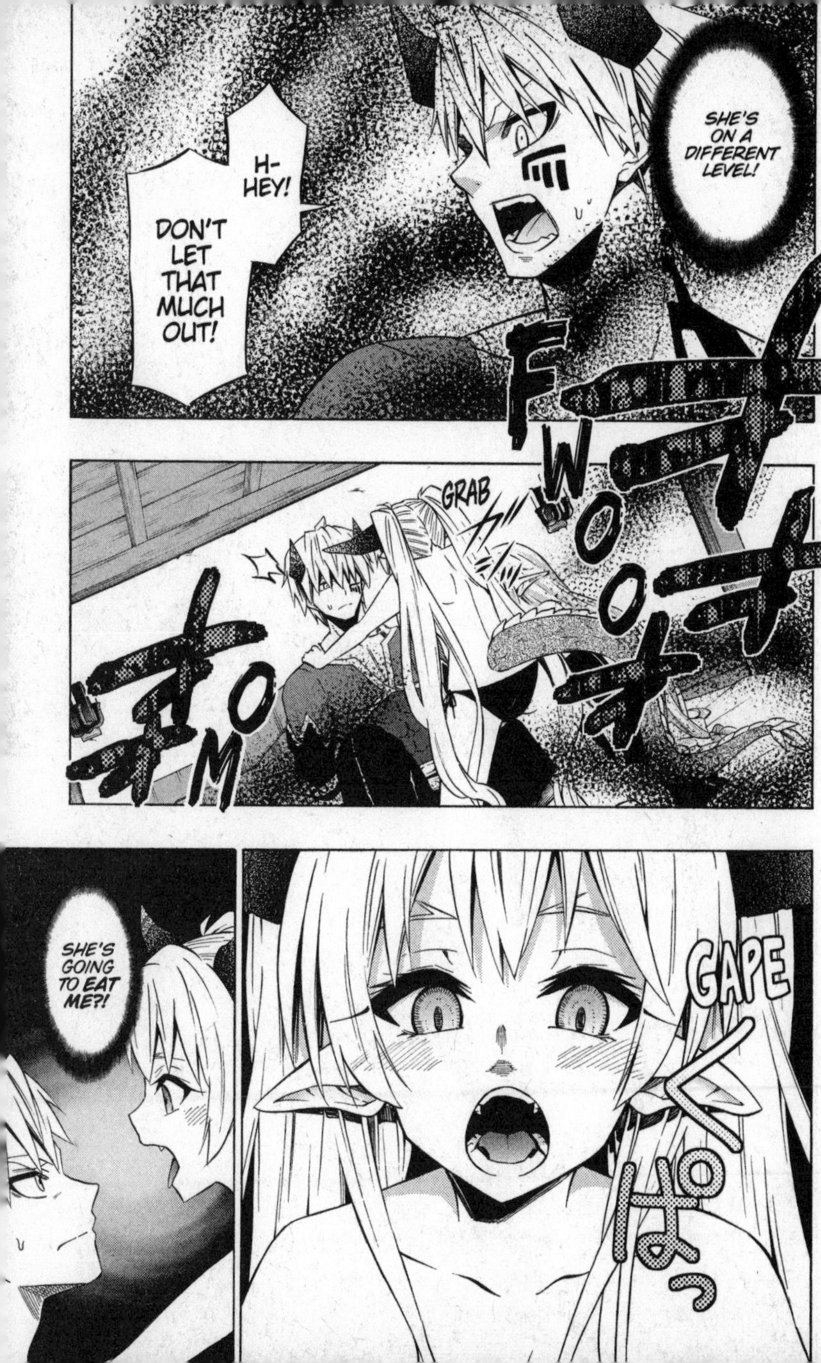
SHE'S ON A DIFFERENT LEVEL!
H-HEY!
DON'T LET THAT MUCH OUT!
FWOOOM
GRAB
GAPE
はっ
SHE'S GOING TO EAT ME?!

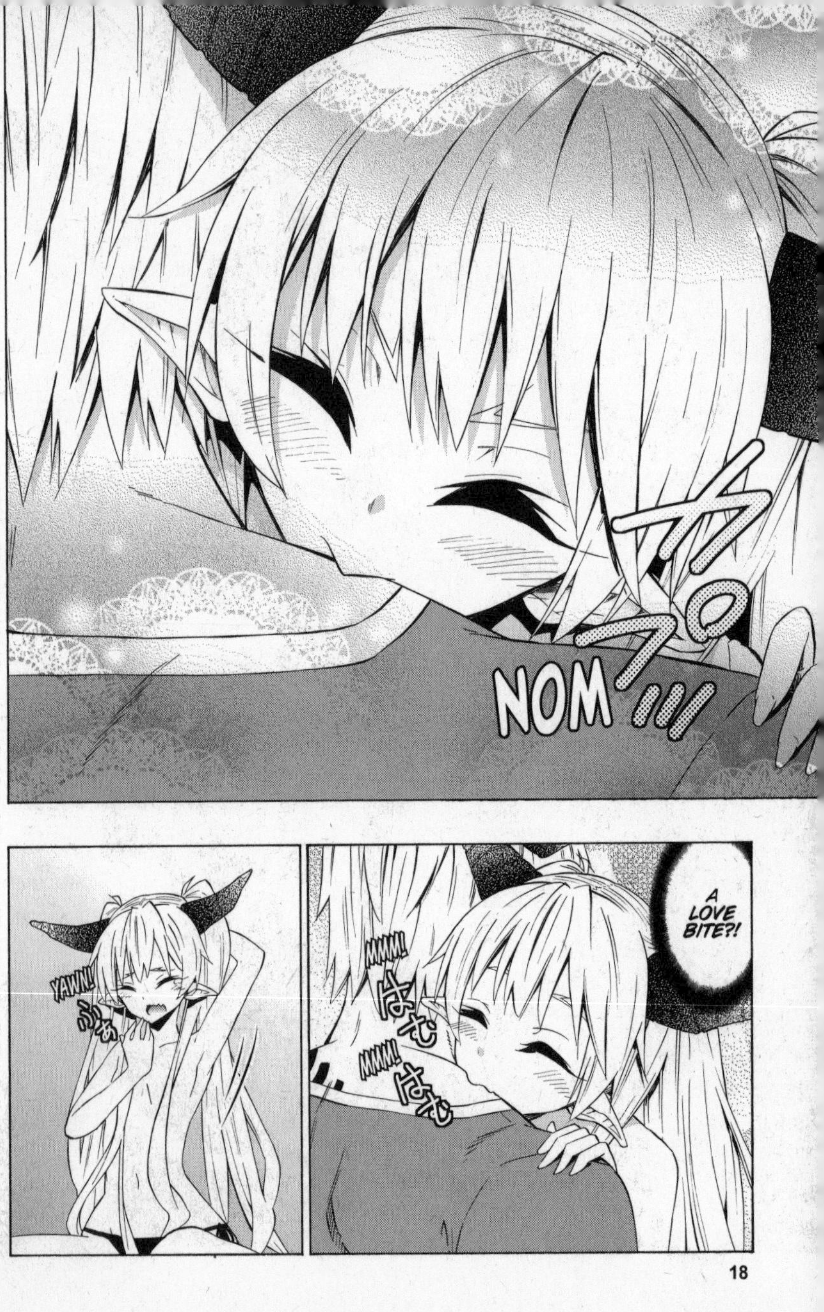
NOM
A LOVE BITE?!
MMM! はむ
MMM! はむ
YAWN! ふぁ

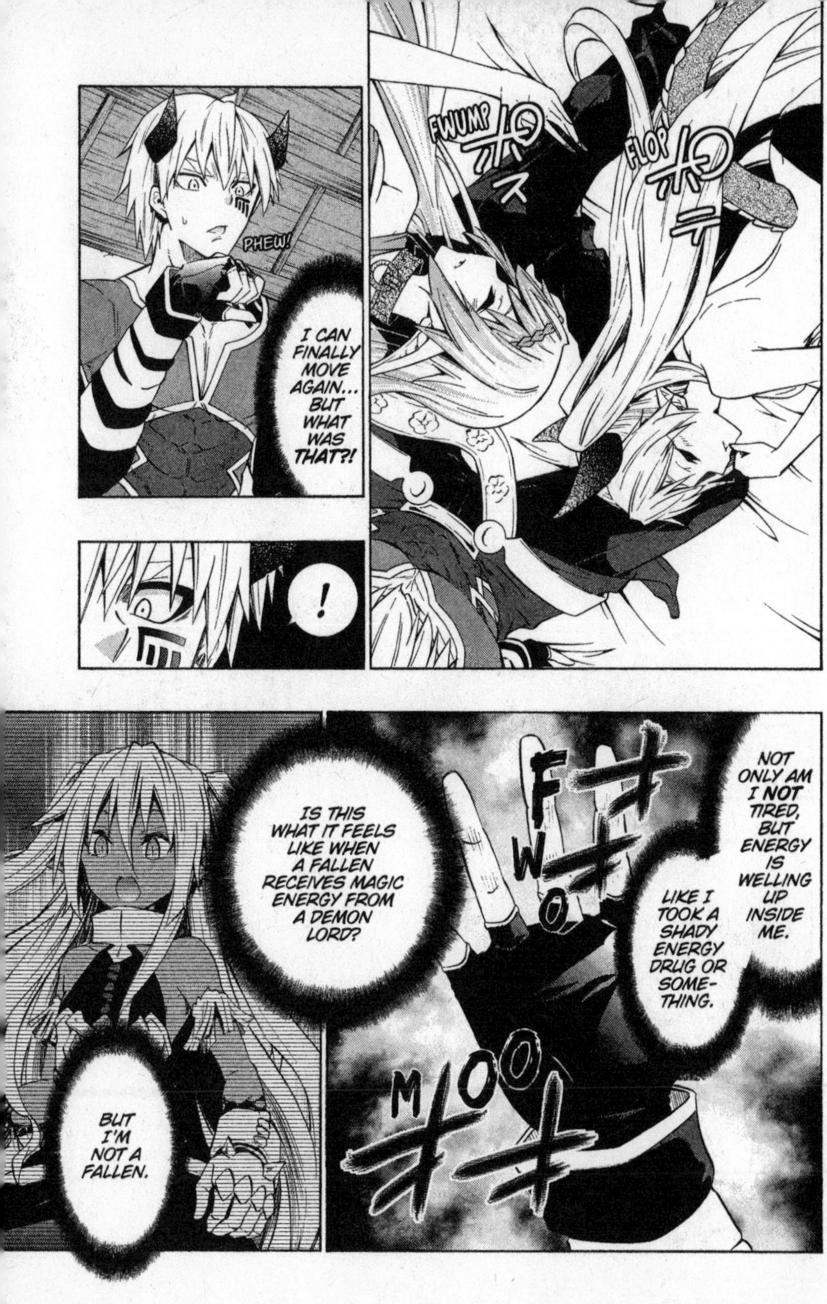
FWUMP
FLOP
PHEW!
I CAN FINALLY MOVE AGAIN... BUT WHAT WAS THAT?!
!
FWO
NOT ONLY AM I NOT TIRED, BUT ENERGY IS WELLING UP INSIDE ME.
LIKE I TOOK A SHADY ENERGY DRUG OR SOME-THING.
MOO
IS THIS WHAT IT FEELS LIKE WHEN A FALLEN RECEIVES MAGIC ENERGY FROM A DEMON LORD?
BUT I'M NOT A FALLEN.

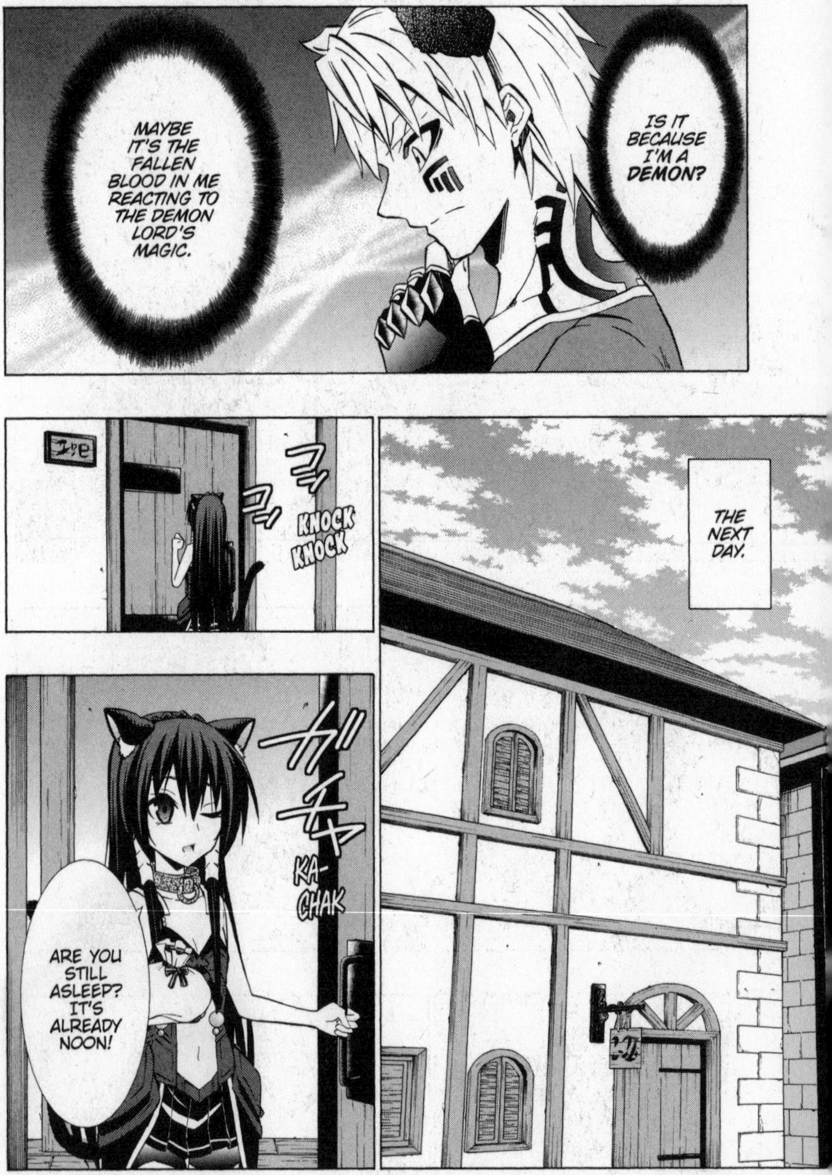
IS IT BECAUSE I'M A DEMON?
MAYBE IT'S THE FALLEN BLOOD IN ME REACTING TO THE DEMON LORD'S MAGIC.
THE NEXT DAY.
KNOCK KNOCK
KA-CHAK
ARE YOU STILL ASLEEP? IT'S ALREADY NOON!

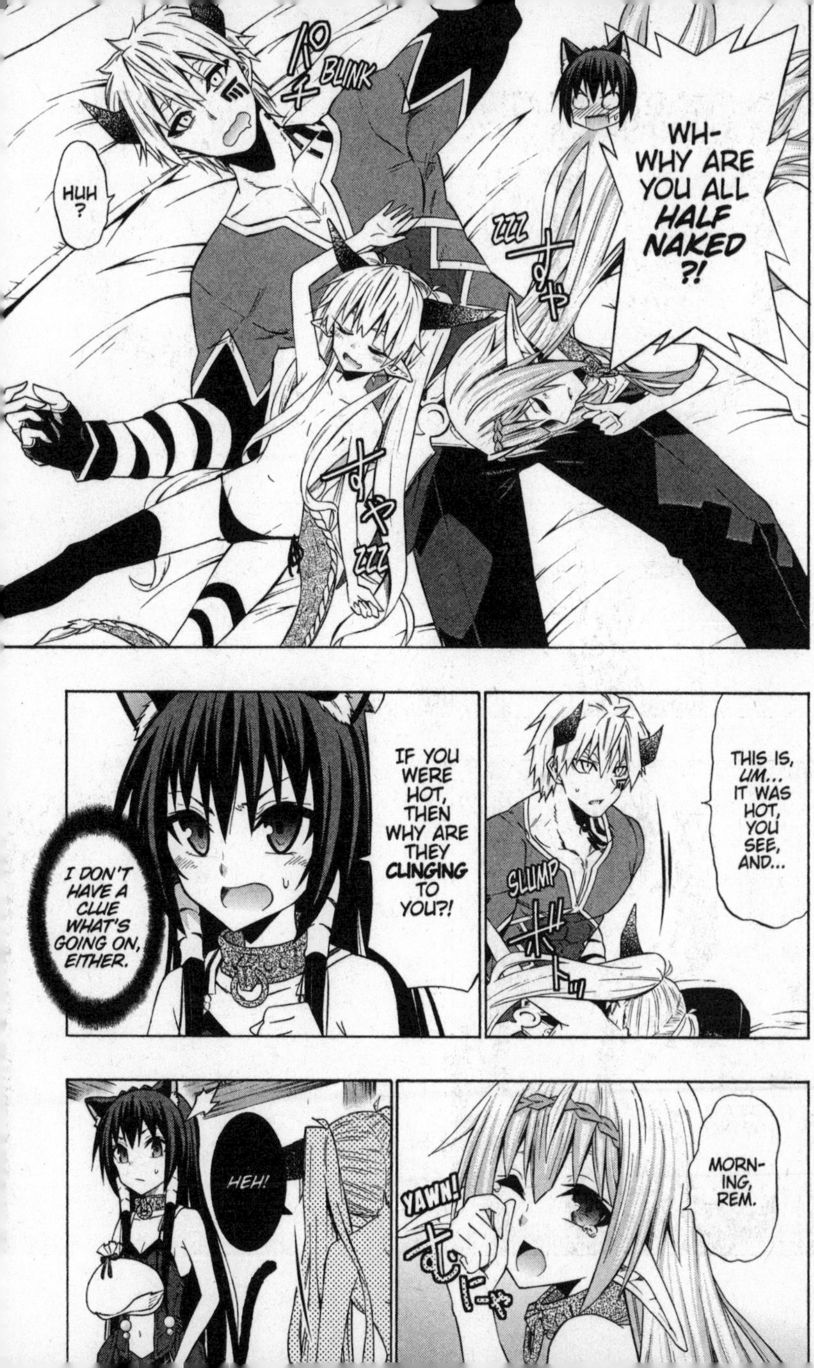
WH- WHY ARE YOU ALL HALF NAKED ?!
ZZZ
BLINK
HUH ?
ZZZ
THIS IS, UM... IT WAS HOT, YOU SEE, AND...
SLUMP
IF YOU WERE HOT, THEN WHY ARE THEY CLINGING TO YOU?!
I DON'T HAVE A CLUE WHAT'S GOING ON, EITHER.
MORNING, REM.
YAWN!
HEH!

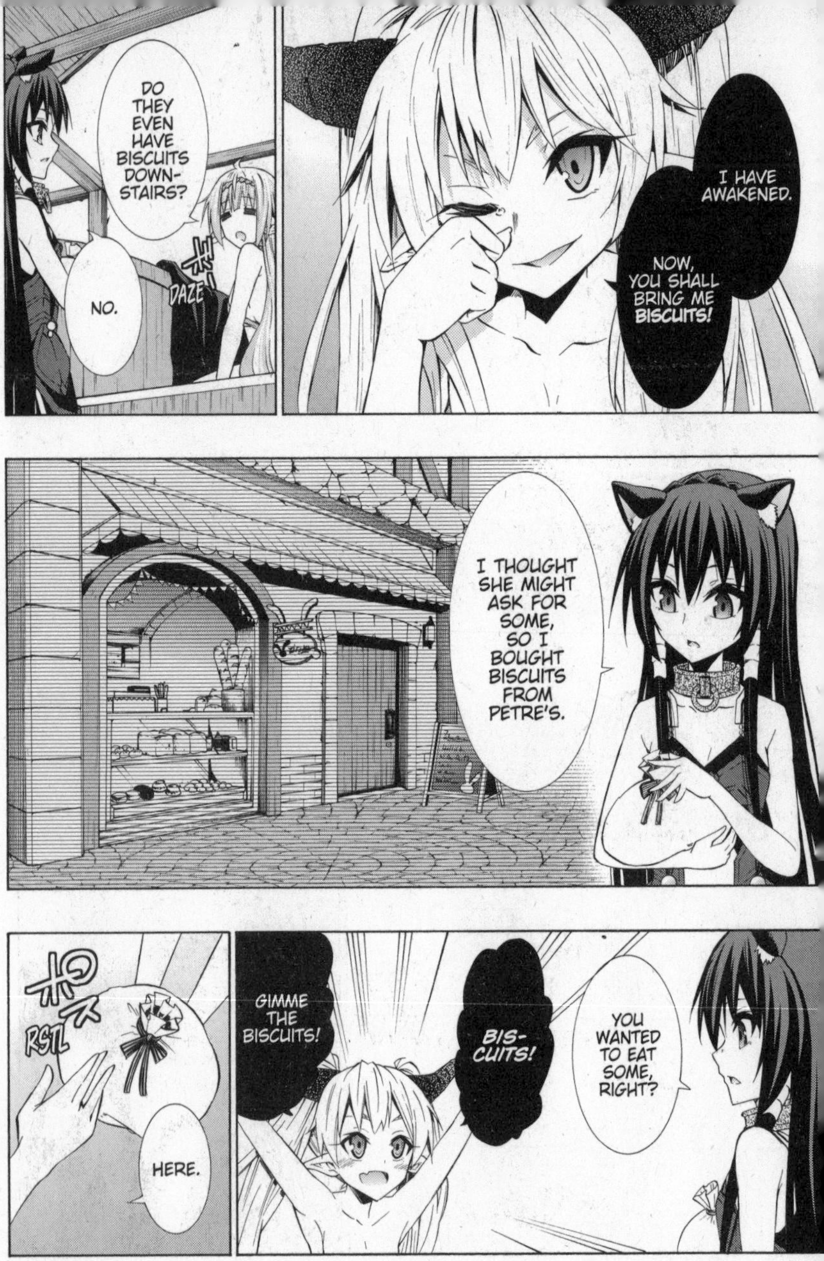
I HAVE AWAKENED.
NOW, YOU SHALL BRING ME BISCUITS!
DO THEY EVEN HAVE BISCUITS DOWN-STAIRS?
DAZE
NO.
I THOUGHT SHE MIGHT ASK FOR SOME, SO I BOUGHT BISCUITS FROM PETRE'S.
YOU WANTED TO EAT SOME, RIGHT?
BIS-CUITS!
GIMME THE BISCUITS!
RSTL
HERE.

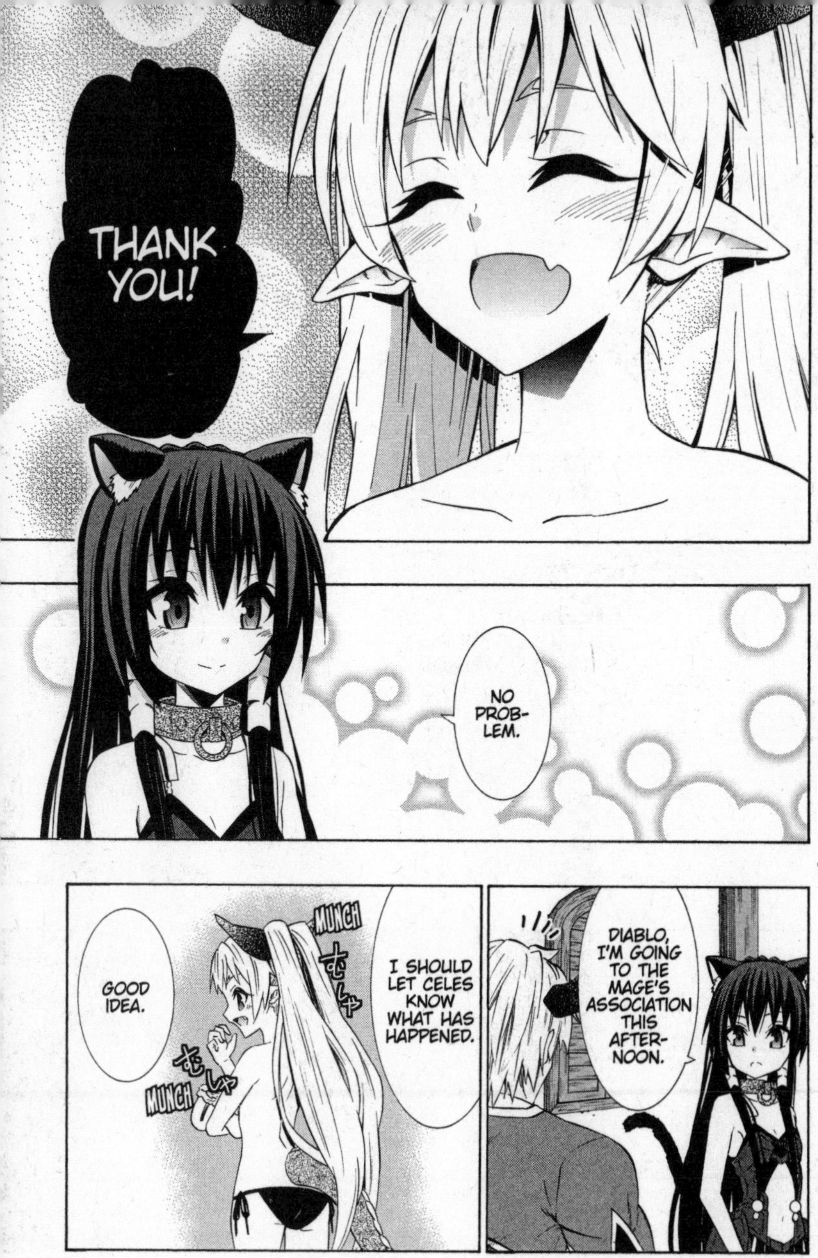
THANK YOU!
NO PROB-LEM.
DIABLO, I'M GOING TO THE MAGE'S ASSOCIATION THIS AFTER-NOON.
I SHOULD LET CELES KNOW WHAT HAS HAPPENED.
MUNCH
むしゃ
GOOD IDEA.
むしゃ
MUNCH

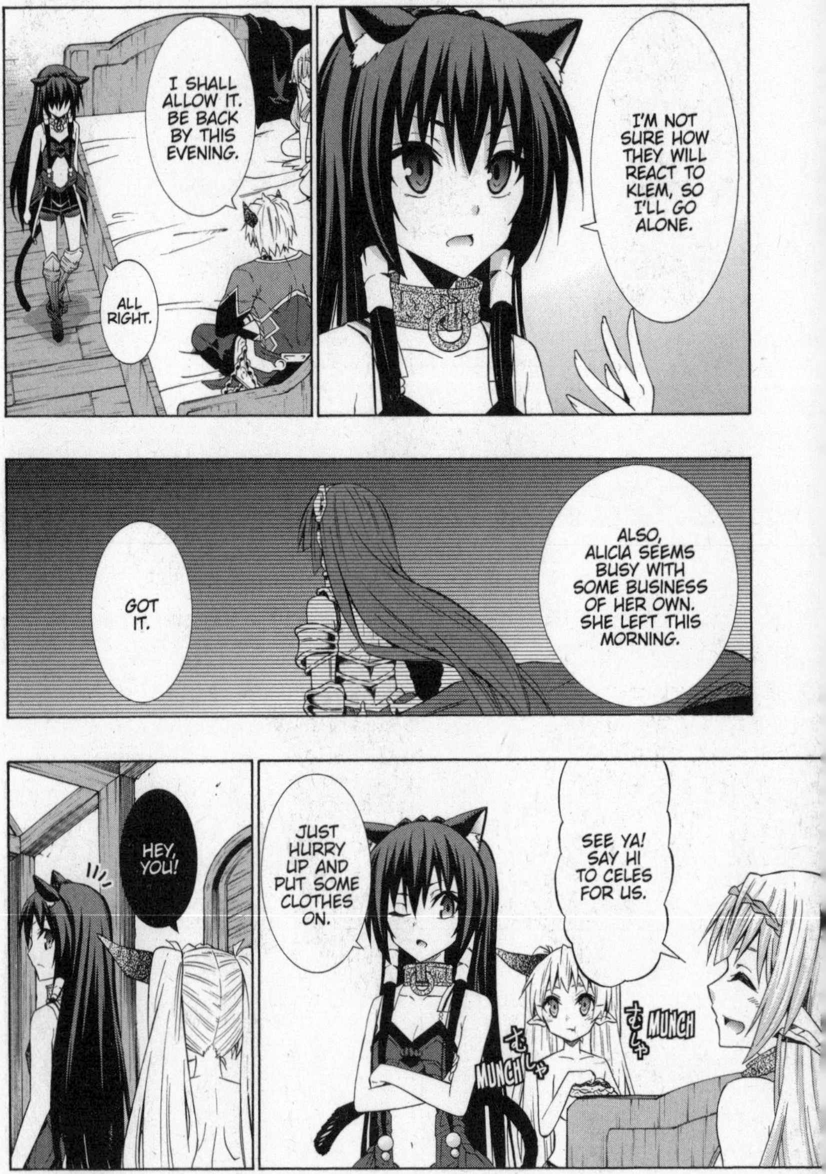
I'M NOT SURE HOW THEY WILL REACT TO KLEM, SO I'LL GO ALONE.
I SHALL ALLOW IT. BE BACK BY THIS EVENING.
ALL RIGHT.
ALSO, ALICIA SEEMS BUSY WITH SOME BUSINESS OF HER OWN. SHE LEFT THIS MORNING.
GOT IT.
SEE YA! SAY HI TO CELES FOR US.
JUST HURRY UP AND PUT SOME CLOTHES ON.
むしゃ MUNCH
むしゃ MUNCH
HEY, YOU!

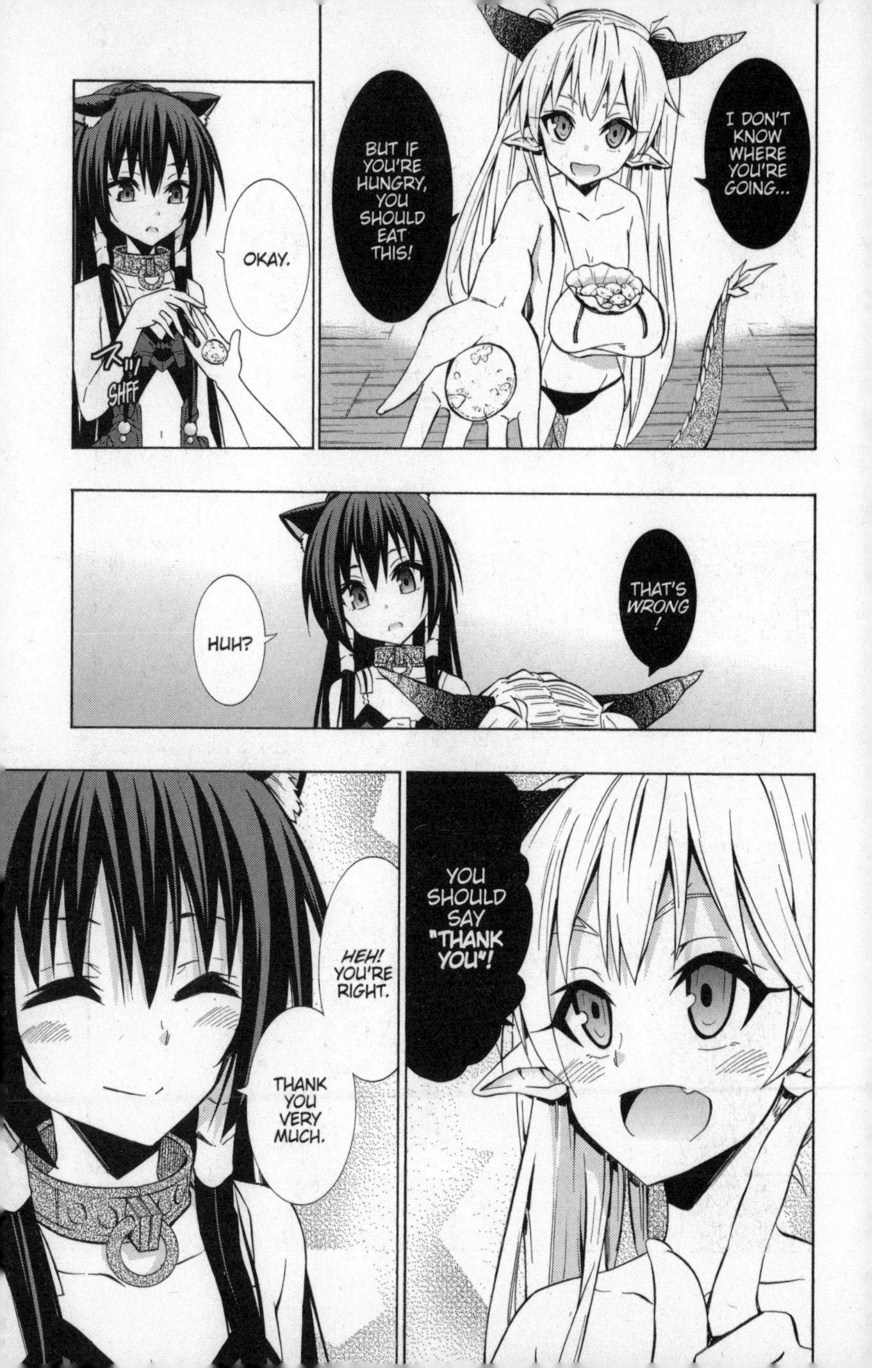
I DON'T KNOW WHERE YOU'RE GOING...
BUT IF YOU'RE HUNGRY, YOU SHOULD EAT THIS!
OKAY.
SHFF
THAT'S WRONG!
HUH?
YOU SHOULD SAY "THANK YOU"!
HEH! YOU'RE RIGHT.
THANK YOU VERY MUCH.

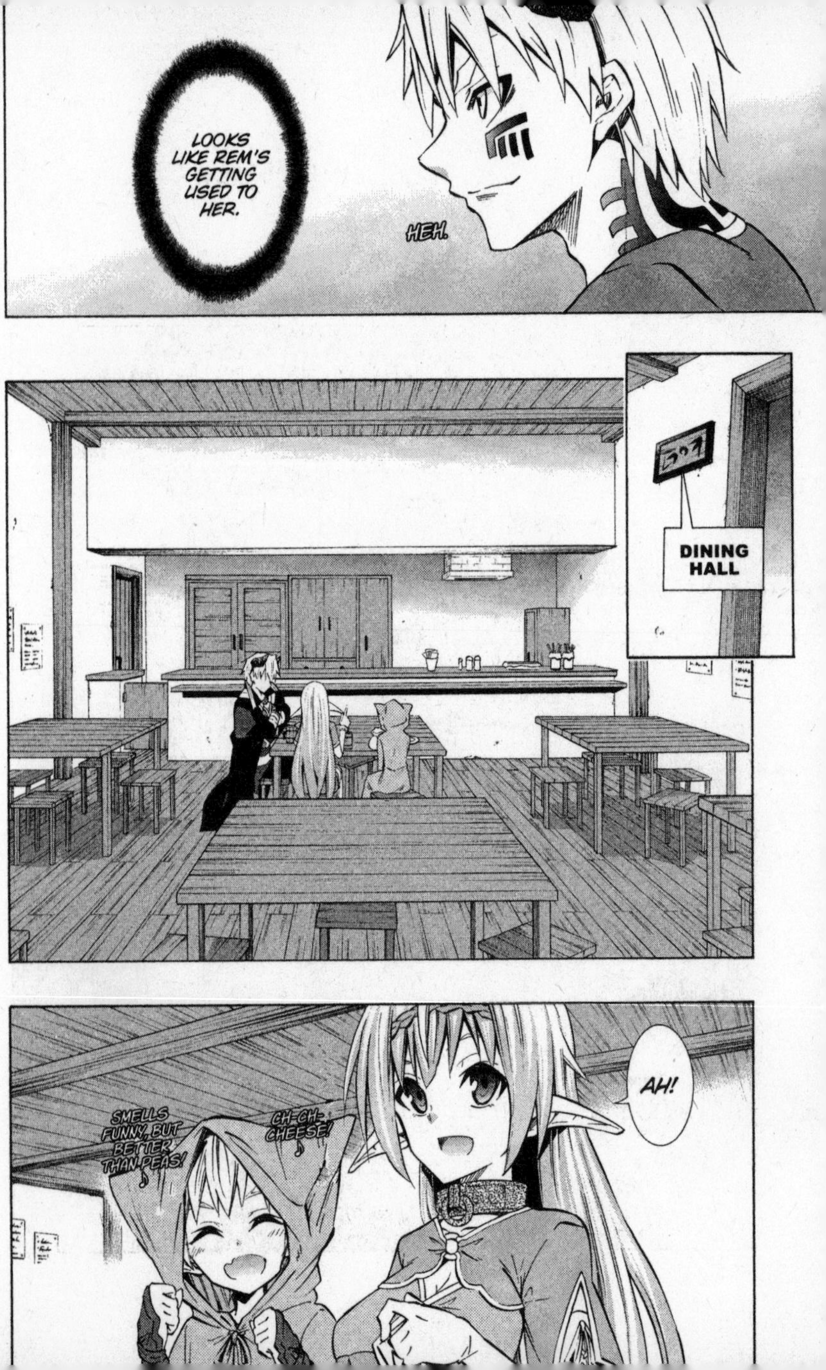
LOOKS LIKE REM'S GETTING USED TO HER.
HEH.
DINING HALL
AH!
CH-CH-CHEESE!
SMELLS FUNNY, BUT BETTER THAN PEAS!

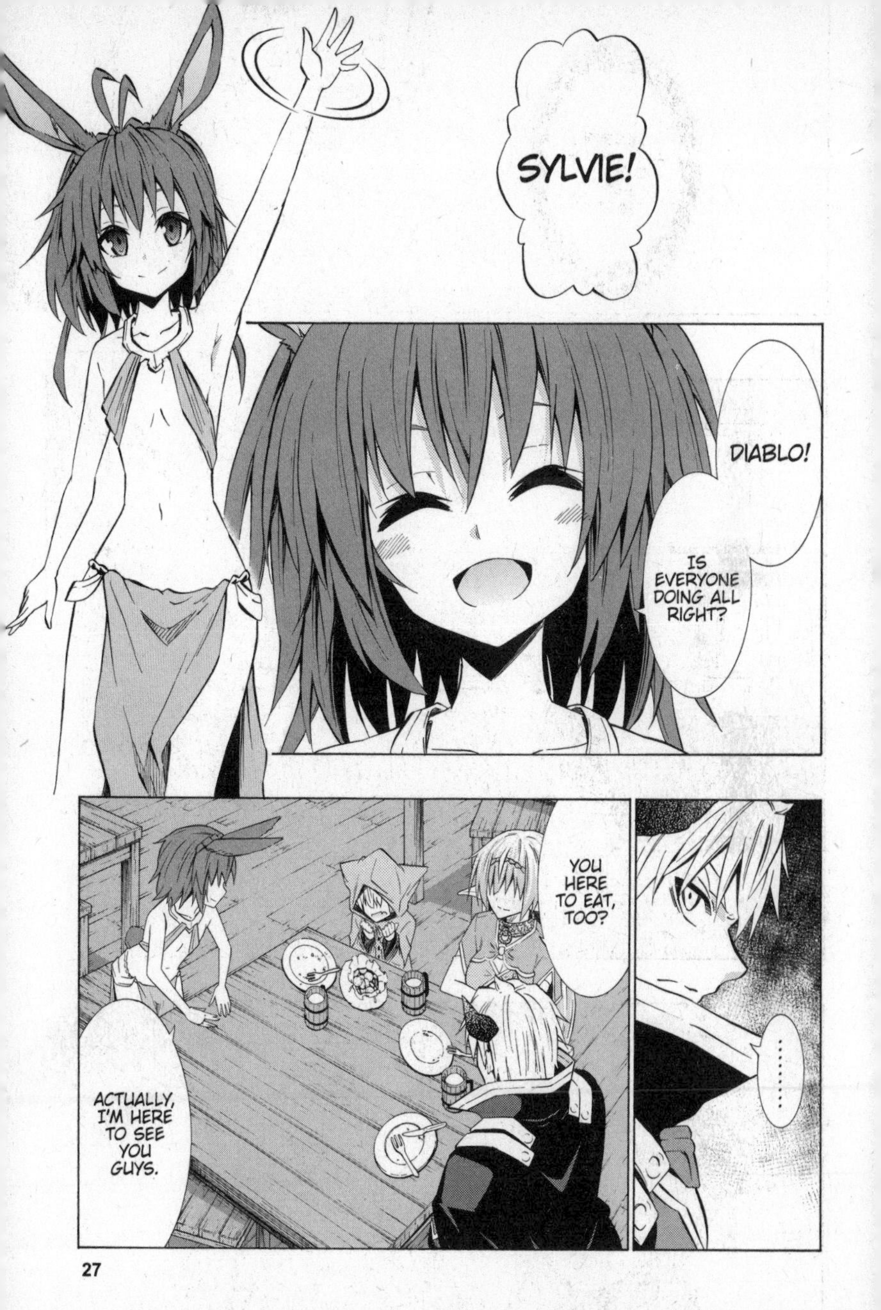
SYLVIE!
DIABLO!
IS EVERYONE DOING ALL RIGHT?
......
YOU HERE TO EAT, TOO?
ACTUALLY, I'M HERE TO SEE YOU GUYS.

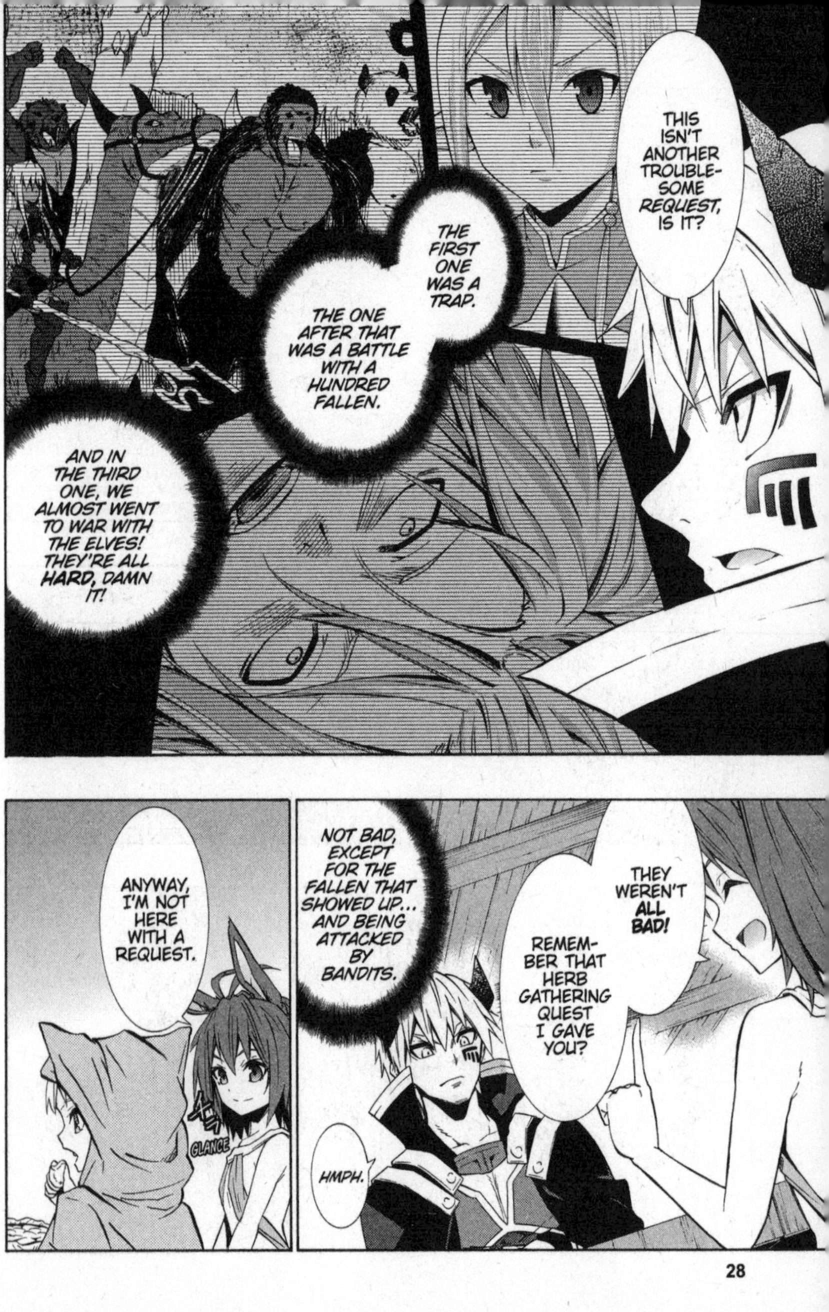
THIS ISN'T ANOTHER TROUBLE-SOME REQUEST, IS IT?
THE FIRST ONE WAS A TRAP.
THE ONE AFTER THAT WAS A BATTLE WITH A HUNDRED FALLEN.
AND IN THE THIRD ONE, WE ALMOST WENT TO WAR WITH THE ELVES! THEY'RE ALL **HARD**, DAMN IT!
THEY WEREN'T **ALL** BAD!
REMEM-BER THAT HERB GATHERING QUEST I GAVE YOU?
NOT BAD, EXCEPT FOR THE FALLEN THAT SHOWED UP... AND BEING ATTACKED BY BANDITS.
HMPH.
ANYWAY, I'M NOT HERE WITH A REQUEST.
GLANCE

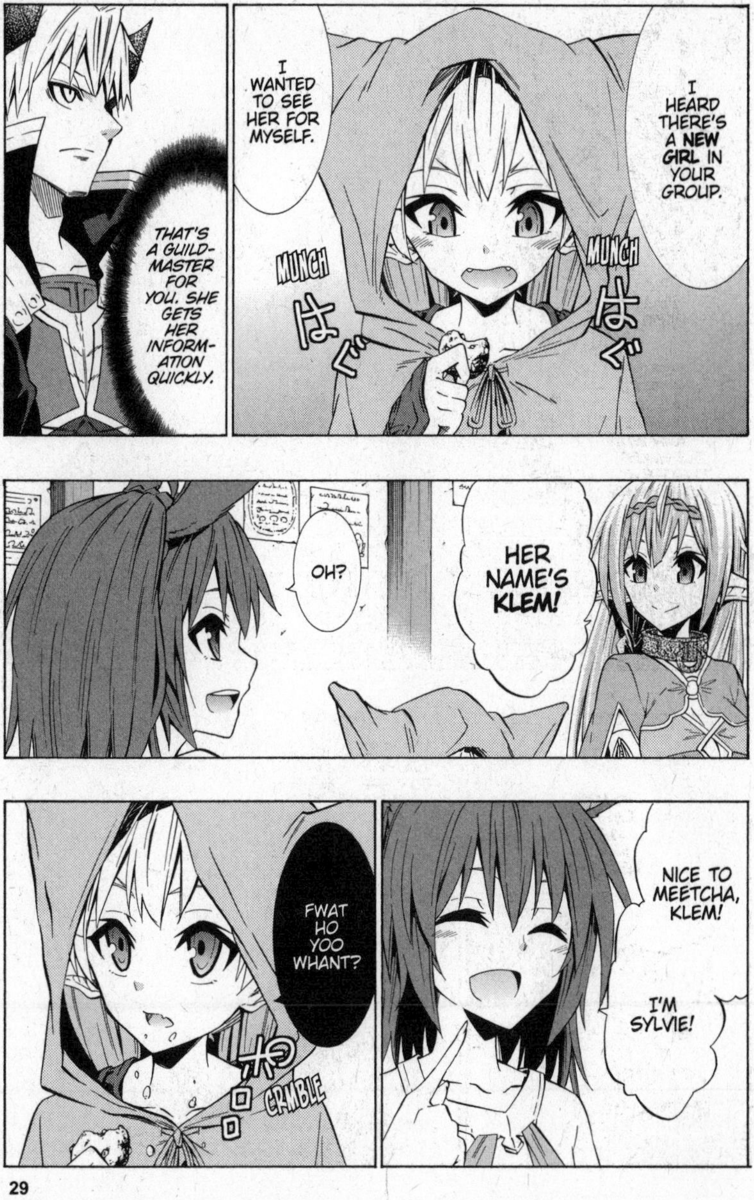
I HEARD THERE'S A **NEW GIRL** IN YOUR GROUP.
MUNCH はぐ
I WANTED TO SEE HER FOR MYSELF.
MUNCH はぐ
THAT'S A GUILD-MASTER FOR YOU. SHE GETS HER INFORMATION QUICKLY.
HER NAME'S **KLEM!**
OH?
NICE TO MEETCHA, KLEM!
I'M SYLVIE!
FWAT HO YOO WHANT?
CRMBLE

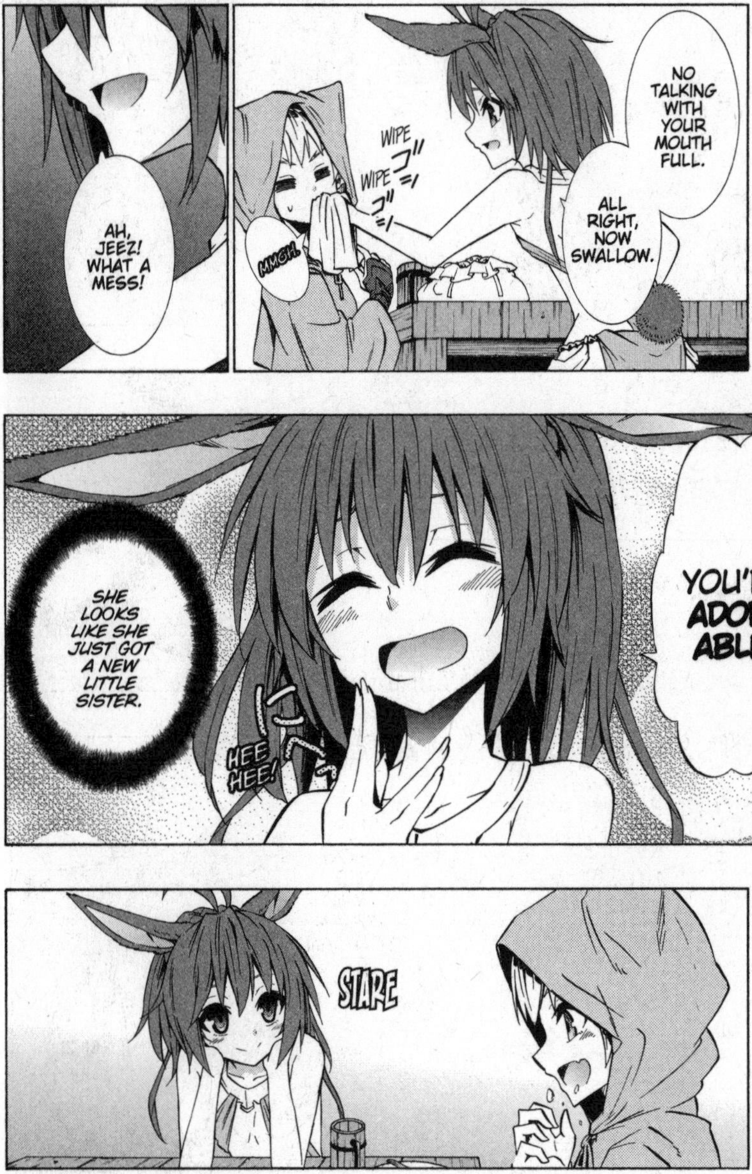
NO TALKING WITH YOUR MOUTH FULL.
ALL RIGHT, NOW SWALLOW.
WIPE
WIPE
MMGH.
AH, JEEZ! WHAT A MESS!
YOU'RE ADORABLE!
HEE HEE!
SHE LOOKS LIKE SHE JUST GOT A NEW LITTLE SISTER.
STARE

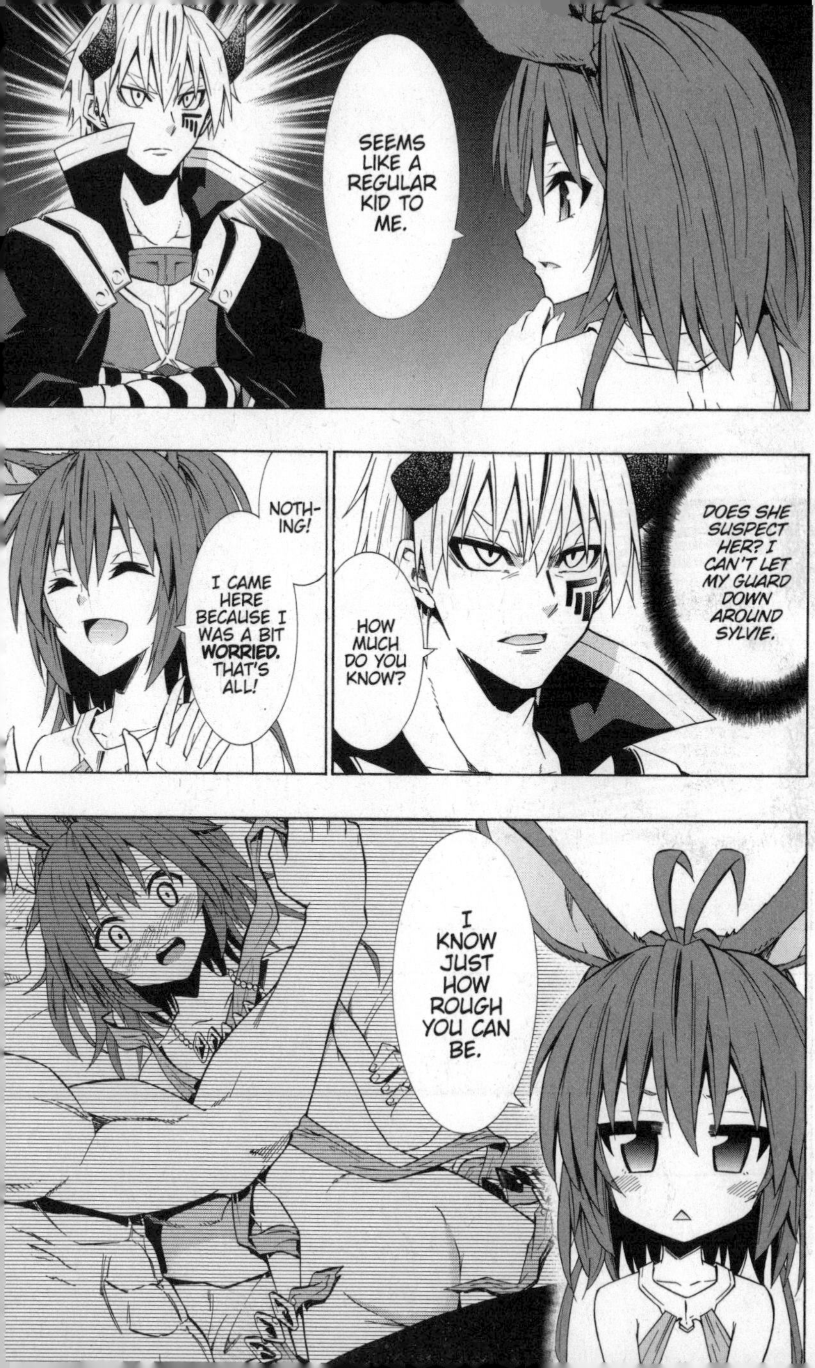
SEEMS LIKE A REGULAR KID TO ME.
DOES SHE SUSPECT HER? I CAN'T LET MY GUARD DOWN AROUND SYLVIE.
HOW MUCH DO YOU KNOW?
NOTH-ING!
I CAME HERE BECAUSE I WAS A BIT WORRIED. THAT'S ALL!
I KNOW JUST HOW ROUGH YOU CAN BE.

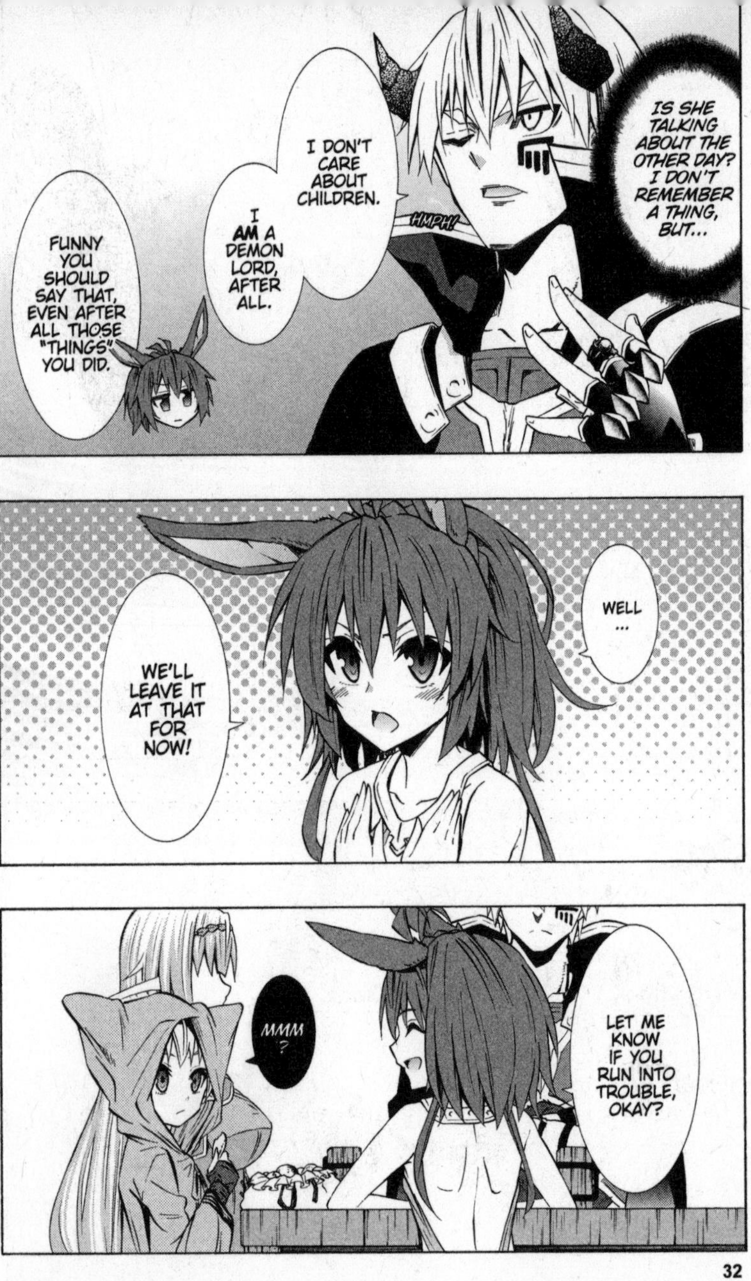
IS SHE TALKING ABOUT THE OTHER DAY? I DON'T REMEMBER A THING, BUT...
HMPH!
I DON'T CARE ABOUT CHILDREN.
I **AM** A DEMON LORD, AFTER ALL.
FUNNY YOU SHOULD SAY THAT, EVEN AFTER ALL THOSE "THINGS" YOU DID.
WELL ...
WE'LL LEAVE IT AT THAT FOR NOW!
LET ME KNOW IF YOU RUN INTO TROUBLE, OKAY?
MMM ?

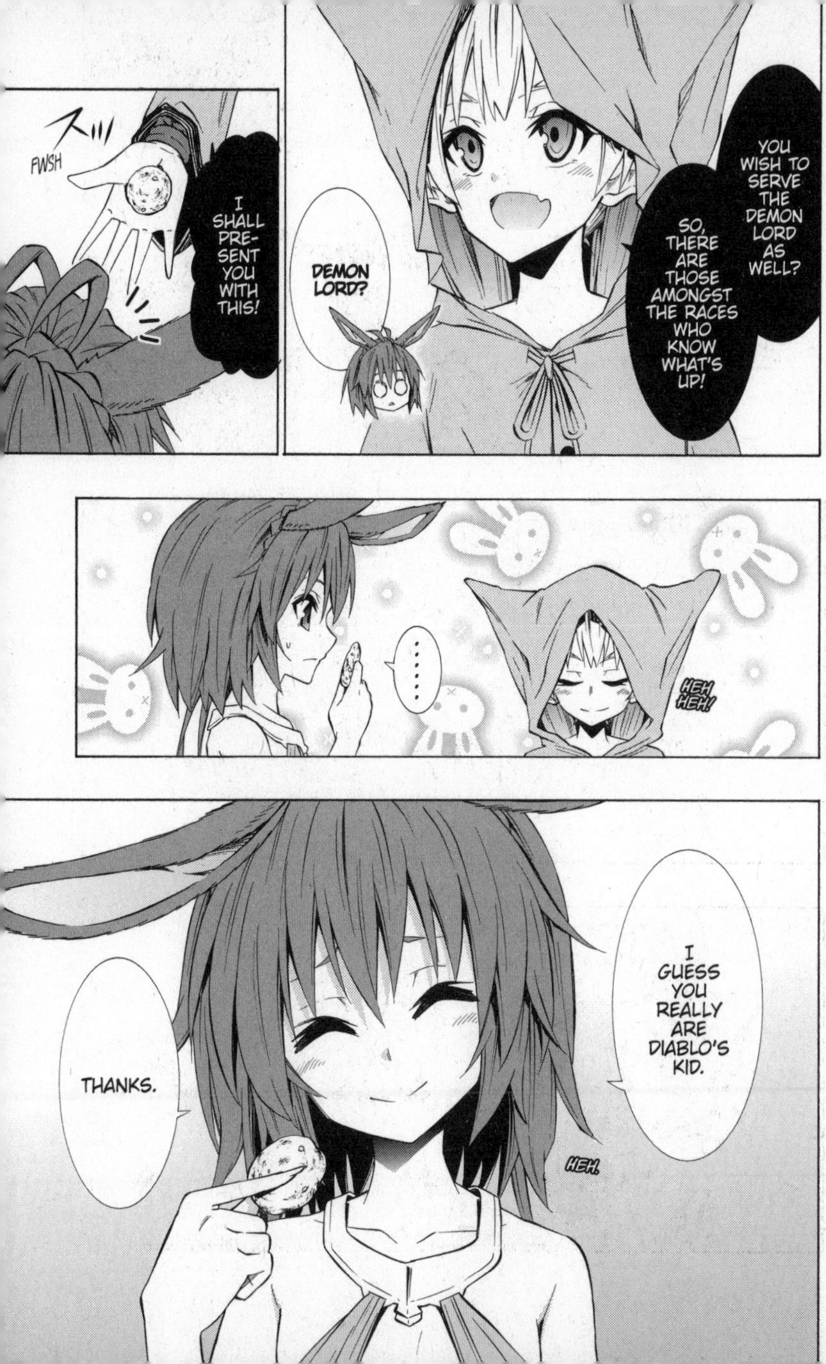
YOU WISH TO SERVE THE DEMON LORD AS WELL?
SO, THERE ARE THOSE AMONGST THE RACES WHO KNOW WHAT'S UP!
DEMON LORD?
I SHALL PRESENT YOU WITH THIS!
FWSH
HEH HEH!
......
I GUESS YOU REALLY ARE DIABLO'S KID.
HEH.
THANKS.

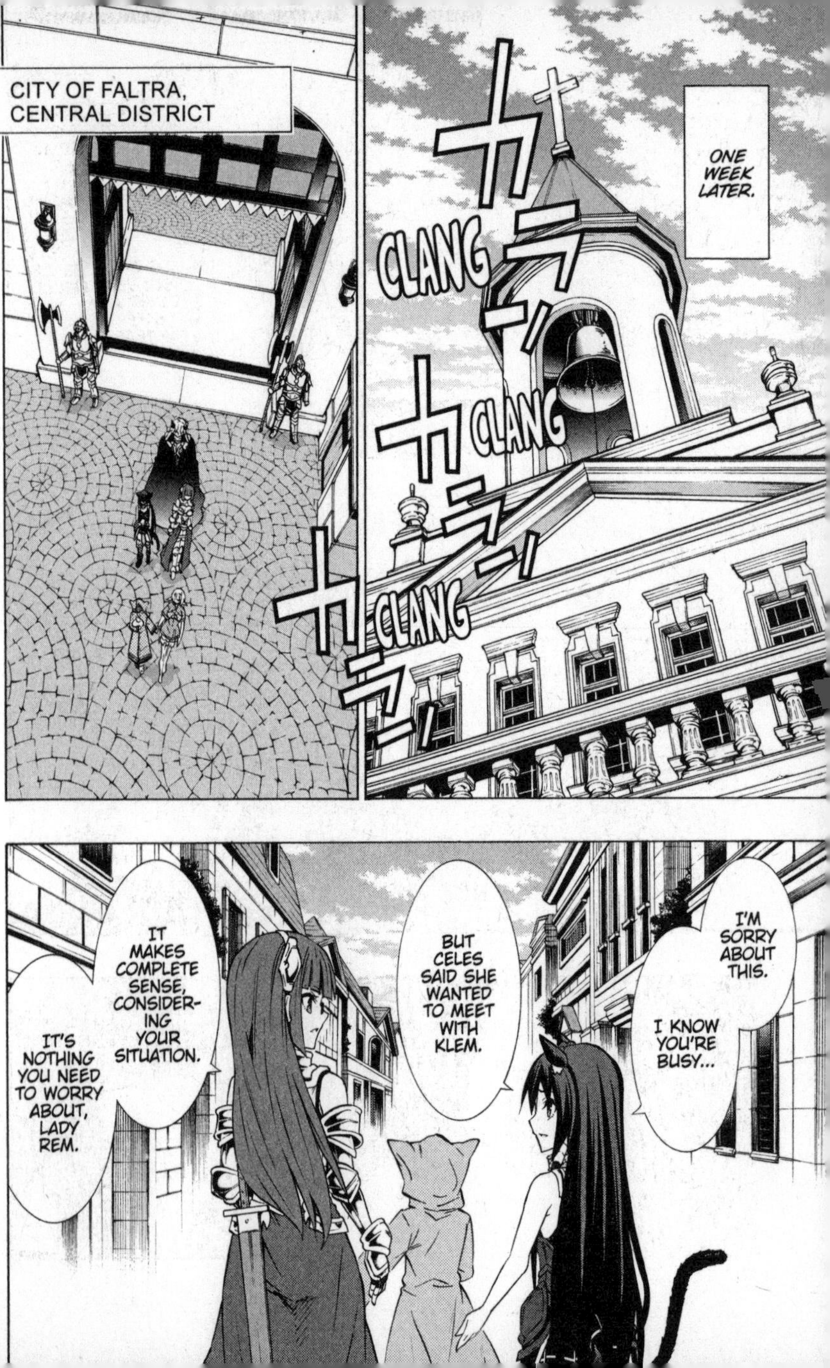
ONE WEEK LATER.
CLANG
CLANG
CLANG
CITY OF FALTRA, CENTRAL DISTRICT
I'M SORRY ABOUT THIS.
I KNOW YOU'RE BUSY...
BUT CELES SAID SHE WANTED TO MEET WITH KLEM.
IT MAKES COMPLETE SENSE, CONSIDERING YOUR SITUATION.
IT'S NOTHING YOU NEED TO WORRY ABOUT, LADY REM.

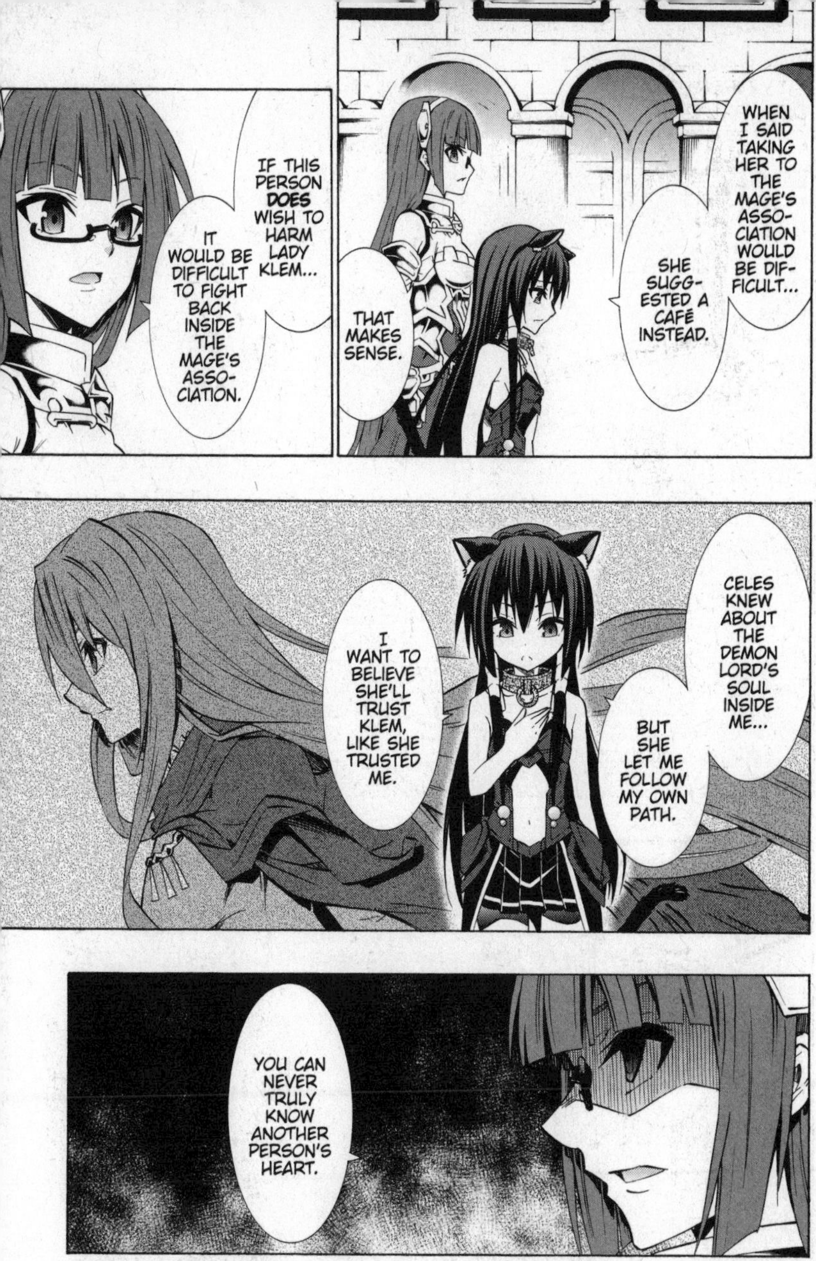
WHEN I SAID TAKING HER TO THE MAGE'S ASSOCIATION WOULD BE DIFFICULT...
SHE SUGGESTED A CAFÉ INSTEAD.
THAT MAKES SENSE.
IF THIS PERSON **DOES** WISH TO HARM LADY KLEM...
IT WOULD BE DIFFICULT TO FIGHT BACK INSIDE THE MAGE'S ASSOCIATION.
CELES KNEW ABOUT THE DEMON LORD'S SOUL INSIDE ME...
BUT SHE LET ME FOLLOW MY OWN PATH.
I WANT TO BELIEVE SHE'LL TRUST KLEM, LIKE SHE TRUSTED ME.
YOU CAN NEVER TRULY KNOW ANOTHER PERSON'S HEART.

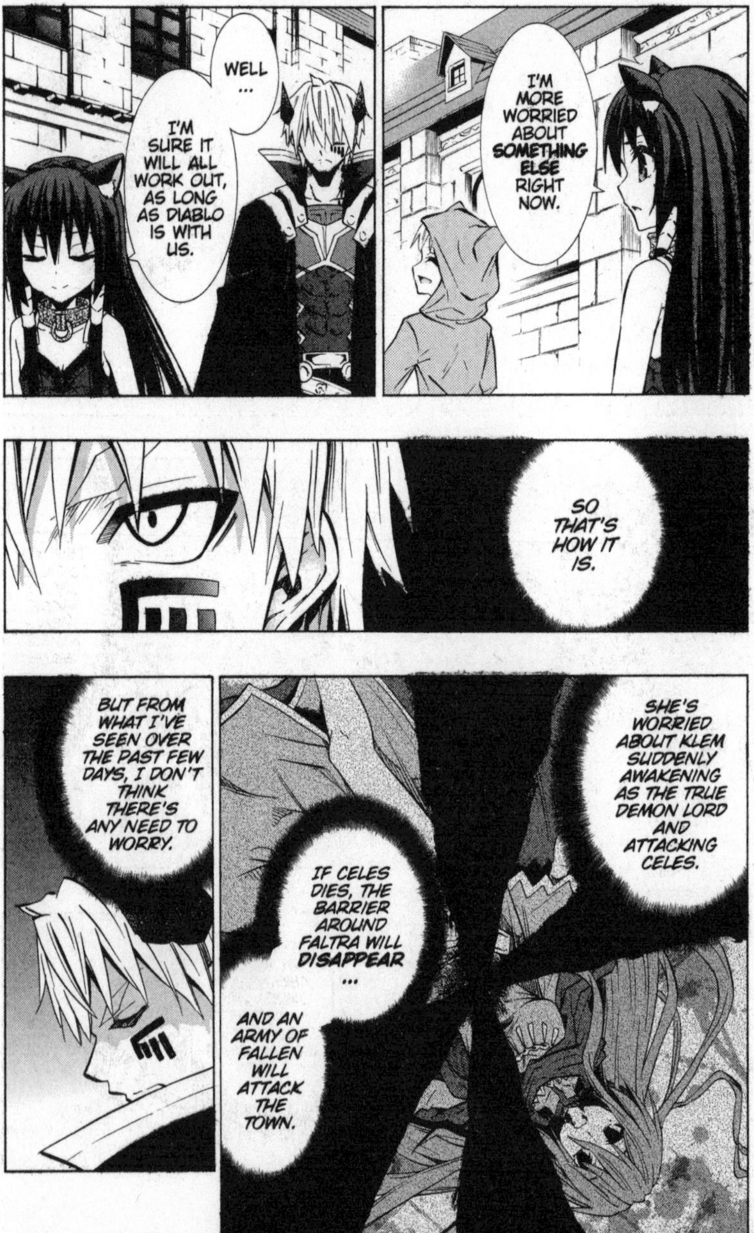
I'M MORE WORRIED ABOUT SOMETHING ELSE RIGHT NOW.
WELL ...
I'M SURE IT WILL ALL WORK OUT, AS LONG AS DIABLO IS WITH US.
SO THAT'S HOW IT IS.
SHE'S WORRIED ABOUT KLEM SUDDENLY AWAKENING AS THE TRUE DEMON LORD AND ATTACKING CELES.
IF CELES DIES, THE BARRIER AROUND FALTRA WILL DISAPPEAR ...
AND AN ARMY OF FALLEN WILL ATTACK THE TOWN.
BUT FROM WHAT I'VE SEEN OVER THE PAST FEW DAYS, I DON'T THINK THERE'S ANY NEED TO WORRY.

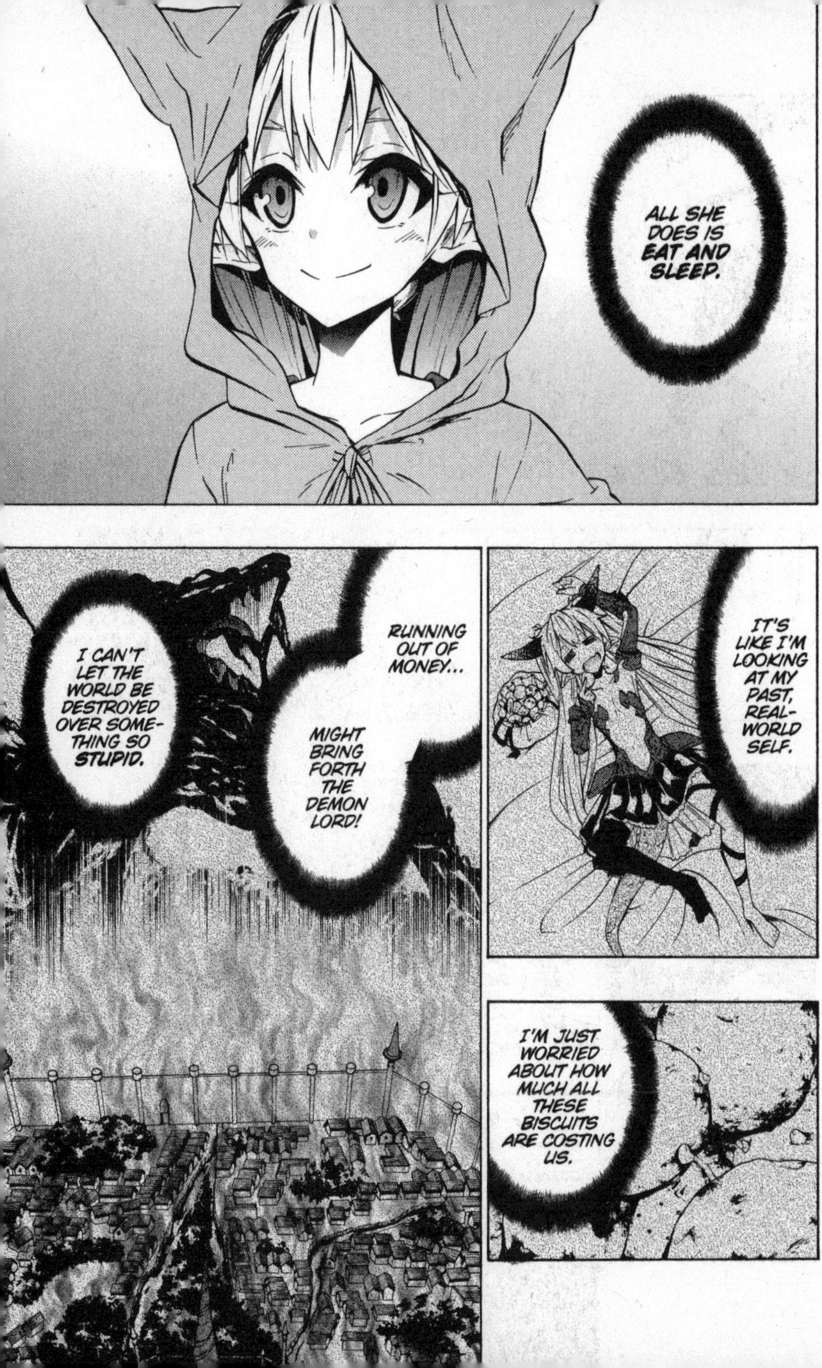
ALL SHE DOES IS EAT AND SLEEP.
IT'S LIKE I'M LOOKING AT MY PAST, REAL-WORLD SELF.
I'M JUST WORRIED ABOUT HOW MUCH ALL THESE BISCUITS ARE COSTING US.
RUNNING OUT OF MONEY...
MIGHT BRING FORTH THE DEMON LORD!
I CAN'T LET THE WORLD BE DESTROYED OVER SOME-THING SO STUPID.

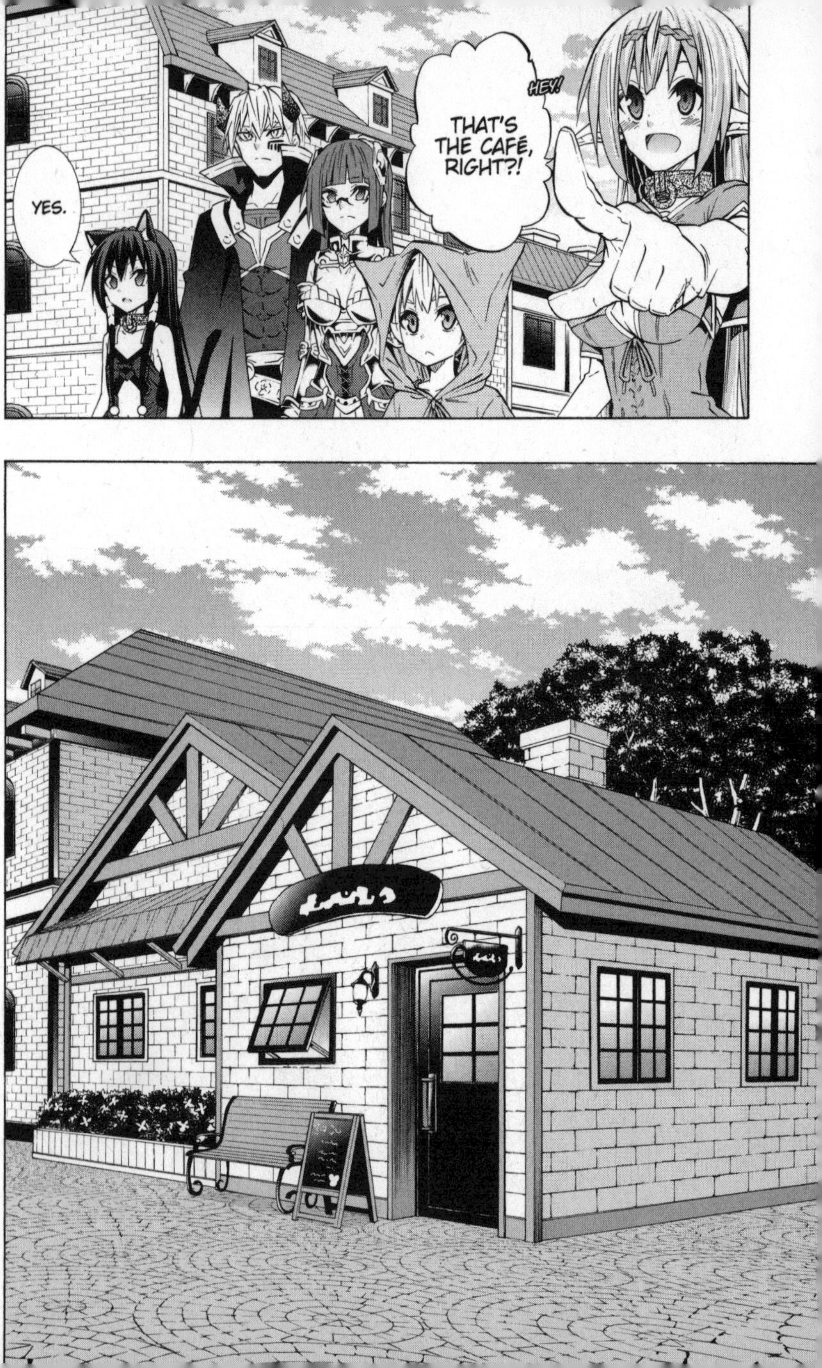
HEY!
THAT'S THE CAFÉ, RIGHT?!
YES.

HOW NOT
TO SUMMON A
DEMON LORD

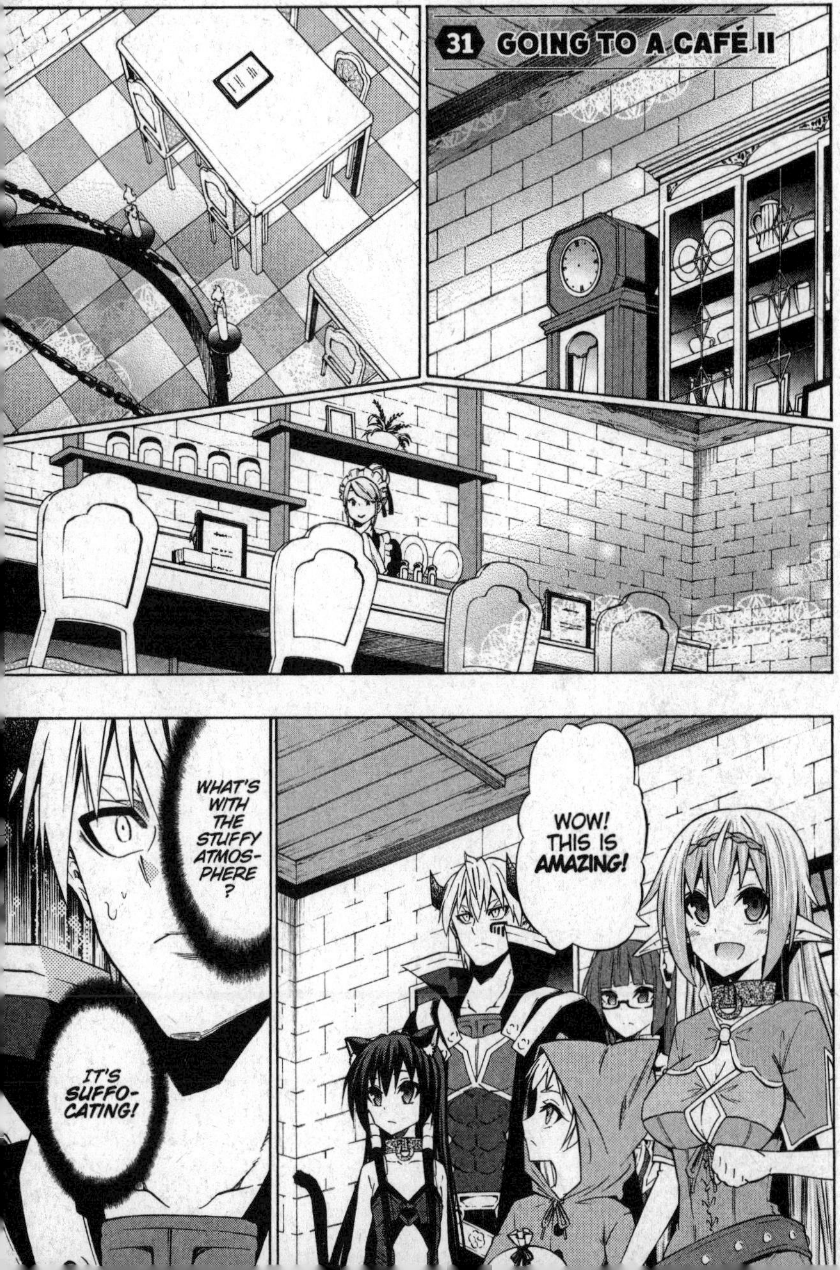
31 GOING TO A CAFÉ II
WOW! THIS IS AMAZING!
WHAT'S WITH THE STUFFY ATMOS-PHERE?
IT'S SUFFO-CATING!

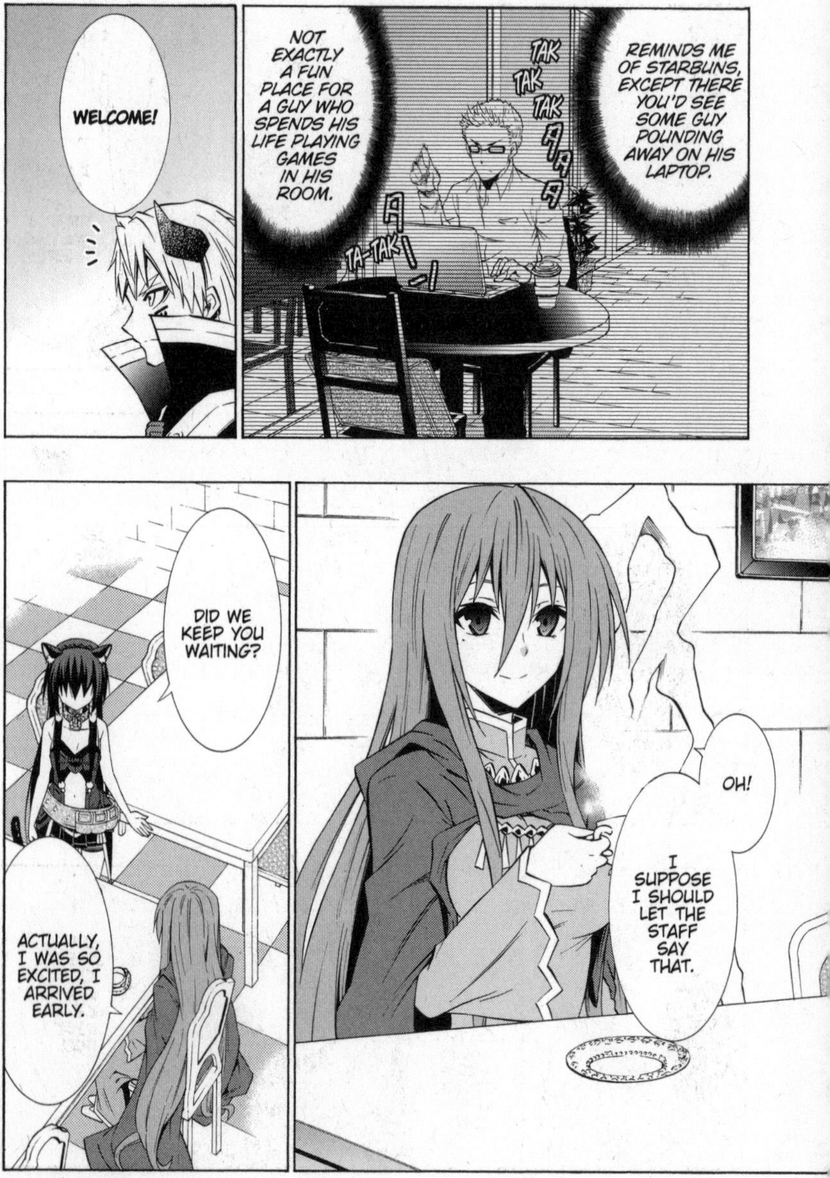
REMINDS ME OF STARBUNS, EXCEPT THERE YOU'D SEE SOME GUY POUNDING AWAY ON HIS LAPTOP.
NOT EXACTLY A FUN PLACE FOR A GUY WHO SPENDS HIS LIFE PLAYING GAMES IN HIS ROOM.
TAK TAK TAK
TA-TAK
WELCOME!
OH!
I SUPPOSE I SHOULD LET THE STAFF SAY THAT.
DID WE KEEP YOU WAITING?
ACTUALLY, I WAS SO EXCITED, I ARRIVED EARLY.

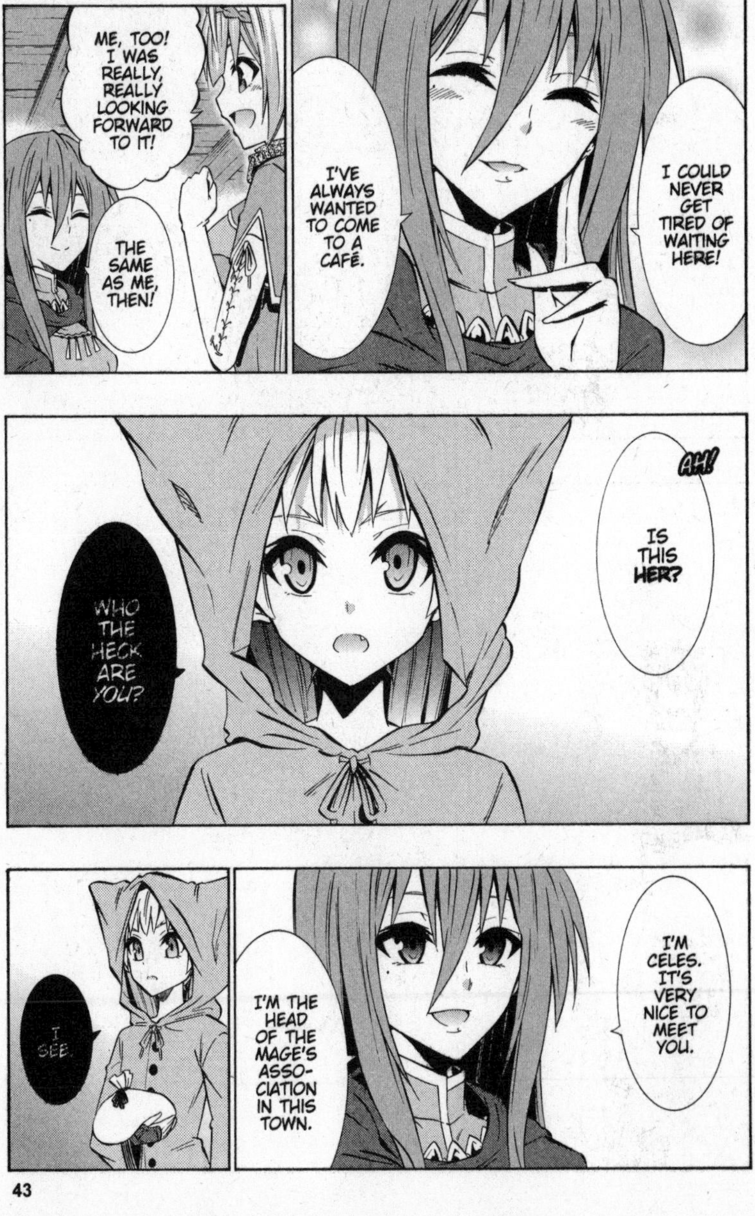
I COULD NEVER GET TIRED OF WAITING HERE!
I'VE ALWAYS WANTED TO COME TO A CAFÉ.
ME, TOO! I WAS REALLY, REALLY LOOKING FORWARD TO IT!
THE SAME AS ME, THEN!
AH!
IS THIS HER?
WHO THE HECK ARE YOU?
I'M CELES. IT'S VERY NICE TO MEET YOU.
I'M THE HEAD OF THE MAGE'S ASSO-CIATION IN THIS TOWN.
I SEE.

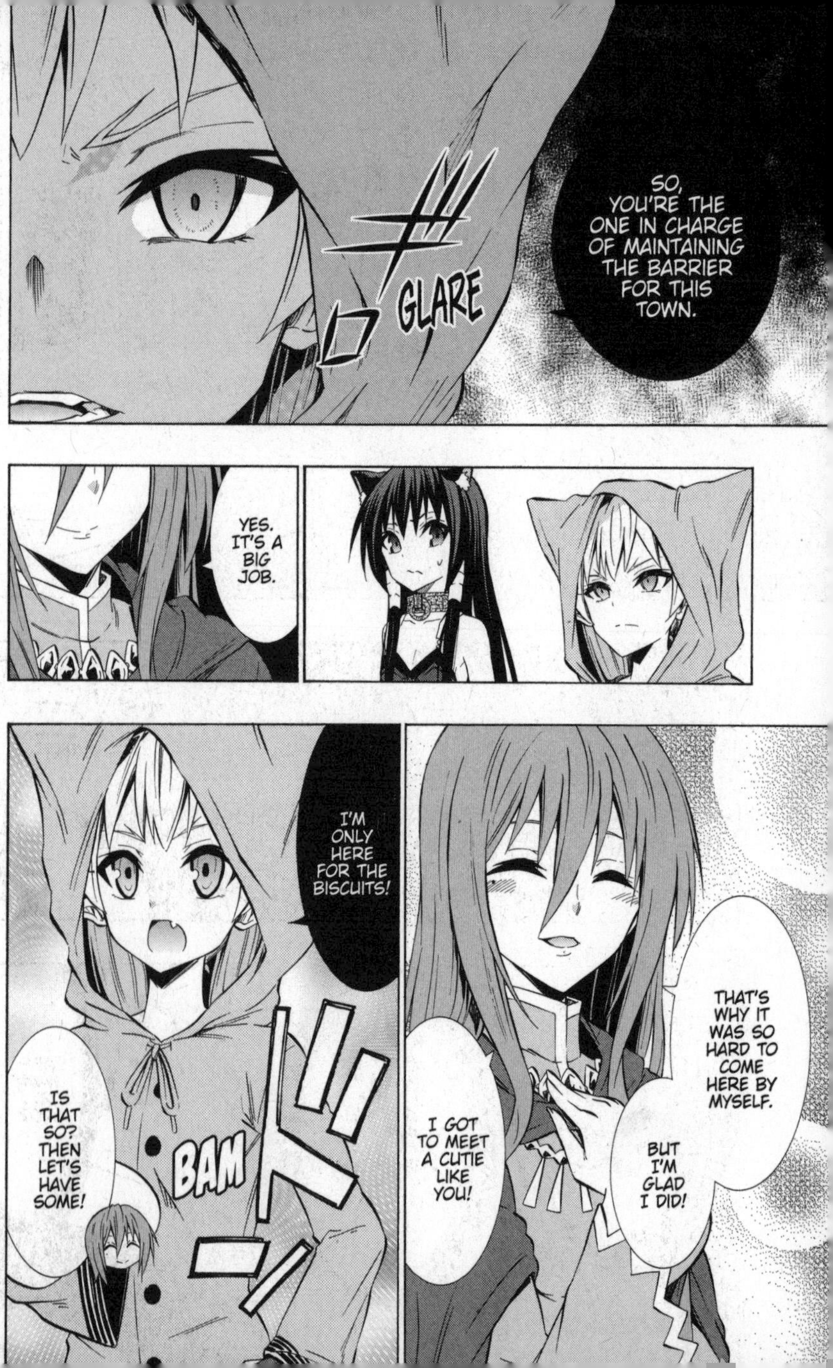
SO, YOU'RE THE ONE IN CHARGE OF MAINTAINING THE BARRIER FOR THIS TOWN.
GLARE
YES. IT'S A BIG JOB.
THAT'S WHY IT WAS SO HARD TO COME HERE BY MYSELF.
BUT I'M GLAD I DID!
I GOT TO MEET A CUTIE LIKE YOU!
I'M ONLY HERE FOR THE BISCUITS!
IS THAT SO? THEN LET'S HAVE SOME!
BAM

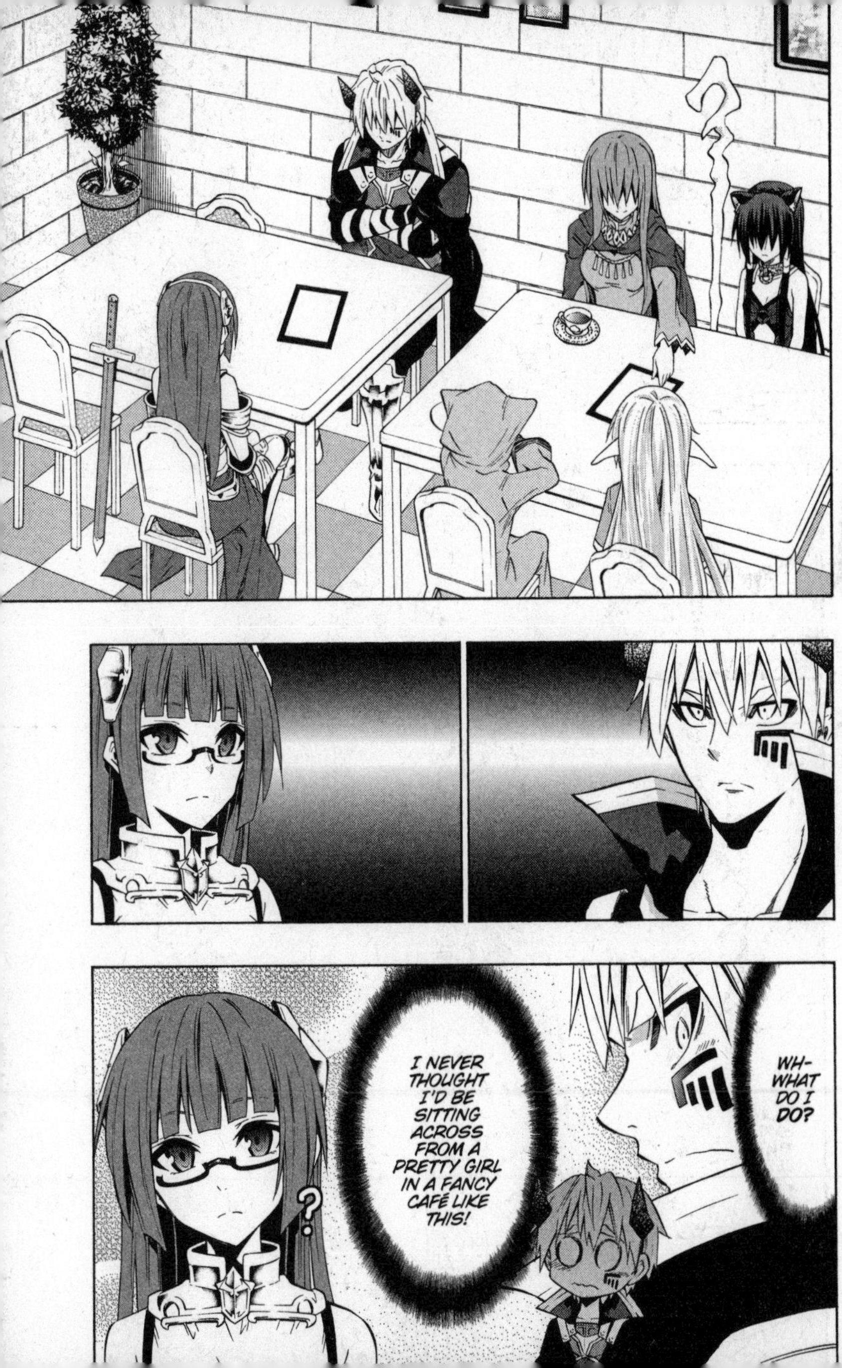
WH- WHAT DO I DO?
I NEVER THOUGHT I'D BE SITTING ACROSS FROM A PRETTY GIRL IN A FANCY CAFÉ LIKE THIS!
? ?

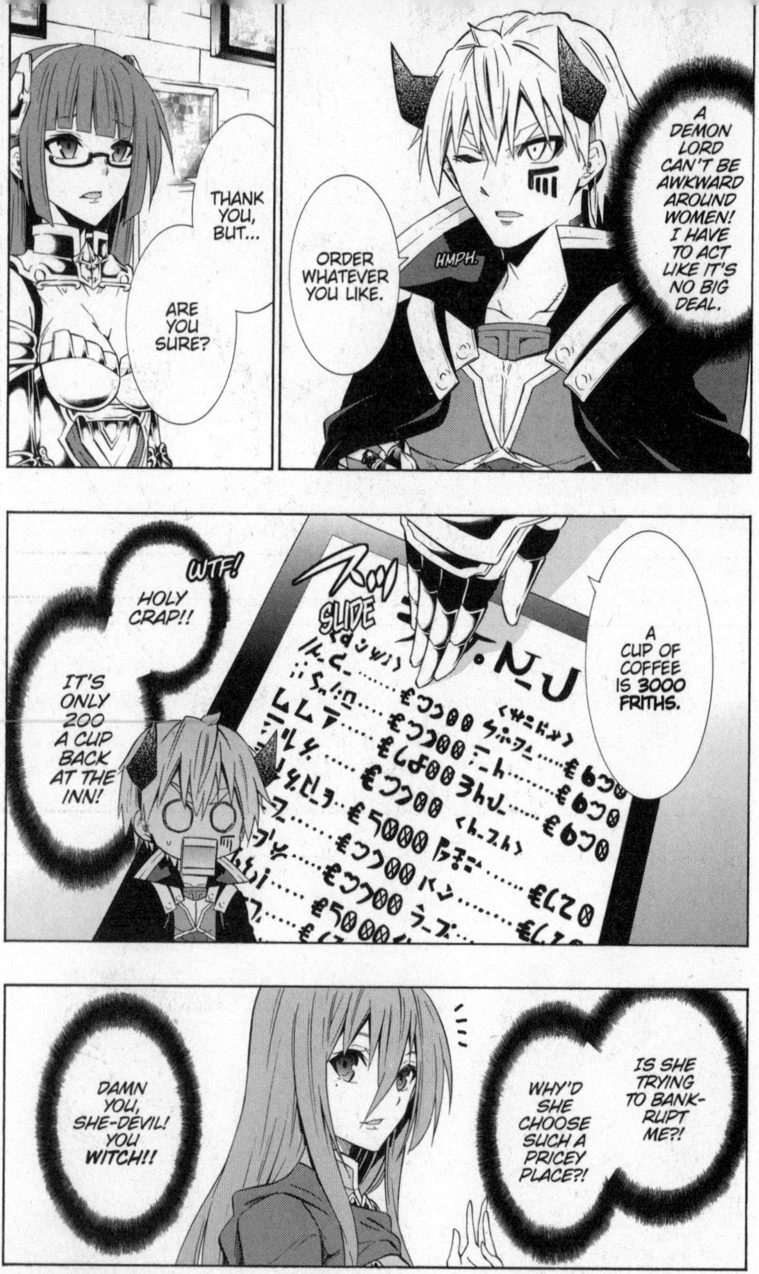
A DEMON LORD CAN'T BE AWKWARD AROUND WOMEN! I HAVE TO ACT LIKE IT'S NO BIG DEAL.
HMPH.
ORDER WHATEVER YOU LIKE.
THANK YOU, BUT...
ARE YOU SURE?
A CUP OF COFFEE IS 3000 FRITHS.
SLIDE
WTF!
HOLY CRAP!!
IT'S ONLY 200 A CUP BACK AT THE INN!
IS SHE TRYING TO BANKRUPT ME?!
WHY'D SHE CHOOSE SUCH A PRICEY PLACE?!
DAMN YOU, SHE-DEVIL! YOU WITCH!!

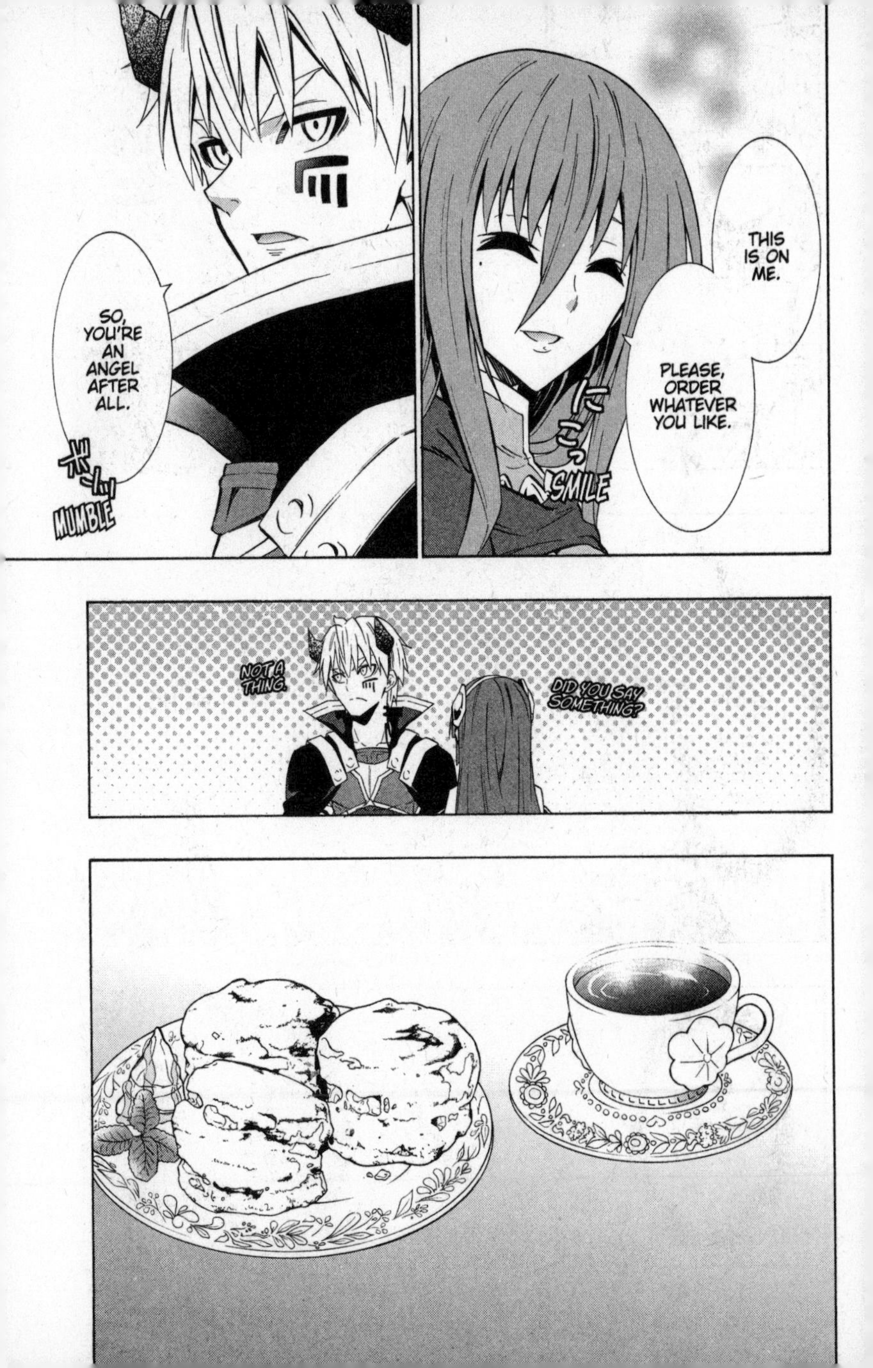
THIS IS ON ME.
PLEASE, ORDER WHATEVER YOU LIKE.
SMILE
SO, YOU'RE AN ANGEL AFTER ALL.
MUMBLE
DID YOU SAY SOMETHING?
NOT A THING.

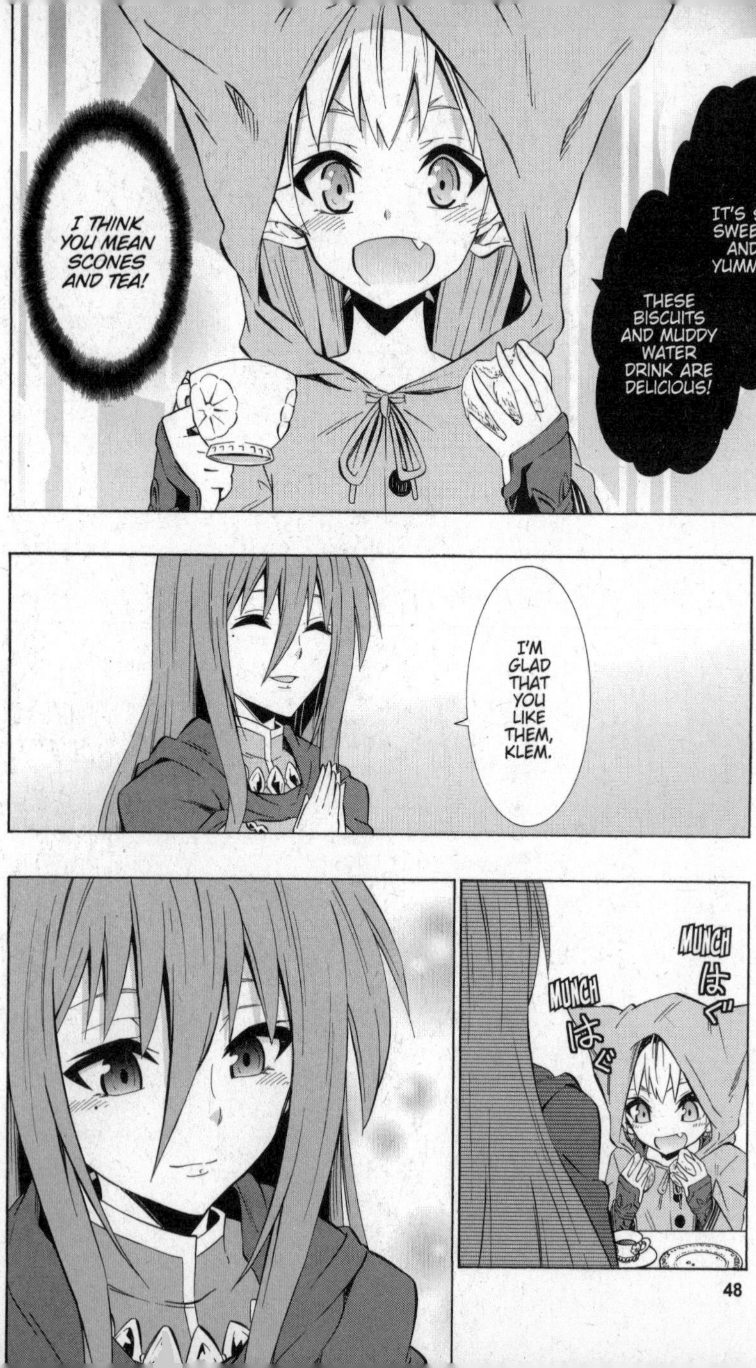
IT'S SO SWEET! AND YUMMY!
THESE BISCUITS AND MUDDY WATER DRINK ARE DELICIOUS!
I THINK YOU MEAN SCONES AND TEA!
I'M GLAD THAT YOU LIKE THEM, KLEM.
MUNCH はぐ
MUNCH はぐ

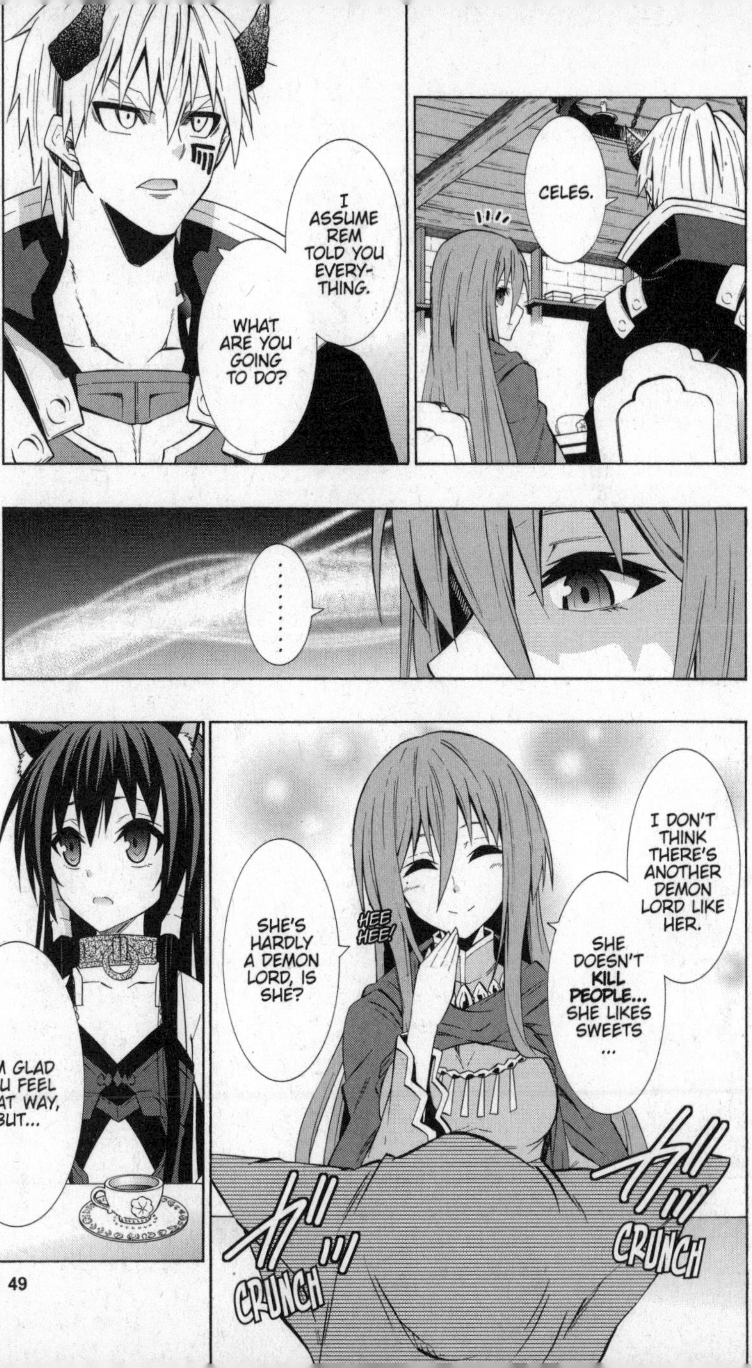
CELES.
I ASSUME REM TOLD YOU EVERYTHING.
WHAT ARE YOU GOING TO DO?
......
I DON'T THINK THERE'S ANOTHER DEMON LORD LIKE HER.
SHE DOESN'T **KILL PEOPLE**... SHE LIKES SWEETS...
HEE HEE!
SHE'S HARDLY A DEMON LORD, IS SHE?
CRUNCH
CRUNCH
I'M GLAD YOU FEEL THAT WAY, BUT...

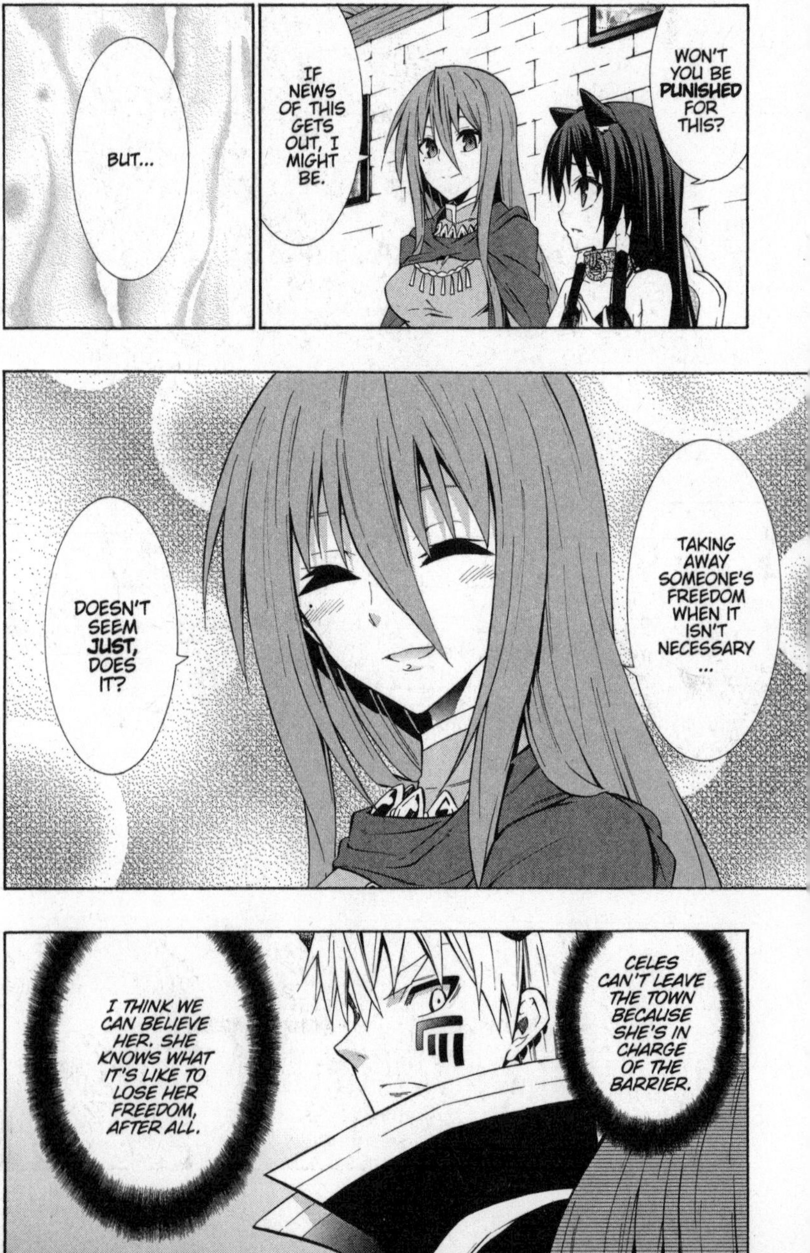
WON'T YOU BE PUNISHED FOR THIS?
IF NEWS OF THIS GETS OUT, I MIGHT BE.
BUT...
TAKING AWAY SOMEONE'S FREEDOM WHEN IT ISN'T NECESSARY ...
DOESN'T SEEM JUST, DOES IT?
CELES CAN'T LEAVE THE TOWN BECAUSE SHE'S IN CHARGE OF THE BARRIER.
I THINK WE CAN BELIEVE HER. SHE KNOWS WHAT IT'S LIKE TO LOSE HER FREEDOM, AFTER ALL.

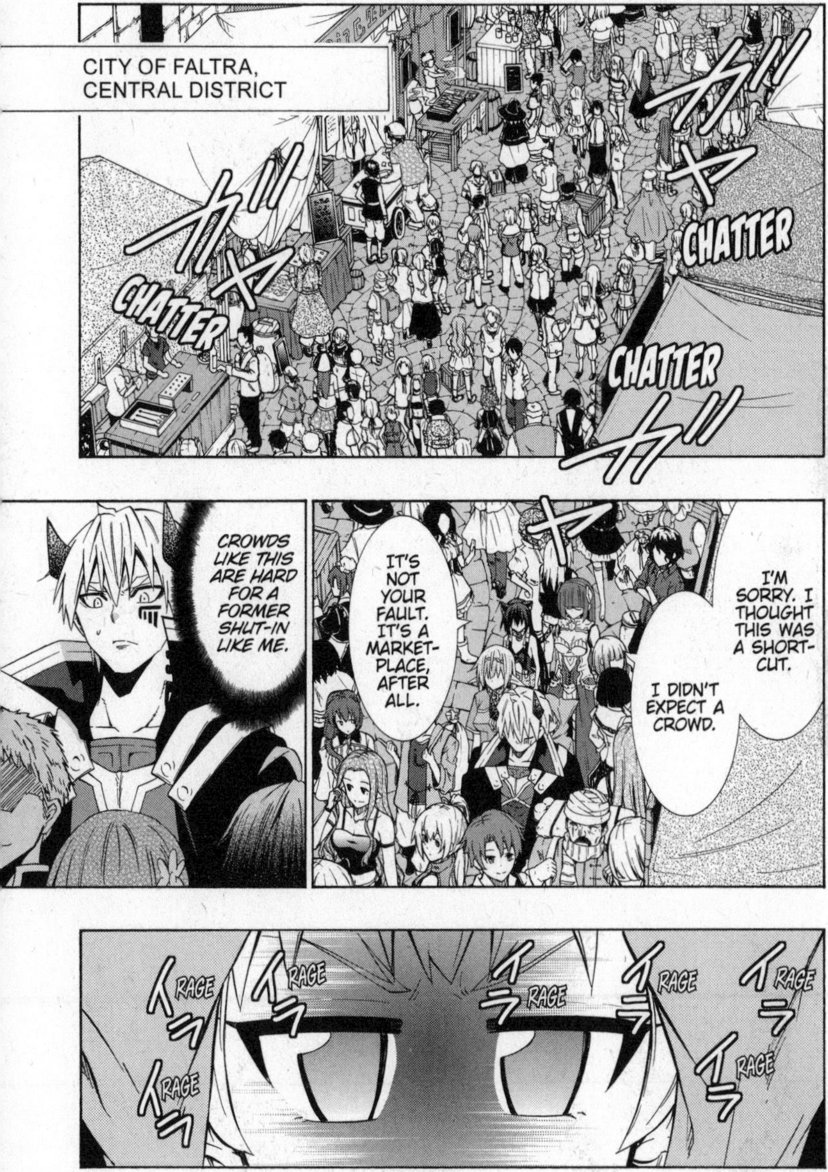
CITY OF FALTRA, CENTRAL DISTRICT
CHATTER
CHATTER
CHATTER
I'M SORRY. I THOUGHT THIS WAS A SHORT-CUT.
I DIDN'T EXPECT A CROWD.
IT'S NOT YOUR FAULT. IT'S A MARKET-PLACE, AFTER ALL.
CROWDS LIKE THIS ARE HARD FOR A FORMER SHUT-IN LIKE ME.
RAGE
RAGE
RAGE
RAGE
RAGE
RAGE
RAGE

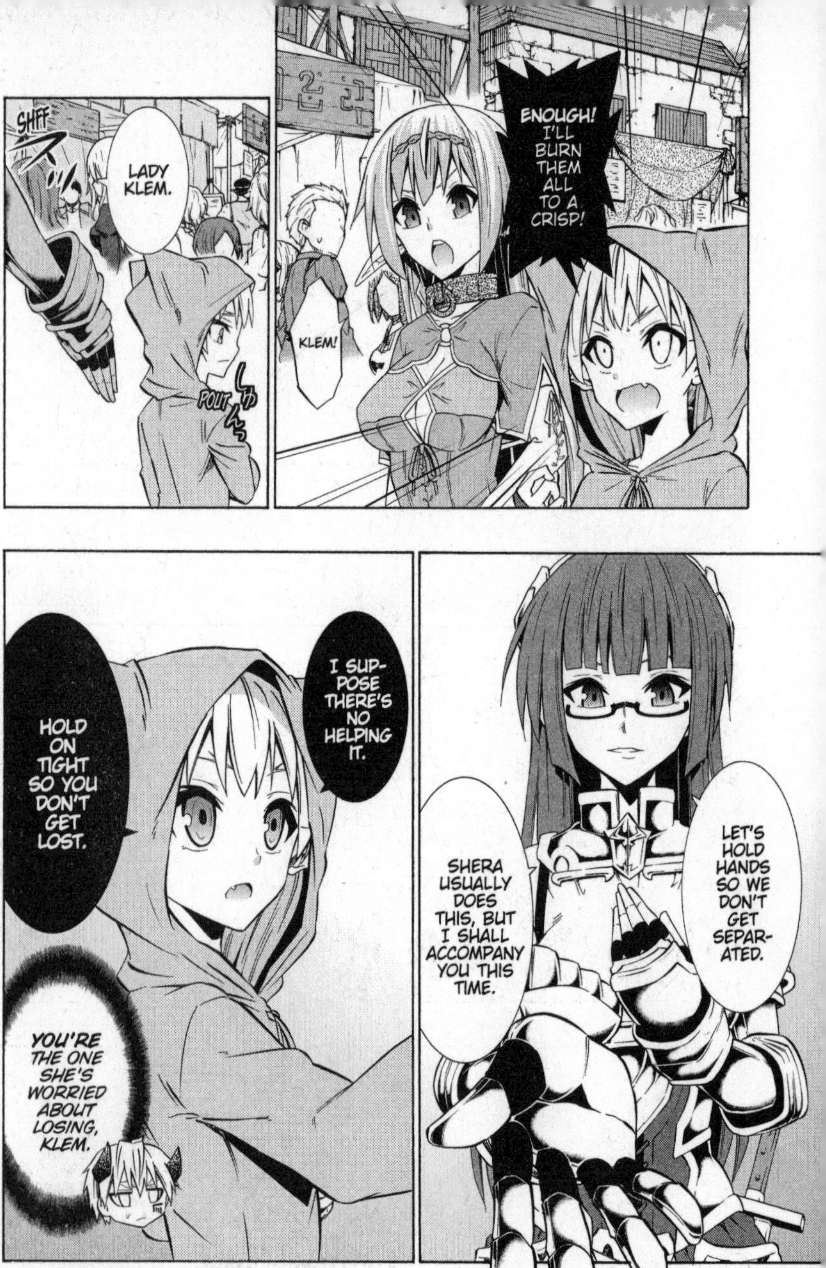
ENOUGH! I'LL BURN THEM ALL TO A CRISP!
KLEM!
SHFF
LADY KLEM.
しゅん
POUT
LET'S HOLD HANDS SO WE DON'T GET SEPAR-ATED.
SHERA USUALLY DOES THIS, BUT I SHALL ACCOMPANY YOU THIS TIME.
I SUP-POSE THERE'S NO HELPING IT.
HOLD ON TIGHT SO YOU DON'T GET LOST.
YOU'RE THE ONE SHE'S WORRIED ABOUT LOSING, KLEM.

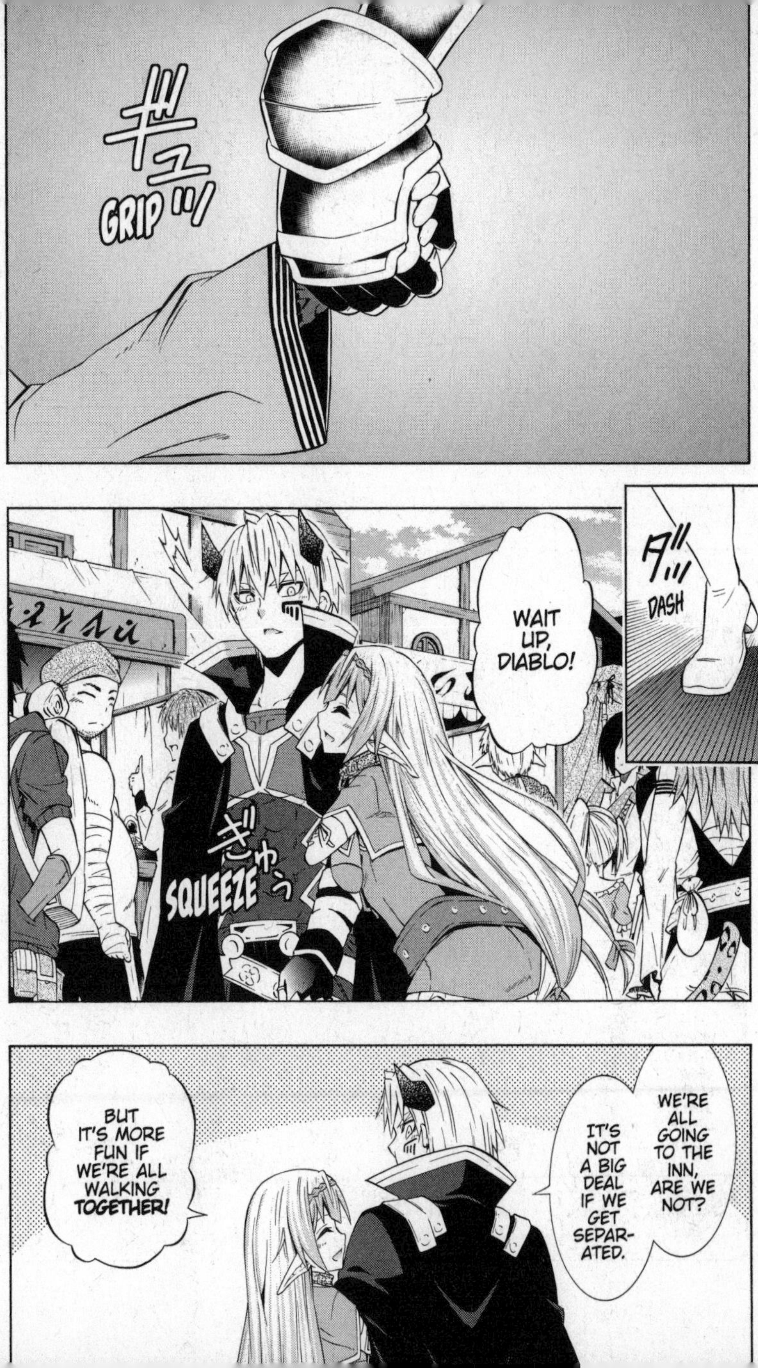
ギュ
GRIP
ダッ
DASH
WAIT UP, DIABLO!
ぎゅう
SQUEEZE
WE'RE ALL GOING TO THE INN, ARE WE NOT?
IT'S NOT A BIG DEAL IF WE GET SEPARATED.
BUT IT'S MORE FUN IF WE'RE ALL WALKING TOGETHER!

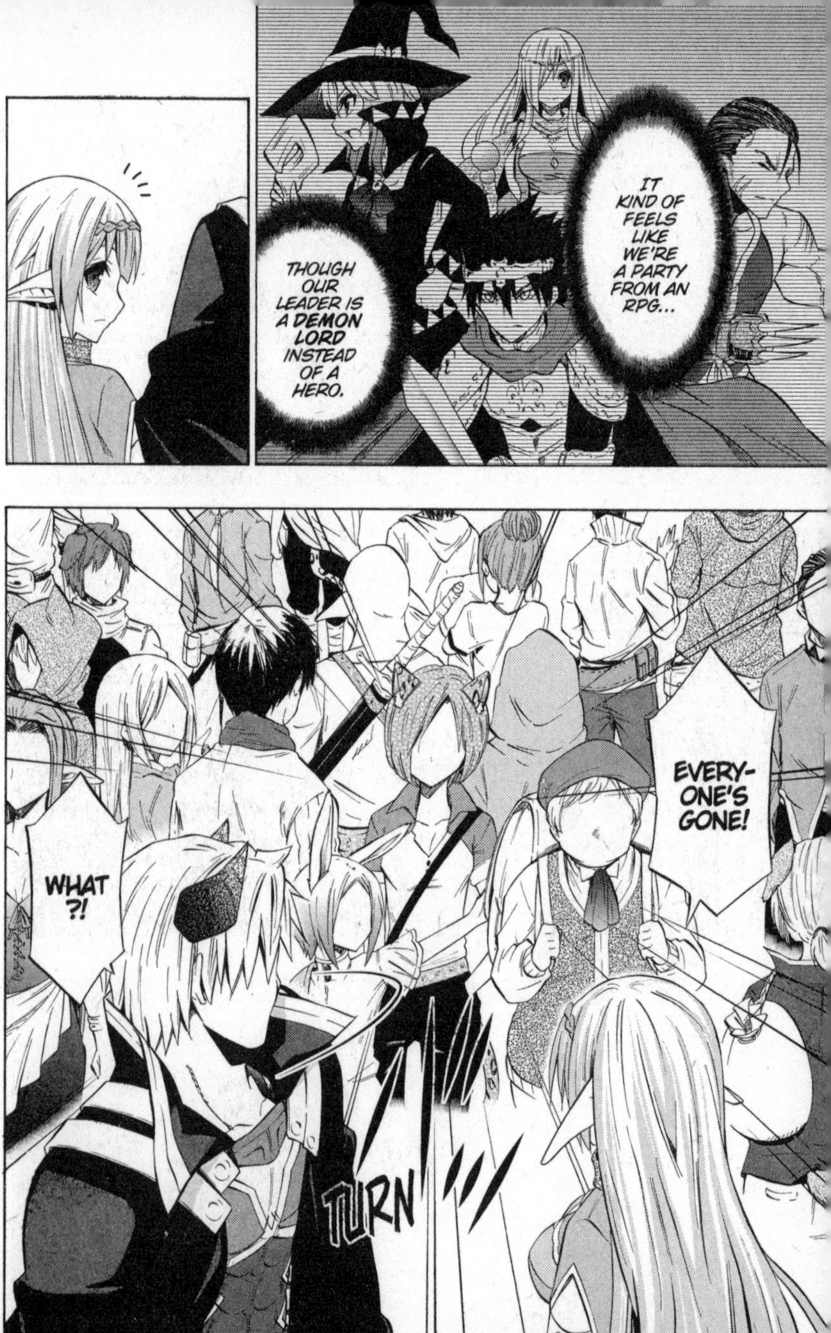
IT KIND OF FEELS LIKE WE'RE A PARTY FROM AN RPG...
THOUGH OUR LEADER IS A DEMON LORD INSTEAD OF A HERO.
EVERY-ONE'S GONE!
WHAT?!
TURN

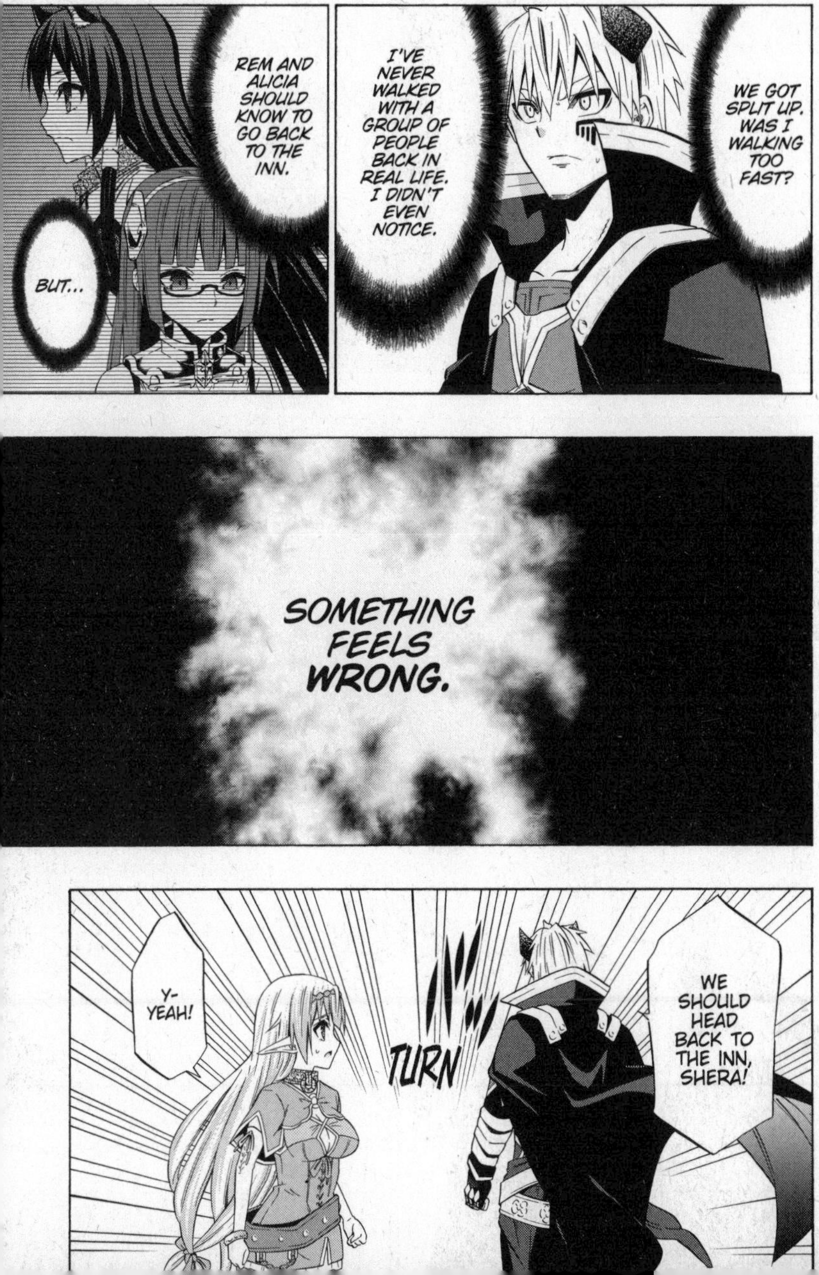
WE GOT SPLIT UP. WAS I WALKING TOO FAST?
I'VE NEVER WALKED WITH A GROUP OF PEOPLE BACK IN REAL LIFE. I DIDN'T EVEN NOTICE.
REM AND ALICIA SHOULD KNOW TO GO BACK TO THE INN.
BUT...
SOMETHING FEELS WRONG.
WE SHOULD HEAD BACK TO THE INN, SHERA!
TURN
Y-YEAH!

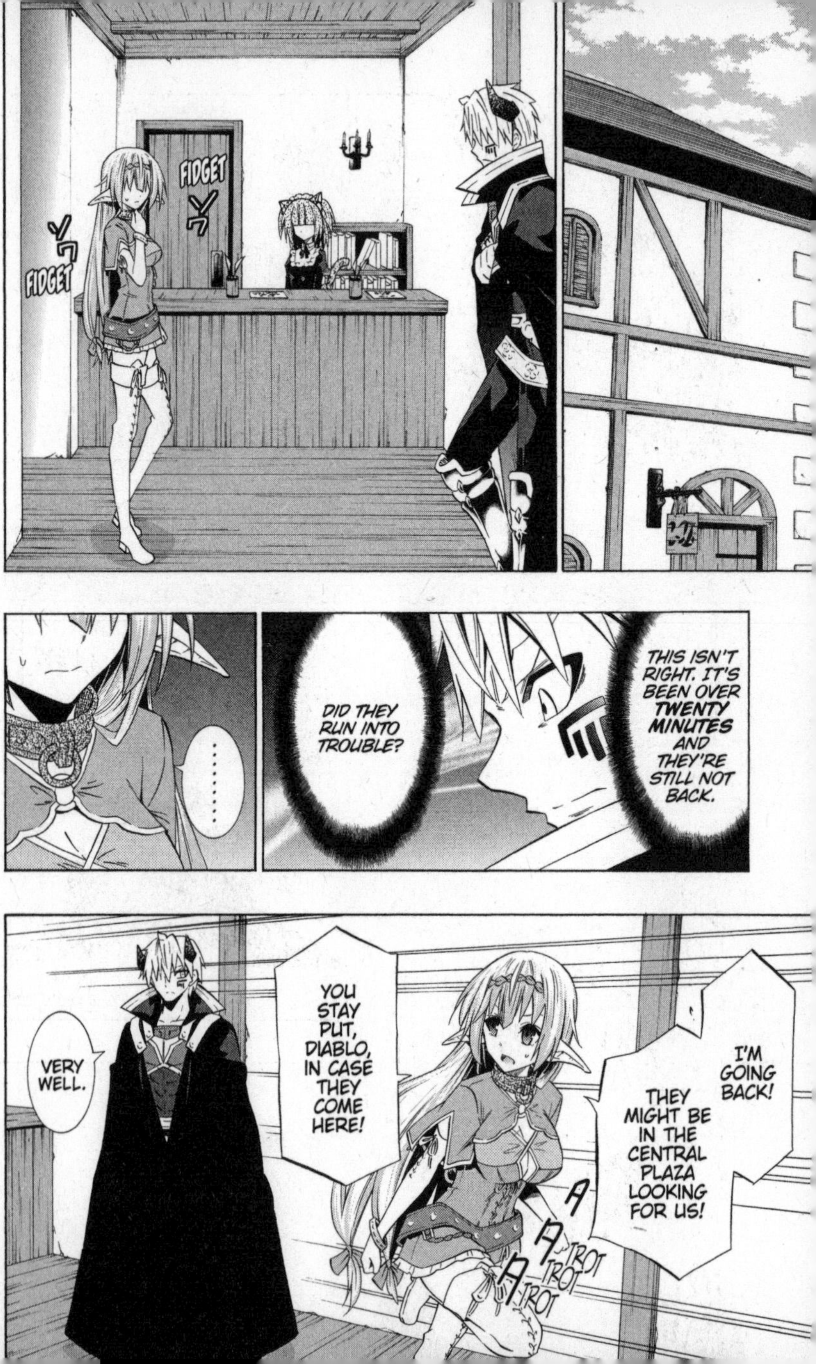
FIDGET
ソワ
FIDGET
ソワ
THIS ISN'T RIGHT. IT'S BEEN OVER TWENTY MINUTES AND THEY'RE STILL NOT BACK.
DID THEY RUN INTO TROUBLE?
......
I'M GOING BACK!
THEY MIGHT BE IN THE CENTRAL PLAZA LOOKING FOR US!
A TROT
A TROT
A TROT
YOU STAY PUT, DIABLO, IN CASE THEY COME HERE!
VERY WELL.

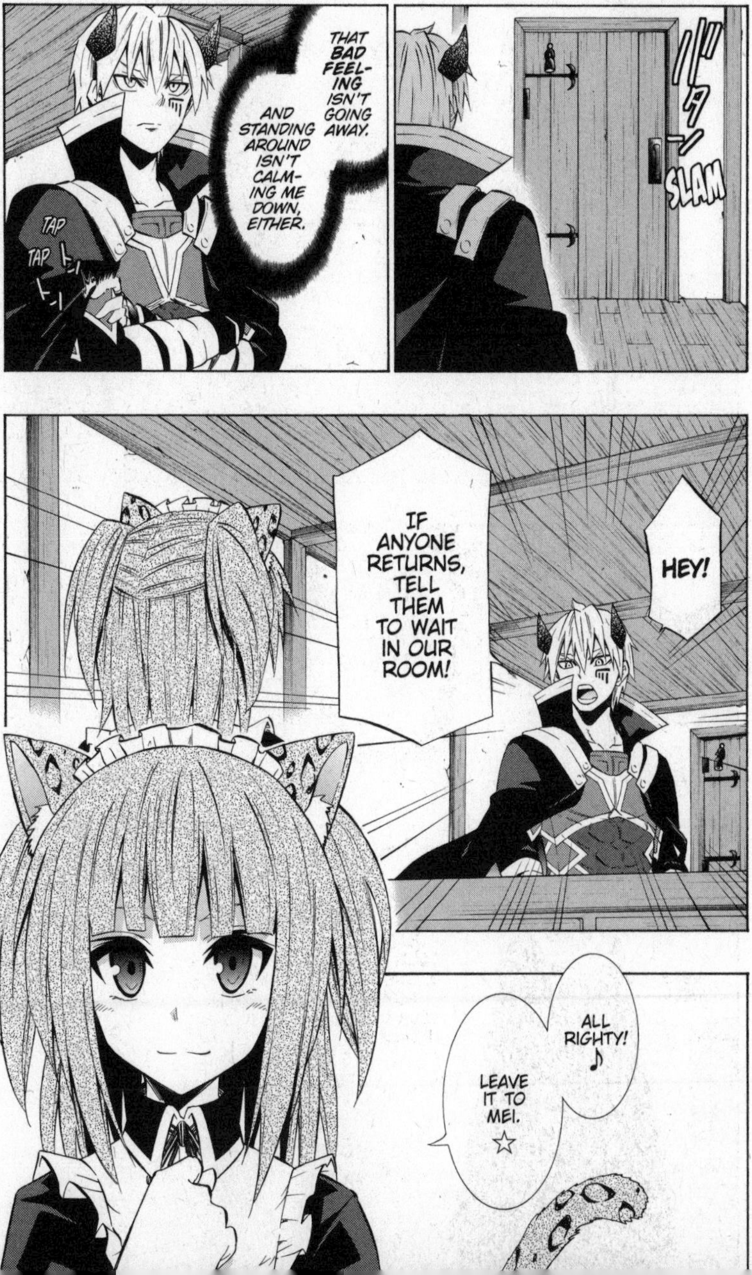
バタン
SLAM
THAT BAD FEELING ISN'T GOING AWAY.
AND STANDING AROUND ISN'T CALMING ME DOWN, EITHER.
TAP TAP
HEY!
IF ANYONE RETURNS, TELL THEM TO WAIT IN OUR ROOM!
ALL RIGHTY! ♪
LEAVE IT TO MEI. ☆

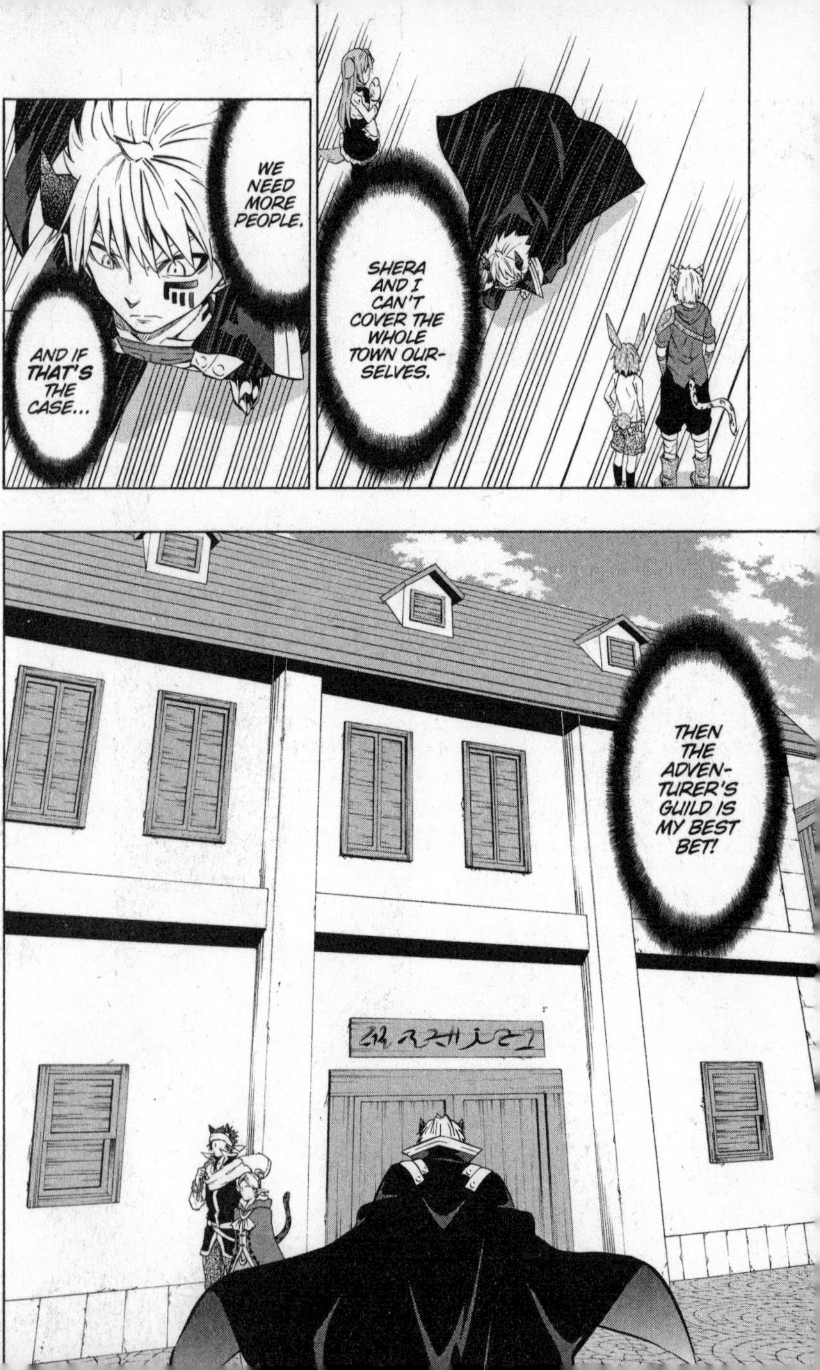
SHERA AND I CAN'T COVER THE WHOLE TOWN OUR-SELVES.
WE NEED MORE PEOPLE.
AND IF THAT'S THE CASE...
THEN THE ADVEN-TURER'S GUILD IS MY BEST BET!

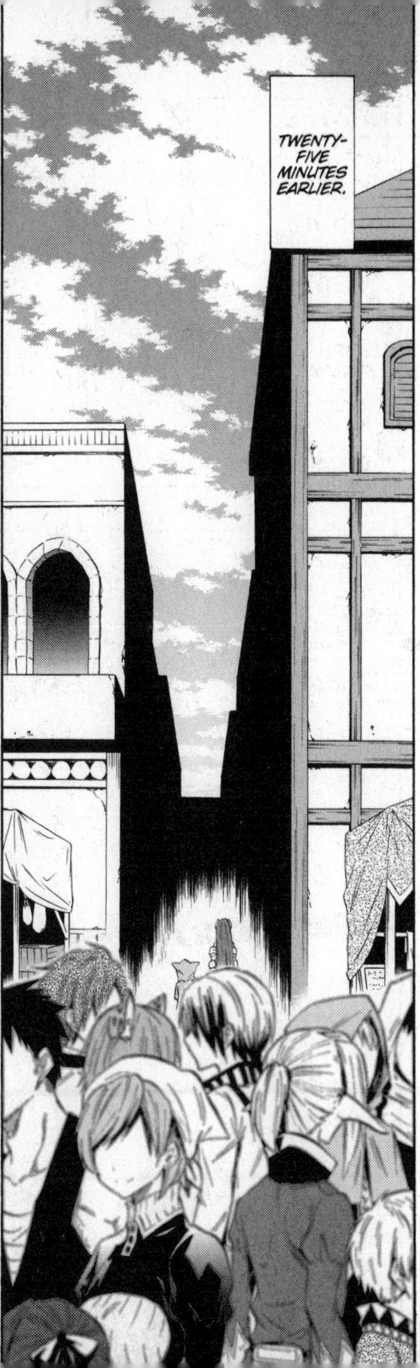
TWENTY-FIVE MINUTES EARLIER.
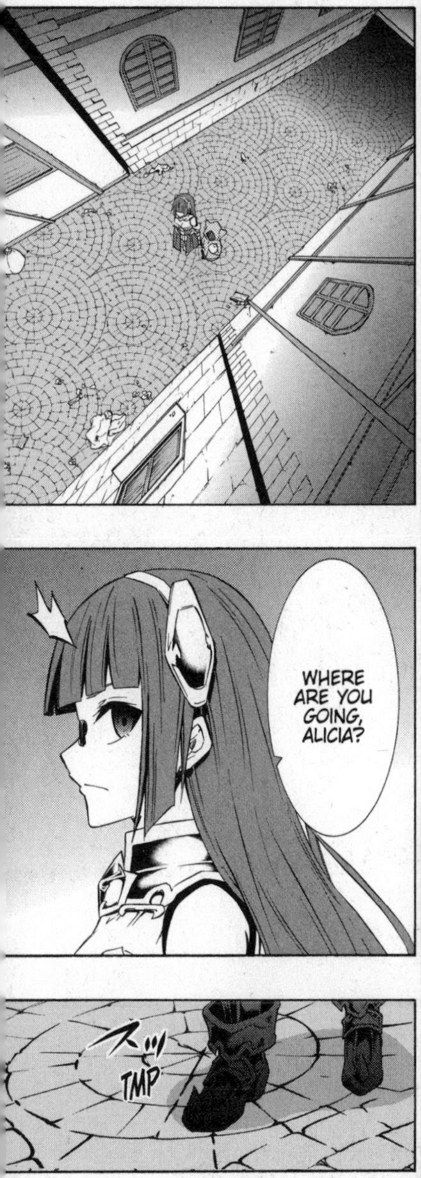
WHERE ARE YOU GOING, ALICIA?
スッ
TMP

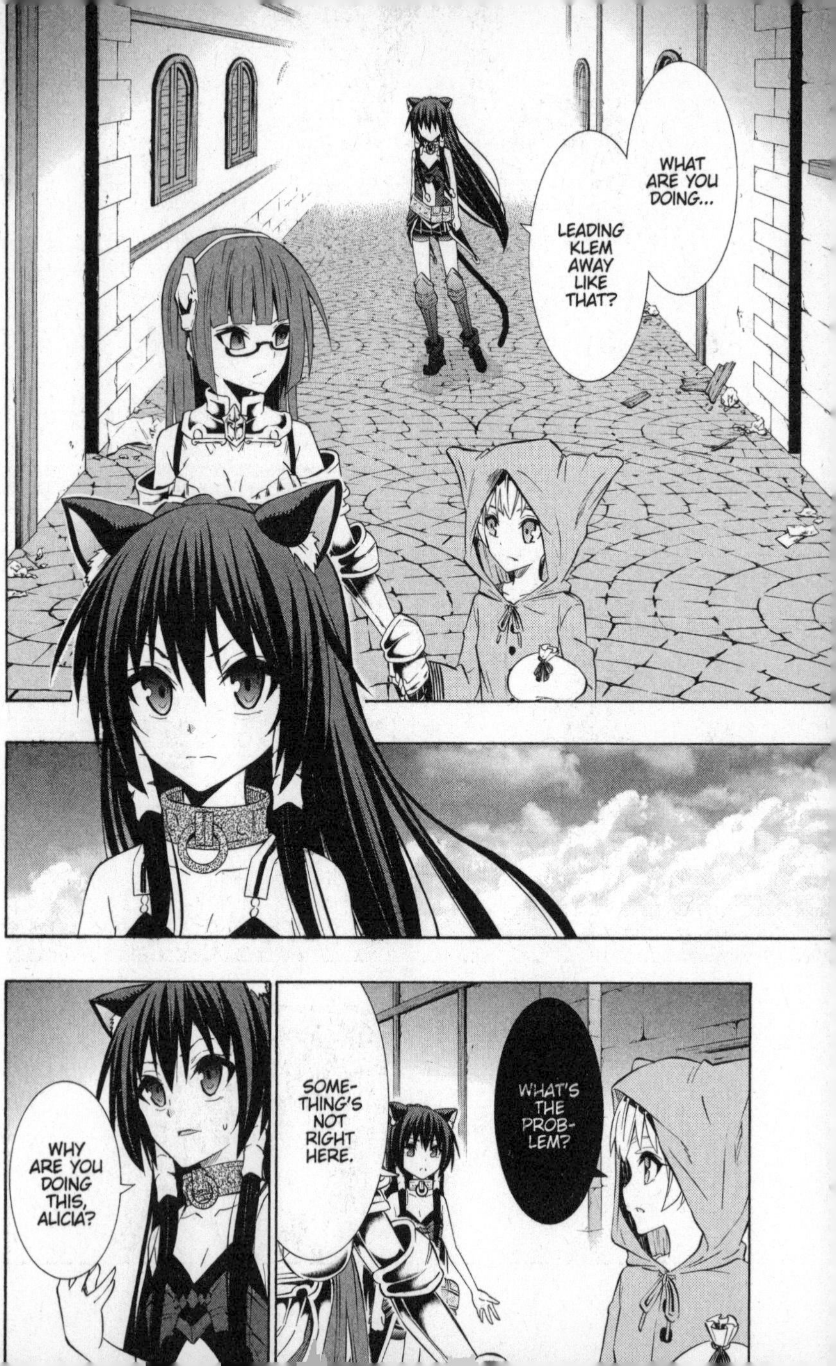
WHAT ARE YOU DOING... LEADING KLEM AWAY LIKE THAT?
WHAT'S THE PROB-LEM?
SOME-THING'S NOT RIGHT HERE.
WHY ARE YOU DOING THIS, ALICIA?

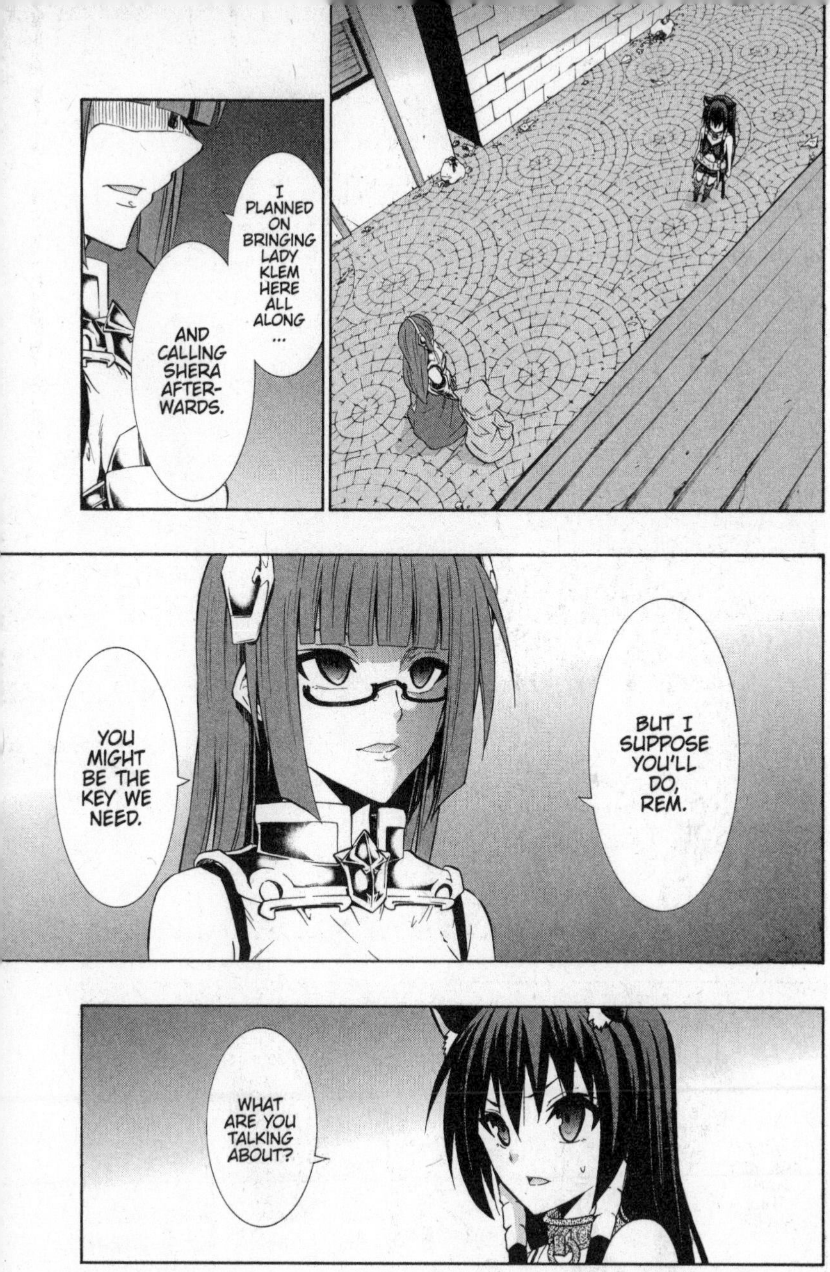
I PLANNED ON BRINGING LADY KLEM HERE ALL ALONG ...
AND CALLING SHERA AFTER-WARDS.
BUT I SUPPOSE YOU'LL DO, REM.
YOU MIGHT BE THE KEY WE NEED.
WHAT ARE YOU TALKING ABOUT?

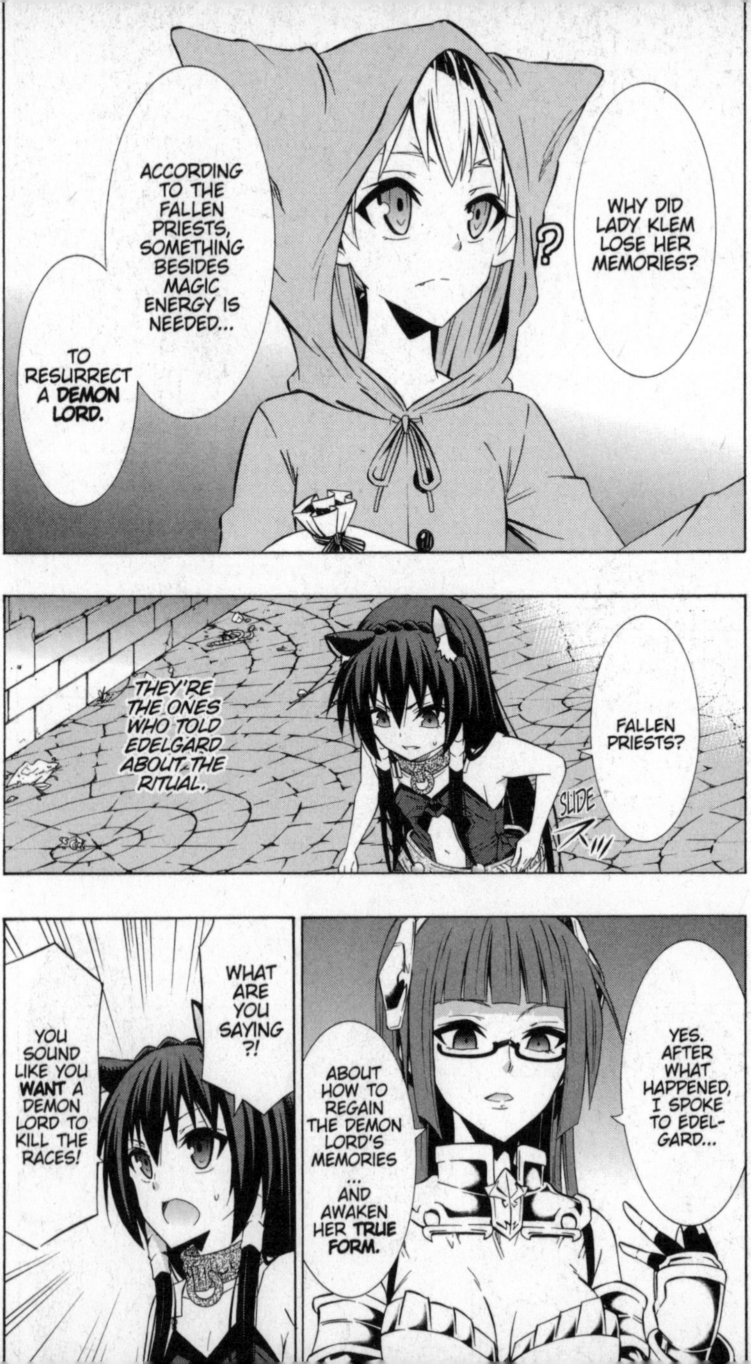
WHY DID LADY KLEM LOSE HER MEMORIES?
?
ACCORDING TO THE FALLEN PRIESTS, SOMETHING BESIDES MAGIC ENERGY IS NEEDED...
TO RESURRECT A **DEMON LORD.**
FALLEN PRIESTS?
SLIDE
THEY'RE THE ONES WHO TOLD EDELGARD ABOUT THE RITUAL.
YES. AFTER WHAT HAPPENED, I SPOKE TO EDEL-GARD...
ABOUT HOW TO REGAIN THE DEMON LORD'S MEMORIES ...
AND AWAKEN HER **TRUE FORM.**
WHAT ARE YOU SAYING?!
YOU SOUND LIKE YOU **WANT** A DEMON LORD TO KILL THE RACES!

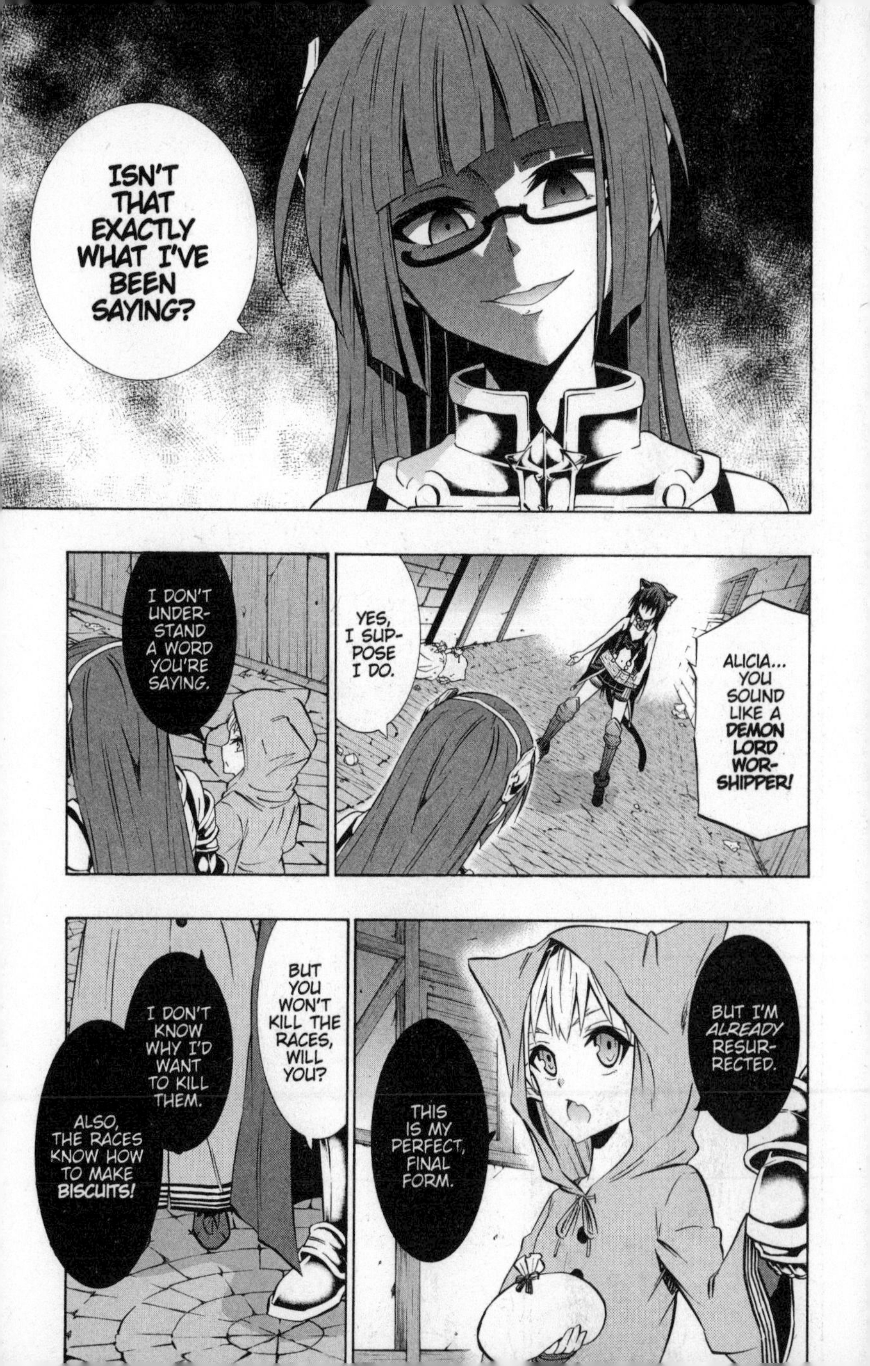
ISN'T THAT EXACTLY WHAT I'VE BEEN SAYING?
ALICIA... YOU SOUND LIKE A DEMON LORD WOR-SHIPPER!
YES, I SUP-POSE I DO.
I DON'T UNDER-STAND A WORD YOU'RE SAYING.
BUT I'M ALREADY RESUR-RECTED.
THIS IS MY PERFECT, FINAL FORM.
BUT YOU WON'T KILL THE RACES, WILL YOU?
I DON'T KNOW WHY I'D WANT TO KILL THEM.
ALSO, THE RACES KNOW HOW TO MAKE BISCUITS!

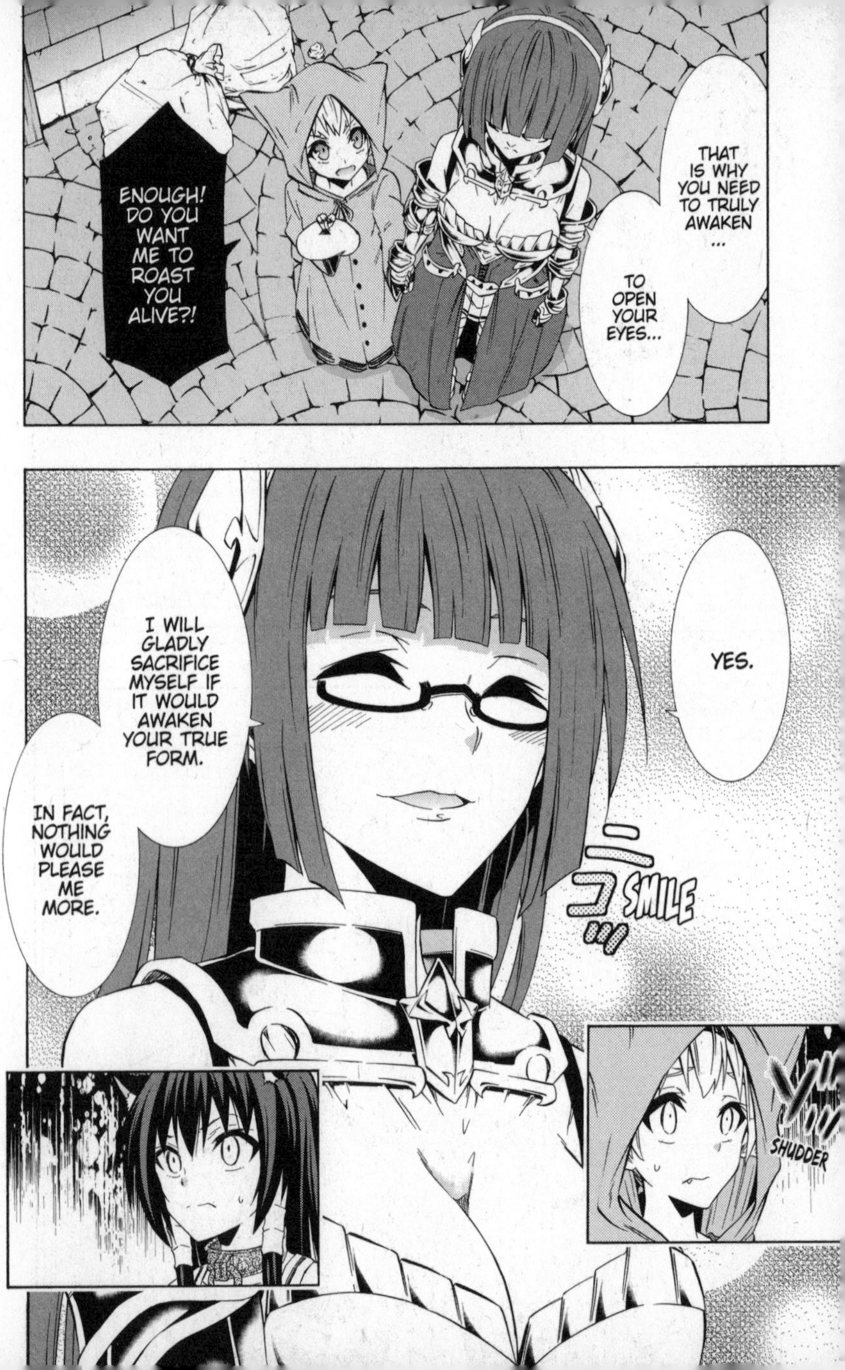
THAT IS WHY YOU NEED TO TRULY AWAKEN ...
TO OPEN YOUR EYES...
ENOUGH! DO YOU WANT ME TO ROAST YOU ALIVE?!
YES.
I WILL GLADLY SACRIFICE MYSELF IF IT WOULD AWAKEN YOUR TRUE FORM.
IN FACT, NOTHING WOULD PLEASE ME MORE.
SMILE
SHUDDER

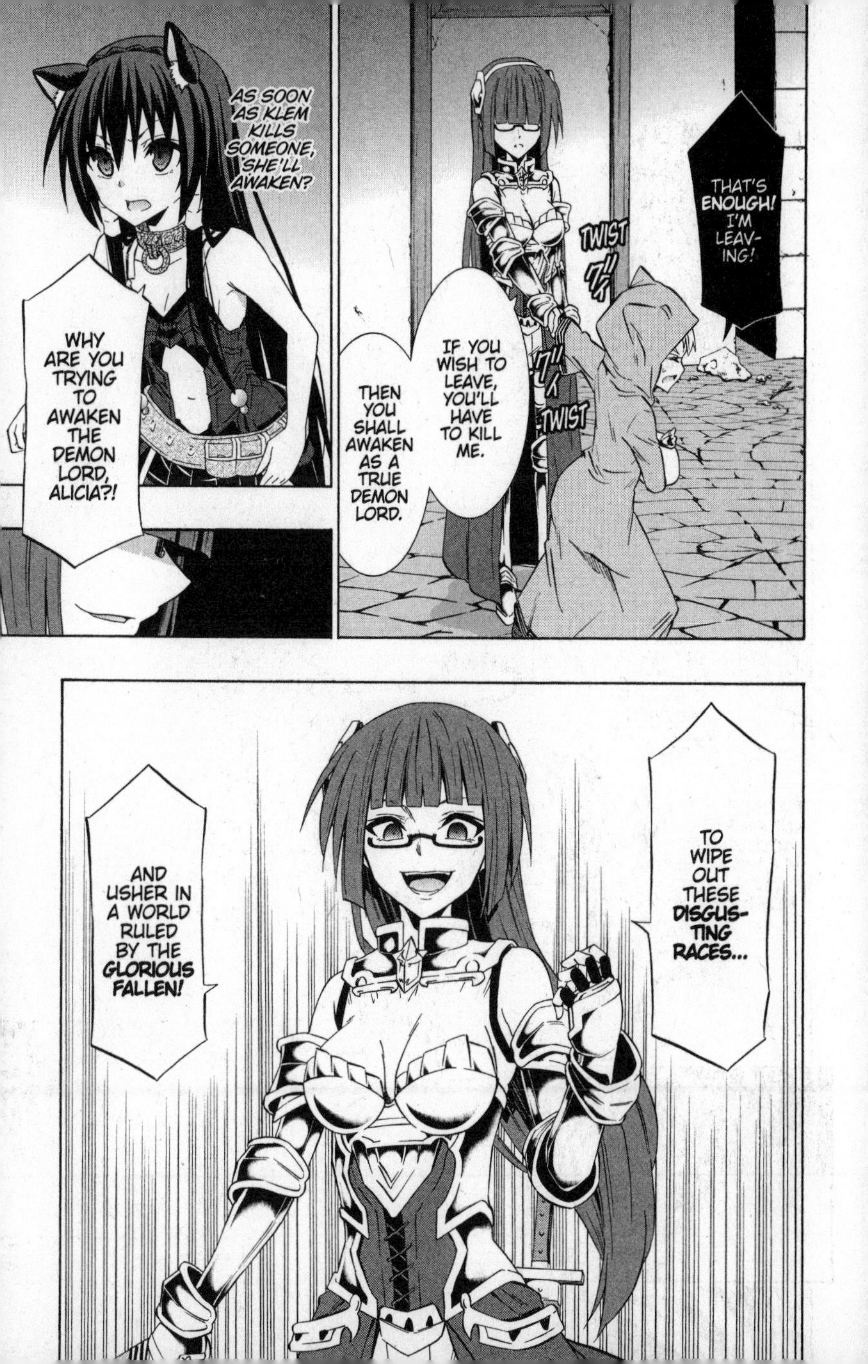
THAT'S ENOUGH! I'M LEAVING!
TWIST
TWIST
IF YOU WISH TO LEAVE, YOU'LL HAVE TO KILL ME.
THEN YOU SHALL AWAKEN AS A TRUE DEMON LORD.
AS SOON AS KLEM KILLS SOMEONE, SHE'LL AWAKEN?
WHY ARE YOU TRYING TO AWAKEN THE DEMON LORD, ALICIA?!
TO WIPE OUT THESE **DISGUSTING RACES...**
AND USHER IN A WORLD RULED BY THE **GLORIOUS FALLEN!**

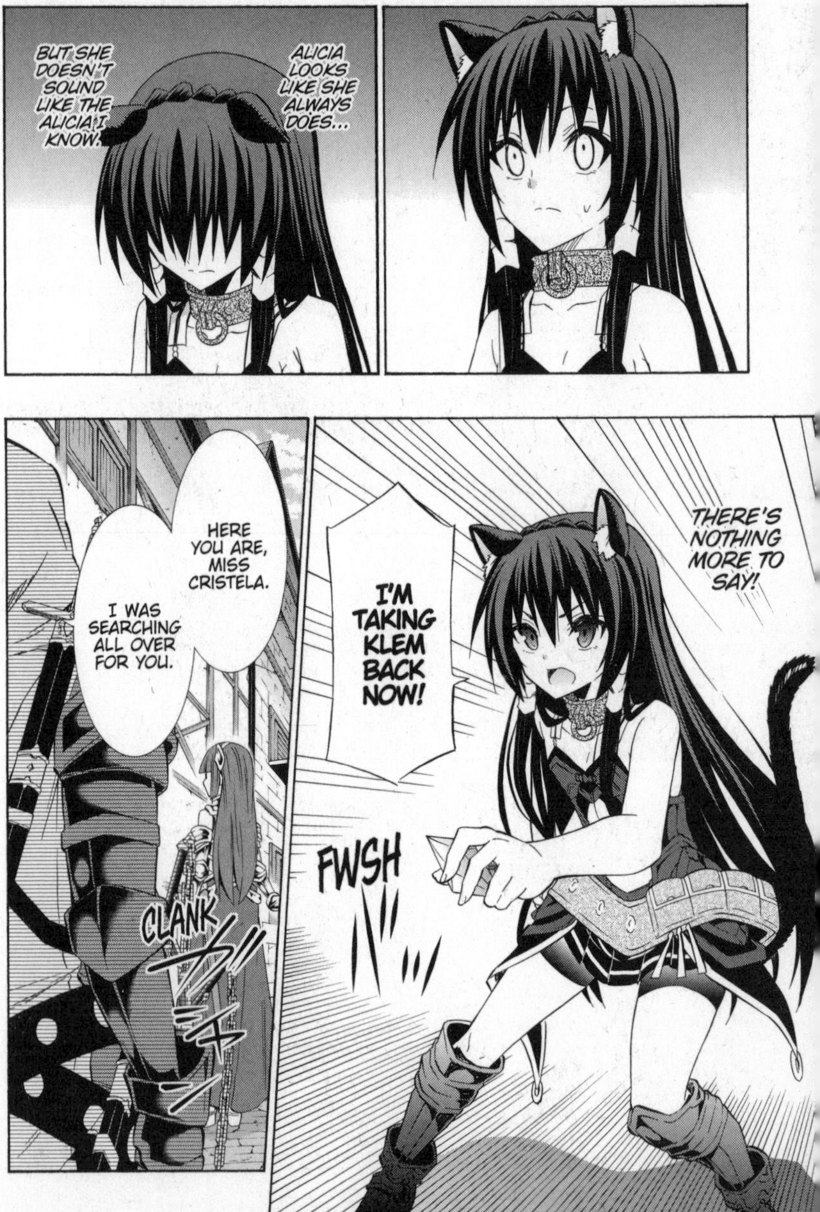
ALICIA LOOKS LIKE SHE ALWAYS DOES...
BUT SHE DOESN'T SOUND LIKE THE ALICIA I KNOW.
THERE'S NOTHING MORE TO SAY!
I'M TAKING KLEM BACK NOW!
FWSH
HERE YOU ARE, MISS CRISTELA.
I WAS SEARCHING ALL OVER FOR YOU.
CLANK

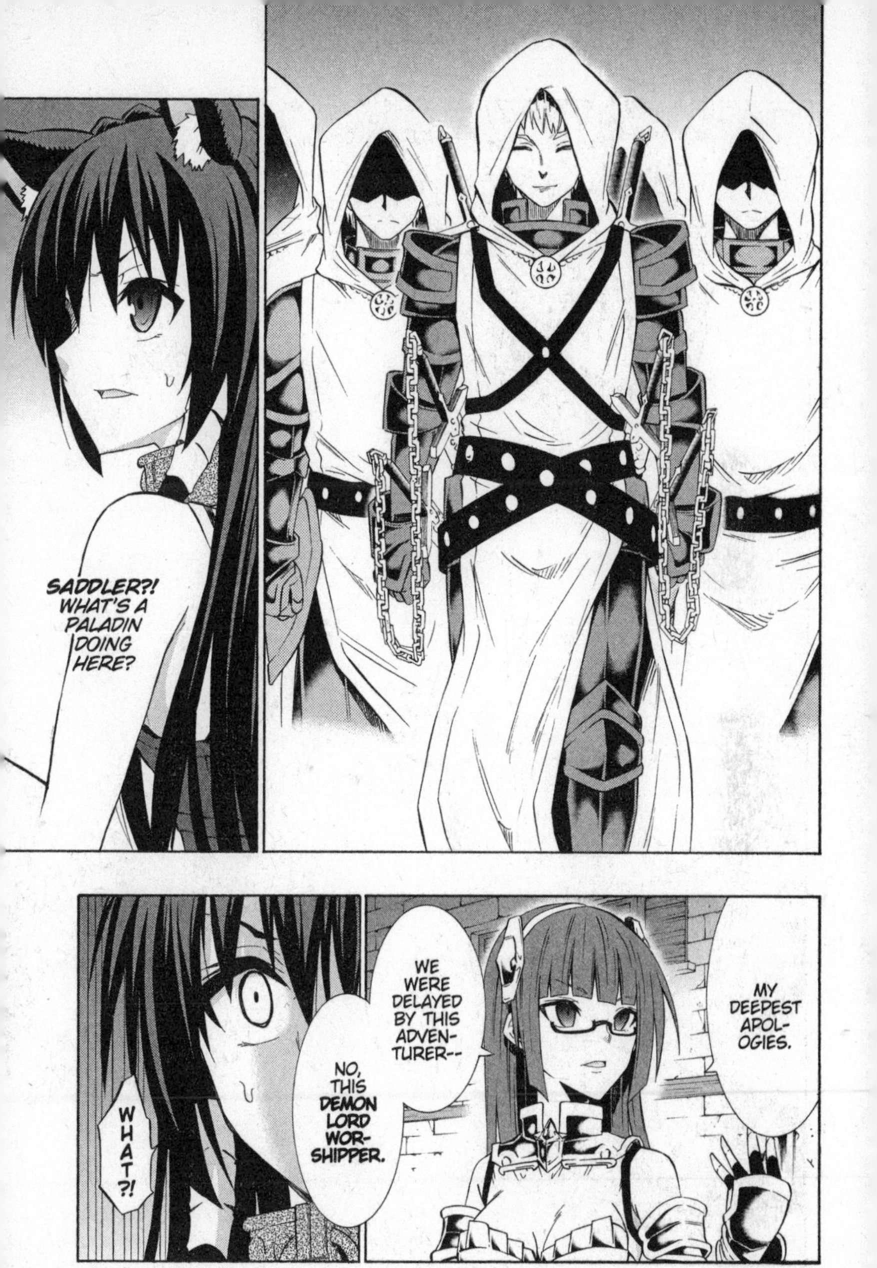
SADDLER?! WHAT'S A PALADIN DOING HERE?
MY DEEPEST APOLOGIES.
WE WERE DELAYED BY THIS ADVENTURER--
NO, THIS DEMON LORD WORSHIPPER.
WHAT?!

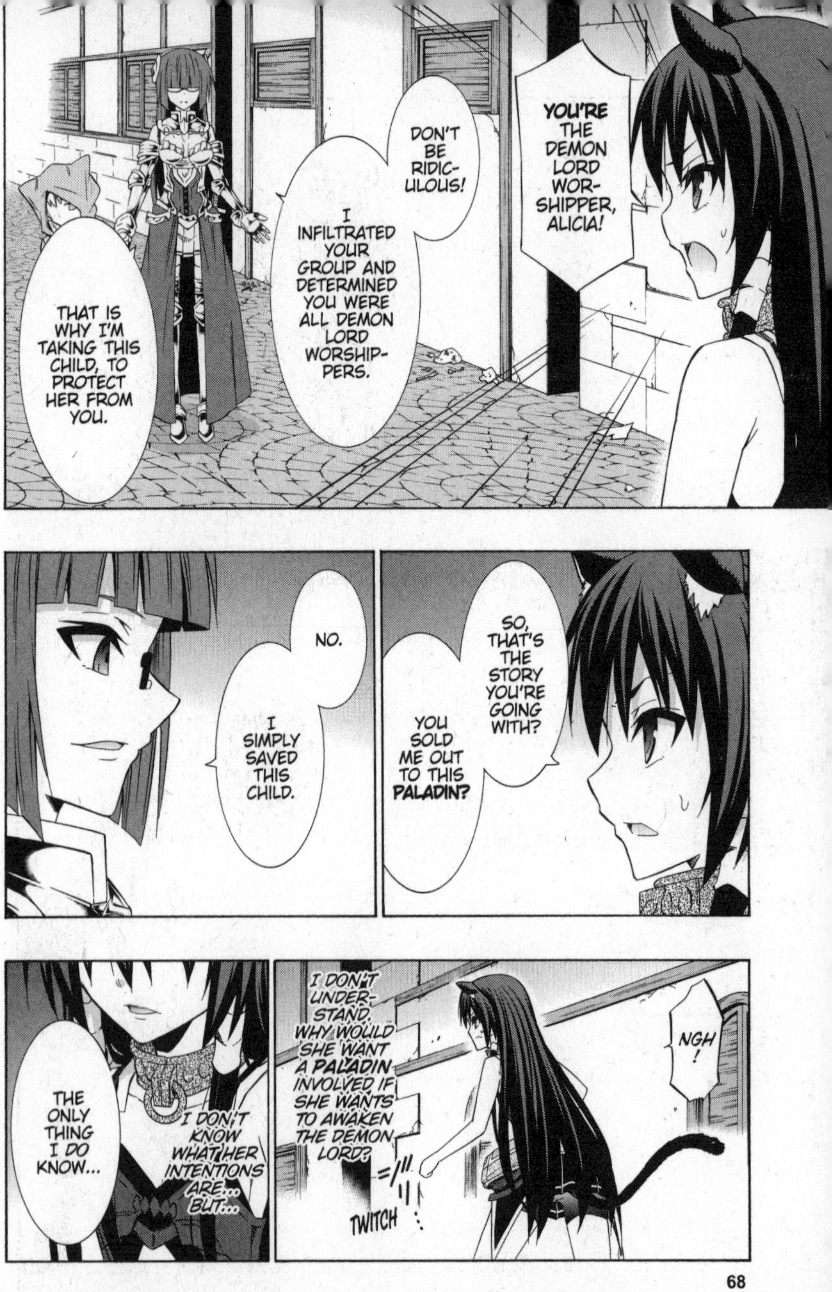
YOU'RE THE DEMON LORD WOR-SHIPPER, ALICIA!
DON'T BE RIDIC-ULOUS!
I INFILTRATED YOUR GROUP AND DETERMINED YOU WERE ALL DEMON LORD WORSHIP-PERS.
THAT IS WHY I'M TAKING THIS CHILD, TO PROTECT HER FROM YOU.
SO, THAT'S THE STORY YOU'RE GOING WITH?
YOU SOLD ME OUT TO THIS PALADIN?
NO.
I SIMPLY SAVED THIS CHILD.
NGH!
I DON'T UNDER-STAND. WHY WOULD SHE WANT A PALADIN INVOLVED IF SHE WANTS TO AWAKEN THE DEMON LORD?
TWITCH
I DON'T KNOW WHAT HER INTENTIONS ARE... BUT...
THE ONLY THING I DO KNOW...

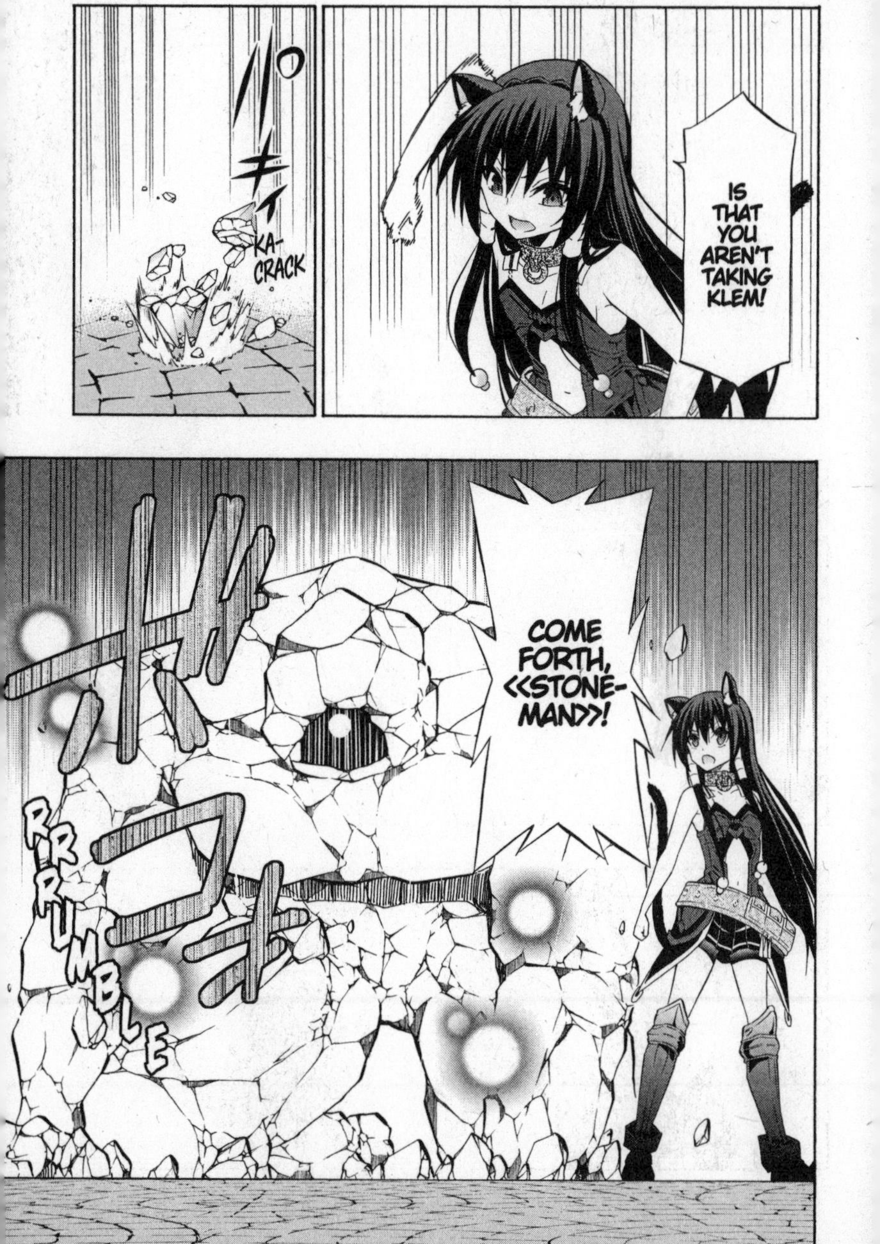
IS THAT YOU AREN'T TAKING KLEM!
パキィ
KA-CRACK
COME FORTH, <<STONE-MAN>>!
RRRUMBLE

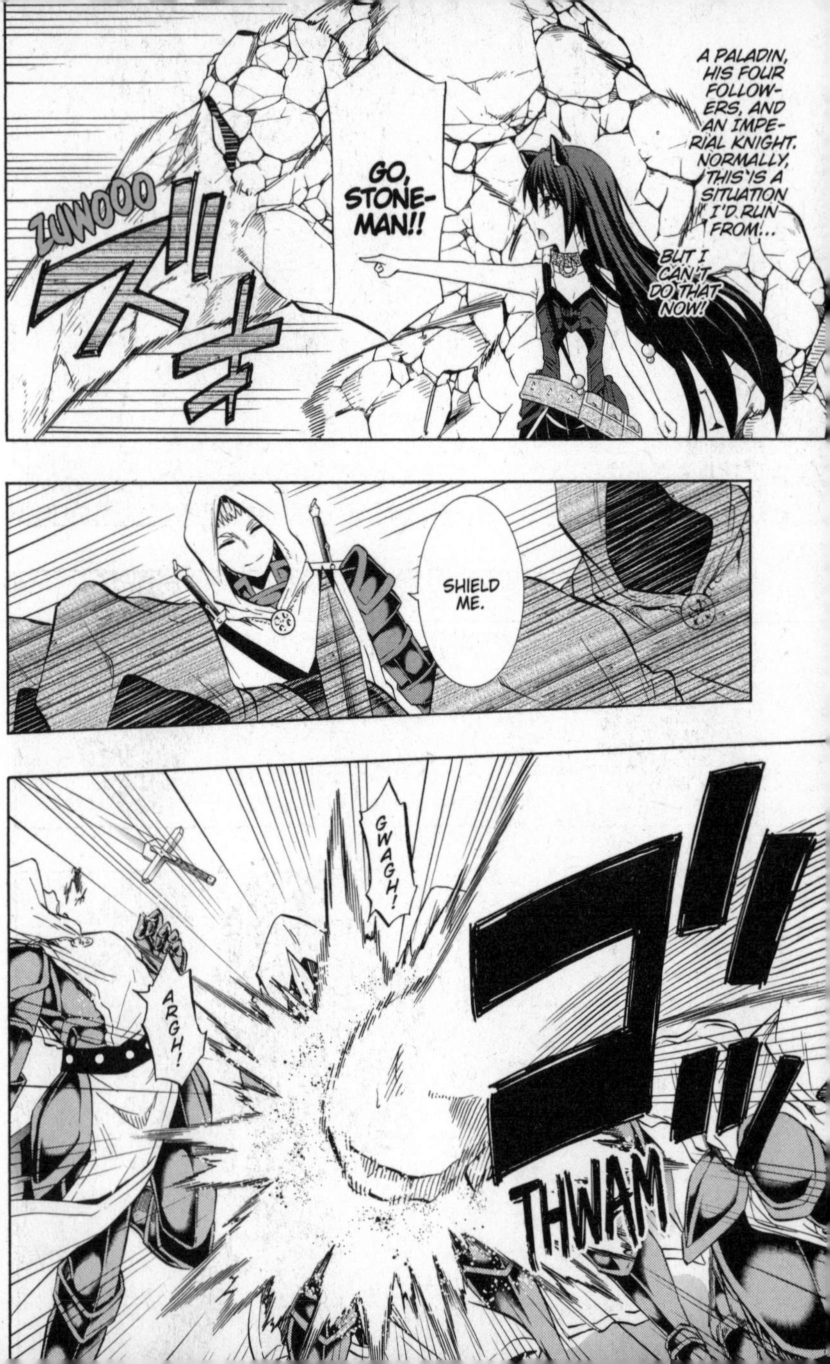
A PALADIN, HIS FOUR FOLLOWERS, AND AN IMPERIAL KNIGHT. NORMALLY, THIS IS A SITUATION I'D RUN FROM...
BUT I CAN'T DO THAT NOW!
GO, STONE-MAN!!
ZUWOOO
SHIELD ME.
THWAM
GWAGH!
ARGH!

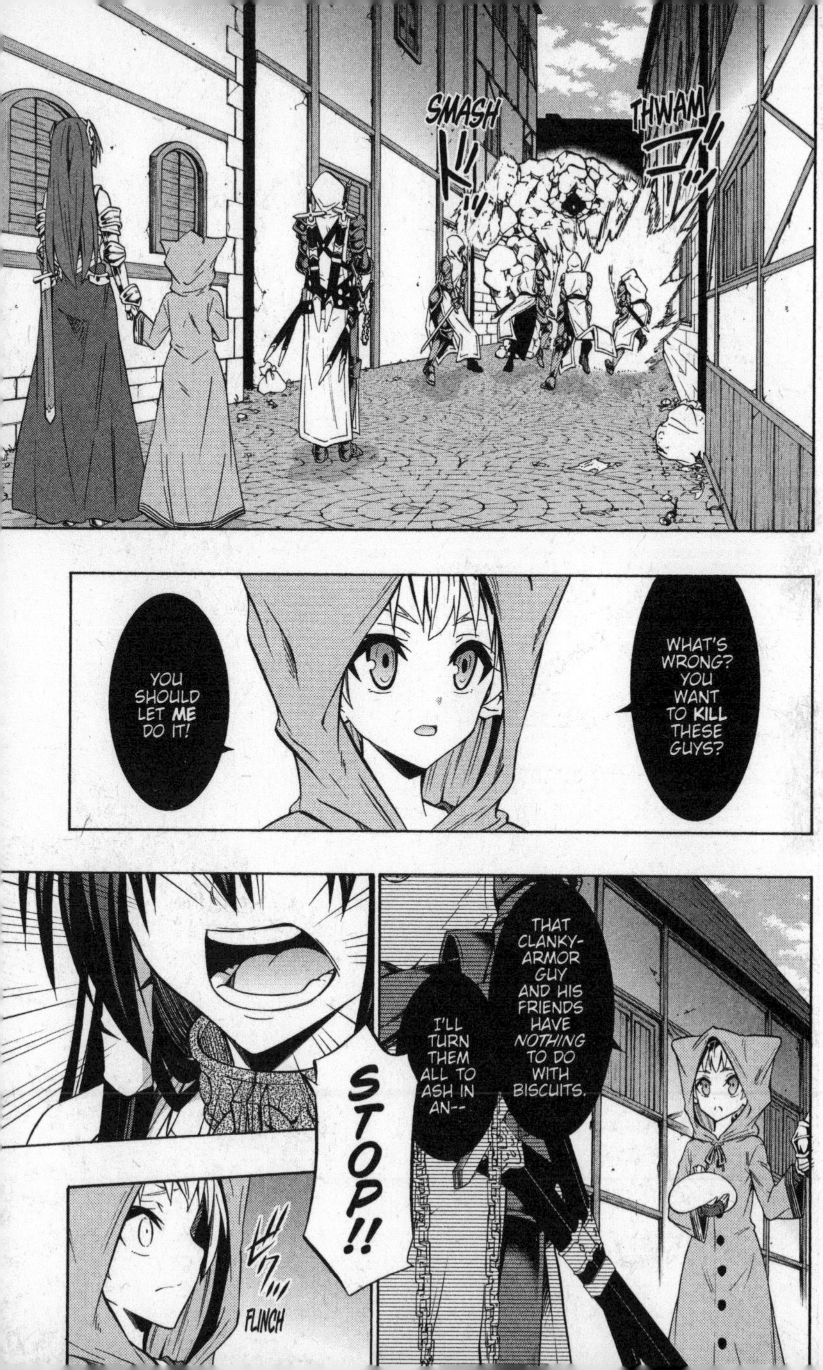
THWAM
SMASH
WHAT'S WRONG? YOU WANT TO **KILL** THESE GUYS?
YOU SHOULD LET **ME** DO IT!
THAT CLANKY-ARMOR GUY AND HIS FRIENDS HAVE *NOTHING* TO DO WITH BISCUITS.
I'LL TURN THEM ALL TO ASH IN AN--
STOP!!
FLINCH

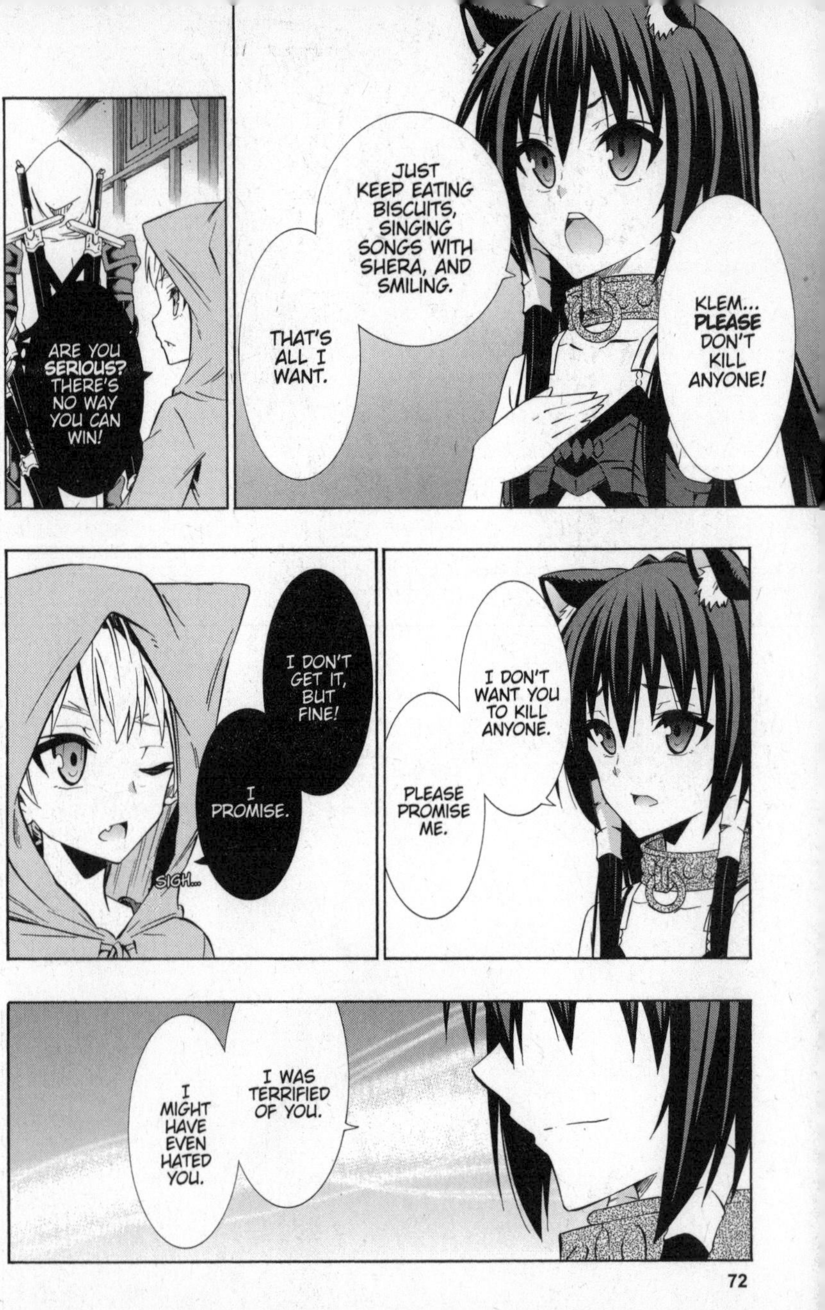
KLEM... **PLEASE** DON'T KILL ANYONE!
JUST KEEP EATING BISCUITS, SINGING SONGS WITH SHERA, AND SMILING.
THAT'S ALL I WANT.
ARE YOU **SERIOUS?** THERE'S NO WAY YOU CAN WIN!
I DON'T WANT YOU TO KILL ANYONE.
PLEASE PROMISE ME.
I DON'T GET IT, BUT FINE!
I PROMISE.
SIGH...
I WAS TERRIFIED OF YOU.
I MIGHT HAVE EVEN HATED YOU.

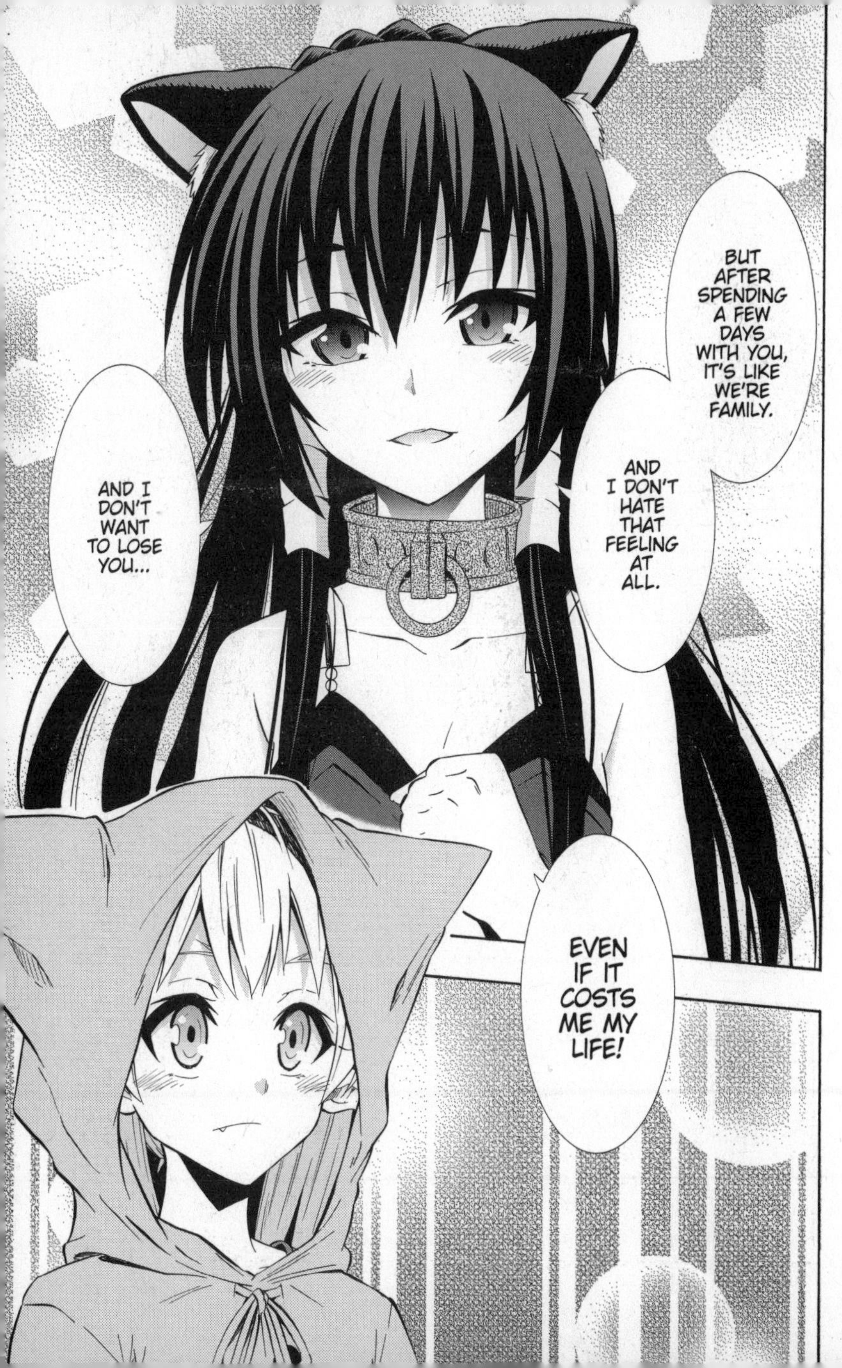
BUT AFTER SPENDING A FEW DAYS WITH YOU, IT'S LIKE WE'RE FAMILY.
AND I DON'T HATE THAT FEELING AT ALL.
AND I DON'T WANT TO LOSE YOU...
EVEN IF IT COSTS ME MY LIFE!

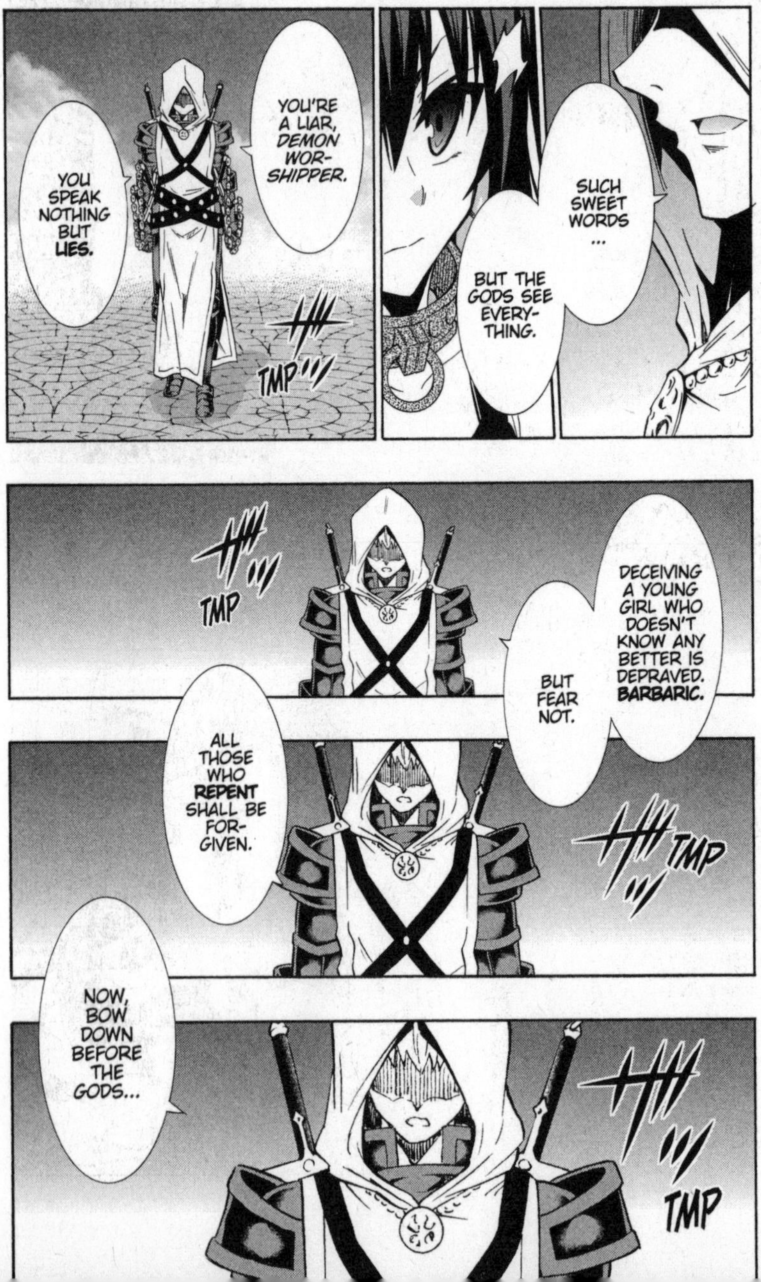
SUCH SWEET WORDS ...
BUT THE GODS SEE EVERYTHING.
YOU'RE A LIAR, DEMON WORSHIPPER.
YOU SPEAK NOTHING BUT **LIES.**
TMP
DECEIVING A YOUNG GIRL WHO DOESN'T KNOW ANY BETTER IS DEPRAVED. **BARBARIC.**
TMP
BUT FEAR NOT.
ALL THOSE WHO **REPENT** SHALL BE FORGIVEN.
TMP
NOW, BOW DOWN BEFORE THE GODS...
TMP

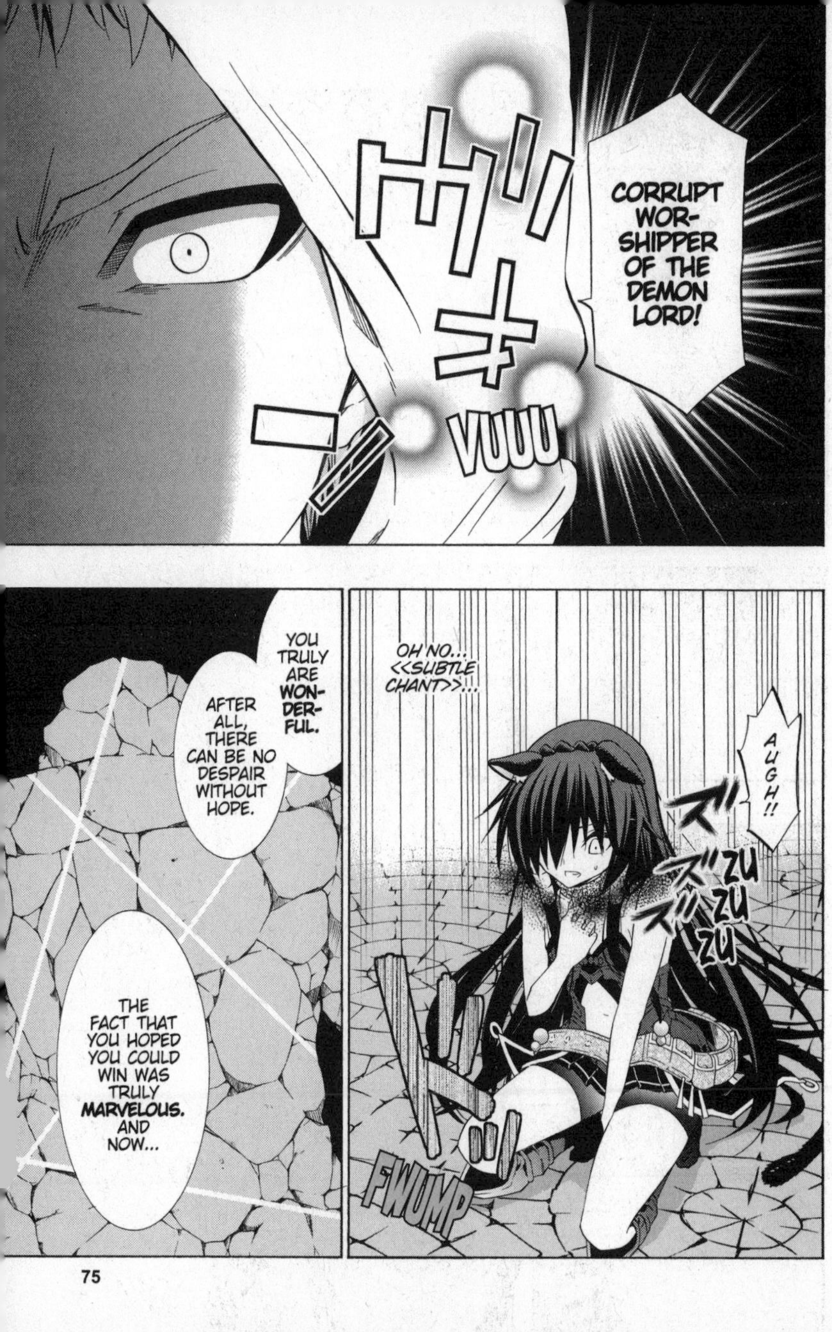
CORRUPT WOR-SHIPPER OF THE DEMON LORD!
VUUU
OH NO... <<SUBTLE CHANT>>...
AUGH!!
ZU ZU ZU
FWUMP
YOU TRULY ARE **WON-DER-FUL.**
AFTER ALL, THERE CAN BE NO DESPAIR WITHOUT HOPE.
THE FACT THAT YOU HOPED YOU COULD WIN WAS TRULY **MARVELOUS.** AND NOW...

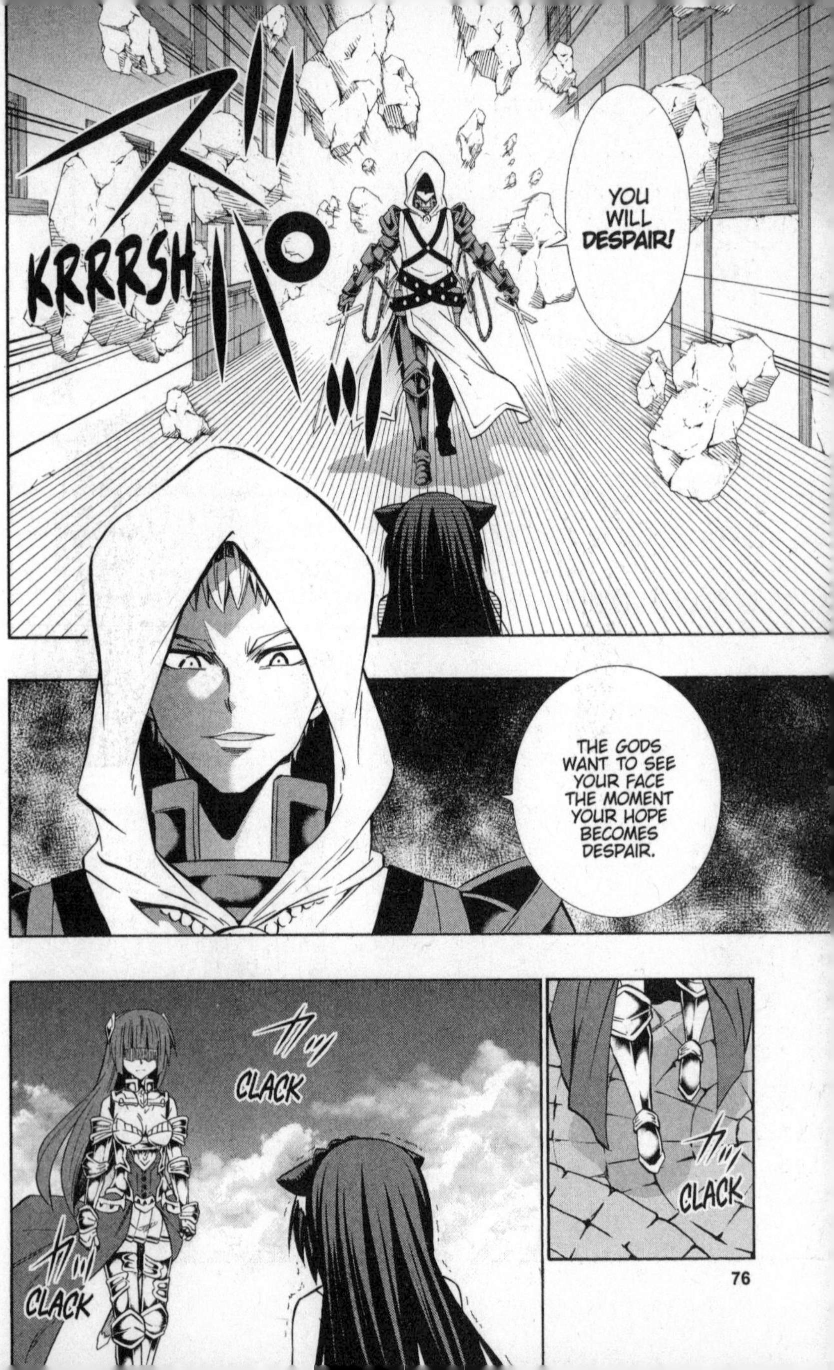
KRRRSH
YOU WILL DESPAIR!
THE GODS WANT TO SEE YOUR FACE THE MOMENT YOUR HOPE BECOMES DESPAIR.
CLACK
CLACK
CLACK

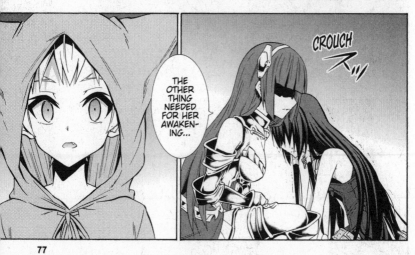

THE OTHER THING NEEDED FOR HER AWAKENING...

CROUCH

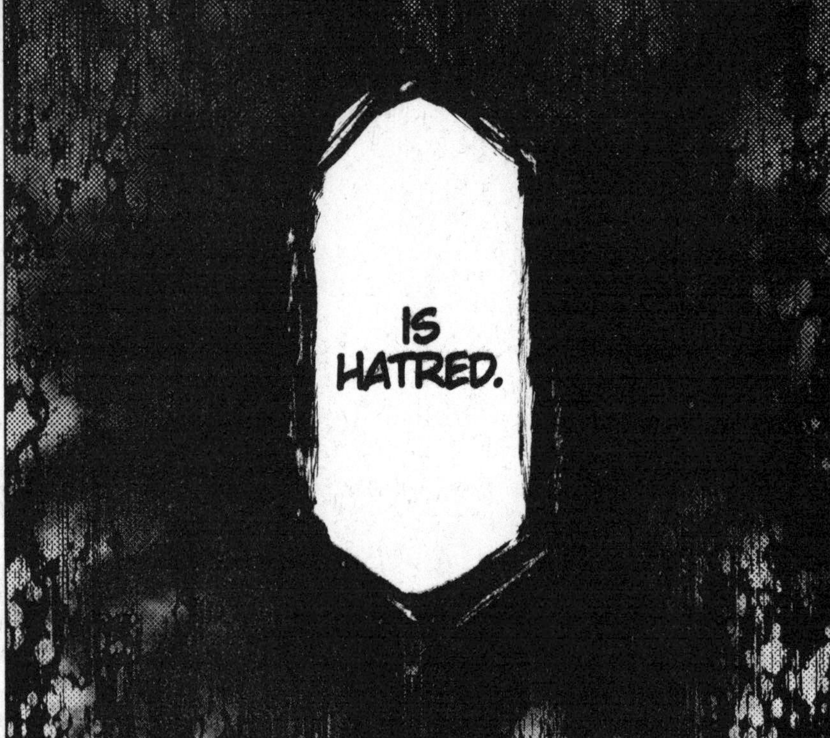
IS HATRED.

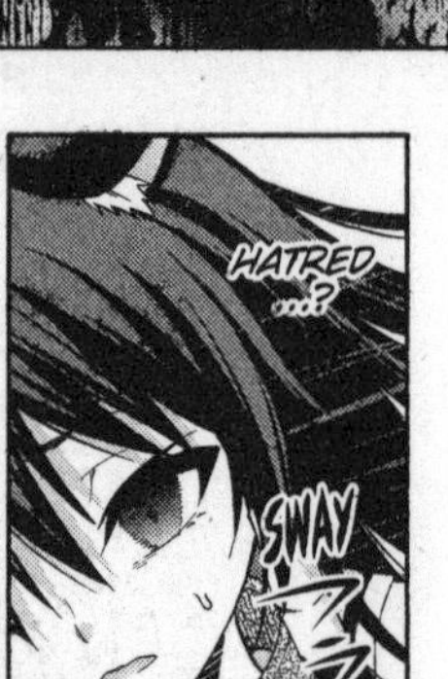
HATRED ...?
SWAY

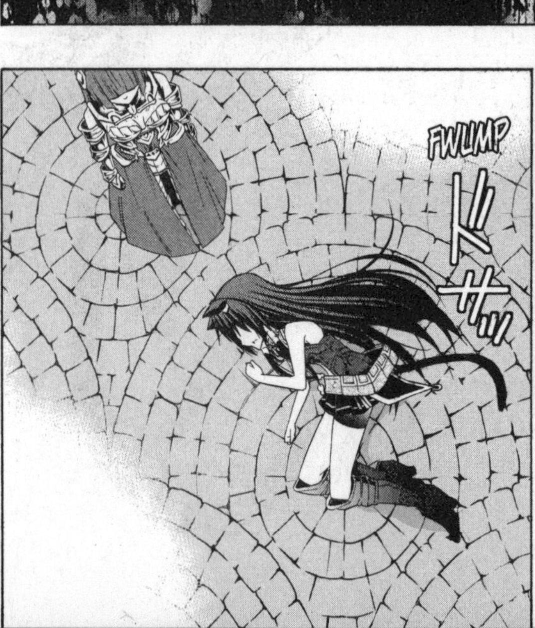
FWUMP

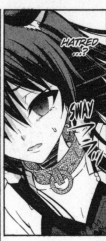

32 REM'S STORY I

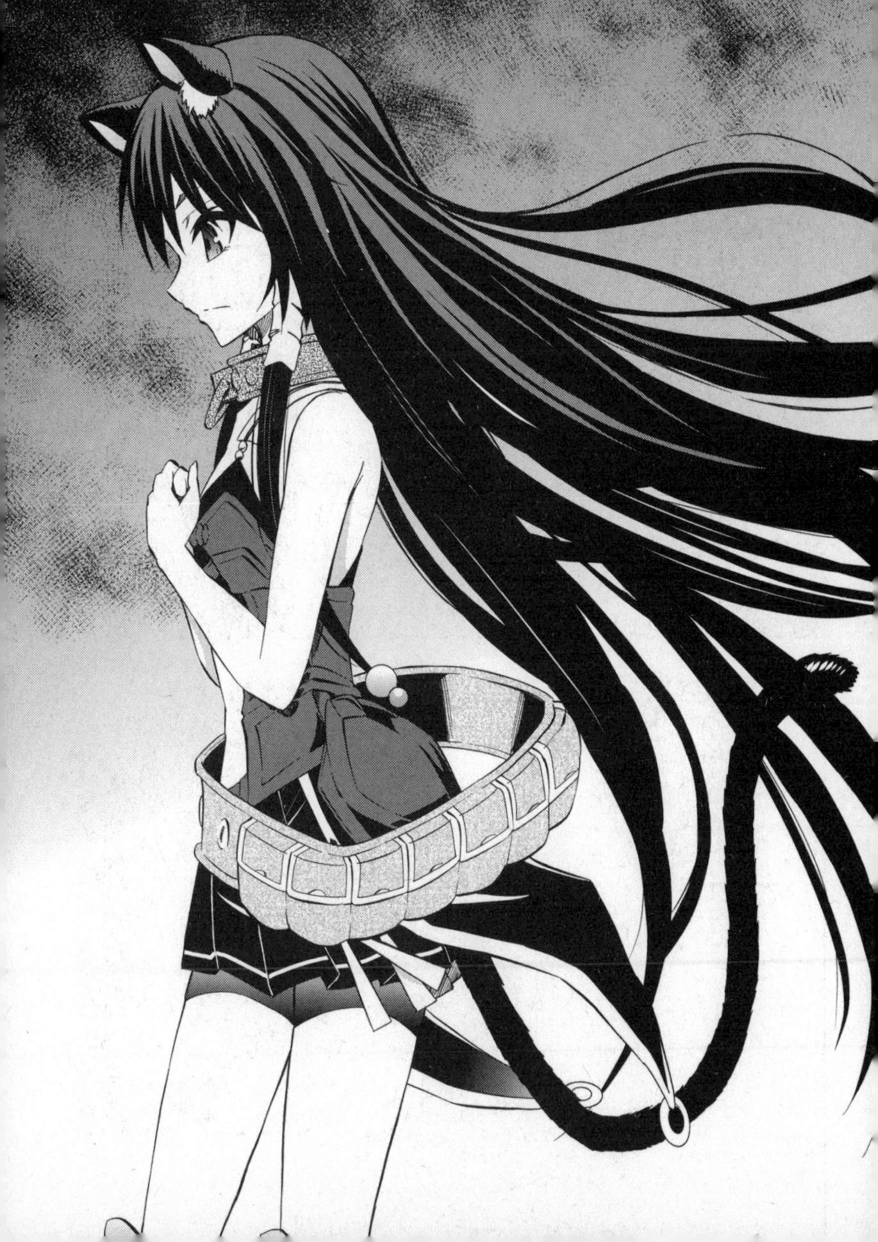

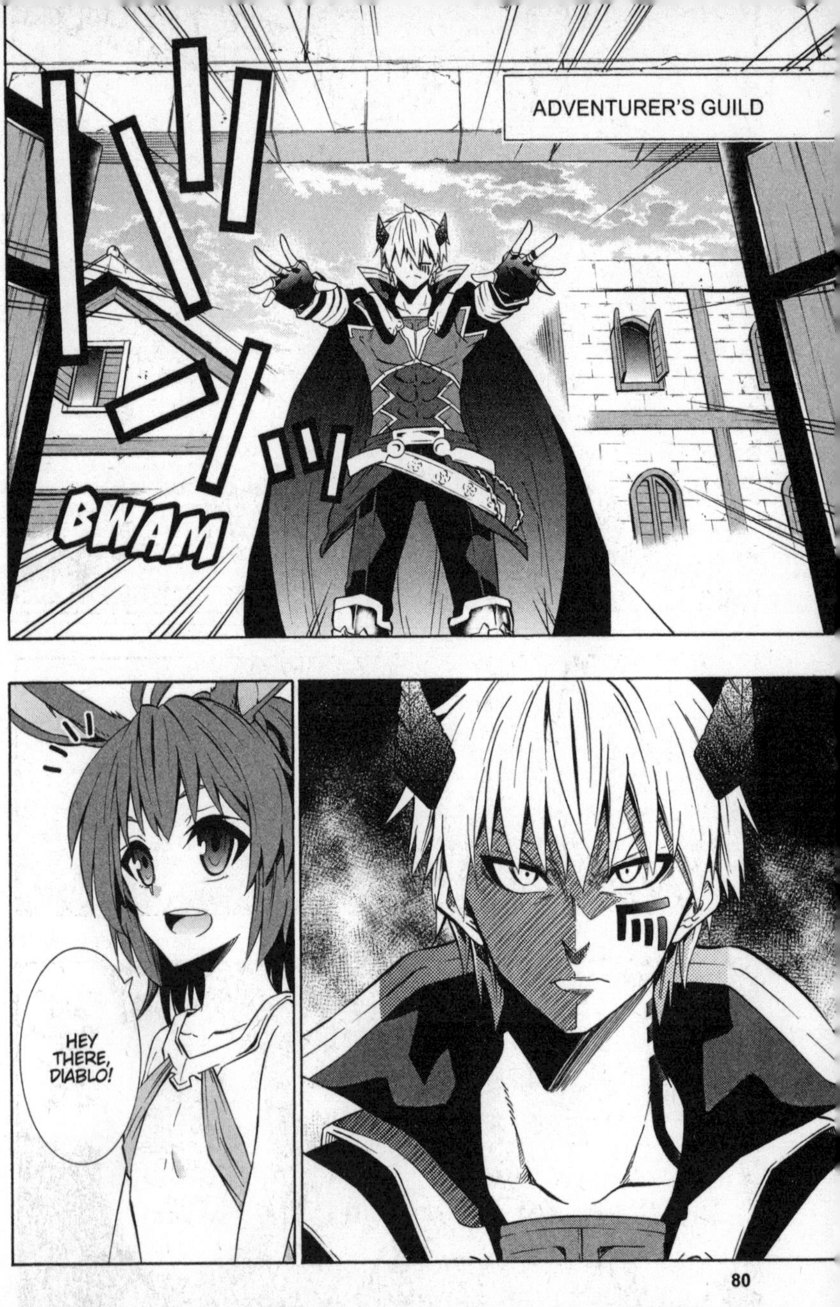
ADVENTURER'S GUILD
BWAM
HEY THERE, DIABLO!

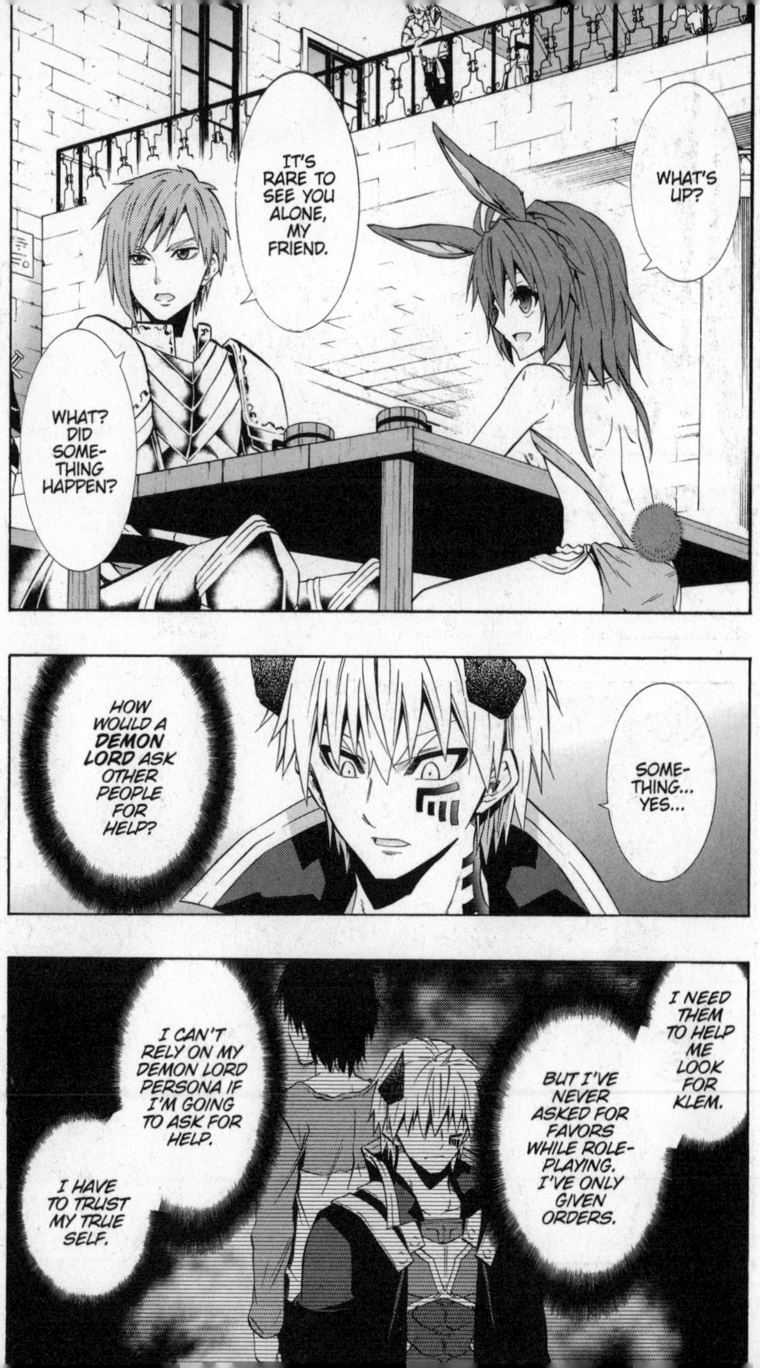
WHAT'S UP?
IT'S RARE TO SEE YOU ALONE, MY FRIEND.
WHAT? DID SOME-THING HAPPEN?
SOME-THING... YES...
HOW WOULD A **DEMON LORD** ASK OTHER PEOPLE FOR HELP?
I NEED THEM TO HELP ME LOOK FOR KLEM.
BUT I'VE NEVER ASKED FOR FAVORS WHILE ROLE-PLAYING. I'VE ONLY GIVEN ORDERS.
I CAN'T RELY ON MY DEMON LORD PERSONA IF I'M GOING TO ASK FOR HELP.
I HAVE TO TRUST MY TRUE SELF.

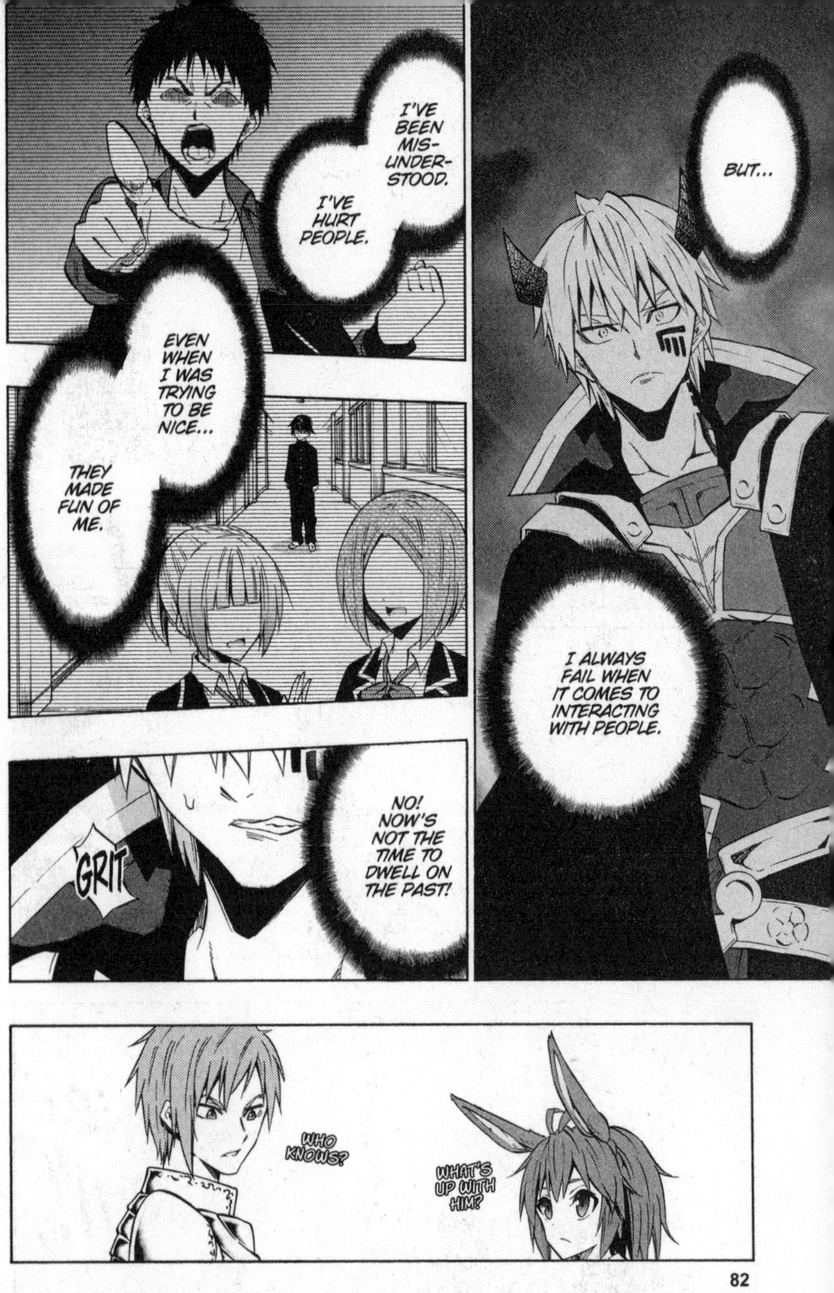
BUT...
I ALWAYS FAIL WHEN IT COMES TO INTERACTING WITH PEOPLE.
I'VE BEEN MIS-UNDER-STOOD.
I'VE HURT PEOPLE.
EVEN WHEN I WAS TRYING TO BE NICE...
THEY MADE FUN OF ME.
NO! NOW'S NOT THE TIME TO DWELL ON THE PAST!
GRIT
WHAT'S UP WITH HIM?
WHO KNOWS?

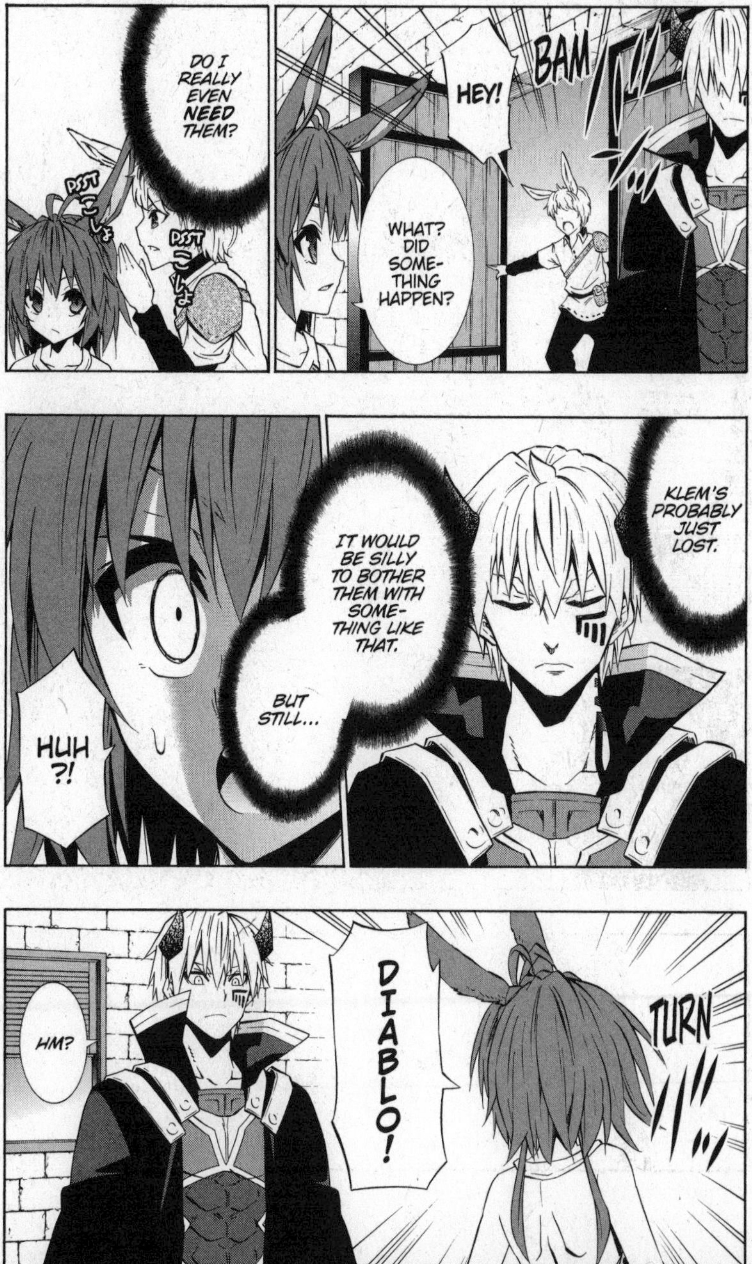
BAM
HEY!
WHAT? DID SOME-THING HAPPEN?
DO I REALLY EVEN NEED THEM?
PSST こしょ
PSST こしょ
KLEM'S PROBABLY JUST LOST.
IT WOULD BE SILLY TO BOTHER THEM WITH SOME-THING LIKE THAT.
BUT STILL...
HUH?!
TURN
DIABLO!
HM?

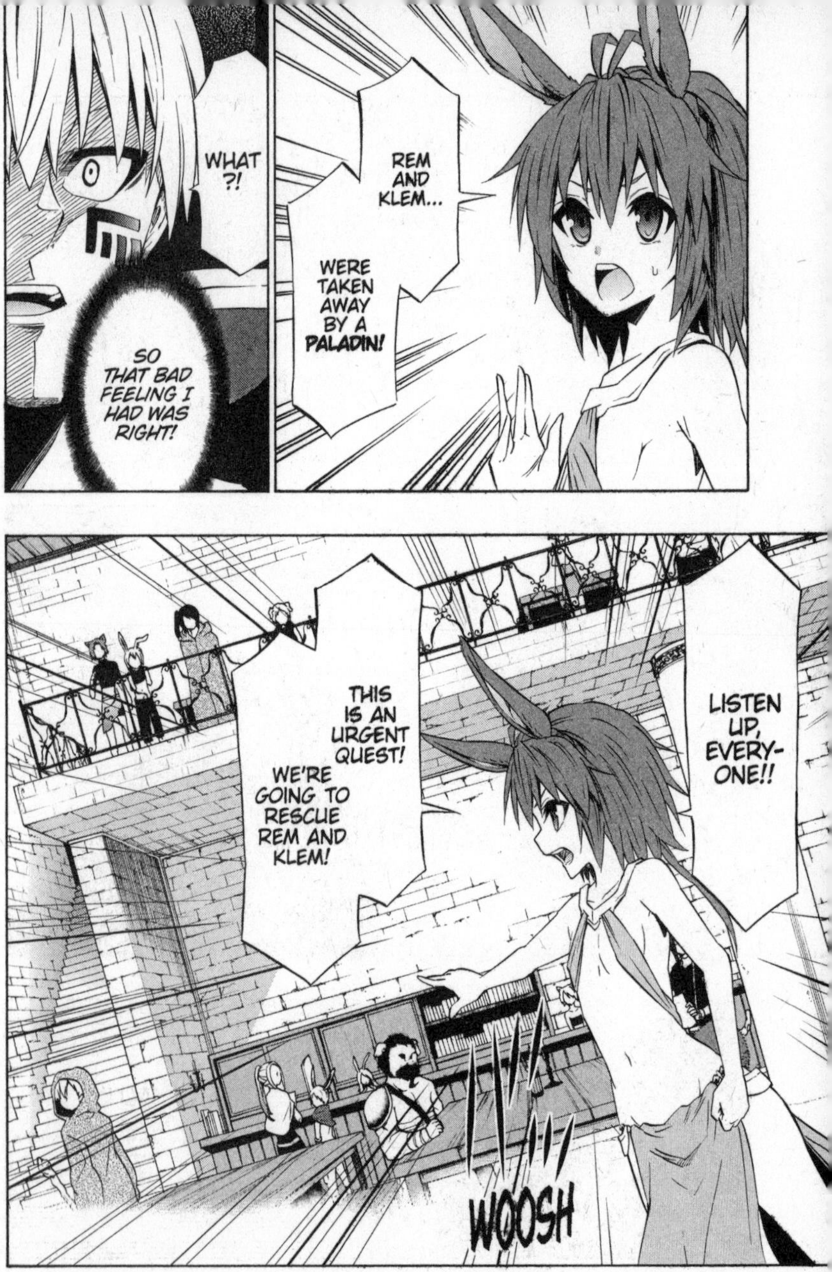
REM AND KLEM...
WERE TAKEN AWAY BY A PALADIN!
WHAT ?!
SO THAT BAD FEELING I HAD WAS RIGHT!
LISTEN UP, EVERY-ONE!!
THIS IS AN URGENT QUEST!
WE'RE GOING TO RESCUE REM AND KLEM!
WOOSH

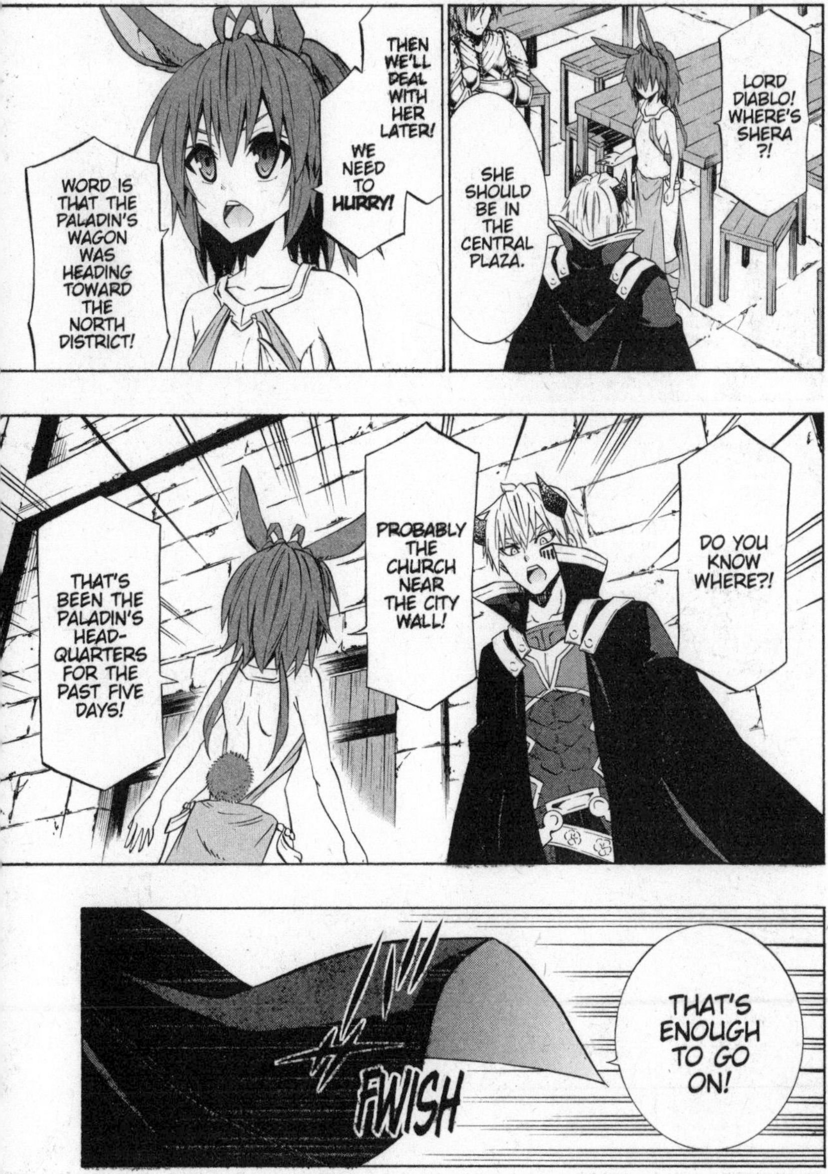
LORD DIABLO! WHERE'S SHERA?!
SHE SHOULD BE IN THE CENTRAL PLAZA.
THEN WE'LL DEAL WITH HER LATER!
WE NEED TO HURRY!
WORD IS THAT THE PALADIN'S WAGON WAS HEADING TOWARD THE NORTH DISTRICT!
DO YOU KNOW WHERE?!
PROBABLY THE CHURCH NEAR THE CITY WALL!
THAT'S BEEN THE PALADIN'S HEAD-QUARTERS FOR THE PAST FIVE DAYS!
THAT'S ENOUGH TO GO ON!
FWISH

YOU HAVE MY THANKS!

HUH ?

DASH

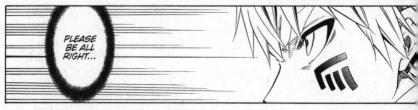

PLEASE BE ALL RIGHT...

HE DID.

DID HE JUST SAY THANKS?

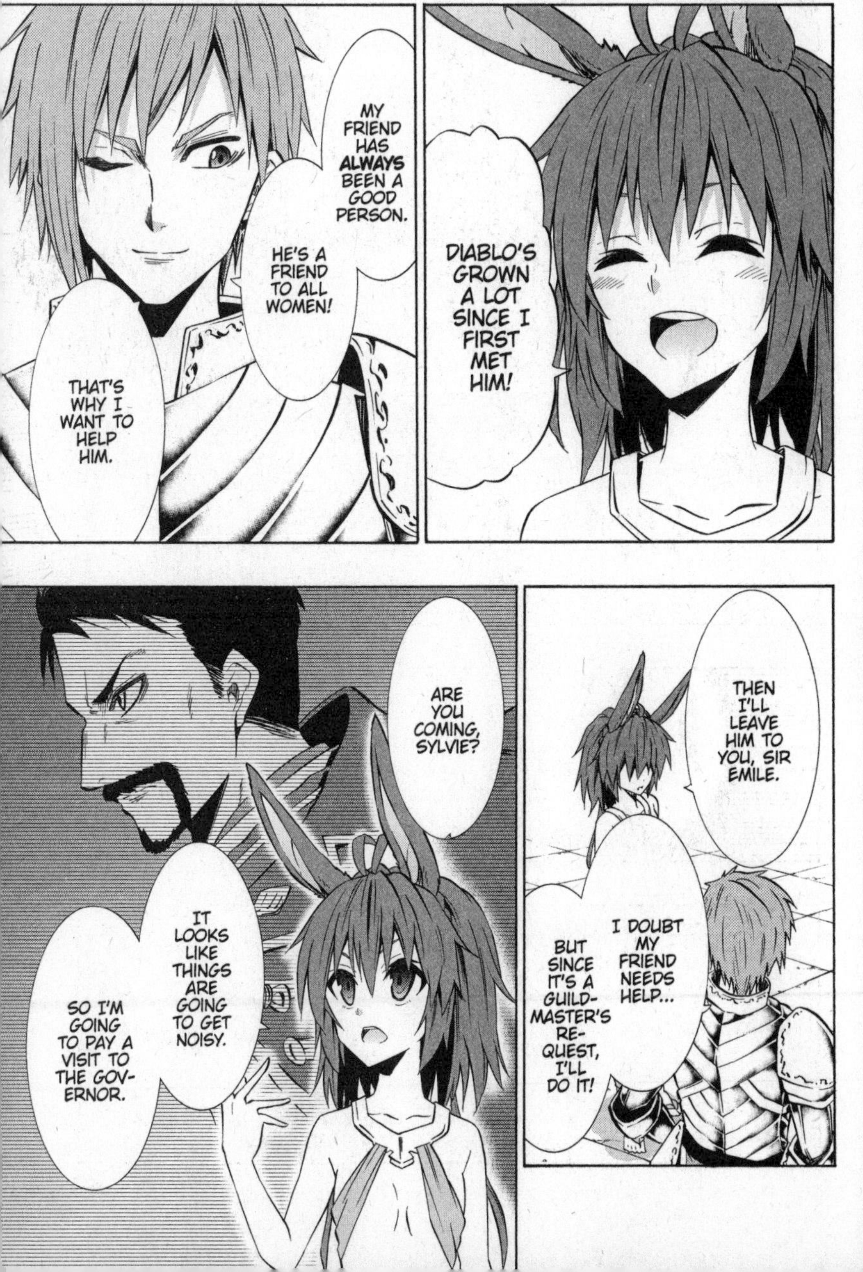
DIABLO'S GROWN A LOT SINCE I FIRST MET HIM!
MY FRIEND HAS **ALWAYS** BEEN A GOOD PERSON.
HE'S A FRIEND TO ALL WOMEN!
THAT'S WHY I WANT TO HELP HIM.
THEN I'LL LEAVE HIM TO YOU, SIR EMILE.
I DOUBT MY FRIEND NEEDS HELP...
BUT SINCE IT'S A GUILD-MASTER'S RE-QUEST, I'LL DO IT!
ARE YOU COMING, SYLVIE?
IT LOOKS LIKE THINGS ARE GOING TO GET NOISY.
SO I'M GOING TO PAY A VISIT TO THE GOV-ERNOR.

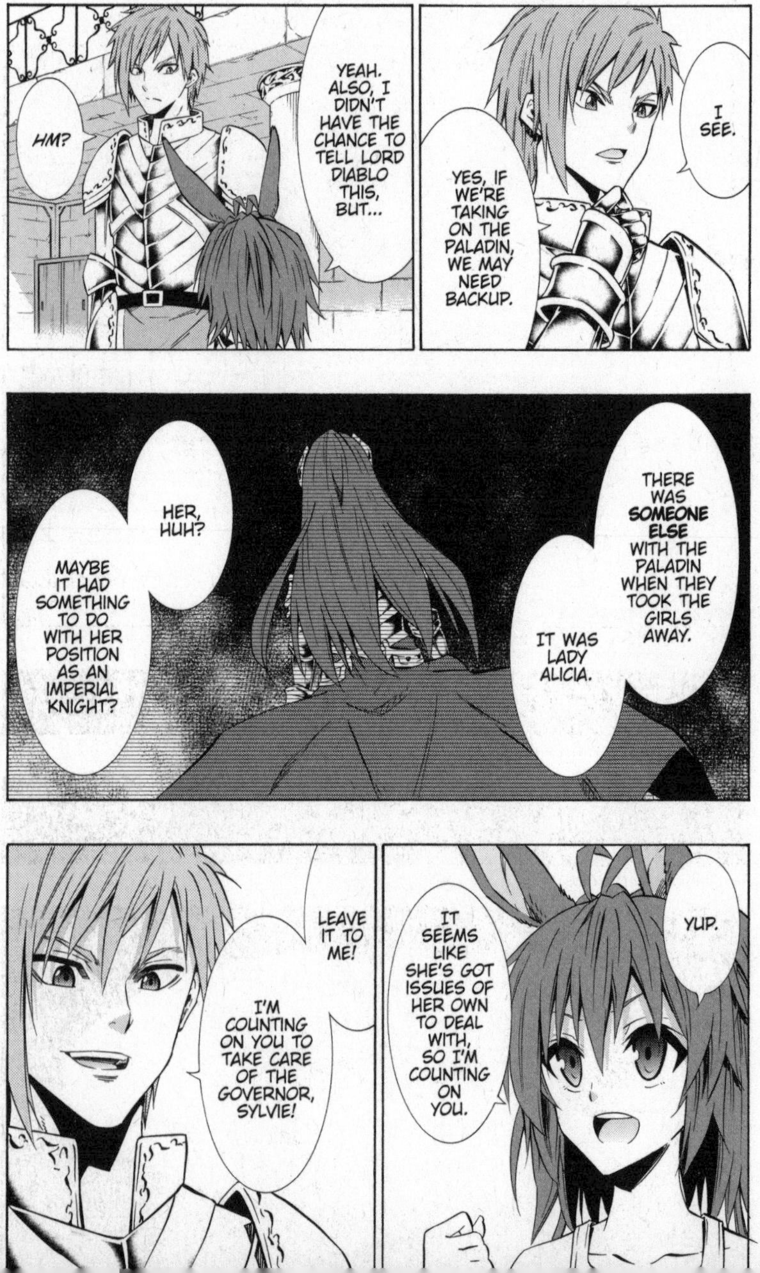
I SEE.
YES, IF WE'RE TAKING ON THE PALADIN, WE MAY NEED BACKUP.
YEAH. ALSO, I DIDN'T HAVE THE CHANCE TO TELL LORD DIABLO THIS, BUT...
HM?
THERE WAS **SOMEONE ELSE** WITH THE PALADIN WHEN THEY TOOK THE GIRLS AWAY.
IT WAS LADY ALICIA.
HER, HUH?
MAYBE IT HAD SOMETHING TO DO WITH HER POSITION AS AN IMPERIAL KNIGHT?
YUP.
IT SEEMS LIKE SHE'S GOT ISSUES OF HER OWN TO DEAL WITH, SO I'M COUNTING ON YOU.
LEAVE IT TO ME!
I'M COUNTING ON YOU TO TAKE CARE OF THE GOVERNOR, SYLVIE!

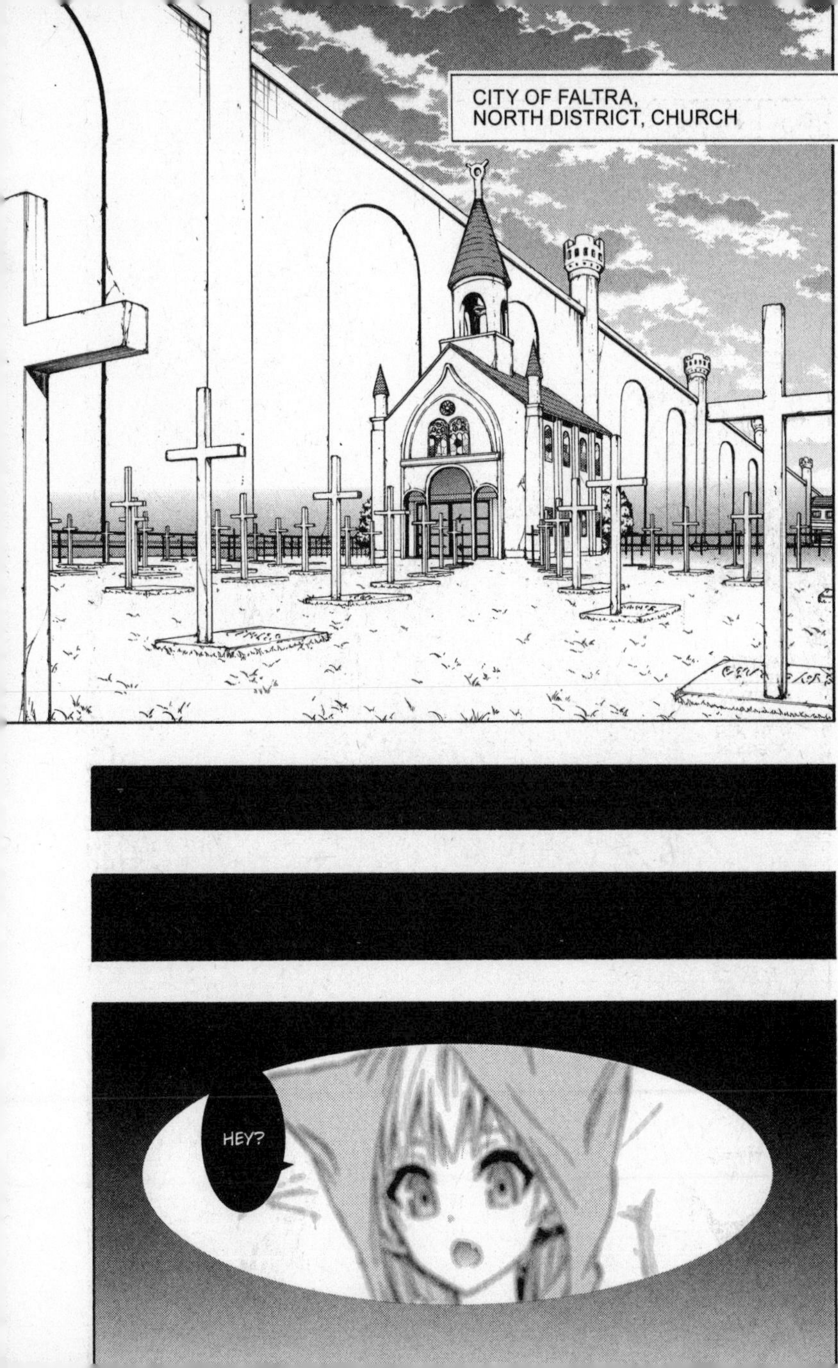
CITY OF FALTRA, NORTH DISTRICT, CHURCH
HEY?

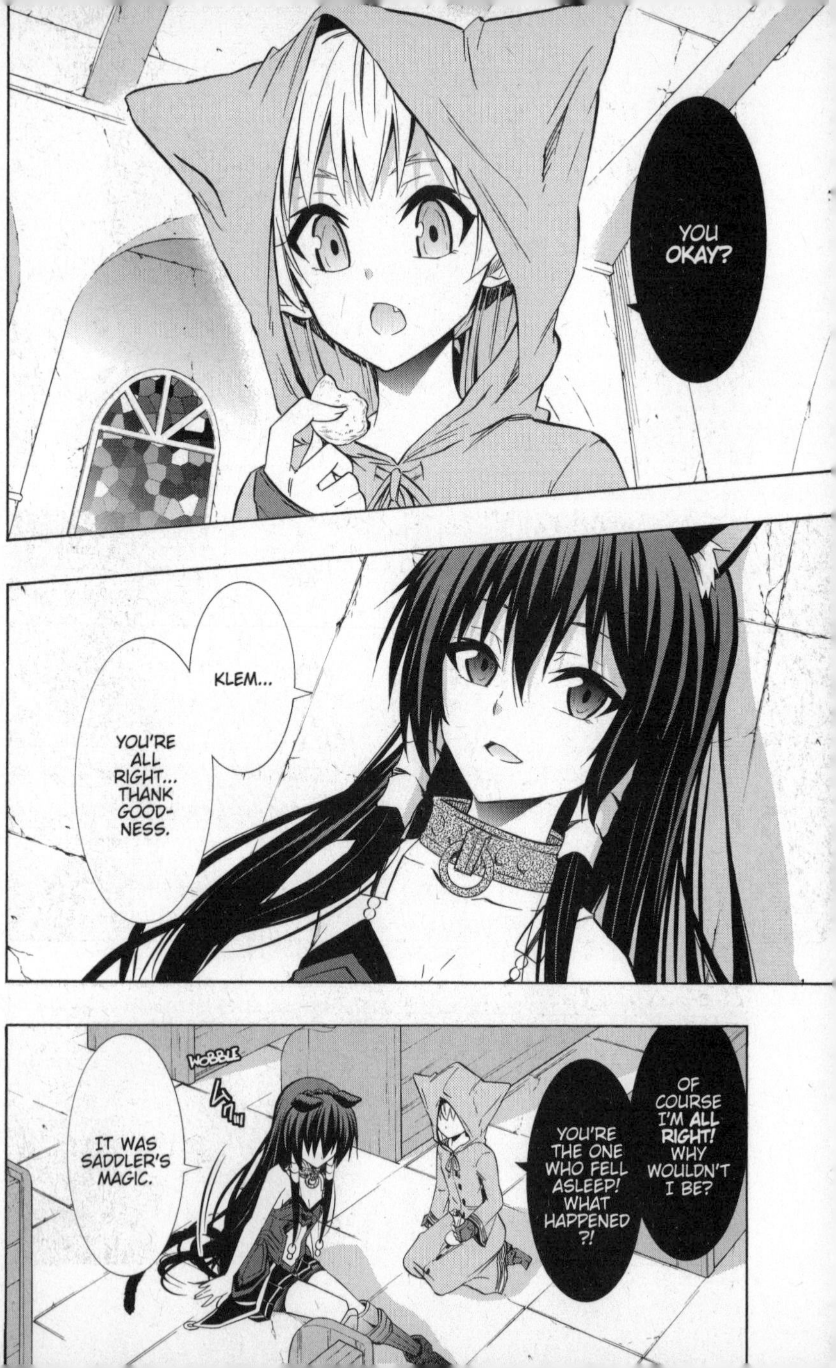
YOU OKAY?
KLEM...
YOU'RE ALL RIGHT... THANK GOOD-NESS.
OF COURSE I'M **ALL RIGHT!** WHY WOULDN'T I BE?
YOU'RE THE ONE WHO FELL ASLEEP! WHAT HAPPENED?!
WOBBLE
IT WAS SADDLER'S MAGIC.

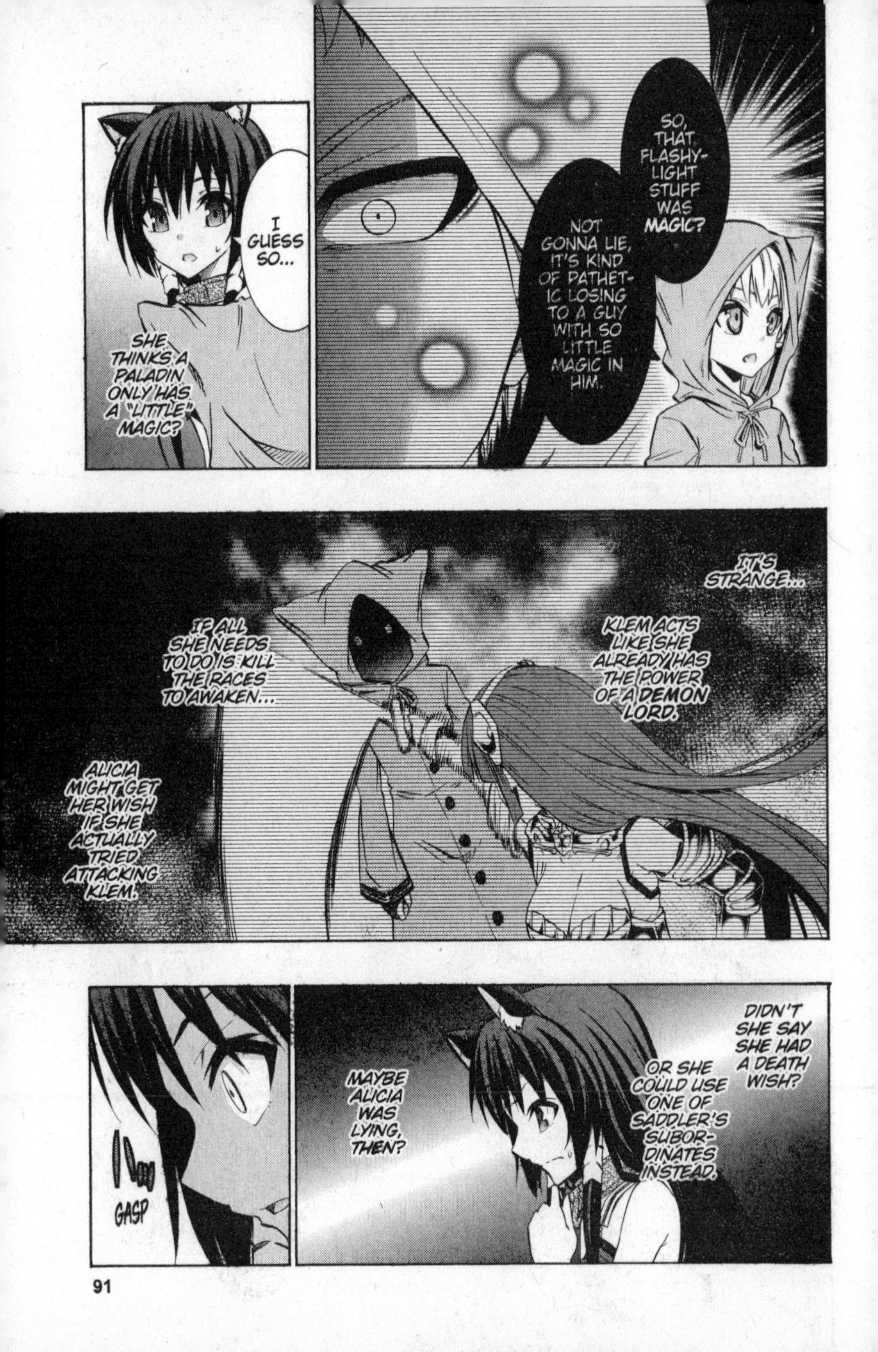

SO, THAT FLASHY-LIGHT STUFF WAS MAGIC?
NOT GONNA LIE, IT'S KIND OF PATHETIC LOSING TO A GUY WITH SO LITTLE MAGIC IN HIM.
I GUESS SO...
SHE THINKS A PALADIN ONLY HAS A "LITTLE" MAGIC?
IT'S STRANGE...
KLEM ACTS LIKE SHE ALREADY HAS THE POWER OF A DEMON LORD.
IF ALL SHE NEEDS TO DO IS KILL THE RACES TO AWAKEN...
ALICIA MIGHT GET HER WISH IF SHE ACTUALLY TRIED ATTACKING KLEM.
DIDN'T SHE SAY SHE HAD A DEATH WISH?
OR SHE COULD USE ONE OF SADDLER'S SUBORDINATES INSTEAD.
MAYBE ALICIA WAS LYING, THEN?
GASP

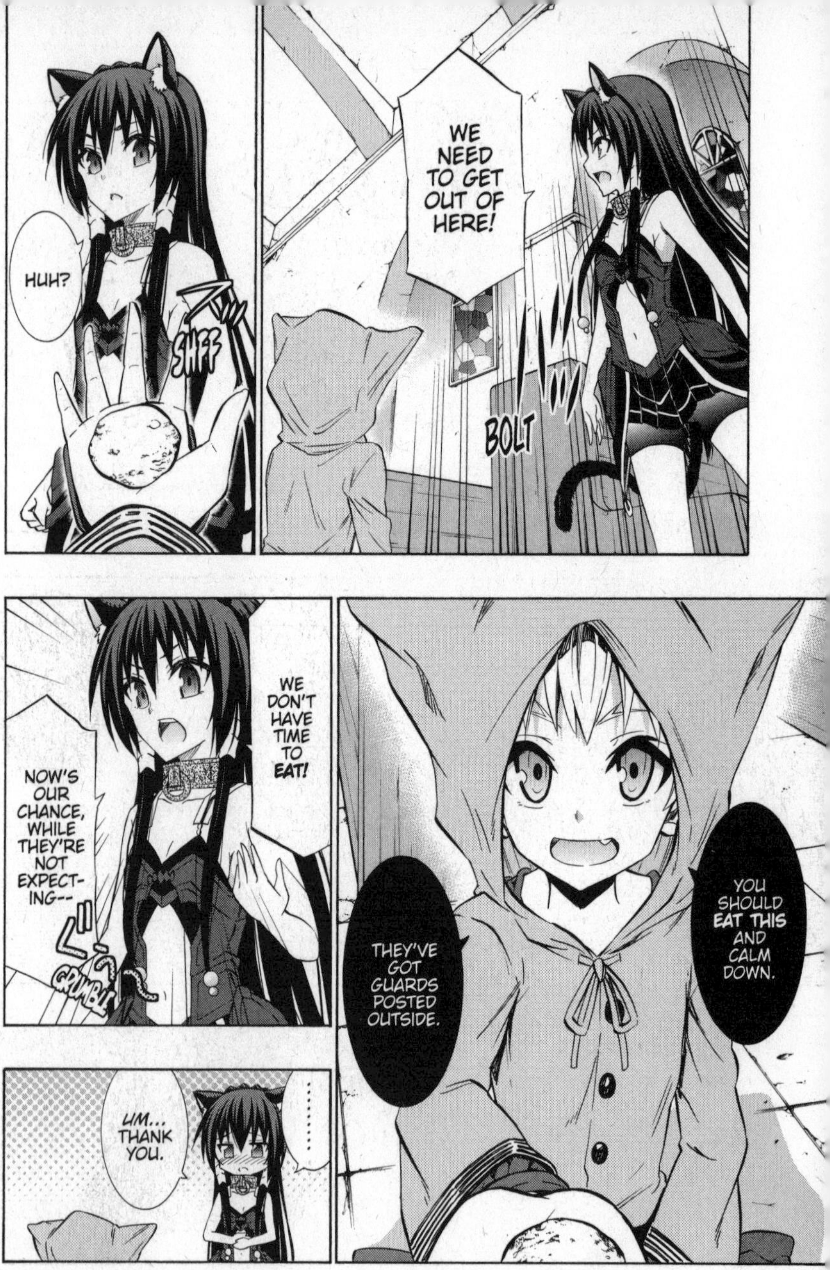
WE NEED TO GET OUT OF HERE!
BOLT
HUH?
SHFF
YOU SHOULD EAT THIS AND CALM DOWN.
THEY'VE GOT GUARDS POSTED OUTSIDE.
WE DON'T HAVE TIME TO EAT!
NOW'S OUR CHANCE, WHILE THEY'RE NOT EXPECTING--
GRUMBLE
......
UM... THANK YOU.

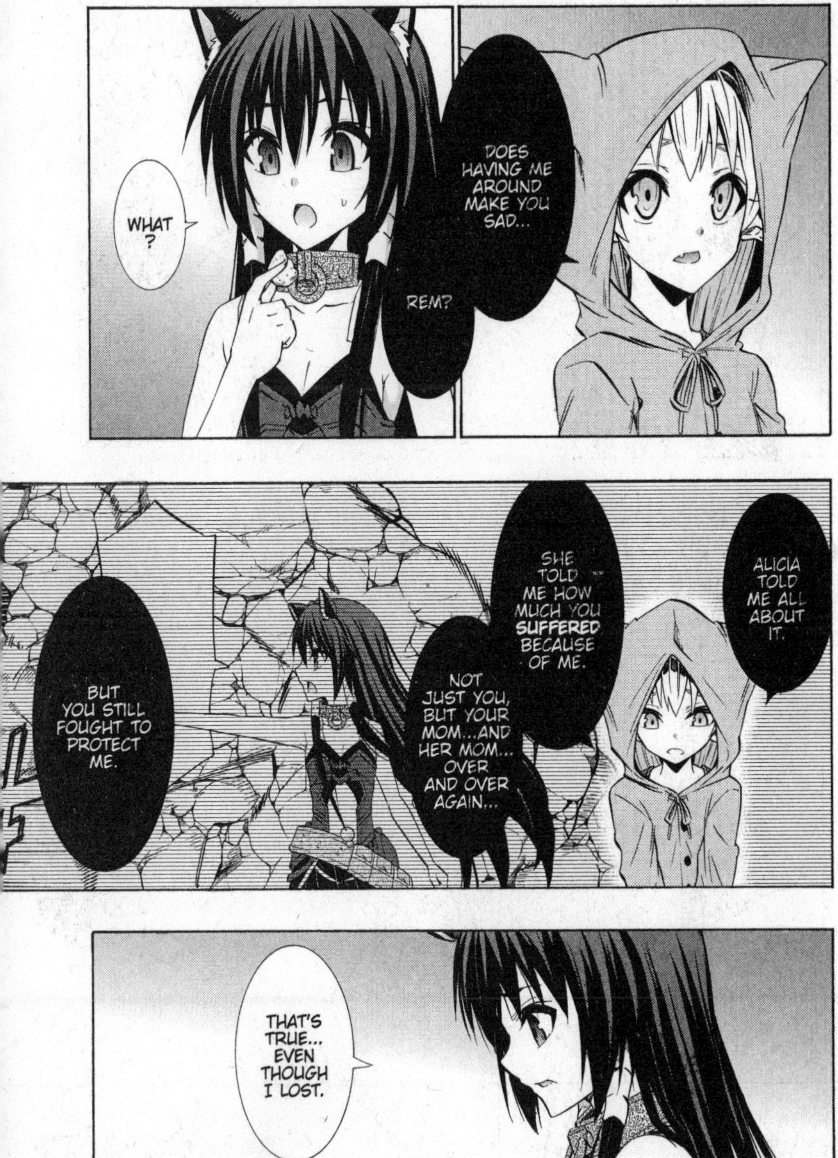
DOES HAVING ME AROUND MAKE YOU SAD...
REM?
WHAT?
ALICIA TOLD ME ALL ABOUT IT.
SHE TOLD ME HOW MUCH YOU **SUFFERED** BECAUSE OF ME.
NOT JUST YOU, BUT YOUR MOM...AND HER MOM... OVER AND OVER AGAIN...
BUT YOU STILL FOUGHT TO PROTECT ME.
THAT'S TRUE... EVEN THOUGH I LOST.

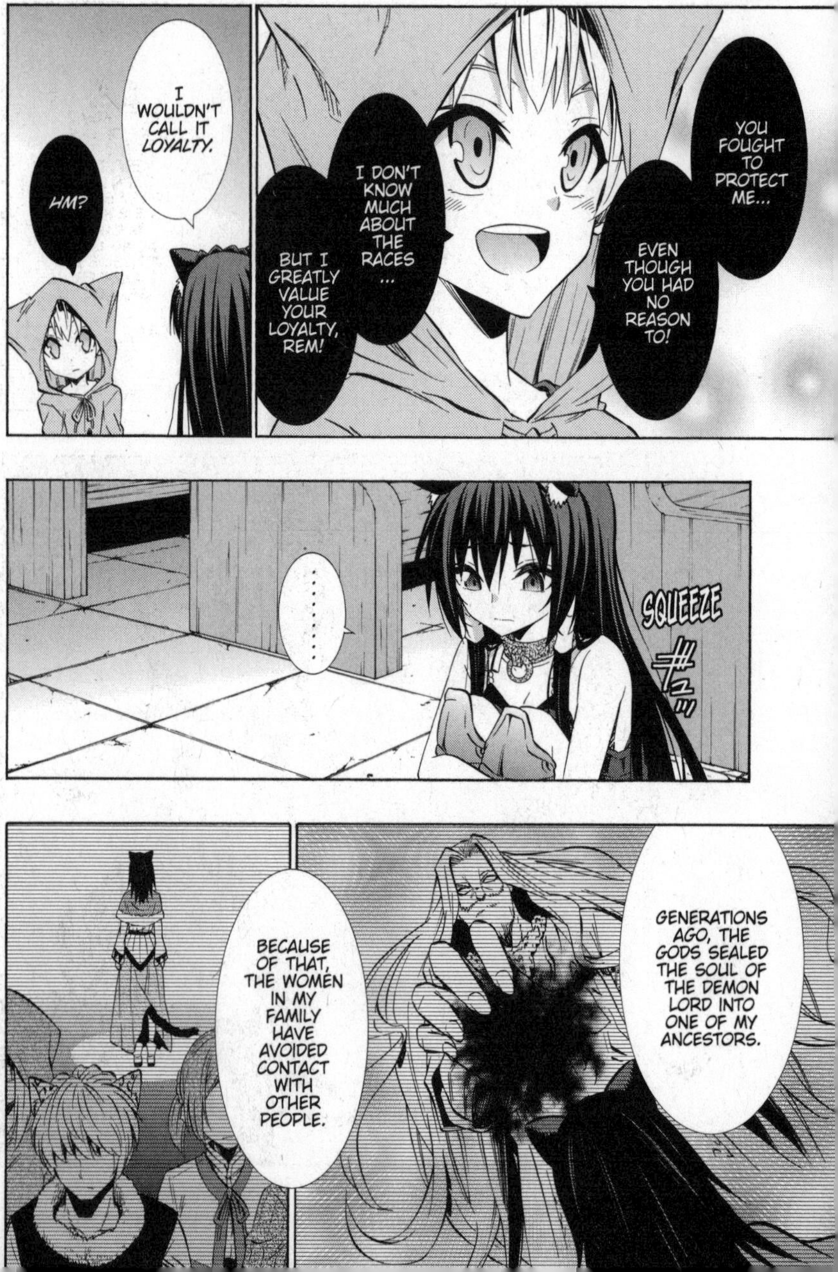
YOU FOUGHT TO PROTECT ME...
EVEN THOUGH YOU HAD NO REASON TO!
I DON'T KNOW MUCH ABOUT THE RACES ...
BUT I GREATLY VALUE YOUR LOYALTY, REM!
I WOULDN'T CALL IT *LOYALTY.*
HM?
......
SQUEEZE
GENERATIONS AGO, THE GODS SEALED THE SOUL OF THE DEMON LORD INTO ONE OF MY ANCESTORS.
BECAUSE OF THAT, THE WOMEN IN MY FAMILY HAVE AVOIDED CONTACT WITH OTHER PEOPLE.

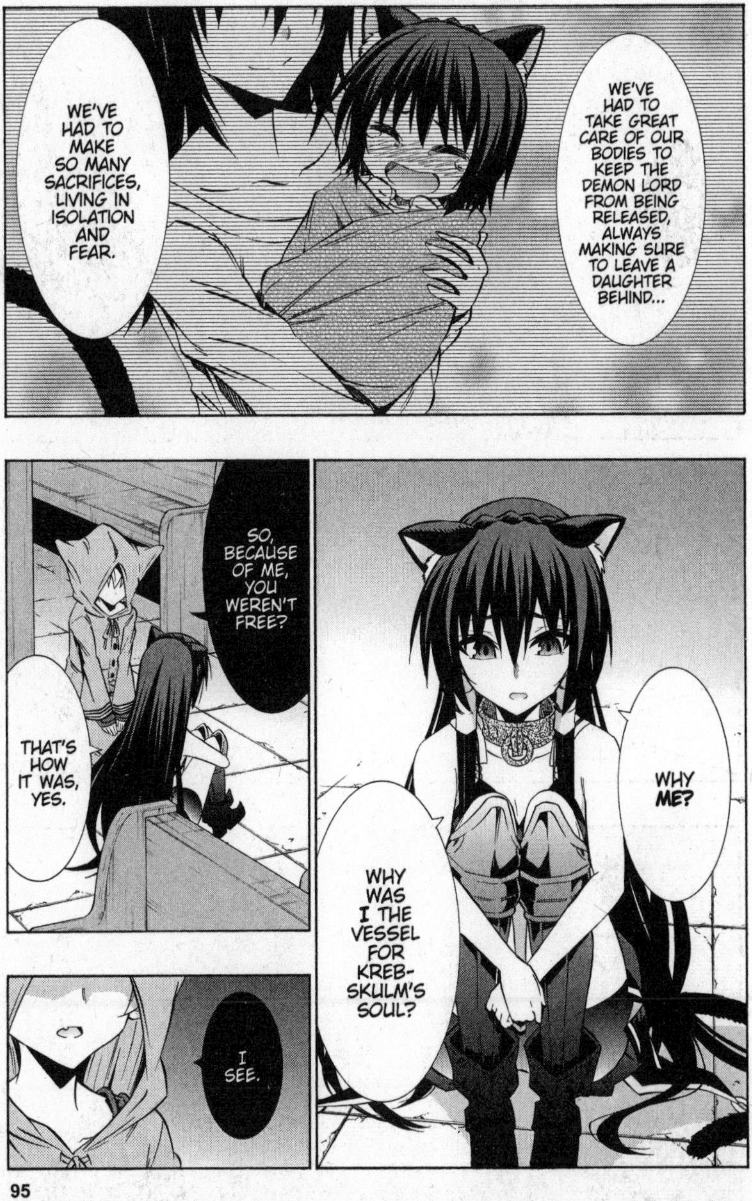
WE'VE HAD TO TAKE GREAT CARE OF OUR BODIES TO KEEP THE DEMON LORD FROM BEING RELEASED, ALWAYS MAKING SURE TO LEAVE A DAUGHTER BEHIND...
WE'VE HAD TO MAKE SO MANY SACRIFICES, LIVING IN ISOLATION AND FEAR.
WHY **ME?**
WHY WAS **I** THE VESSEL FOR KREB-SKULM'S SOUL?
SO, BECAUSE OF ME, YOU WEREN'T FREE?
THAT'S HOW IT WAS, YES.
I SEE.

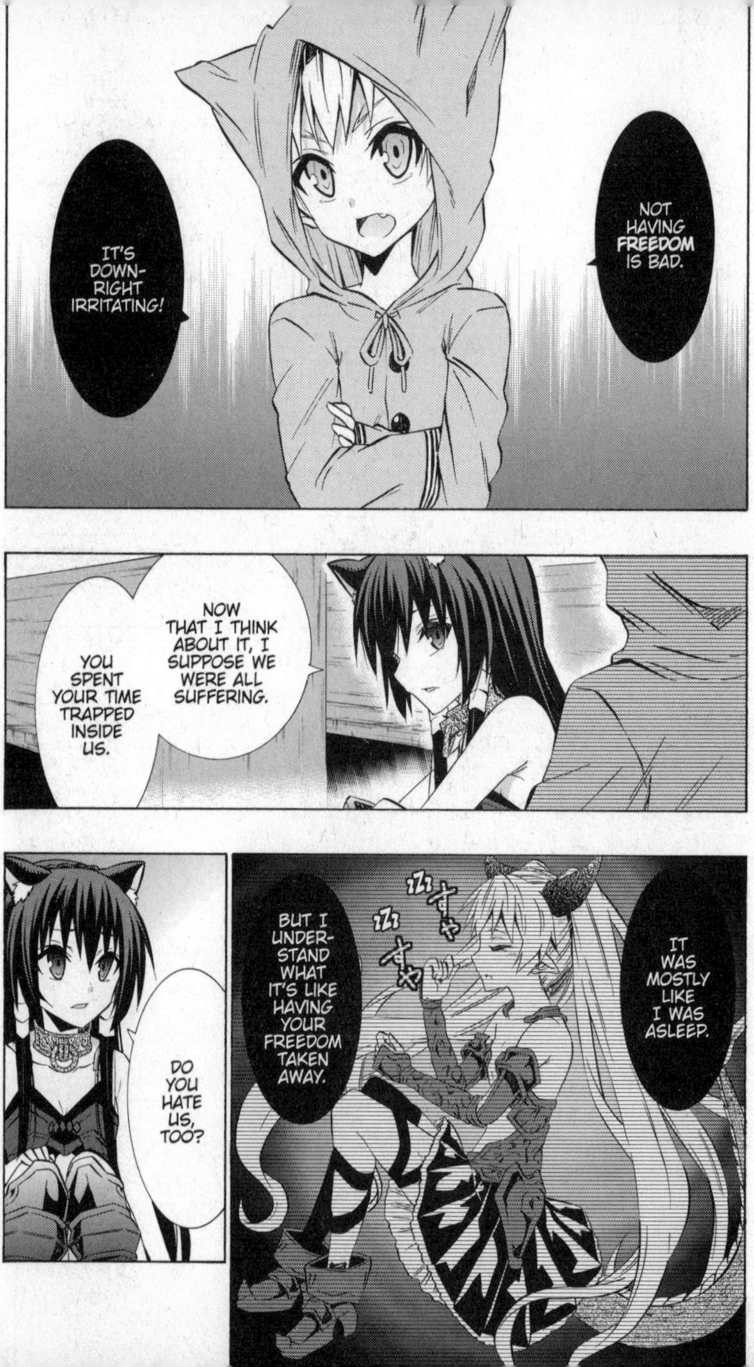
NOT HAVING FREEDOM IS BAD.
IT'S DOWN-RIGHT IRRITATING!
NOW THAT I THINK ABOUT IT, I SUPPOSE WE WERE ALL SUFFERING.
YOU SPENT YOUR TIME TRAPPED INSIDE US.
IT WAS MOSTLY LIKE I WAS ASLEEP.
BUT I UNDER-STAND WHAT IT'S LIKE HAVING YOUR FREEDOM TAKEN AWAY.
DO YOU HATE US, TOO?

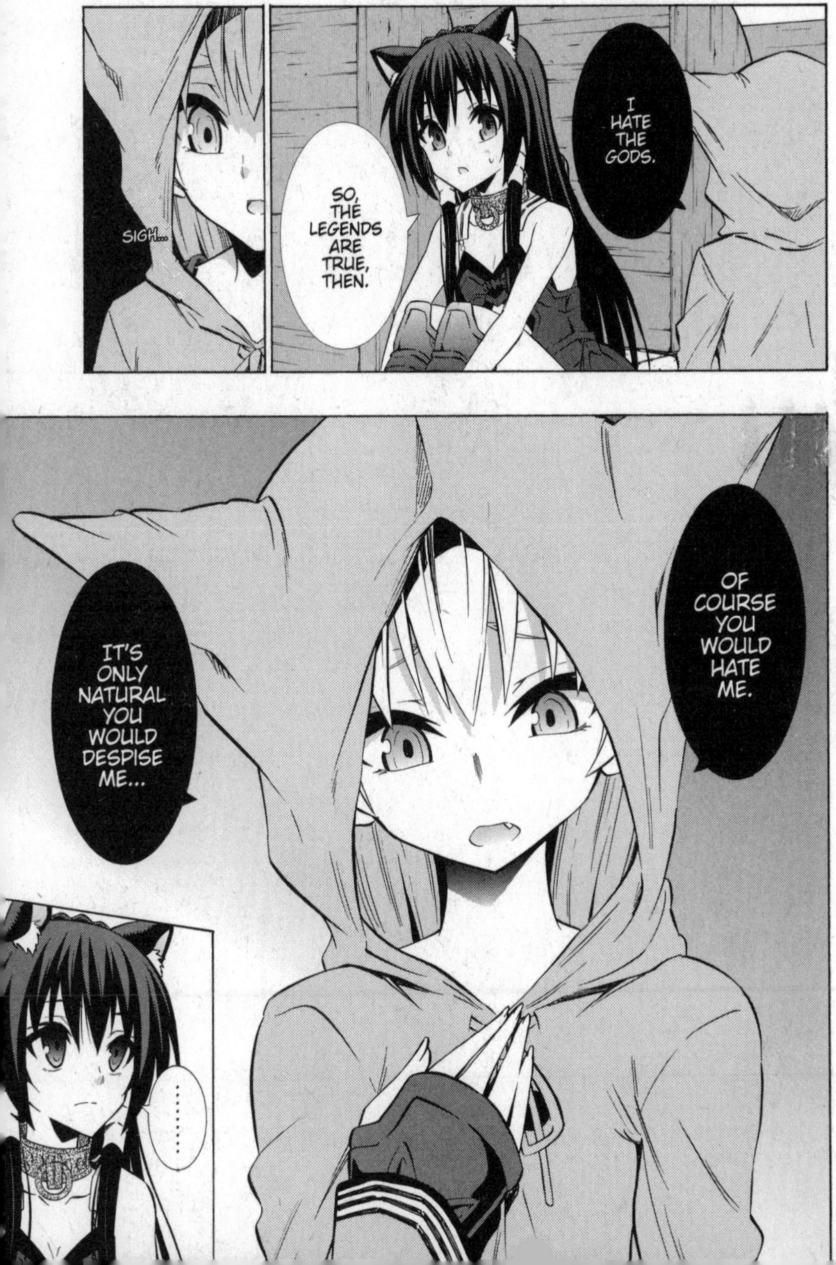
I HATE THE GODS.
SO, THE LEGENDS ARE TRUE, THEN.
SIGH...
OF COURSE YOU WOULD HATE ME.
IT'S ONLY NATURAL YOU WOULD DESPISE ME...
......

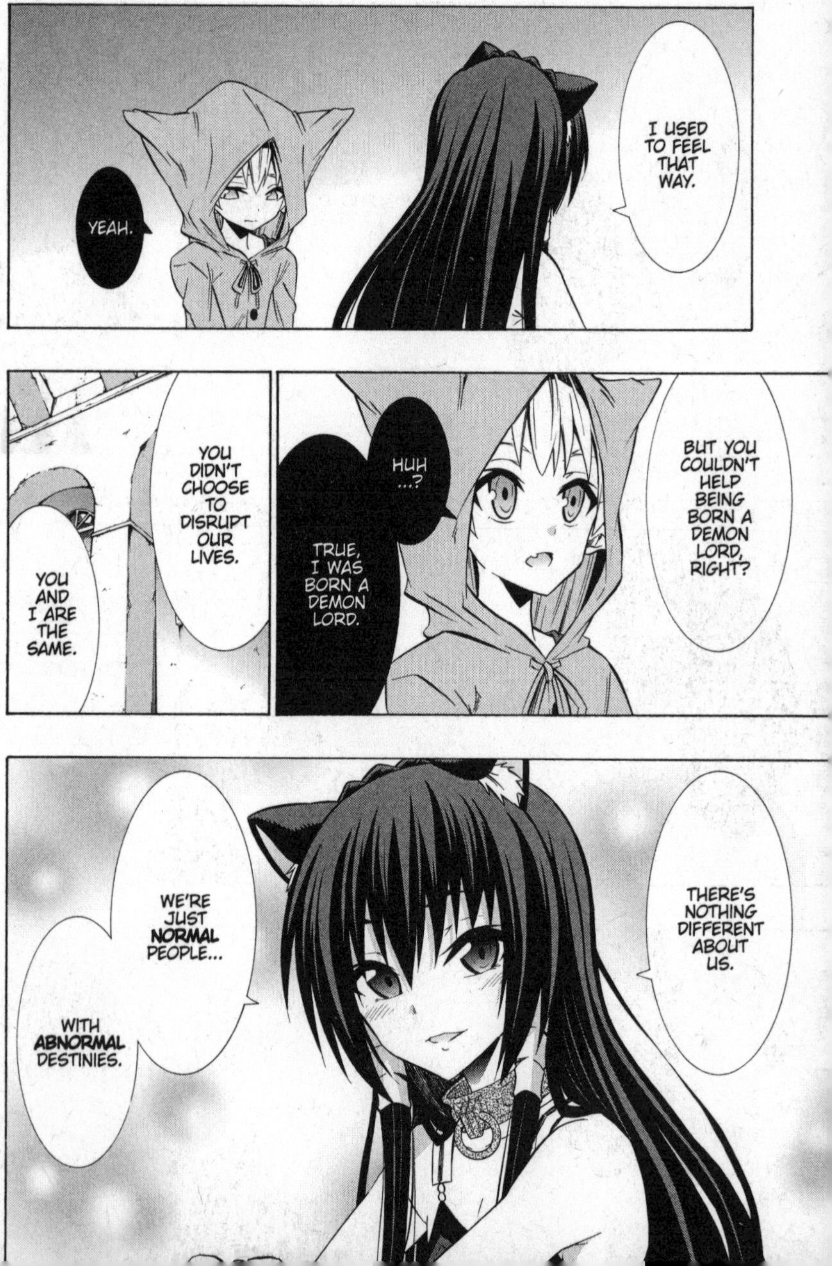
I USED TO FEEL THAT WAY.
YEAH.
BUT YOU COULDN'T HELP BEING BORN A DEMON LORD, RIGHT?
HUH ...?
TRUE, I WAS BORN A DEMON LORD.
YOU DIDN'T CHOOSE TO DISRUPT OUR LIVES.
YOU AND I ARE THE SAME.
THERE'S NOTHING DIFFERENT ABOUT US.
WE'RE JUST **NORMAL** PEOPLE...
WITH **ABNORMAL** DESTINIES.

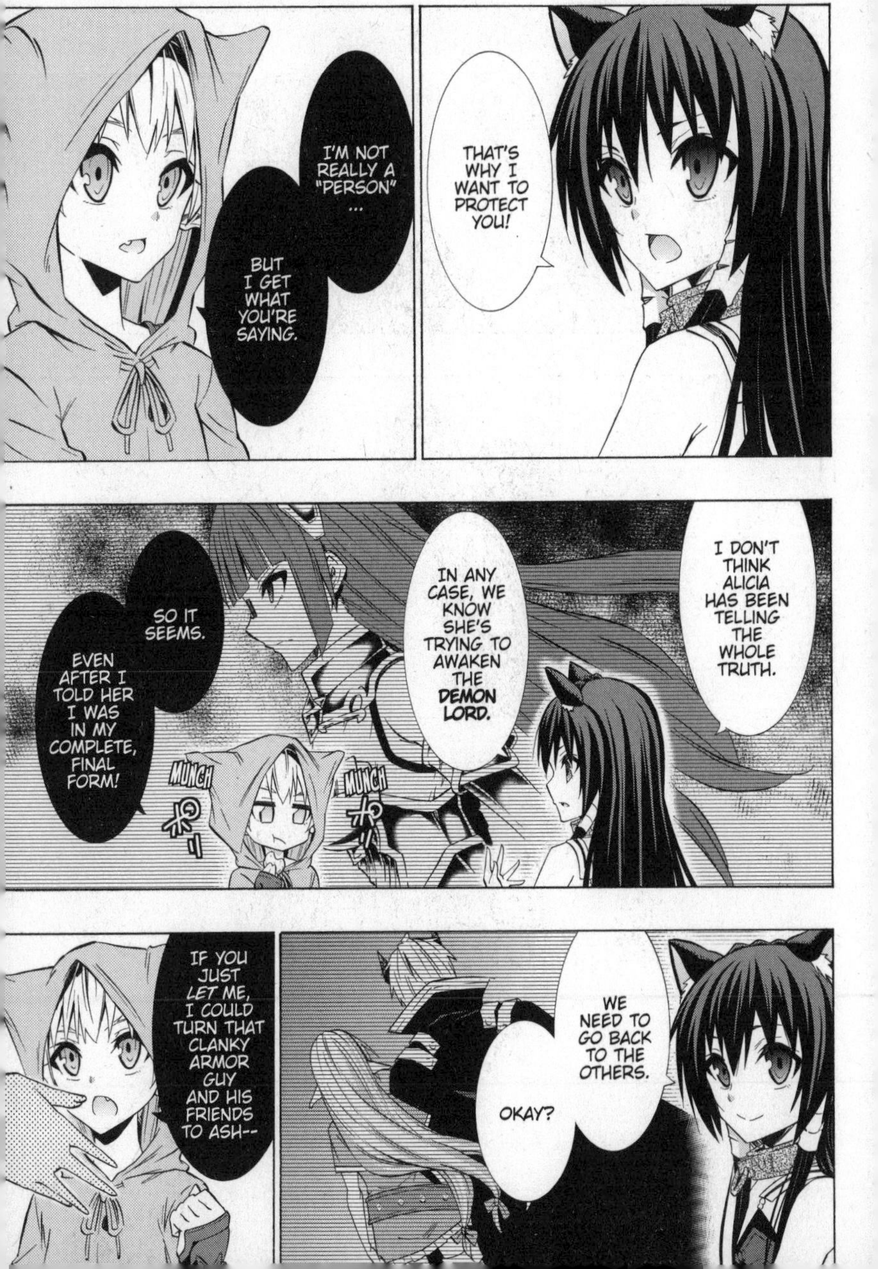
THAT'S WHY I WANT TO PROTECT YOU!
I'M NOT REALLY A "PERSON" ...
BUT I GET WHAT YOU'RE SAYING.
I DON'T THINK ALICIA HAS BEEN TELLING THE WHOLE TRUTH.
IN ANY CASE, WE KNOW SHE'S TRYING TO AWAKEN THE **DEMON LORD.**
MUNCH
SO IT SEEMS.
EVEN AFTER I TOLD HER I WAS IN MY COMPLETE, FINAL FORM!
MUNCH
WE NEED TO GO BACK TO THE OTHERS.
OKAY?
IF YOU JUST *LET ME*, I COULD TURN THAT CLANKY ARMOR GUY AND HIS FRIENDS TO ASH--

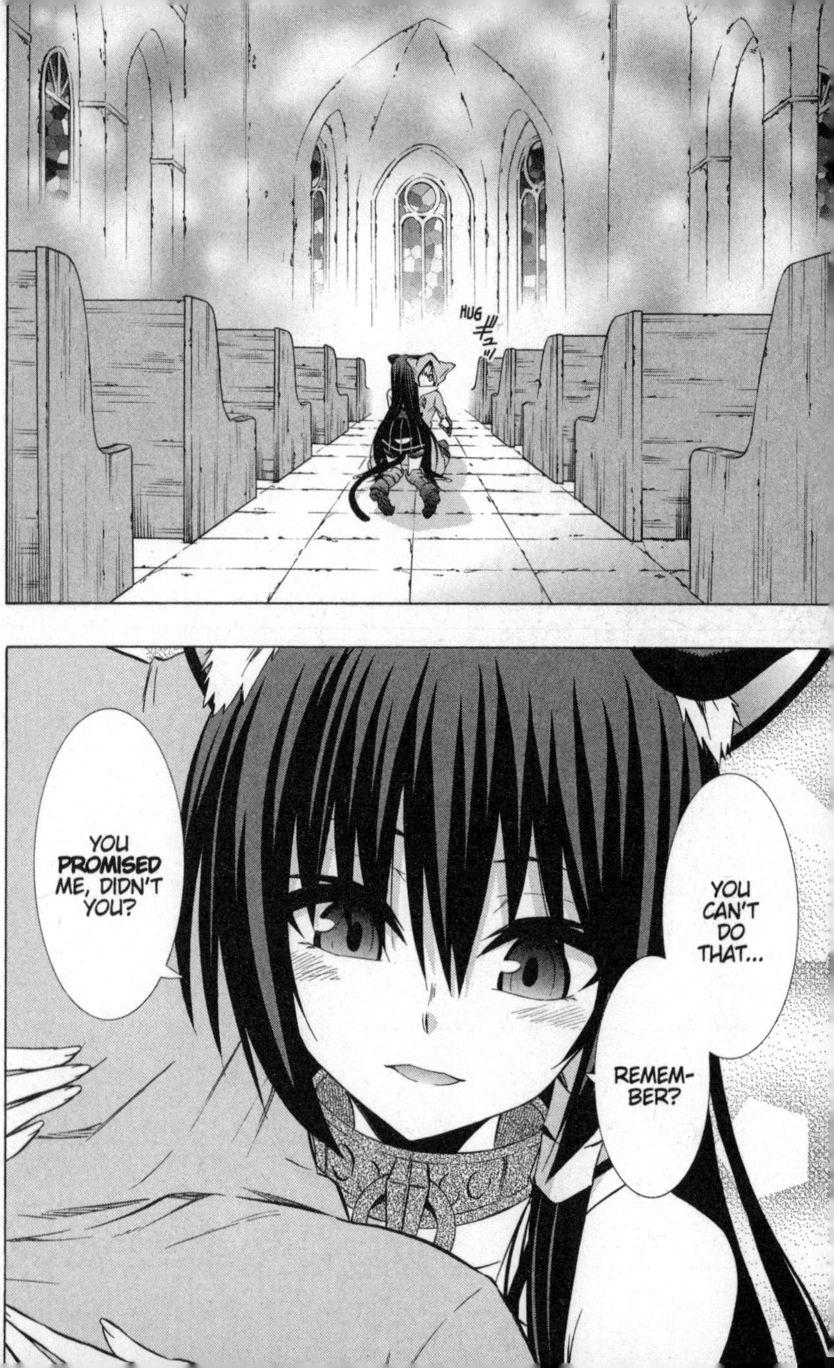
HUG
YOU CAN'T DO THAT...
REMEM-BER?
YOU PROMISED ME, DIDN'T YOU?

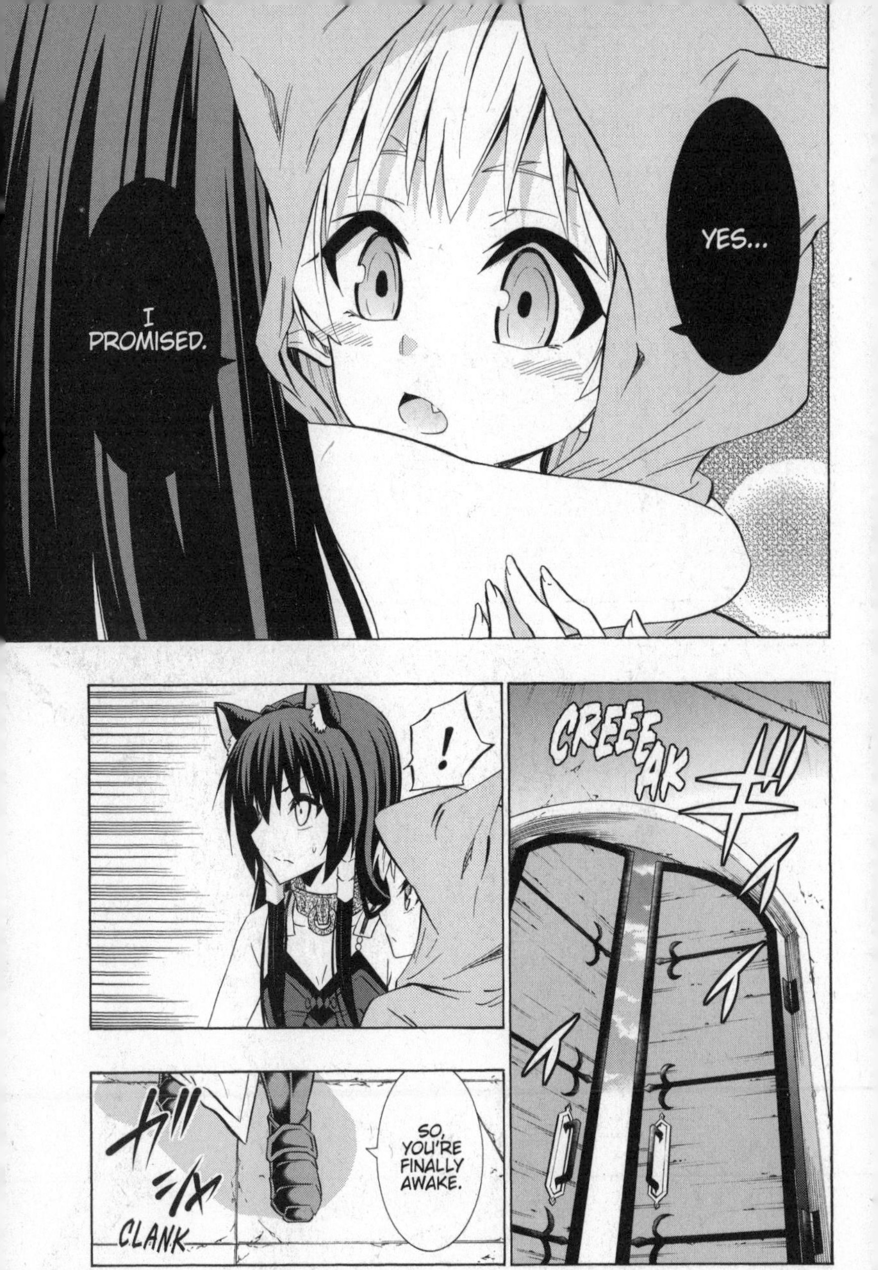
YES...
I PROMISED.
CREEEAK
!
SO, YOU'RE FINALLY AWAKE.
CLANK

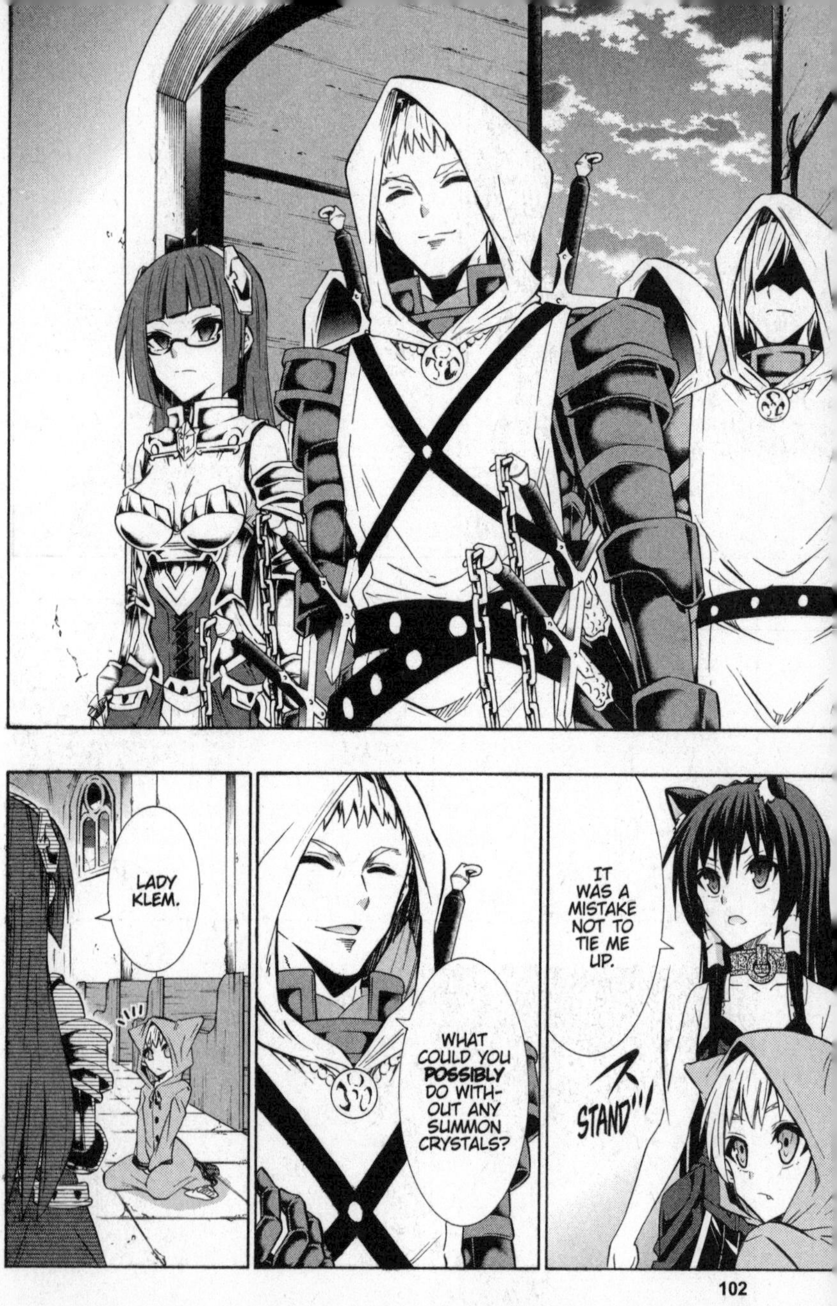
IT WAS A MISTAKE NOT TO TIE ME UP.
ス
STAND
WHAT COULD YOU **POSSIBLY** DO WITH-OUT ANY SUMMON CRYSTALS?
LADY KLEM.

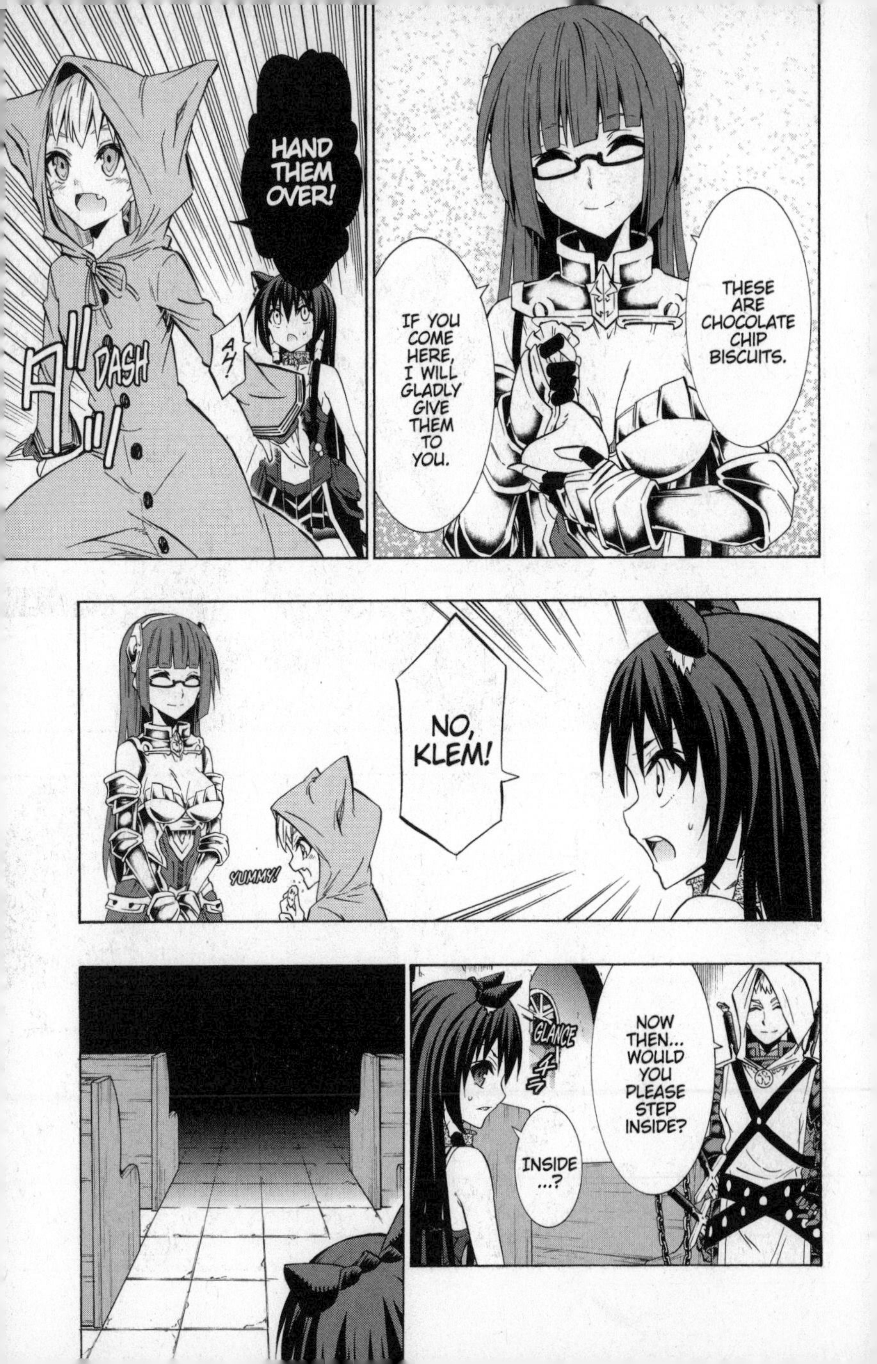
THESE ARE CHOCOLATE CHIP BISCUITS.
IF YOU COME HERE, I WILL GLADLY GIVE THEM TO YOU.
HAND THEM OVER!
DASH
NO, KLEM!
YUMMY!
NOW THEN... WOULD YOU PLEASE STEP INSIDE?
GLANCE
INSIDE ...?

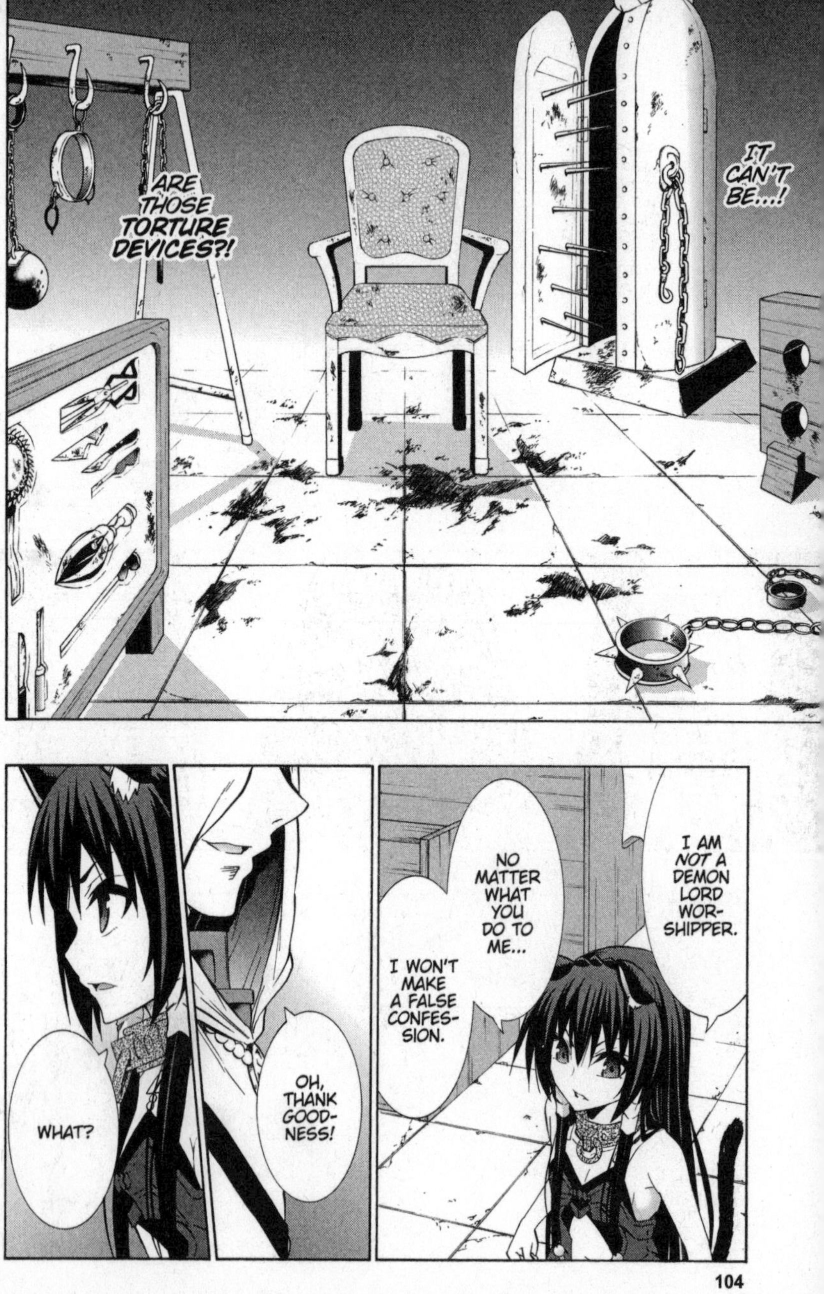
IT CAN'T BE...!
ARE THOSE TORTURE DEVICES?!
I AM *NOT* A DEMON LORD WORSHIPPER.
NO MATTER WHAT YOU DO TO ME...
I WON'T MAKE A FALSE CONFESSION.
OH, THANK GOODNESS!
WHAT?

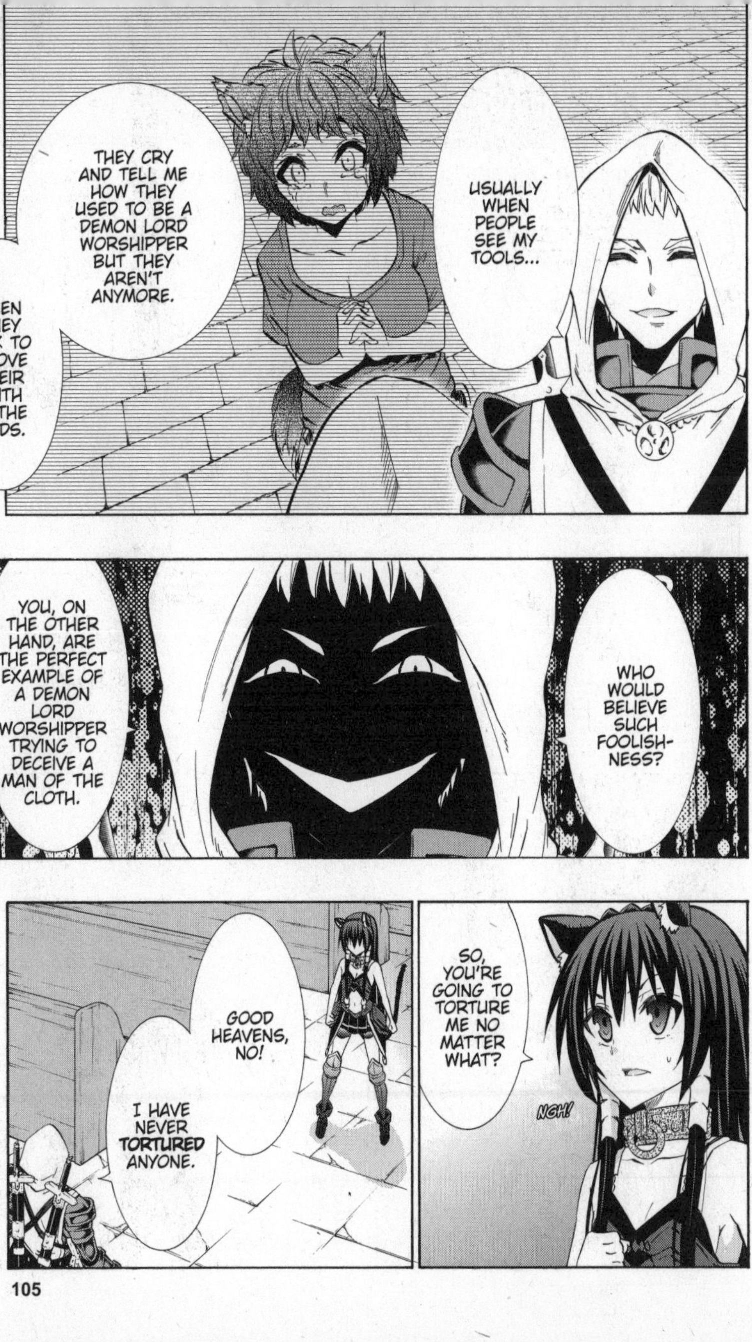
USUALLY WHEN PEOPLE SEE MY TOOLS...
THEY CRY AND TELL ME HOW THEY USED TO BE A DEMON LORD WORSHIPPER BUT THEY AREN'T ANYMORE.
THEN THEY ASK TO PROVE THEIR FAITH IN THE GODS.
WHO WOULD BELIEVE SUCH FOOLISHNESS?
YOU, ON THE OTHER HAND, ARE THE PERFECT EXAMPLE OF A DEMON LORD WORSHIPPER TRYING TO DECEIVE A MAN OF THE CLOTH.
SO, YOU'RE GOING TO TORTURE ME NO MATTER WHAT?
NGH!
GOOD HEAVENS, NO!
I HAVE NEVER **TORTURED** ANYONE.

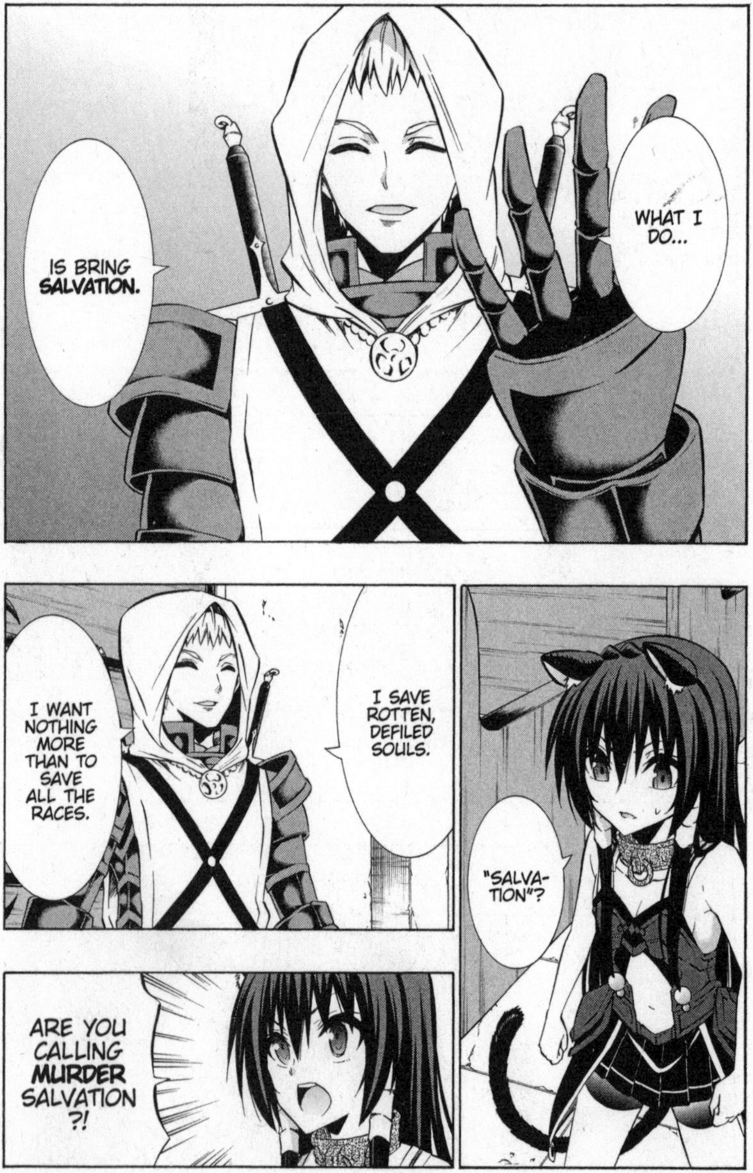
WHAT I DO...
IS BRING SALVATION.
"SALVA-TION"?
I SAVE ROTTEN, DEFILED SOULS.
I WANT NOTHING MORE THAN TO SAVE ALL THE RACES.
ARE YOU CALLING MURDER SALVATION?!

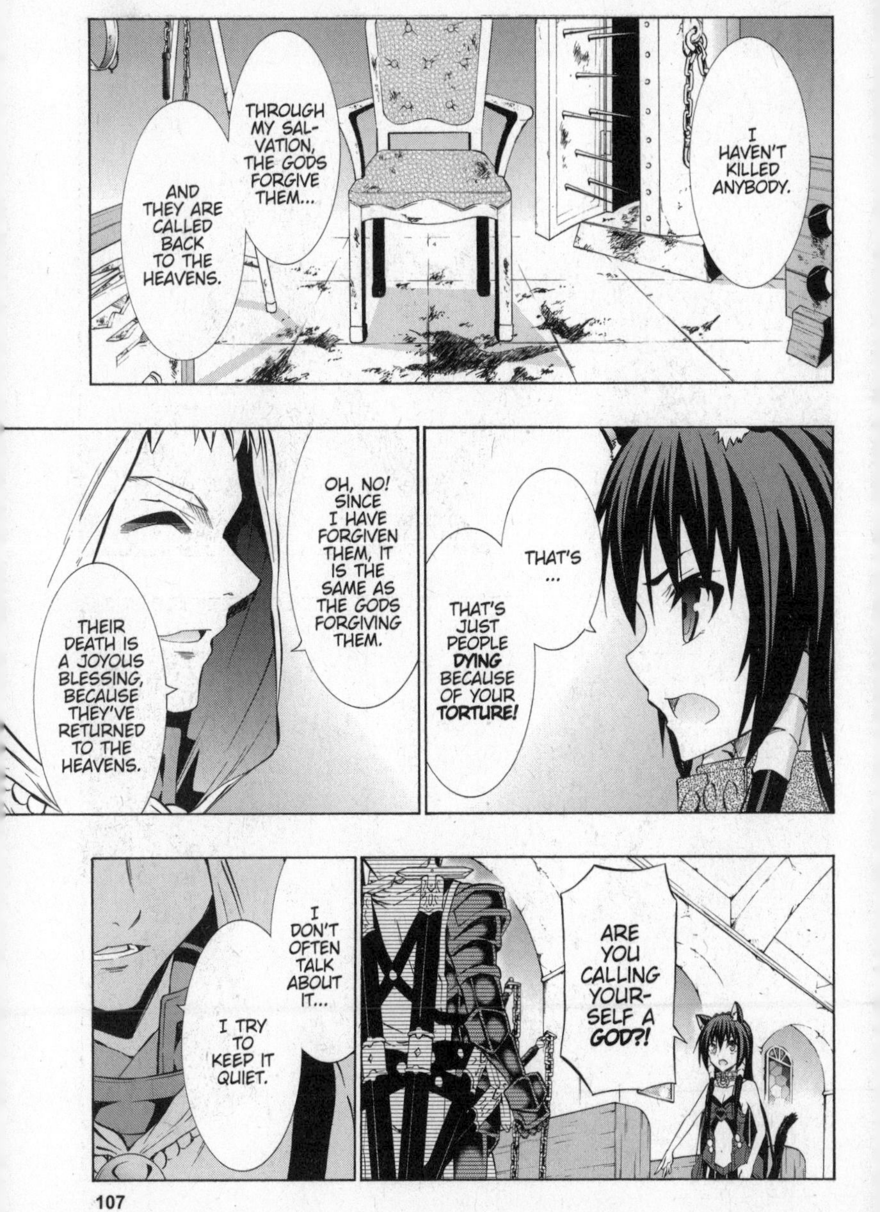
I HAVEN'T KILLED ANYBODY.
THROUGH MY SAL-VATION, THE GODS FORGIVE THEM...
AND THEY ARE CALLED BACK TO THE HEAVENS.
THAT'S ...
THAT'S JUST PEOPLE **DYING** BECAUSE OF YOUR **TORTURE!**
OH, NO! SINCE I HAVE FORGIVEN THEM, IT IS THE SAME AS THE GODS FORGIVING THEM.
THEIR DEATH IS A JOYOUS BLESSING, BECAUSE THEY'VE RETURNED TO THE HEAVENS.
ARE YOU CALLING YOUR-SELF A **GOD?!**
I DON'T OFTEN TALK ABOUT IT...
I TRY TO KEEP IT QUIET.

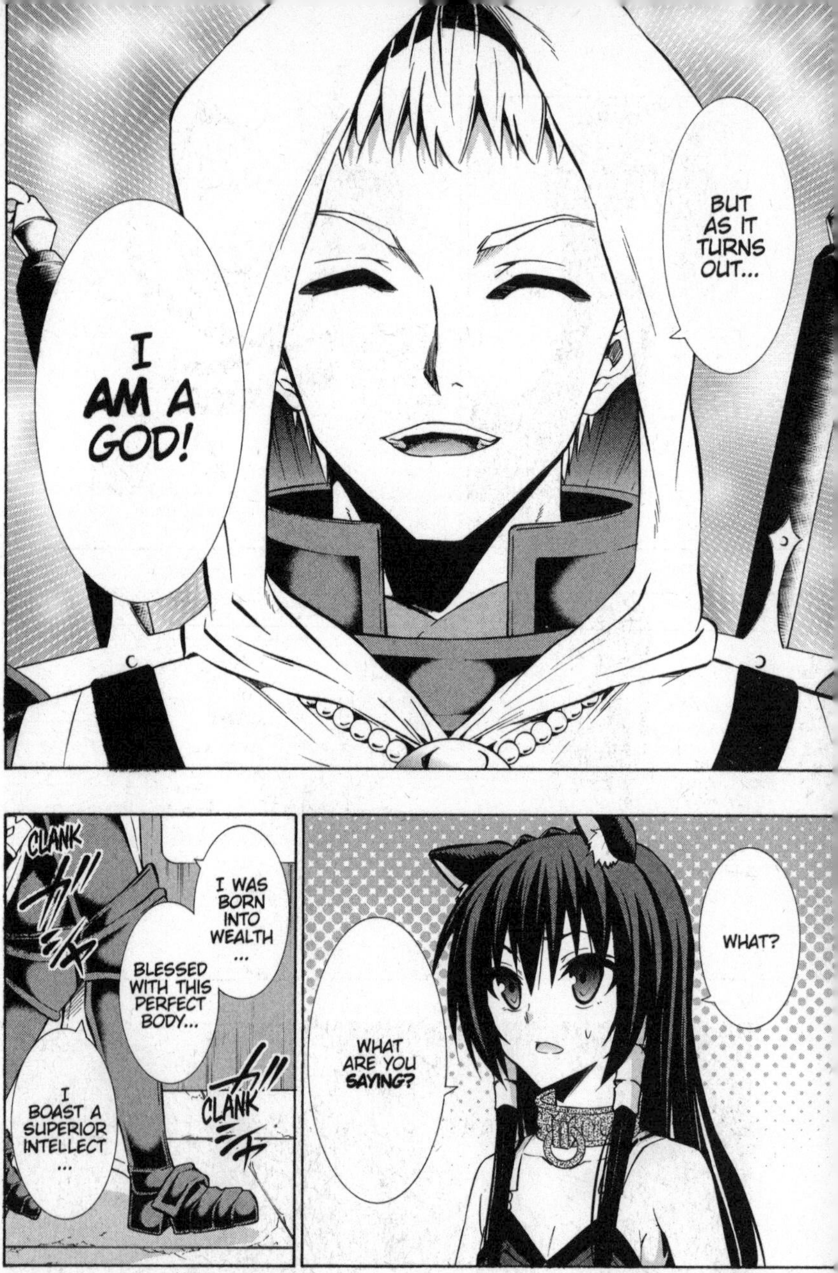
BUT AS IT TURNS OUT...
I AM A GOD!
WHAT?
WHAT ARE YOU SAYING?
CLANK
I WAS BORN INTO WEALTH ...
BLESSED WITH THIS PERFECT BODY...
I BOAST A SUPERIOR INTELLECT ...
CLANK

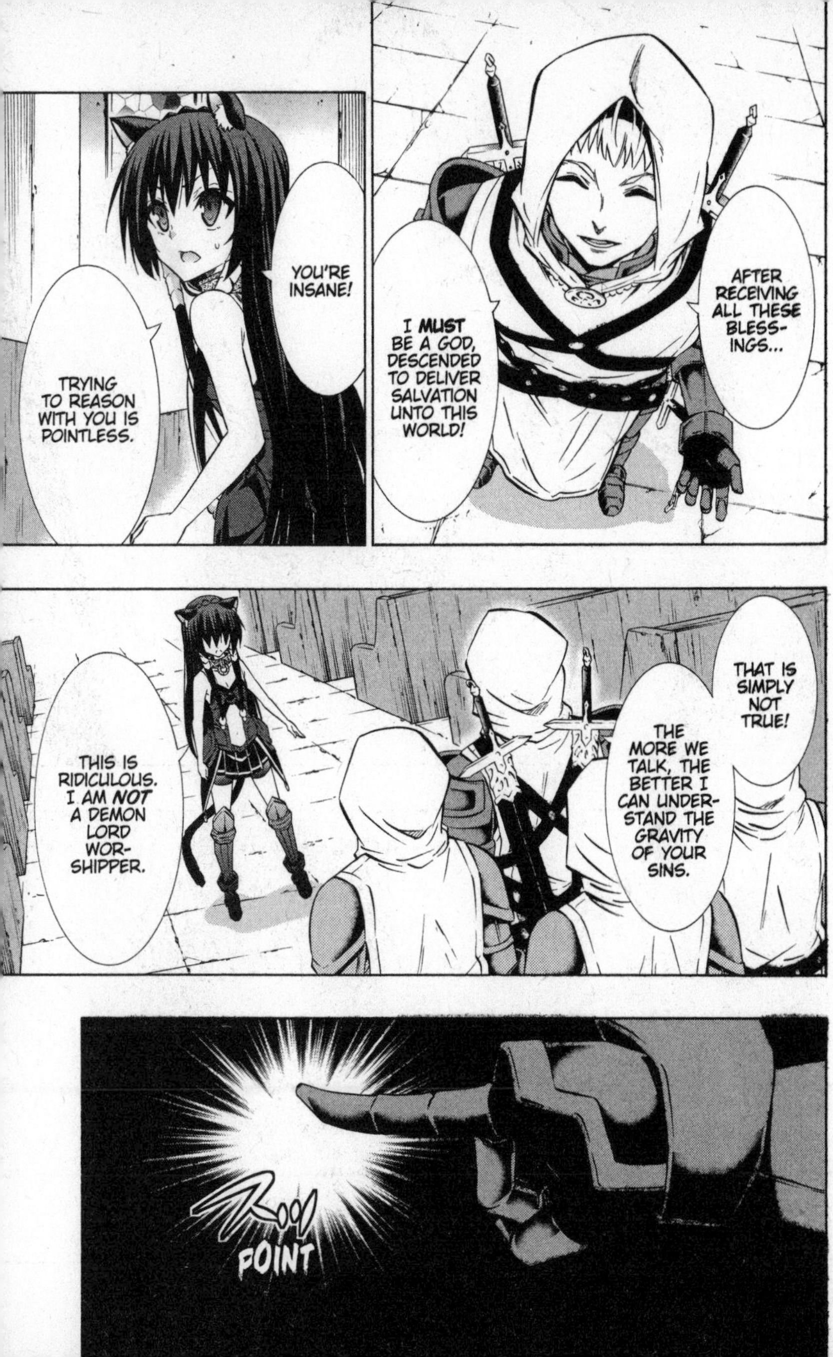
AFTER RECEIVING ALL THESE BLESSINGS...
I MUST BE A GOD, DESCENDED TO DELIVER SALVATION UNTO THIS WORLD!
YOU'RE INSANE!
TRYING TO REASON WITH YOU IS POINTLESS.
THAT IS SIMPLY NOT TRUE!
THE MORE WE TALK, THE BETTER I CAN UNDER-STAND THE GRAVITY OF YOUR SINS.
THIS IS RIDICULOUS. I AM NOT A DEMON LORD WOR-SHIPPER.
POINT

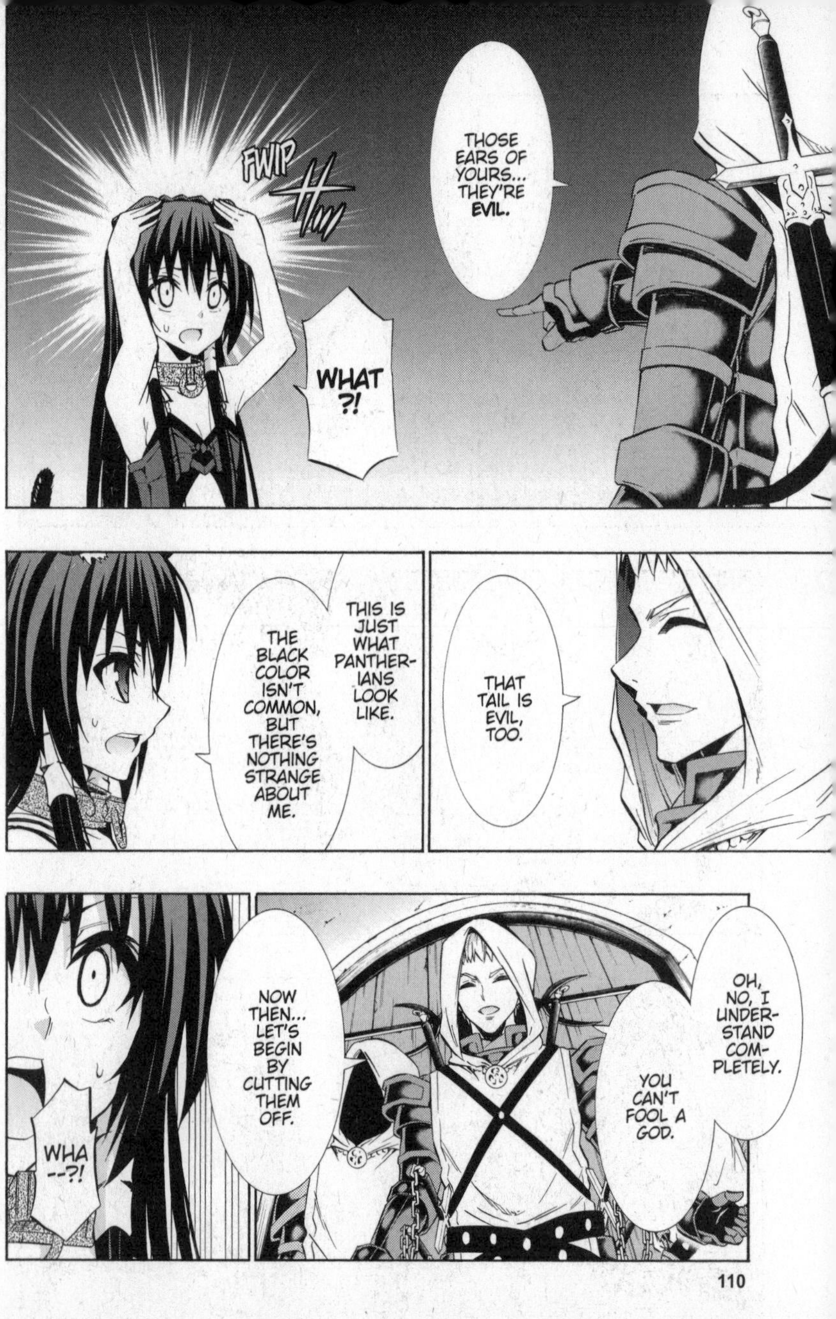
THOSE EARS OF YOURS... THEY'RE EVIL.
FWIP
WHAT?!
THAT TAIL IS EVIL, TOO.
THIS IS JUST WHAT PANTHER-IANS LOOK LIKE.
THE BLACK COLOR ISN'T COMMON, BUT THERE'S NOTHING STRANGE ABOUT ME.
OH, NO, I UNDER-STAND COM-PLETELY.
YOU CAN'T FOOL A GOD.
NOW THEN... LET'S BEGIN BY CUTTING THEM OFF.
WHA--?!

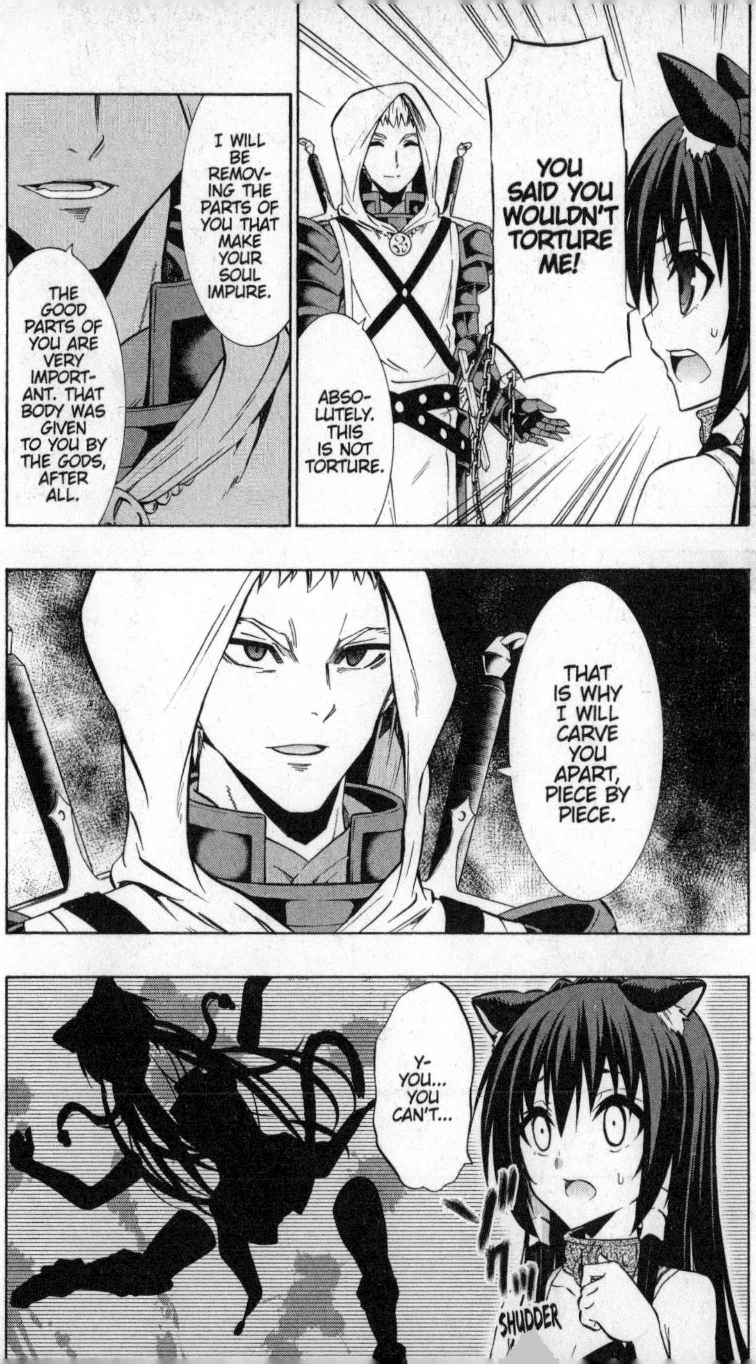
YOU SAID YOU WOULDN'T TORTURE ME!
ABSO-LUTELY. THIS IS NOT TORTURE.
I WILL BE REMOV-ING THE PARTS OF YOU THAT MAKE YOUR SOUL IMPURE.
THE GOOD PARTS OF YOU ARE VERY IMPORT-ANT. THAT BODY WAS GIVEN TO YOU BY THE GODS, AFTER ALL.
THAT IS WHY I WILL CARVE YOU APART, PIECE BY PIECE.
Y-YOU... YOU CAN'T...
SHUDDER

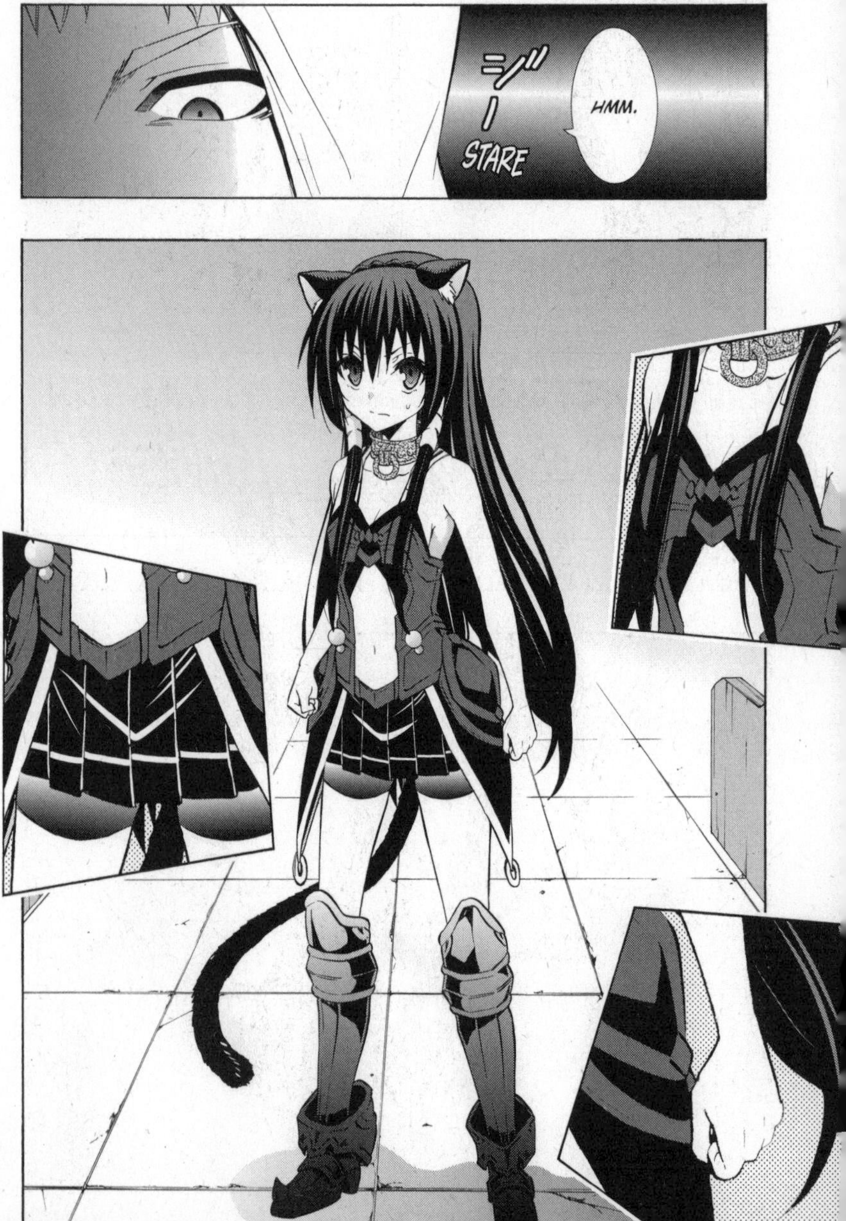
HMM.
ジー
STARE

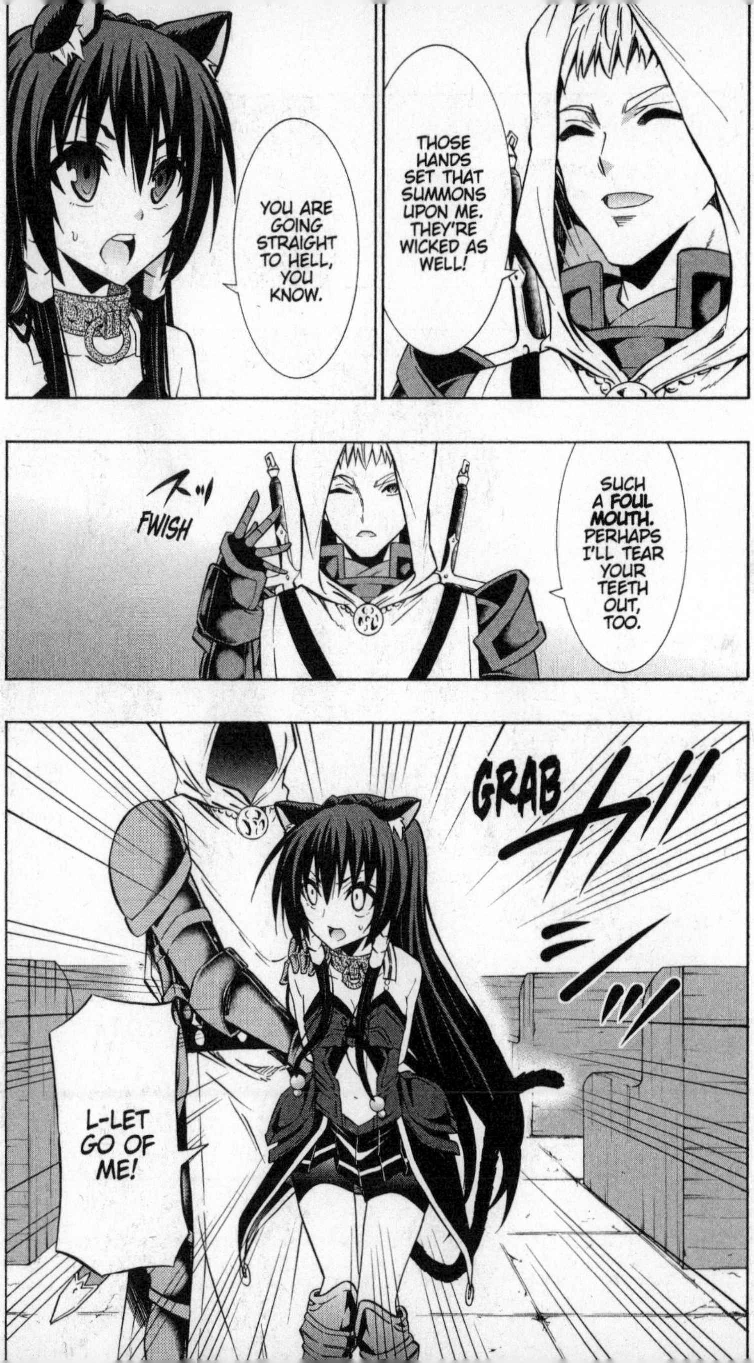

THOSE HANDS SET THAT SUMMONS UPON ME. THEY'RE WICKED AS WELL!
YOU ARE GOING STRAIGHT TO HELL, YOU KNOW.
SUCH A **FOUL MOUTH**. PERHAPS I'LL TEAR YOUR TEETH OUT, TOO.
スッ
FWISH
GRAB
ガッ
L-LET GO OF ME!

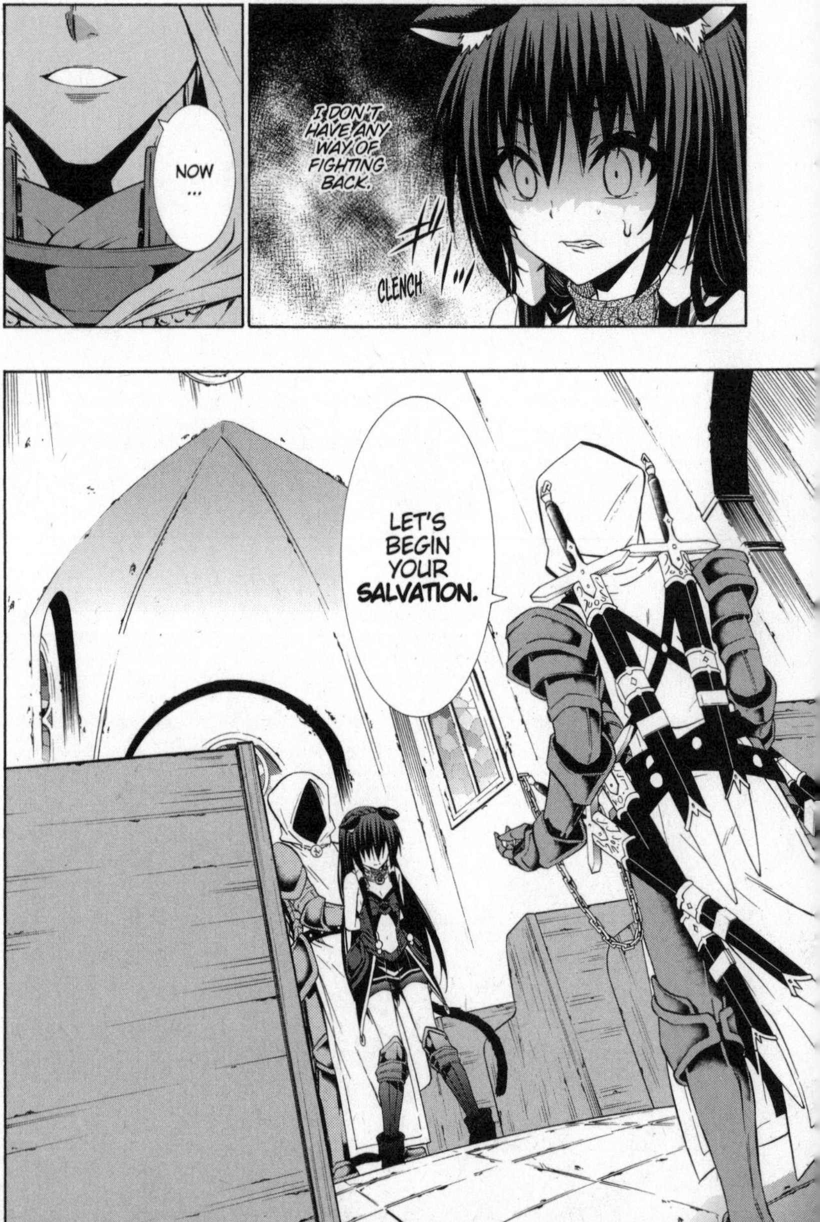
I DON'T HAVE ANY WAY OF FIGHTING BACK.
CLENCH
NOW ...
LET'S BEGIN YOUR **SALVATION.**

HOW NOT
TO SUMMON A
DEMON LORD

33 REM'S STORY II

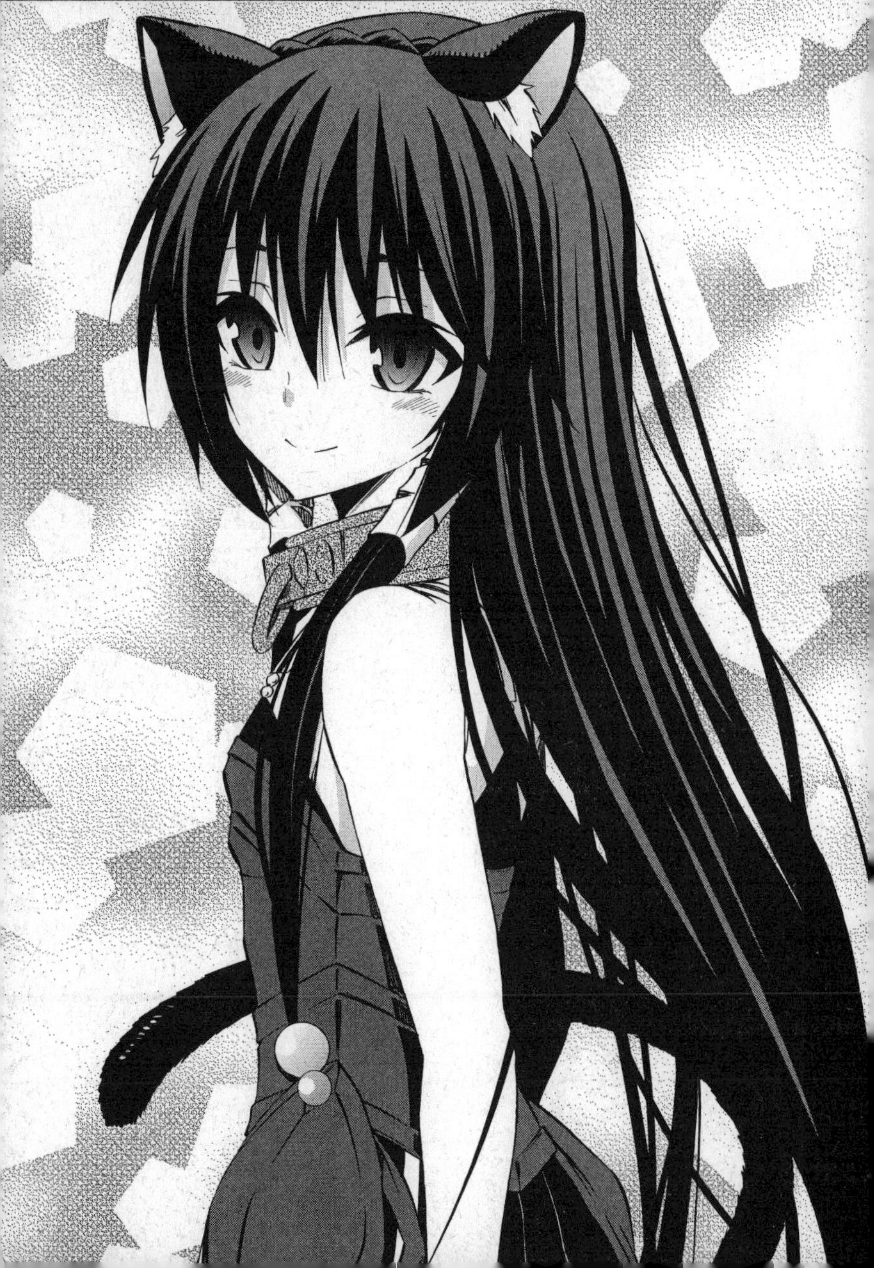

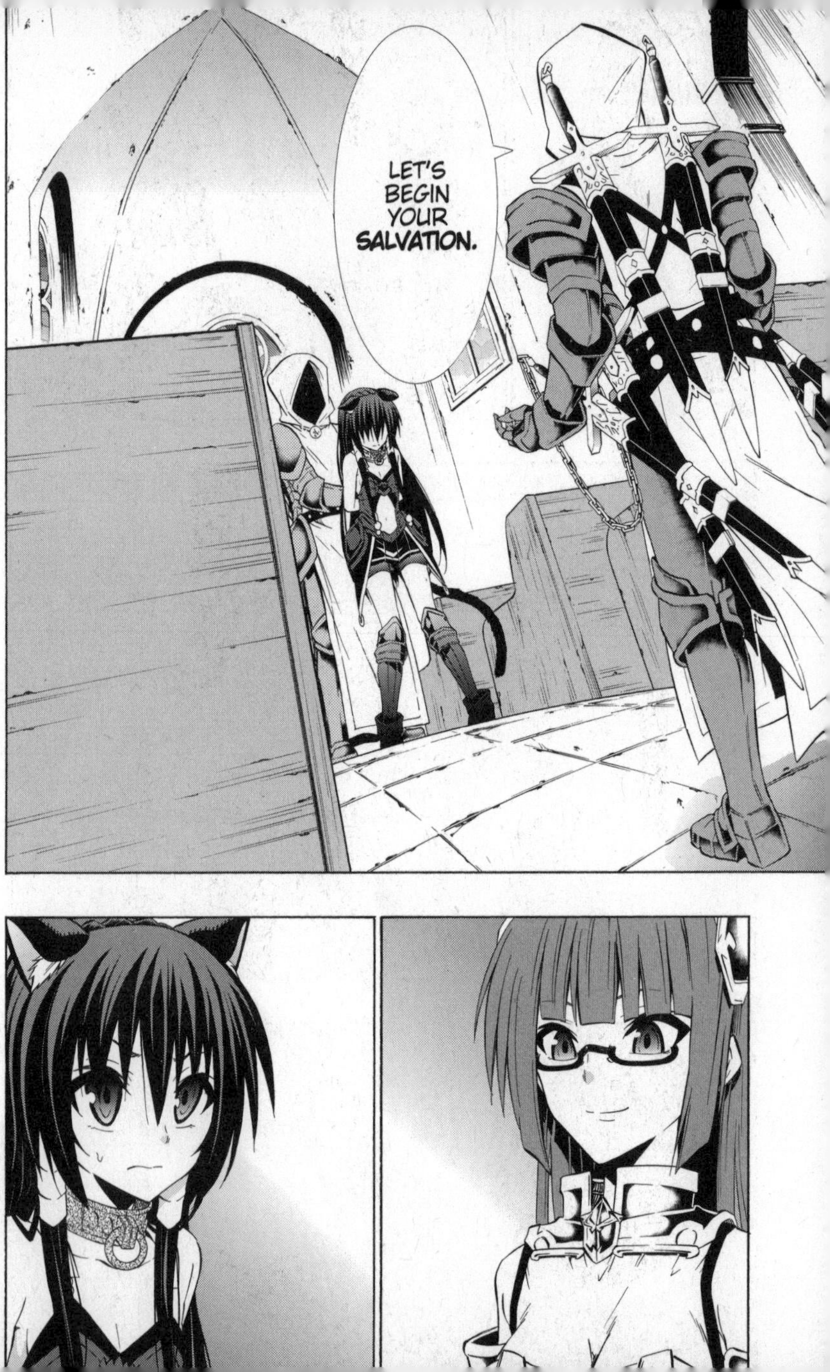
LET'S BEGIN YOUR SALVATION.

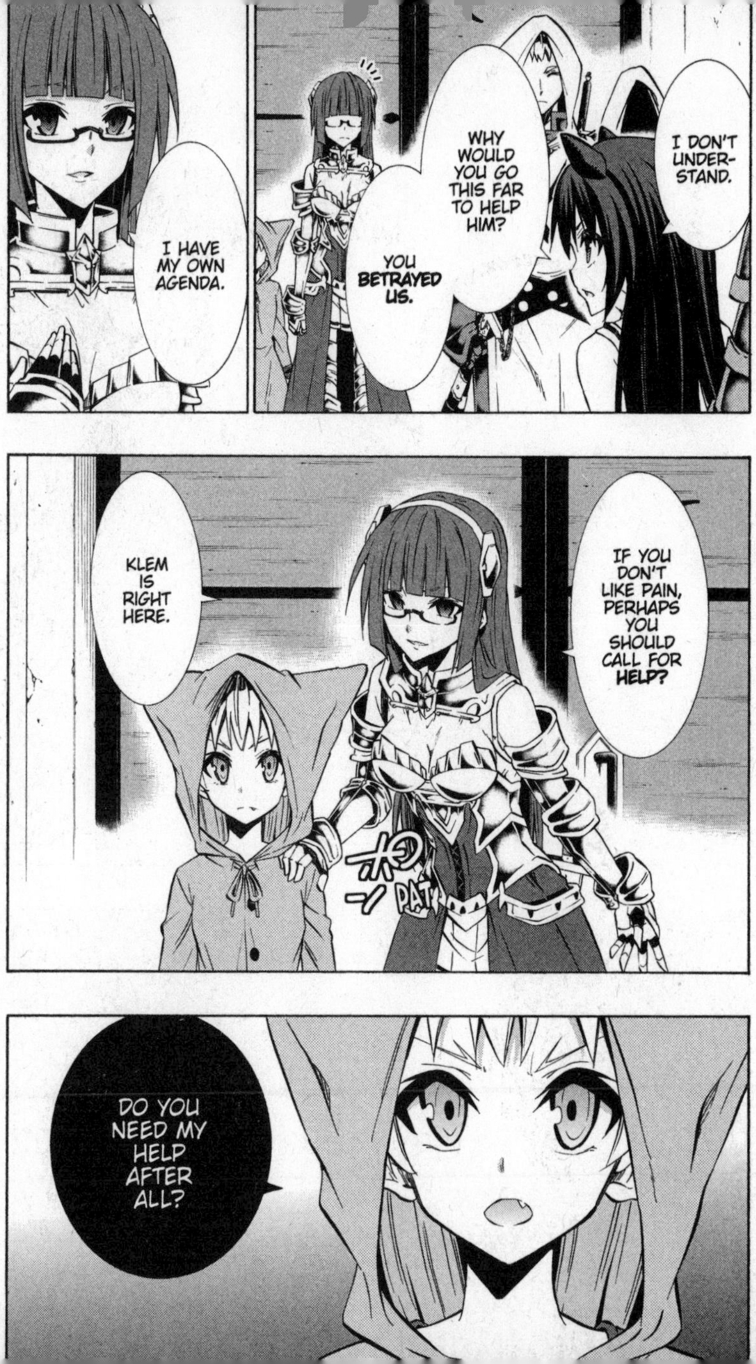
I DON'T UNDER-STAND.
WHY WOULD YOU GO THIS FAR TO HELP HIM?
YOU BETRAYED US.
I HAVE MY OWN AGENDA.
IF YOU DON'T LIKE PAIN, PERHAPS YOU SHOULD CALL FOR HELP?
KLEM IS RIGHT HERE.
PAT
DO YOU NEED MY HELP AFTER ALL?

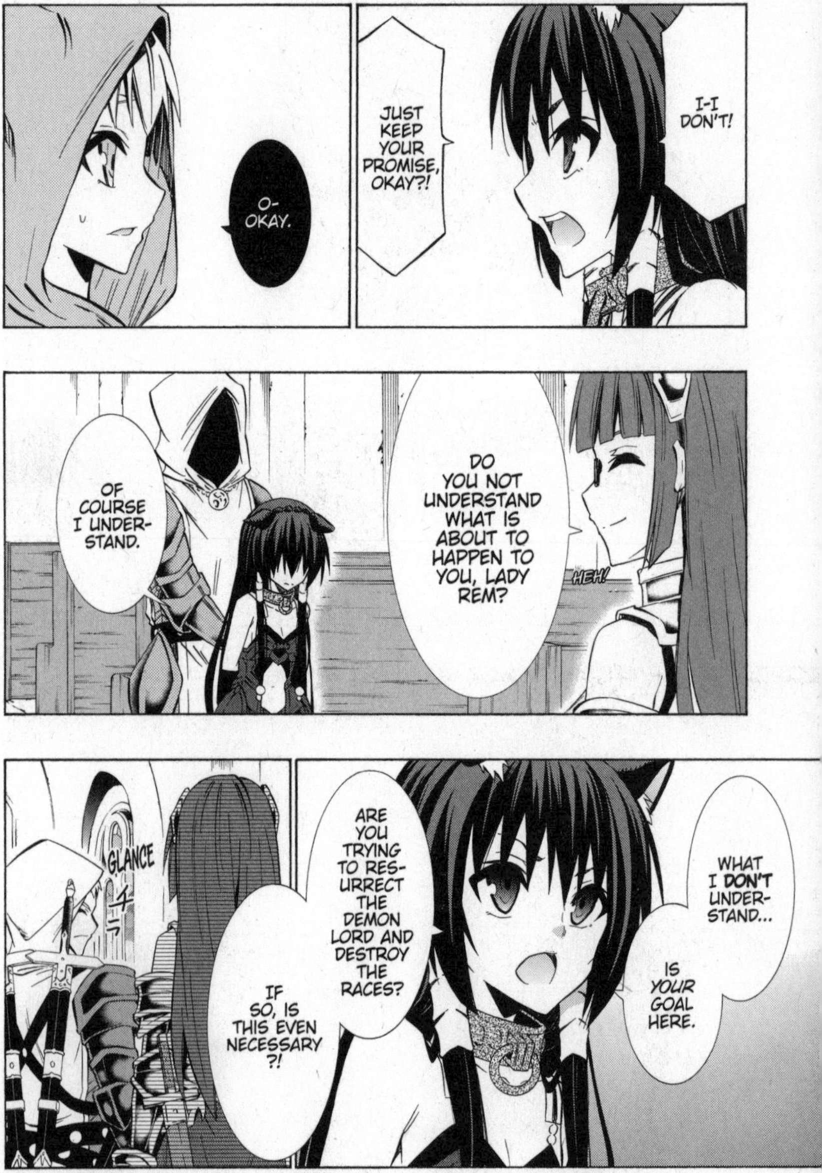
I-I DON'T!
JUST KEEP YOUR PROMISE, OKAY?!
O-OKAY.
DO YOU NOT UNDERSTAND WHAT IS ABOUT TO HAPPEN TO YOU, LADY REM?
HEH!
OF COURSE I UNDER-STAND.
WHAT I **DON'T** UNDER-STAND...
IS *YOUR* GOAL HERE.
ARE YOU TRYING TO RES-URRECT THE DEMON LORD AND DESTROY THE RACES?
IF SO, IS THIS EVEN NECESSARY?!
GLANCE

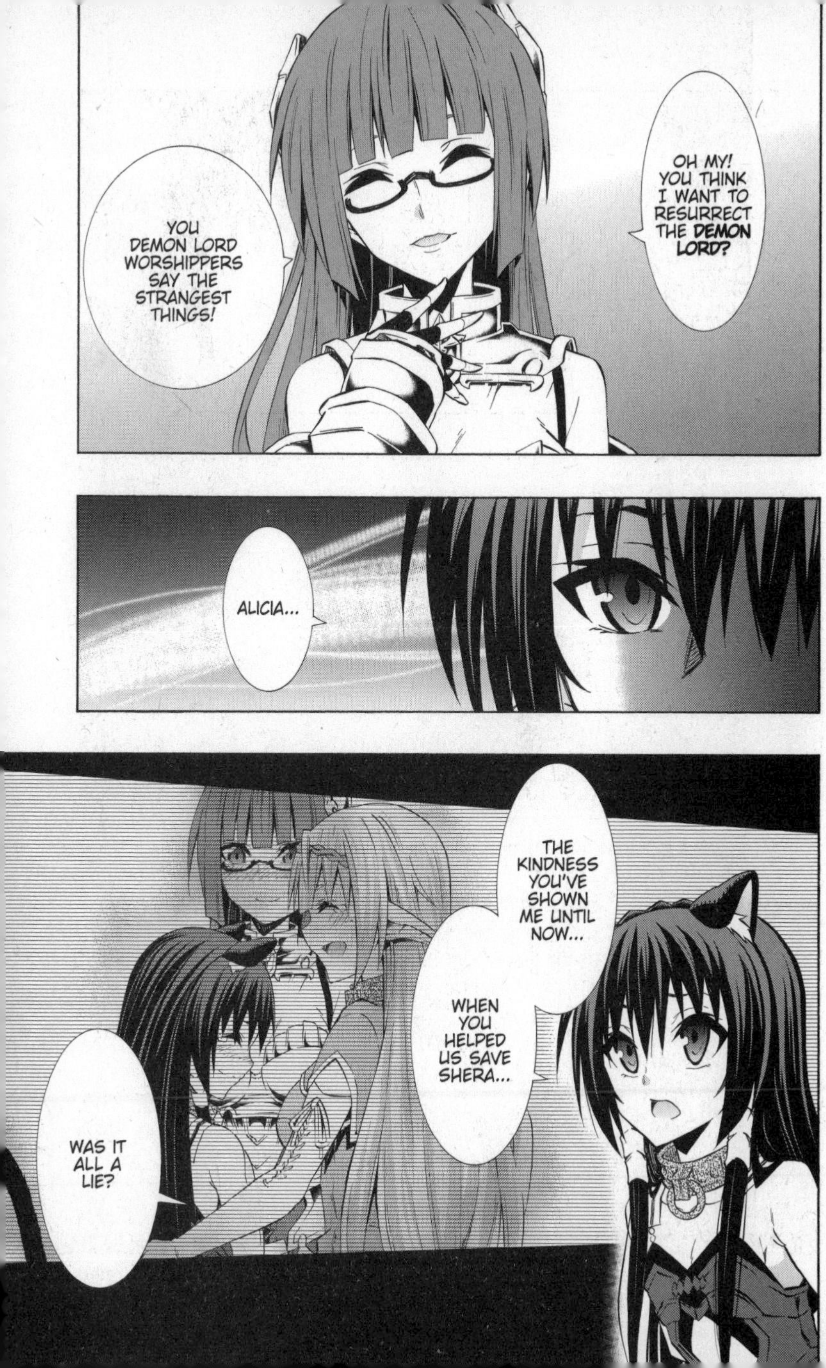
OH MY! YOU THINK I WANT TO RESURRECT THE **DEMON LORD?**
YOU DEMON LORD WORSHIPPERS SAY THE STRANGEST THINGS!
ALICIA...
THE KINDNESS YOU'VE SHOWN ME UNTIL NOW...
WHEN YOU HELPED US SAVE SHERA...
WAS IT ALL A LIE?

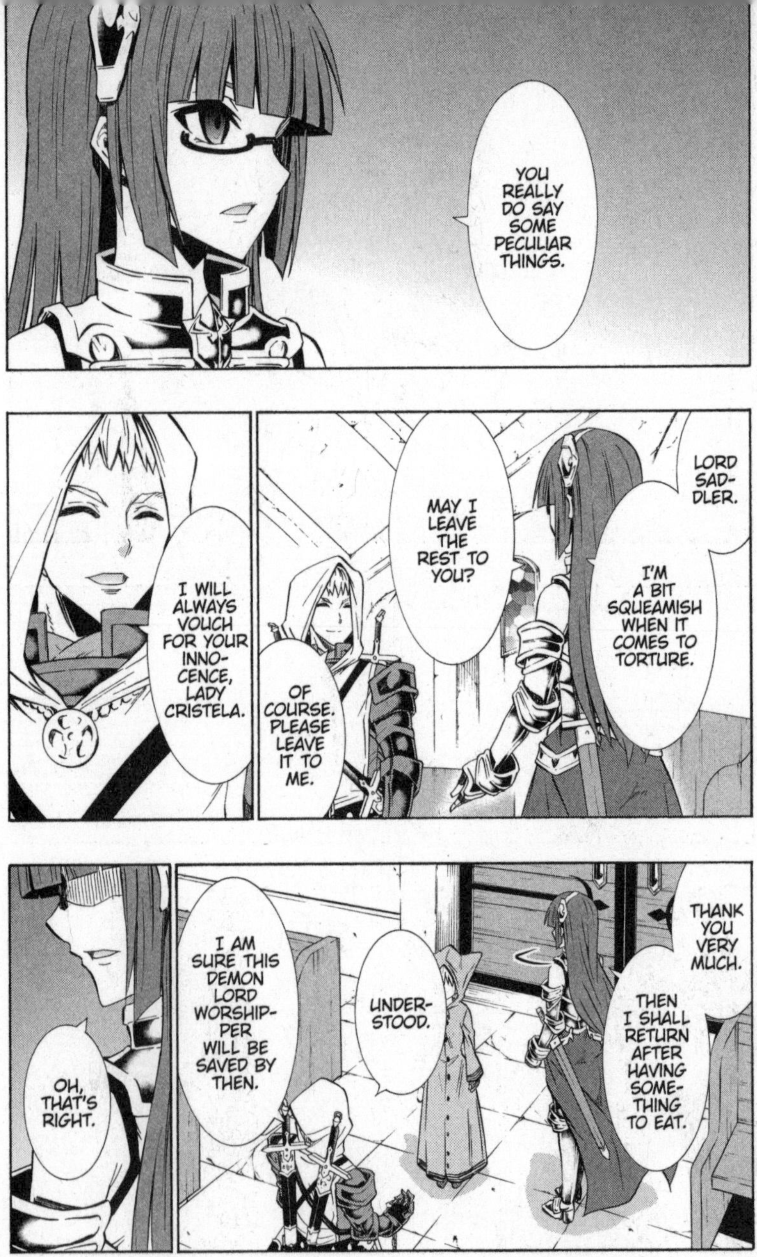
YOU REALLY DO SAY SOME PECULIAR THINGS.
LORD SADDLER.
I'M A BIT SQUEAMISH WHEN IT COMES TO TORTURE.
MAY I LEAVE THE REST TO YOU?
OF COURSE. PLEASE LEAVE IT TO ME.
I WILL ALWAYS VOUCH FOR YOUR INNOCENCE, LADY CRISTELA.
THANK YOU VERY MUCH.
THEN I SHALL RETURN AFTER HAVING SOMETHING TO EAT.
UNDERSTOOD.
I AM SURE THIS DEMON LORD WORSHIPPER WILL BE SAVED BY THEN.
OH, THAT'S RIGHT.

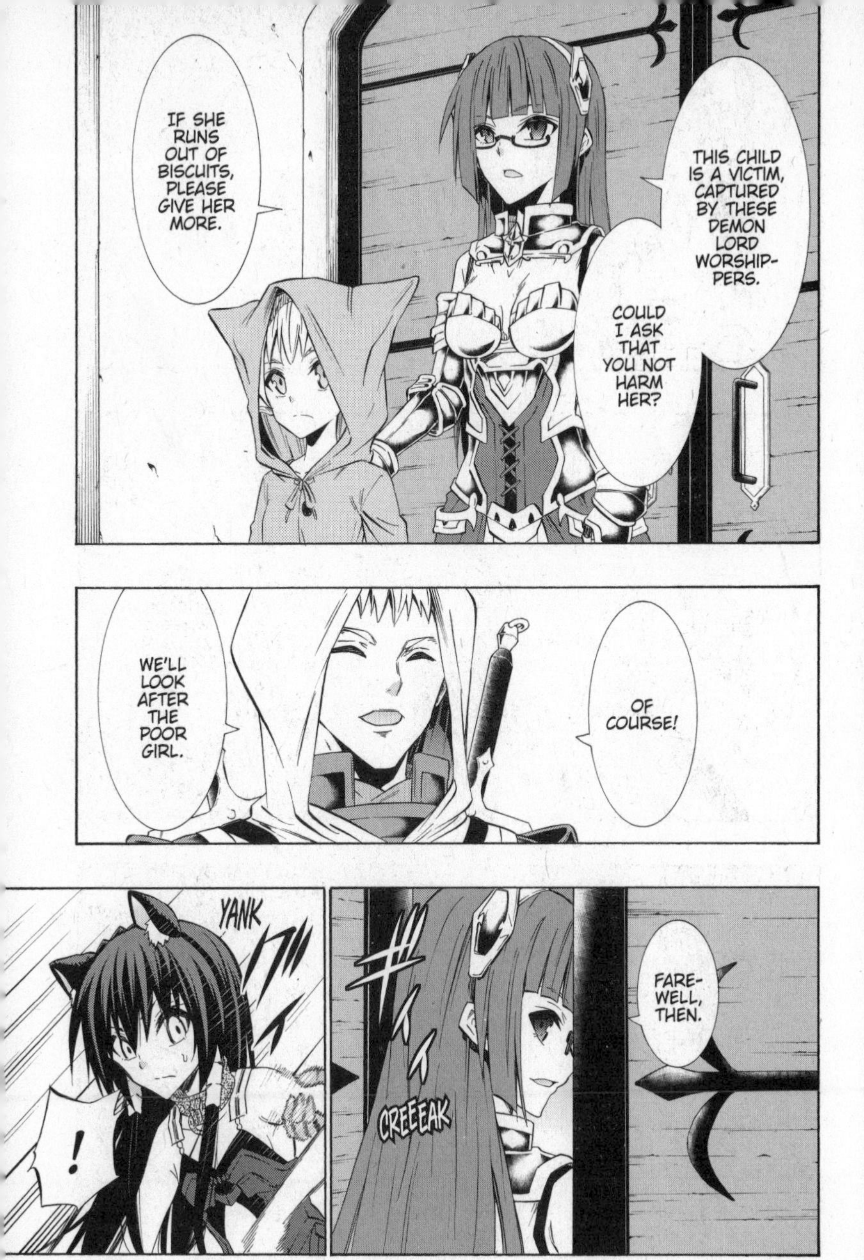
THIS CHILD IS A VICTIM, CAPTURED BY THESE DEMON LORD WORSHIP-PERS.
COULD I ASK THAT YOU NOT HARM HER?
IF SHE RUNS OUT OF BISCUITS, PLEASE GIVE HER MORE.
OF COURSE!
WE'LL LOOK AFTER THE POOR GIRL.
FARE-WELL, THEN.
CREEEAK
YANK
!

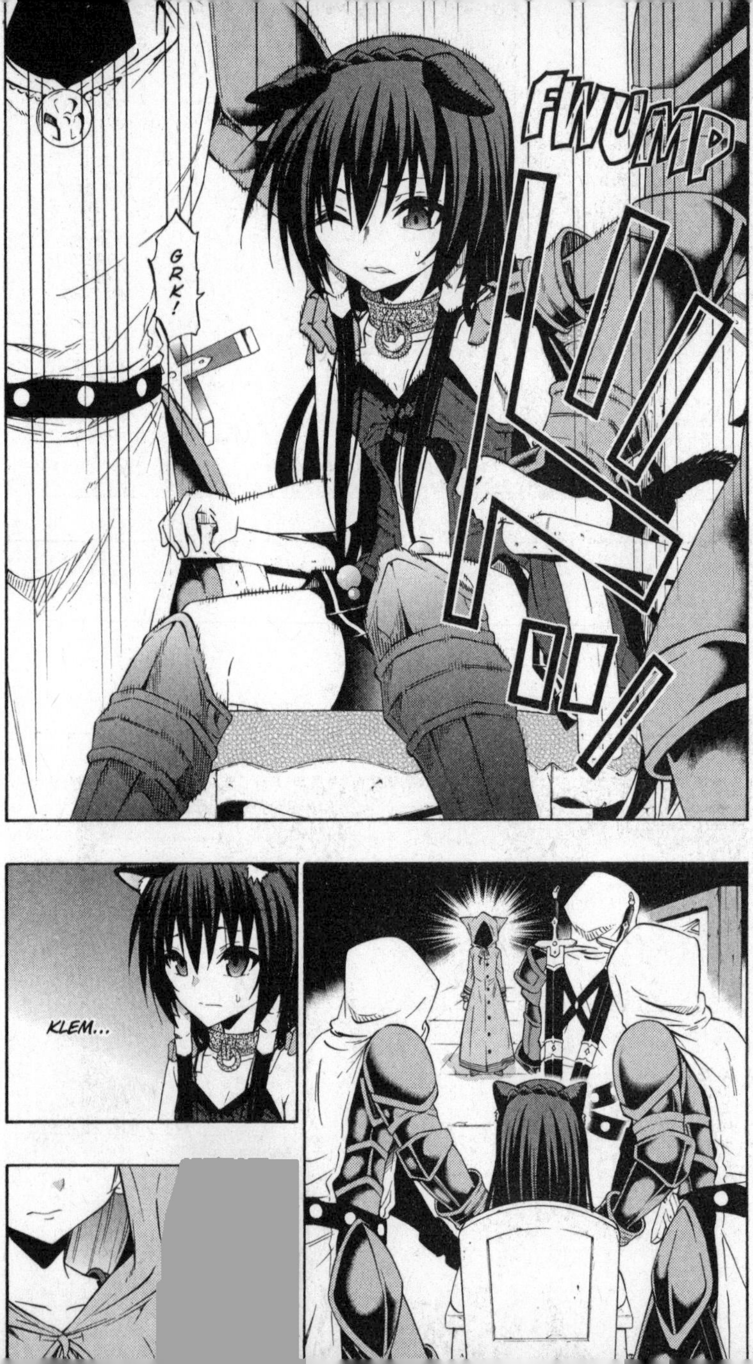
FWUMP
GRK!
KLEM...

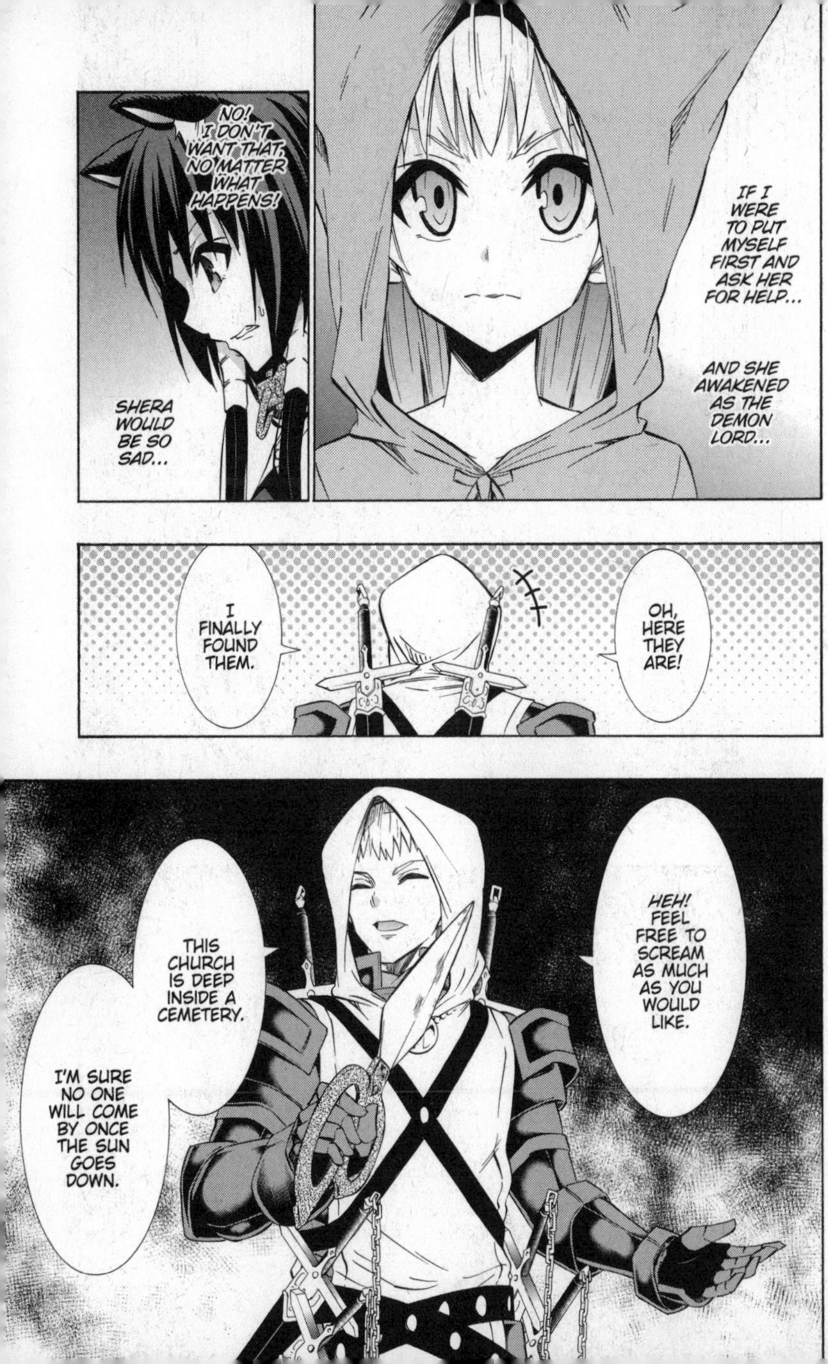
IF I WERE TO PUT MYSELF FIRST AND ASK HER FOR HELP...
AND SHE AWAKENED AS THE DEMON LORD...
SHERA WOULD BE SO SAD...
NO! I DON'T WANT THAT, NO MATTER WHAT HAPPENS!
OH, HERE THEY ARE!
I FINALLY FOUND THEM.
HEH! FEEL FREE TO SCREAM AS MUCH AS YOU WOULD LIKE.
THIS CHURCH IS DEEP INSIDE A CEMETERY.
I'M SURE NO ONE WILL COME BY ONCE THE SUN GOES DOWN.

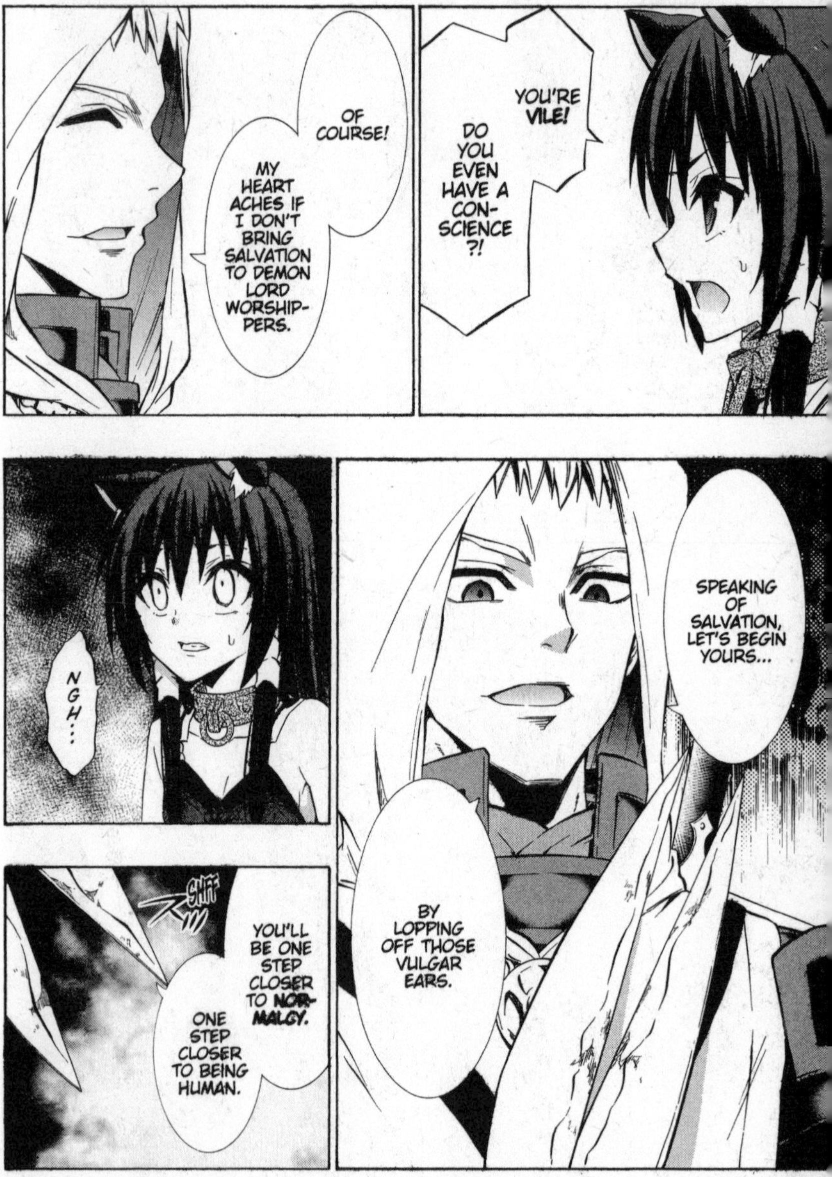
YOU'RE VILE!
DO YOU EVEN HAVE A CON-SCIENCE?!
OF COURSE!
MY HEART ACHES IF I DON'T BRING SALVATION TO DEMON LORD WORSHIP-PERS.
SPEAKING OF SALVATION, LET'S BEGIN YOURS...
BY LOPPING OFF THOSE VULGAR EARS.
NGH...
SHFF
YOU'LL BE ONE STEP CLOSER TO NOR-MALGY.
ONE STEP CLOSER TO BEING HUMAN.

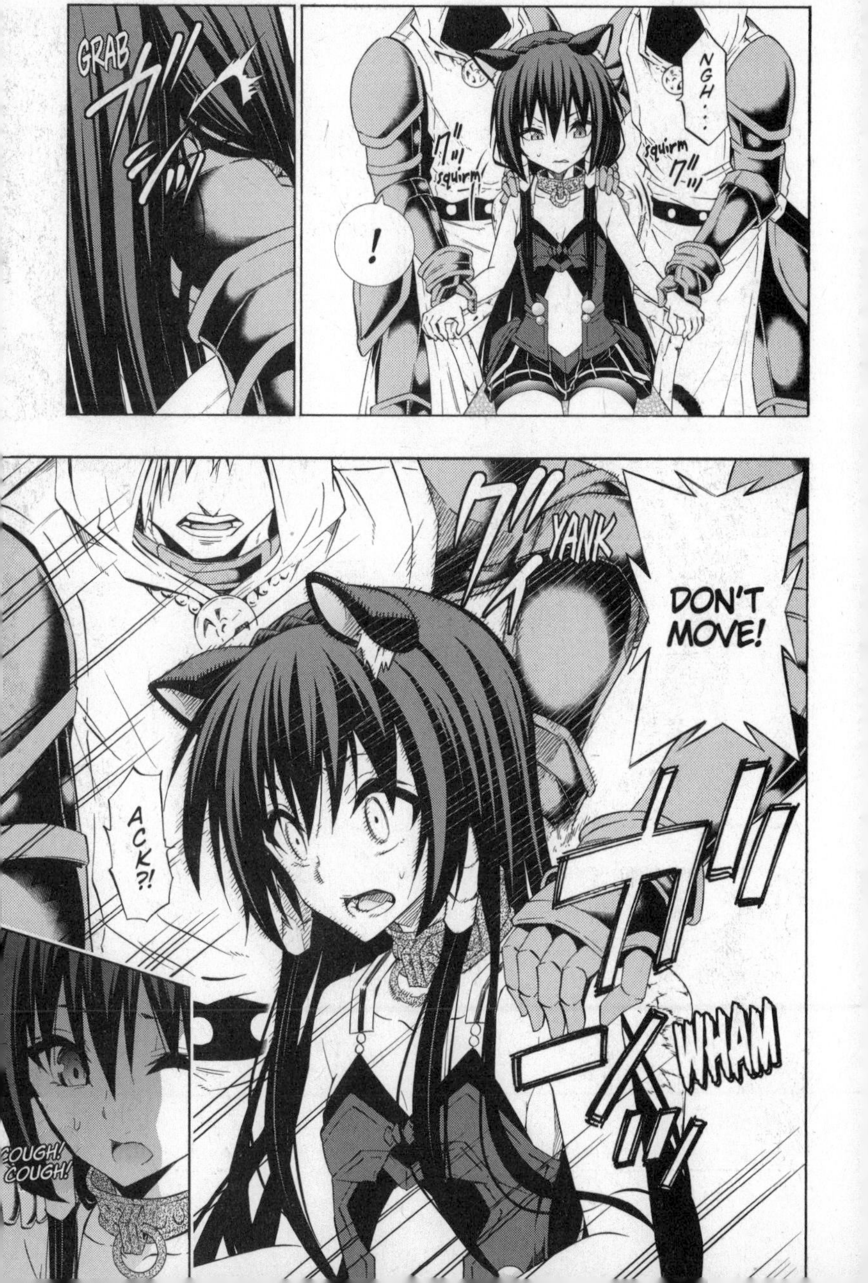
NGH...
squirm
squirm
!
GRAB
YANK
DON'T MOVE!
WHAM
ACK?!
COUGH! COUGH!

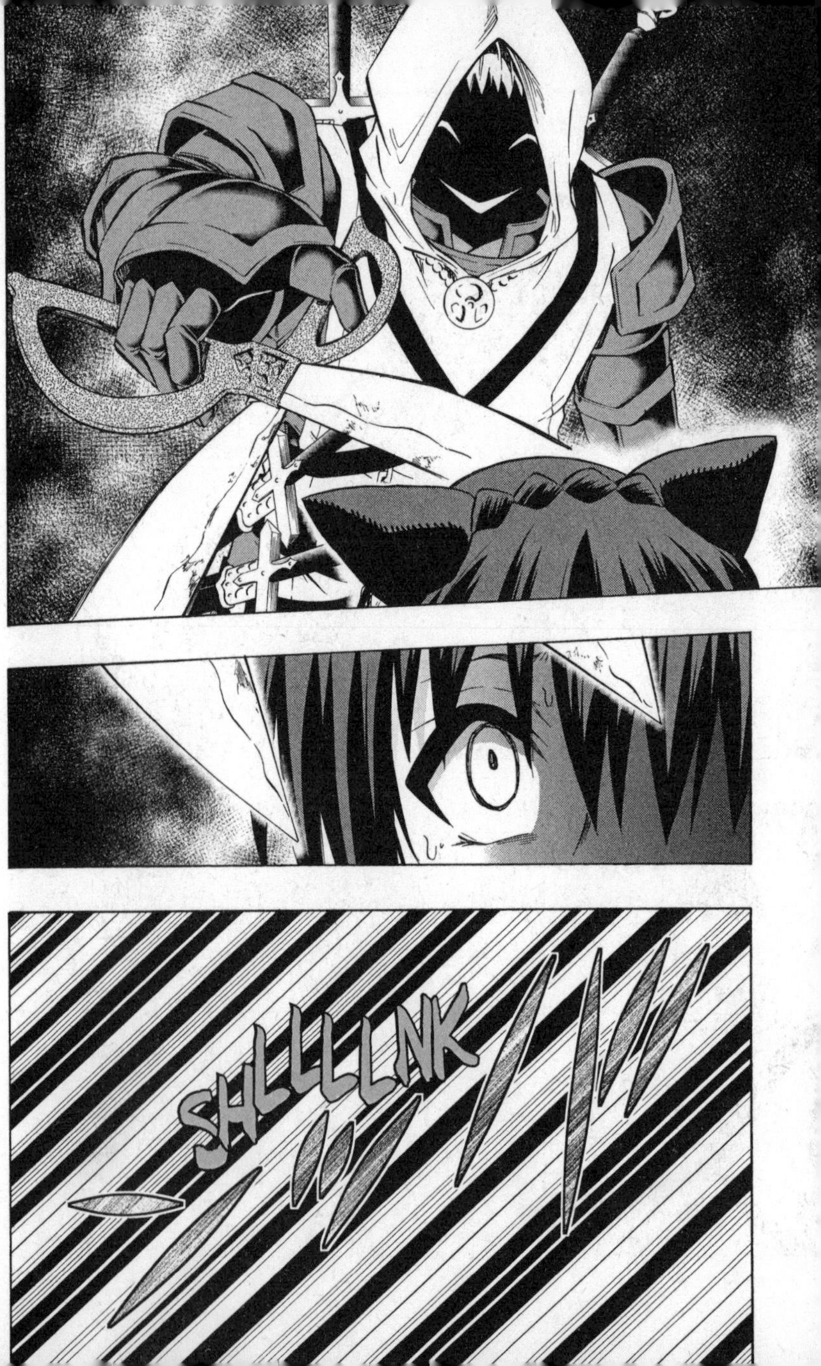
SHLLLLNK

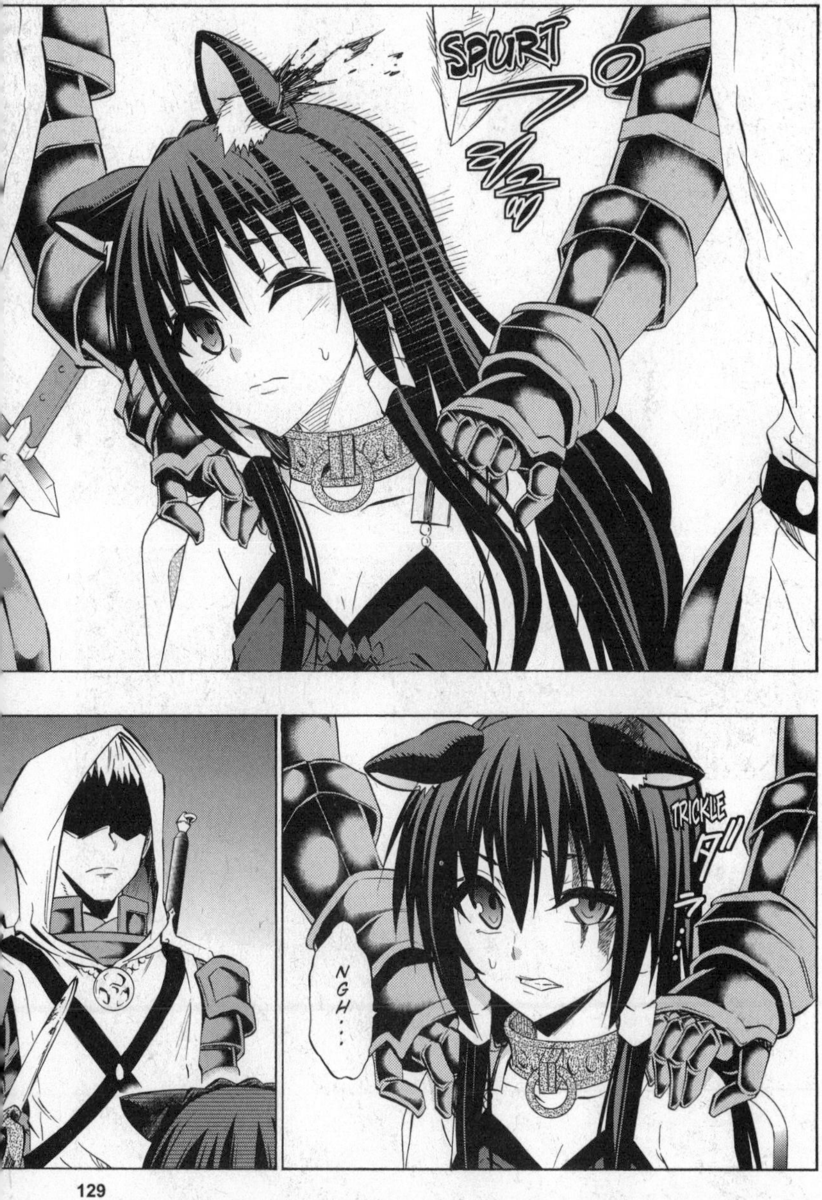
SPURT
TRICKLE
NGH...

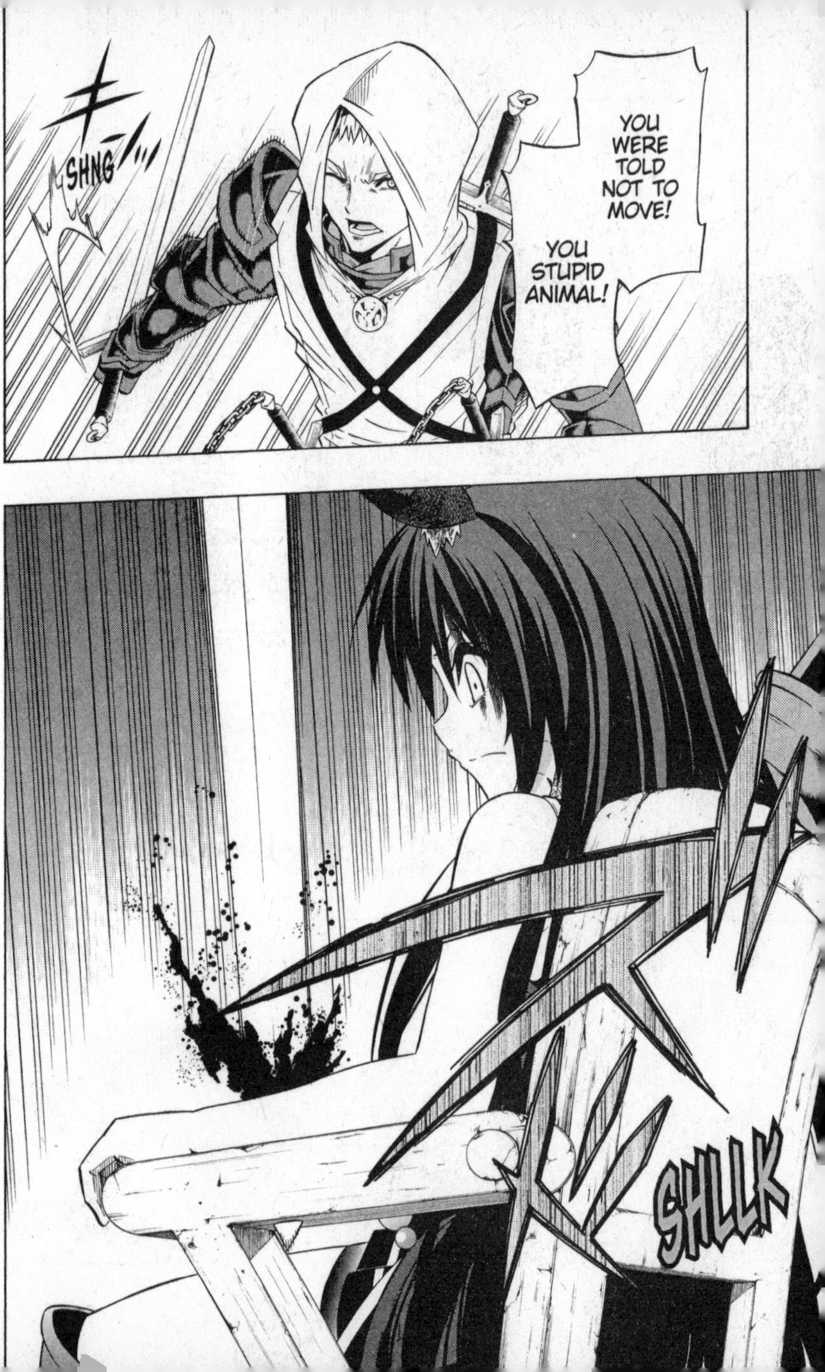
YOU WERE TOLD NOT TO MOVE!
YOU STUPID ANIMAL!
SHNG
SHLLK

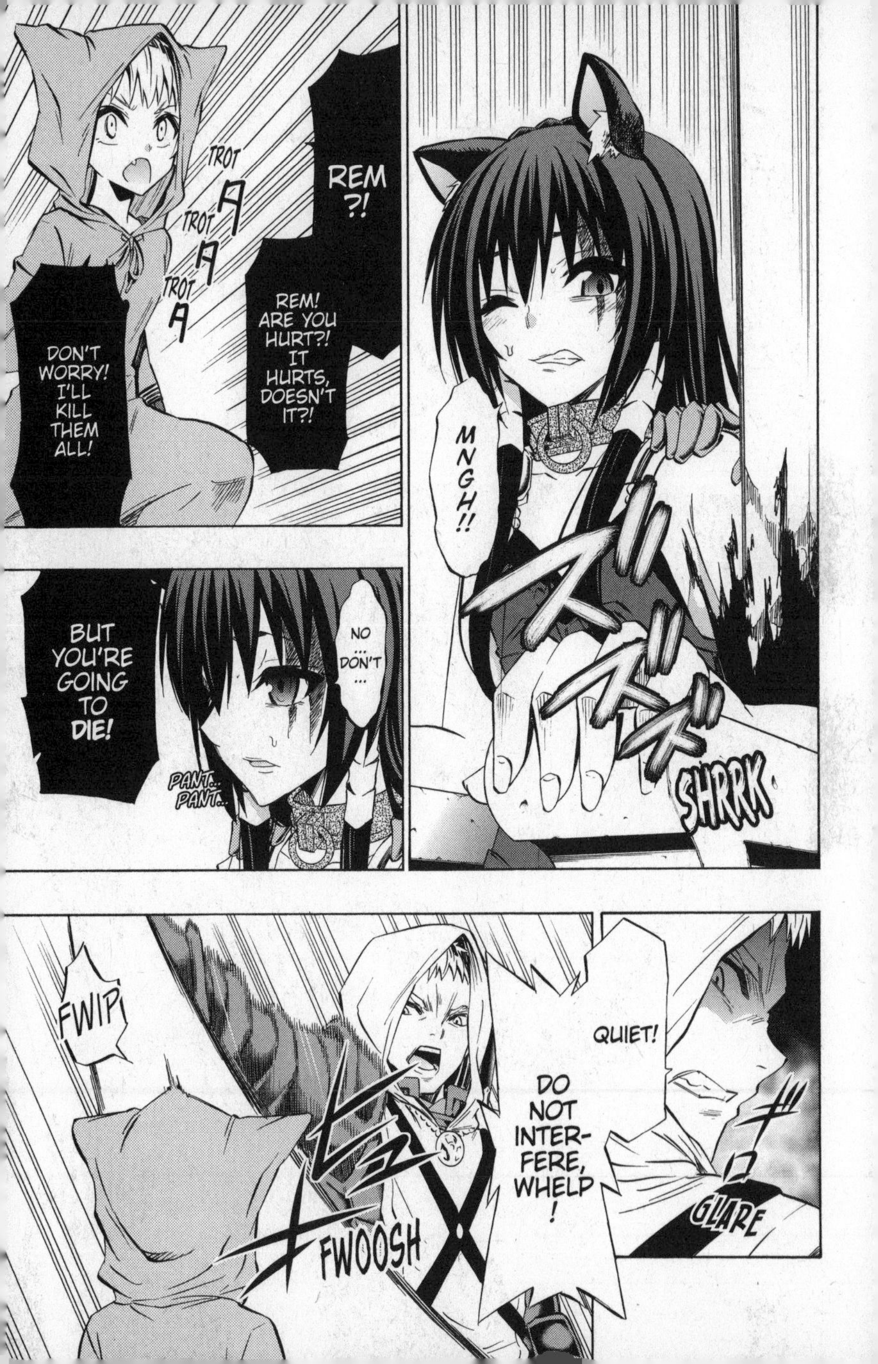
MNGH!!
SHRRK
REM ?!
TROT
TROT
TROT
REM! ARE YOU HURT?! IT HURTS, DOESN'T IT?!
DON'T WORRY! I'LL KILL THEM ALL!
NO ... DON'T ...
BUT YOU'RE GOING TO DIE!
PANT... PANT...
QUIET!
DO NOT INTERFERE, WHELP!
GLARE
FWIP
FWOOSH

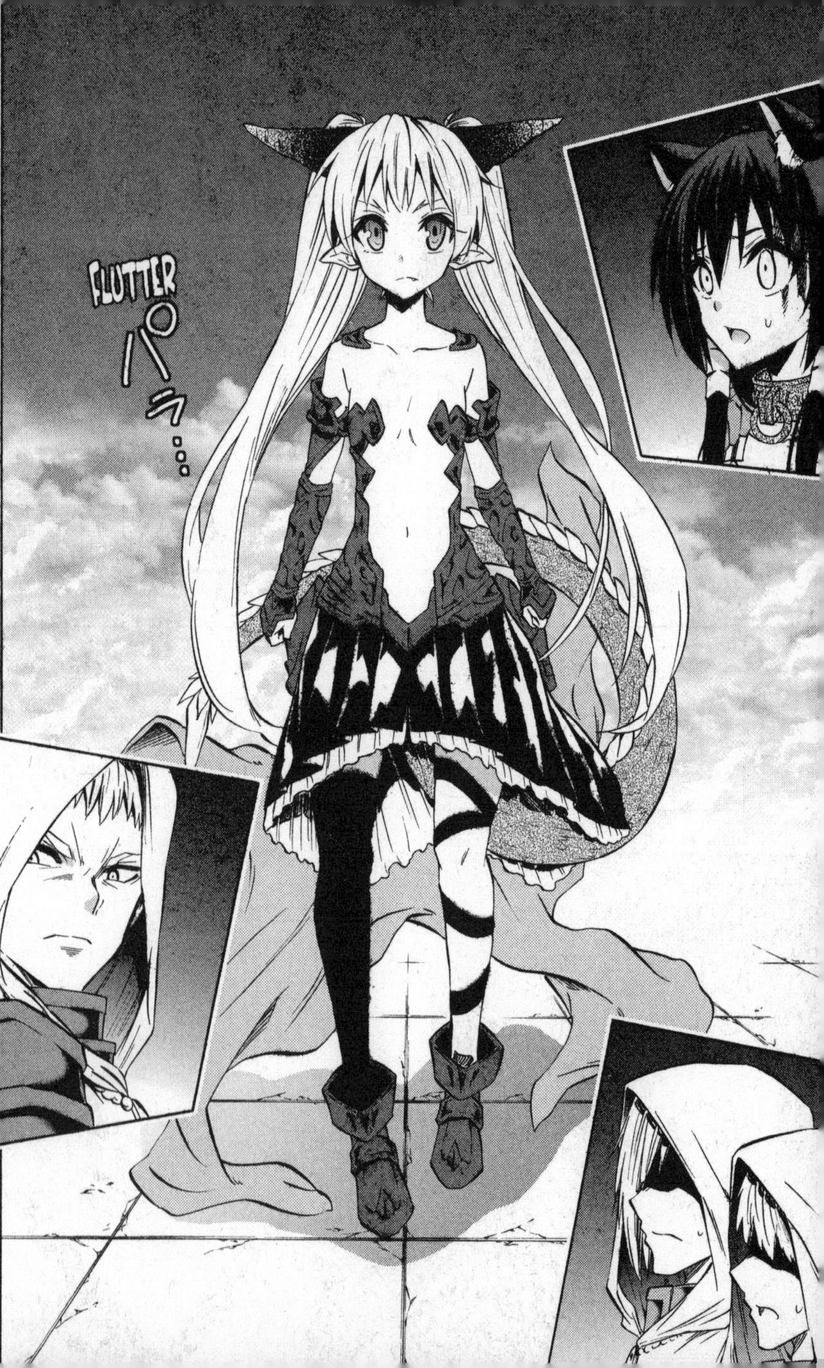
FLUTTER
パラ…

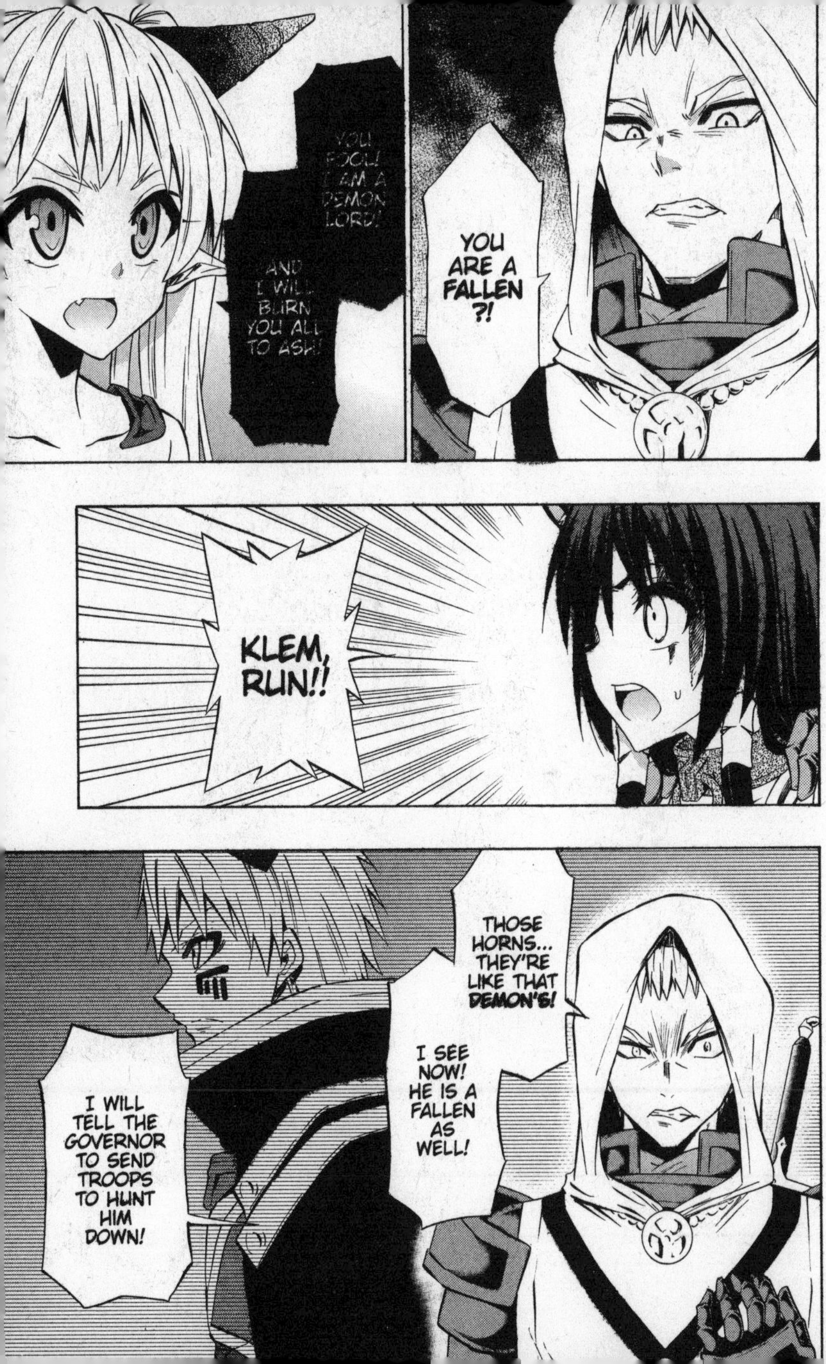
YOU ARE A FALLEN ?!
YOU FOOL! I AM A DEMON LORD!
AND I WILL BURN YOU ALL TO ASH!
KLEM, RUN!!
THOSE HORNS... THEY'RE LIKE THAT DEMON'S!
I SEE NOW! HE IS A FALLEN AS WELL!
I WILL TELL THE GOVERNOR TO SEND TROOPS TO HUNT HIM DOWN!

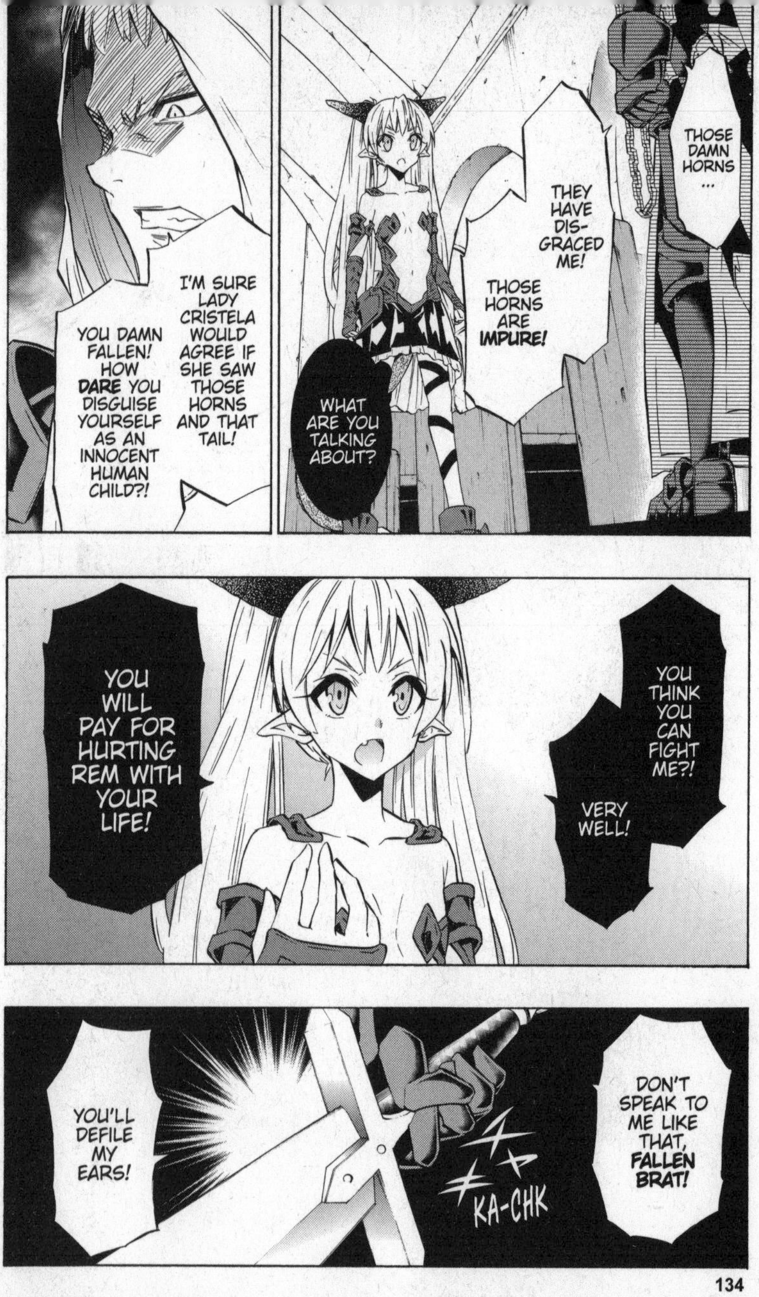
THOSE DAMN HORNS ...
THEY HAVE DIS-GRACED ME!
THOSE HORNS ARE **IMPURE!**
WHAT ARE YOU TALKING ABOUT?
I'M SURE LADY CRISTELA WOULD AGREE IF SHE SAW THOSE HORNS AND THAT TAIL!
YOU DAMN FALLEN! HOW **DARE** YOU DISGUISE YOURSELF AS AN INNOCENT HUMAN CHILD?!
YOU THINK YOU CAN FIGHT ME?!
VERY WELL!
YOU WILL PAY FOR HURTING REM WITH YOUR LIFE!
DON'T SPEAK TO ME LIKE THAT, **FALLEN BRAT!**
KA-CHK
YOU'LL DEFILE MY EARS!

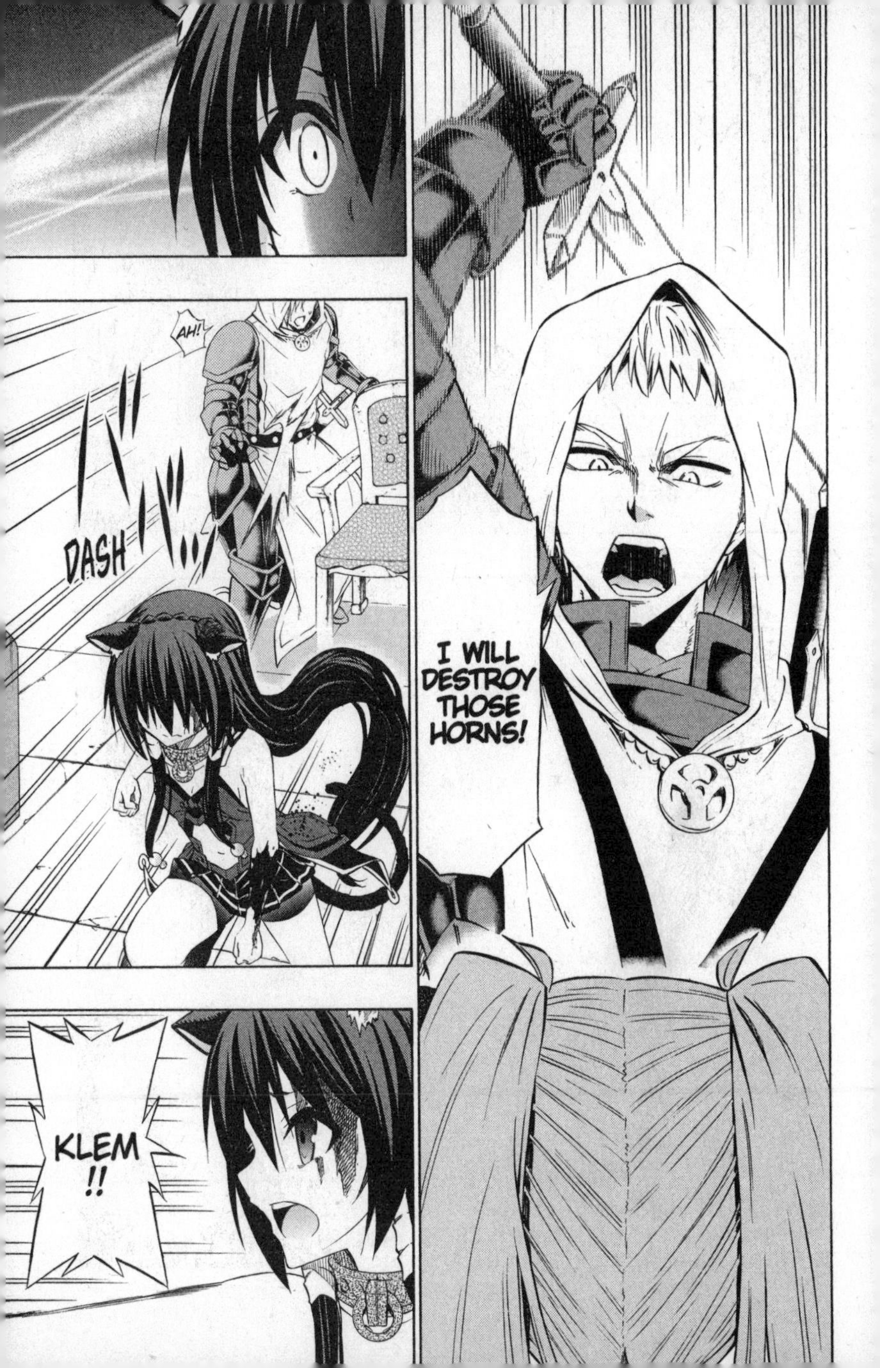
I WILL DESTROY THOSE HORNS!
AH!
DASH
KLEM !!

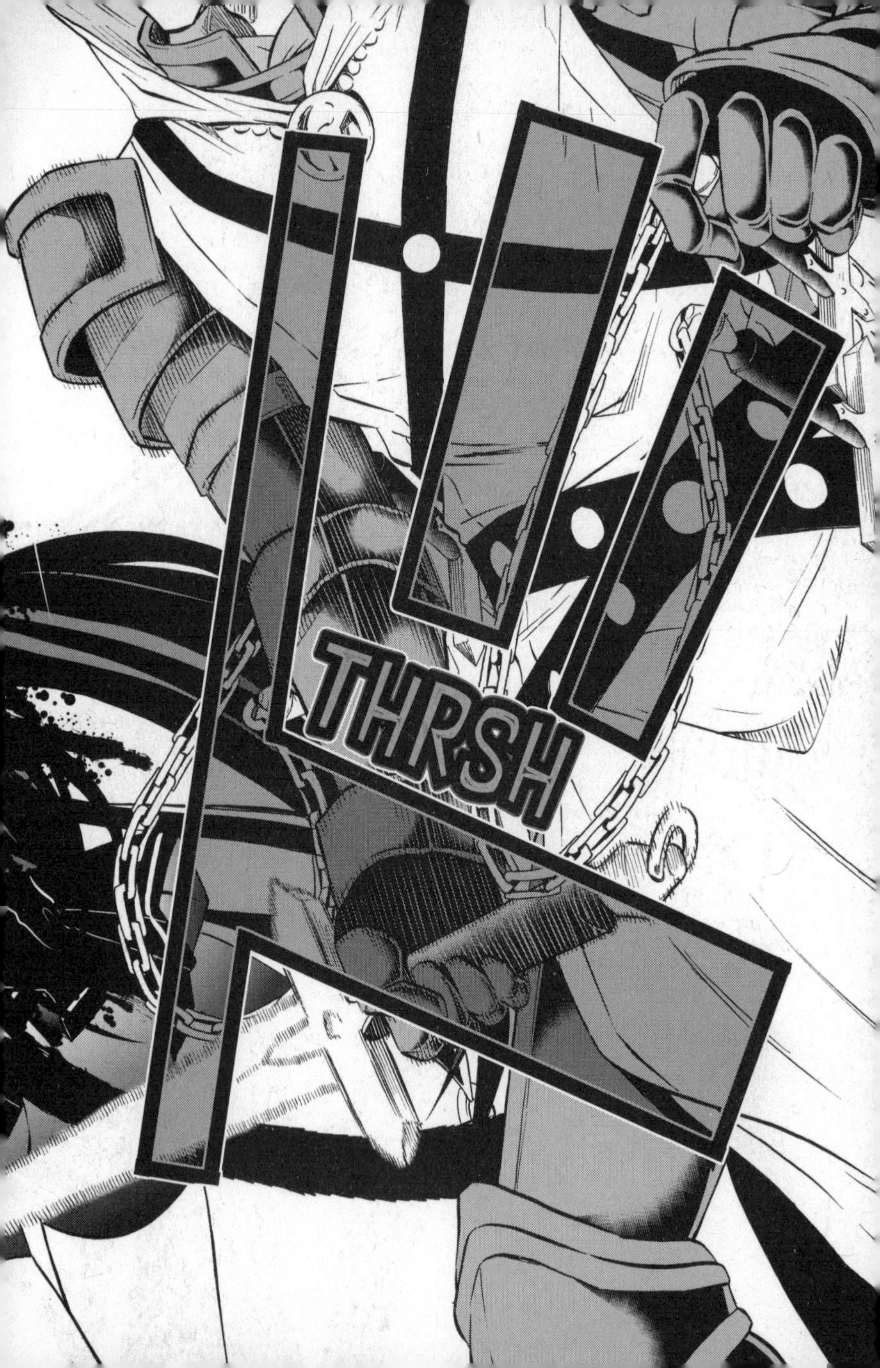
THRSH

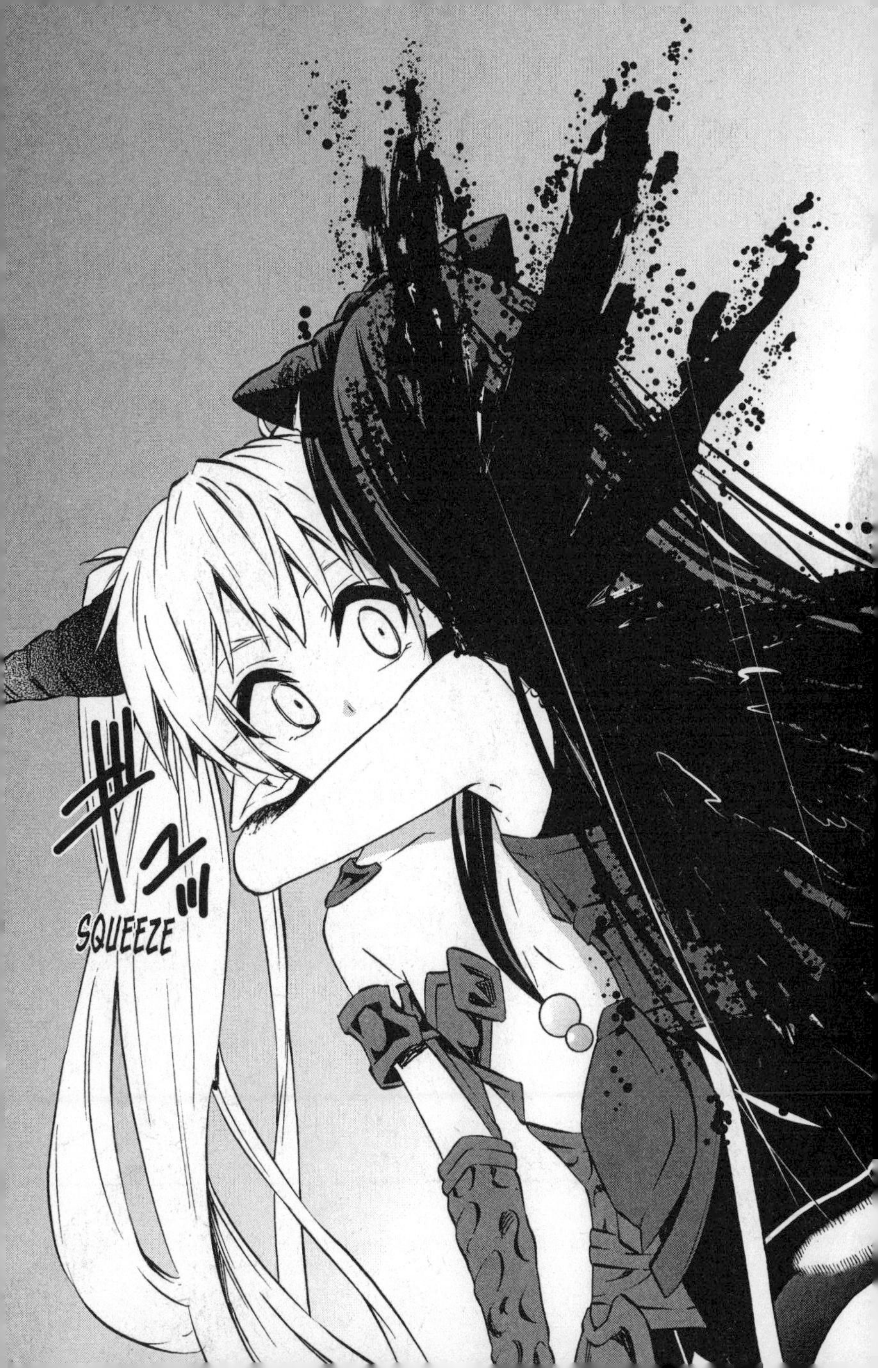
ギュッ
SQUEEZE

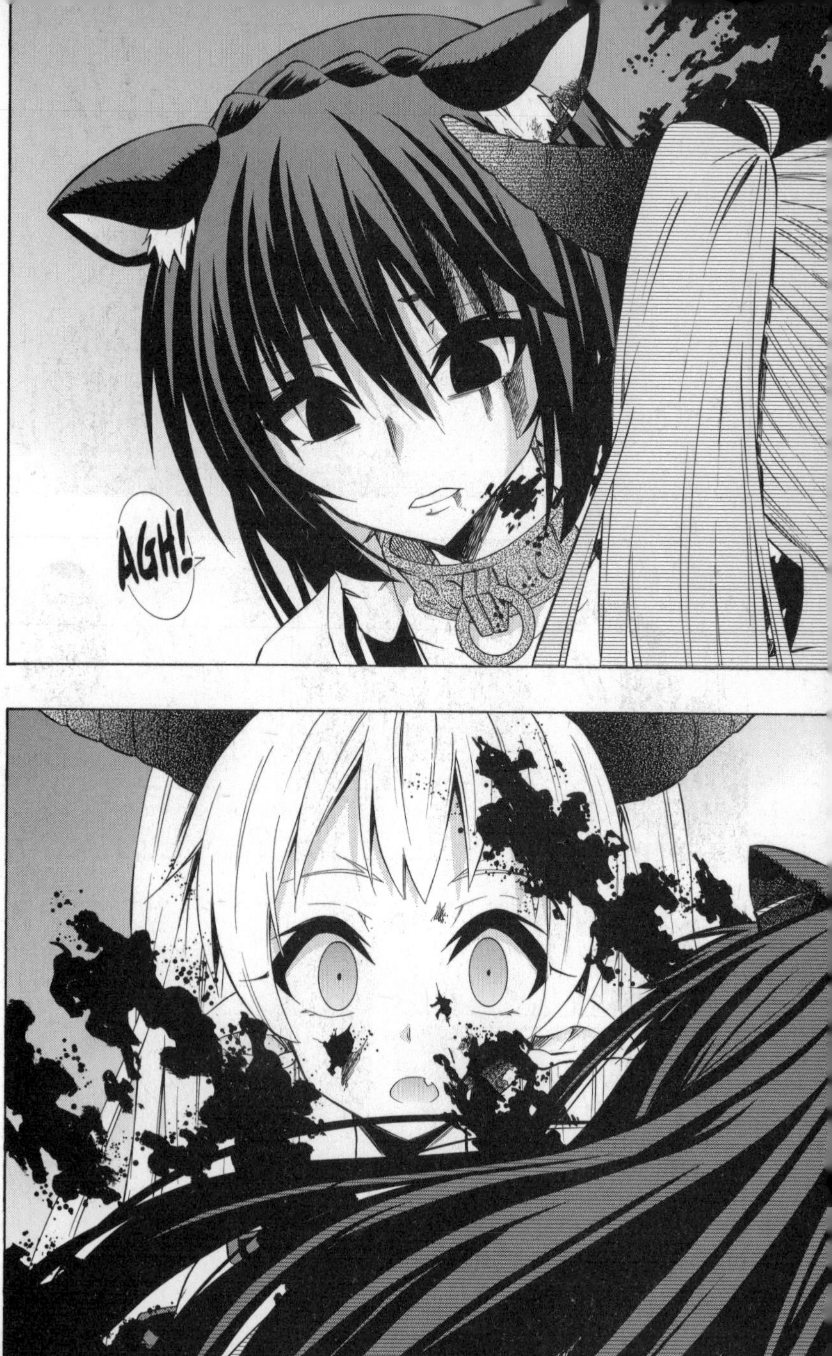
AGH!

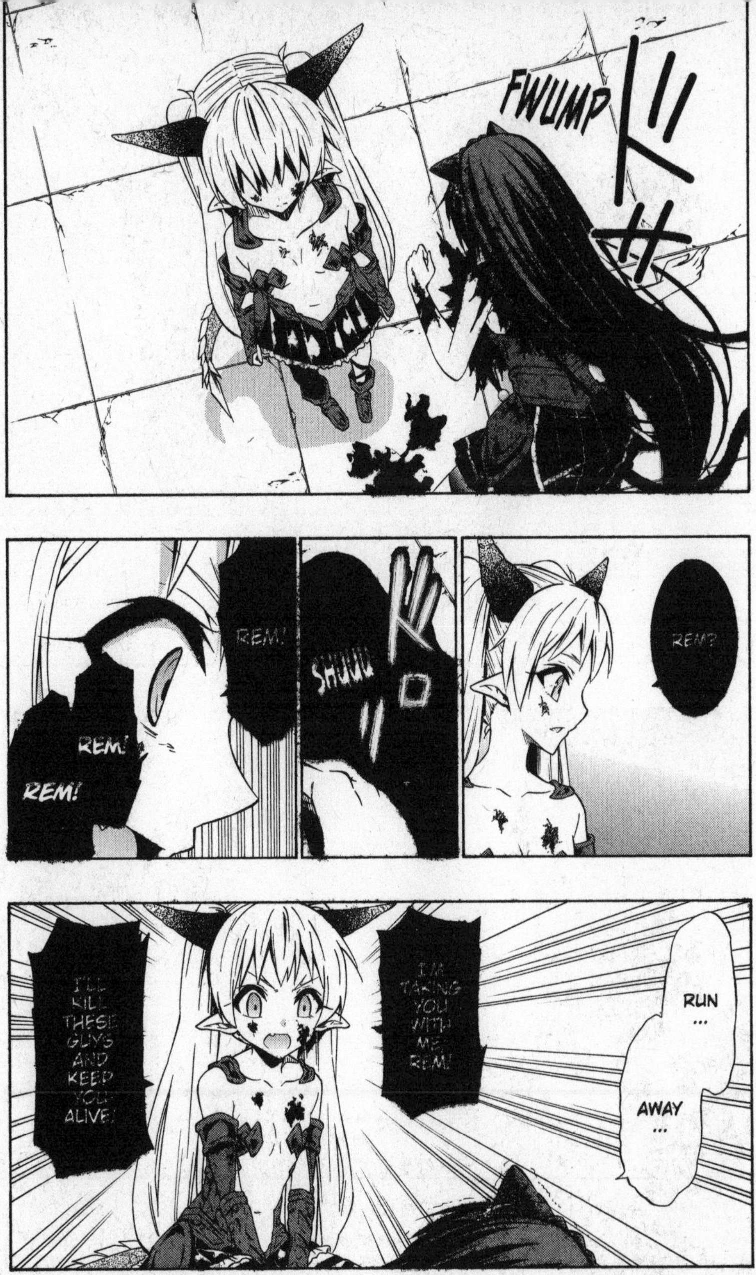

FWUMP
REM?
SHUUU
REM!
REM!
REM!
RUN... AWAY...
I'M TAKING YOU WITH ME, REM!
I'LL KILL THESE GUYS AND KEEP YOU ALIVE!

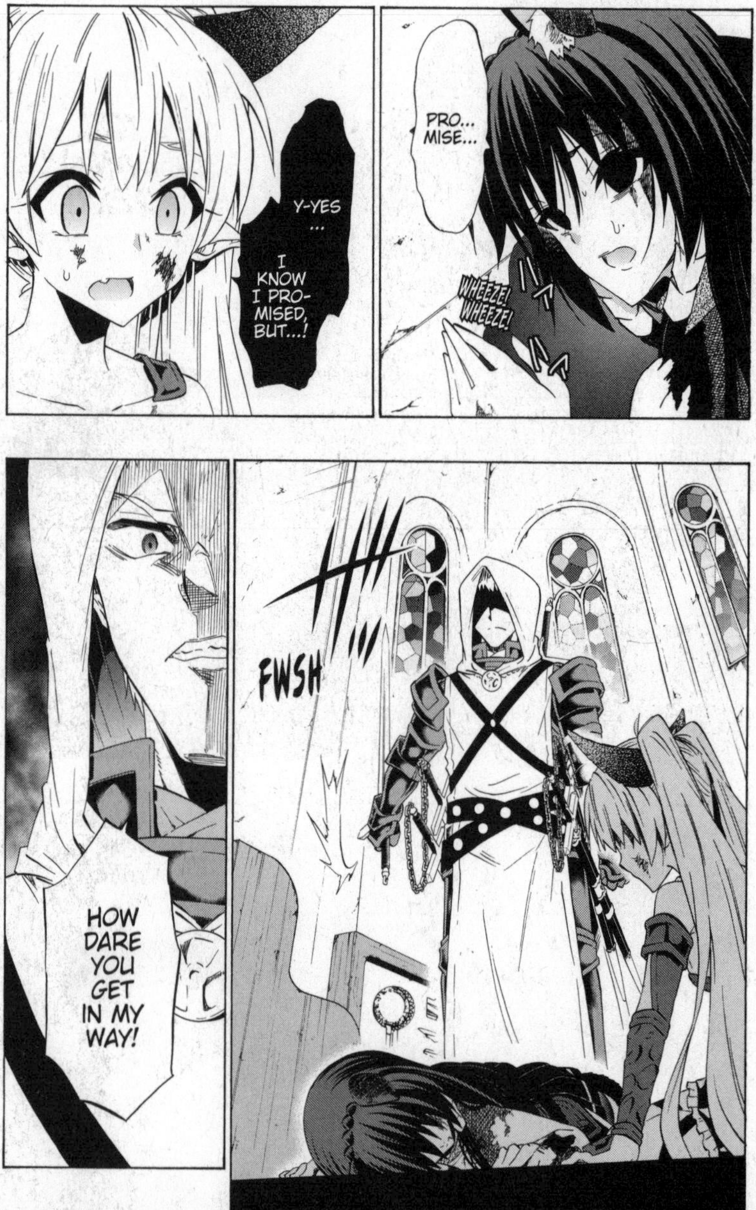

PRO... MISE...
WHEEZE! WHEEZE!
Y-YES ... I KNOW I PRO-MISED, BUT...!
FWSH
HOW DARE YOU GET IN MY WAY!

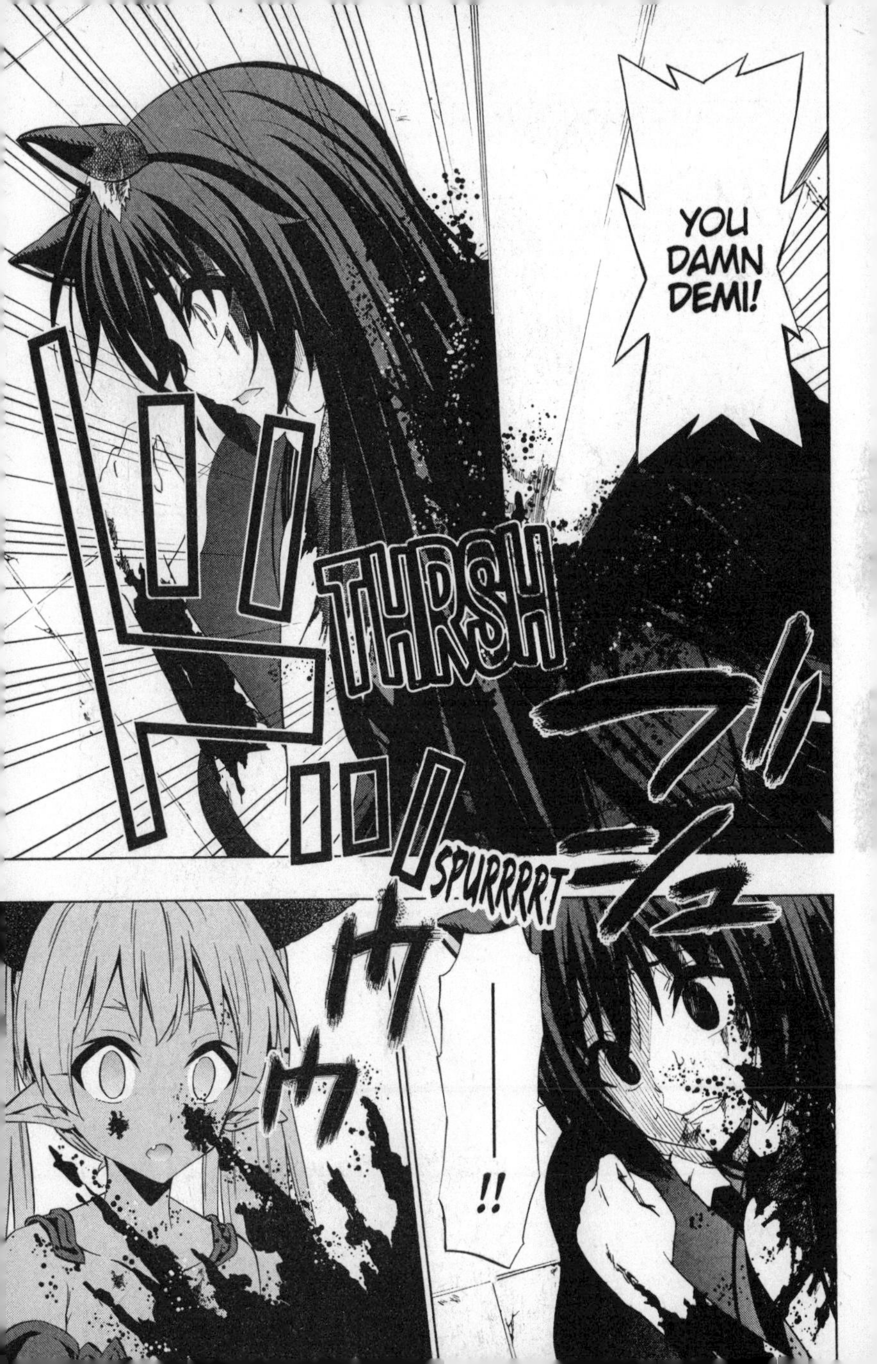
YOU DAMN DEMI!
THRSH
SPURRRRT
—!!

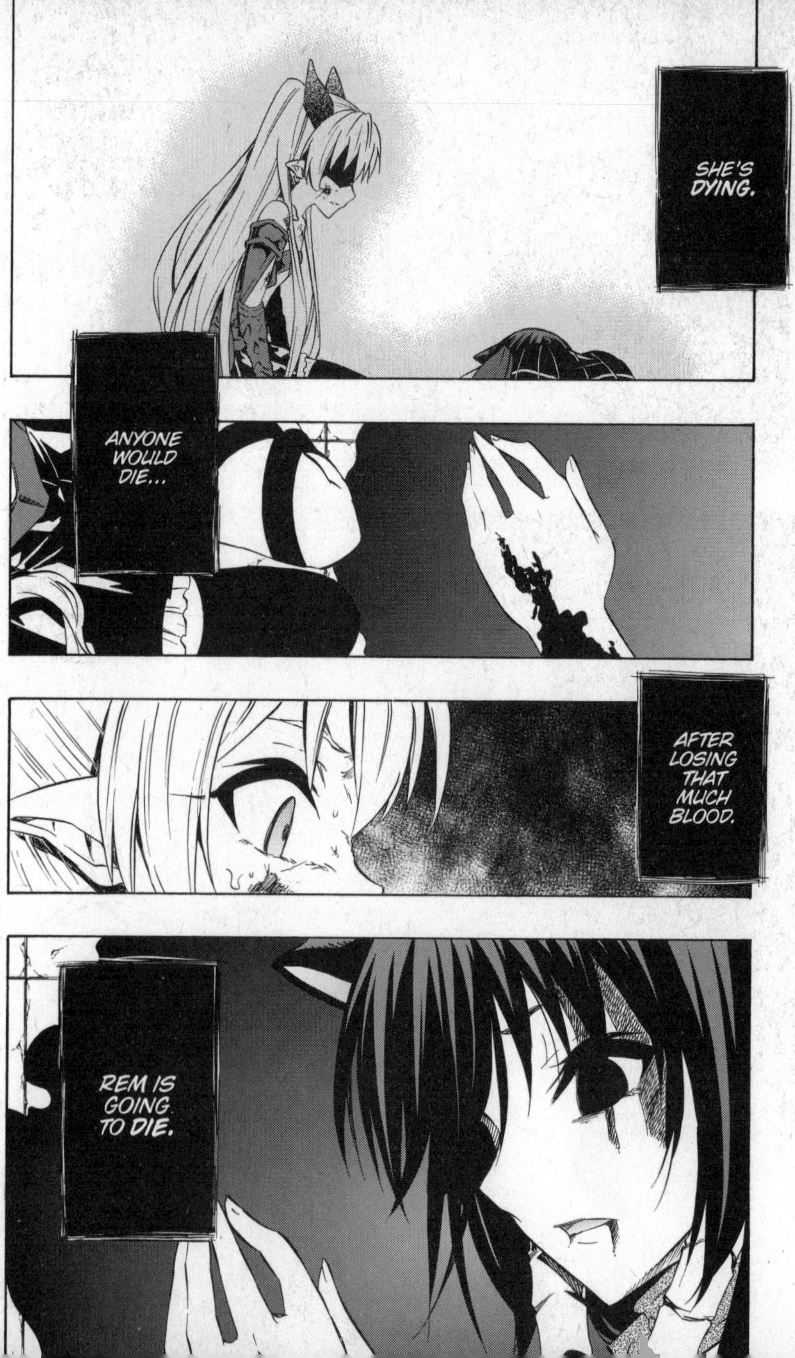
SHE'S DYING.
ANYONE WOULD DIE...
AFTER LOSING THAT MUCH BLOOD.
REM IS GOING TO DIE.

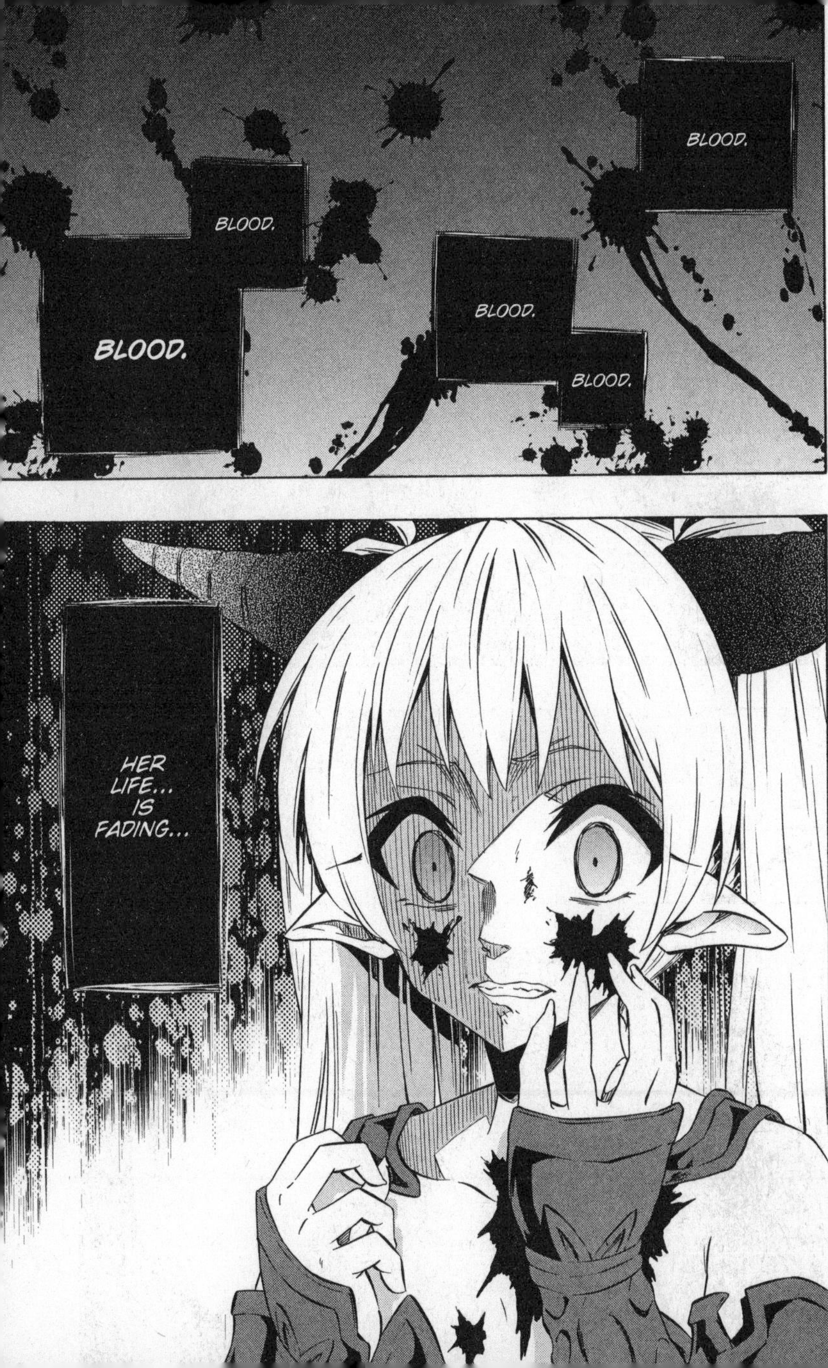
BLOOD.
BLOOD.
BLOOD.
BLOOD.
BLOOD.
HER LIFE... IS FADING...

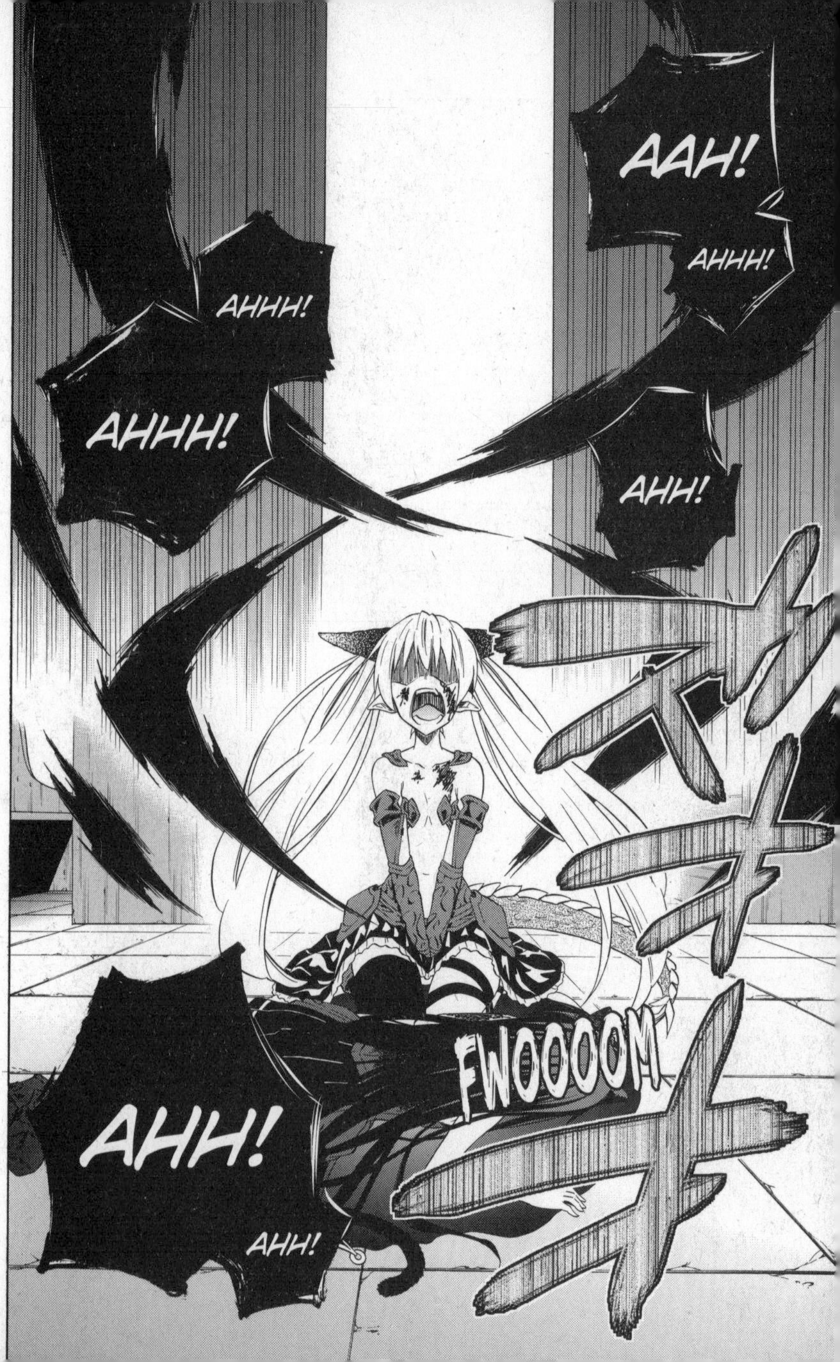
AAH!
AHHH!
AHHH!
AHHH!
AHH!
FWOOOOM
AHH!
AHH!

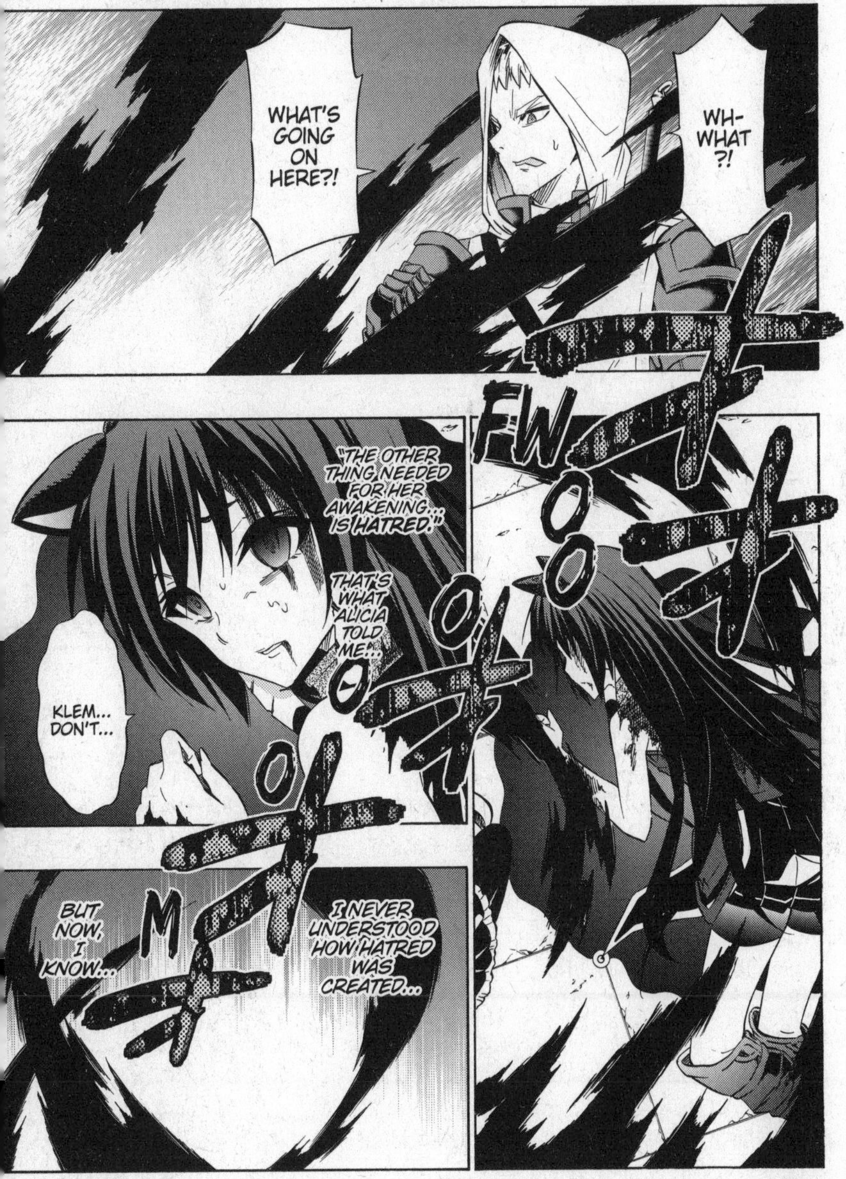
WH-WHAT?!
WHAT'S GOING ON HERE?!
FWOOOOOM
"THE OTHER THING NEEDED FOR HER AWAKENING... IS HATRED."
THAT'S WHAT ALICIA TOLD ME...
KLEM... DON'T...
I NEVER UNDERSTOOD HOW HATRED WAS CREATED...
BUT NOW, I KNOW...

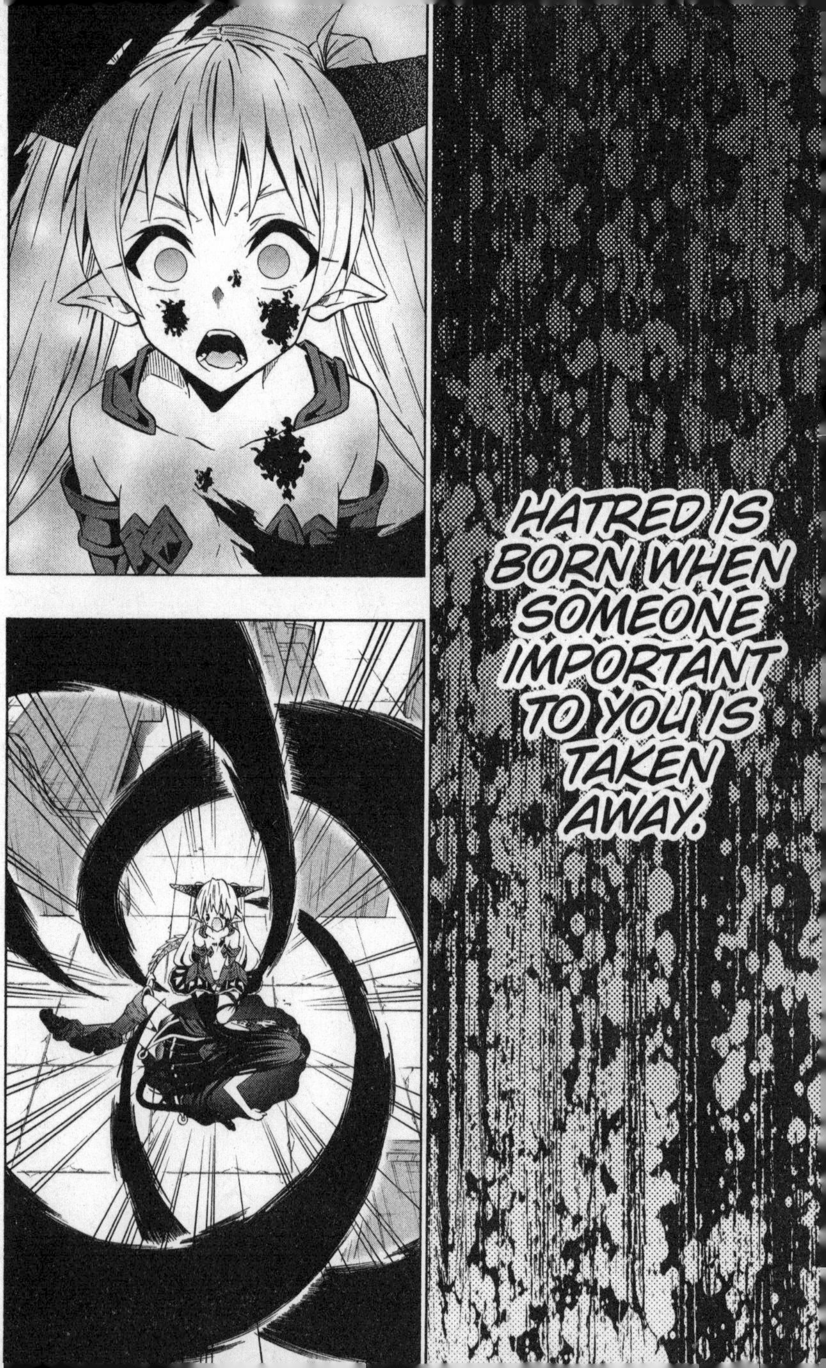
HATRED IS BORN WHEN SOMEONE IMPORTANT TO YOU IS TAKEN AWAY.

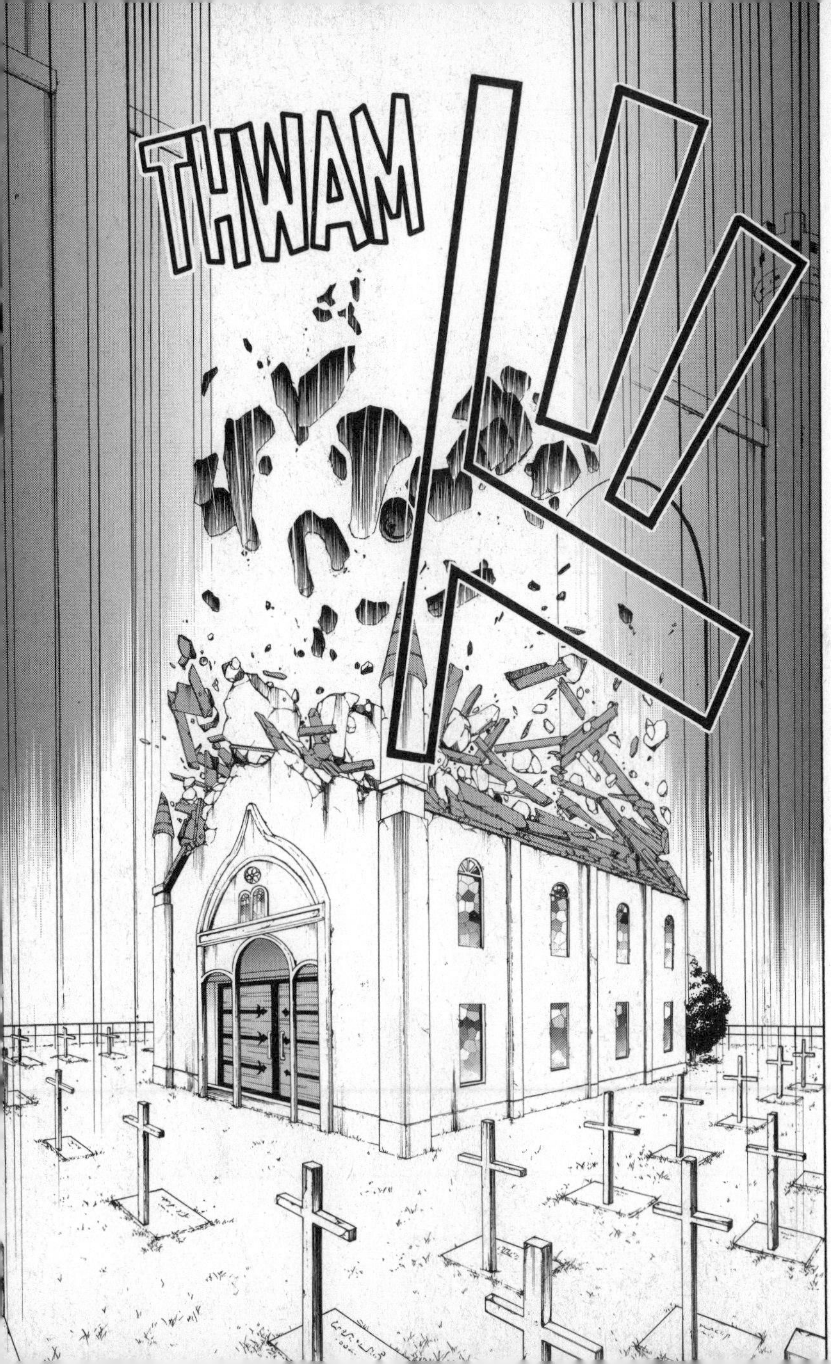
THWAM!!

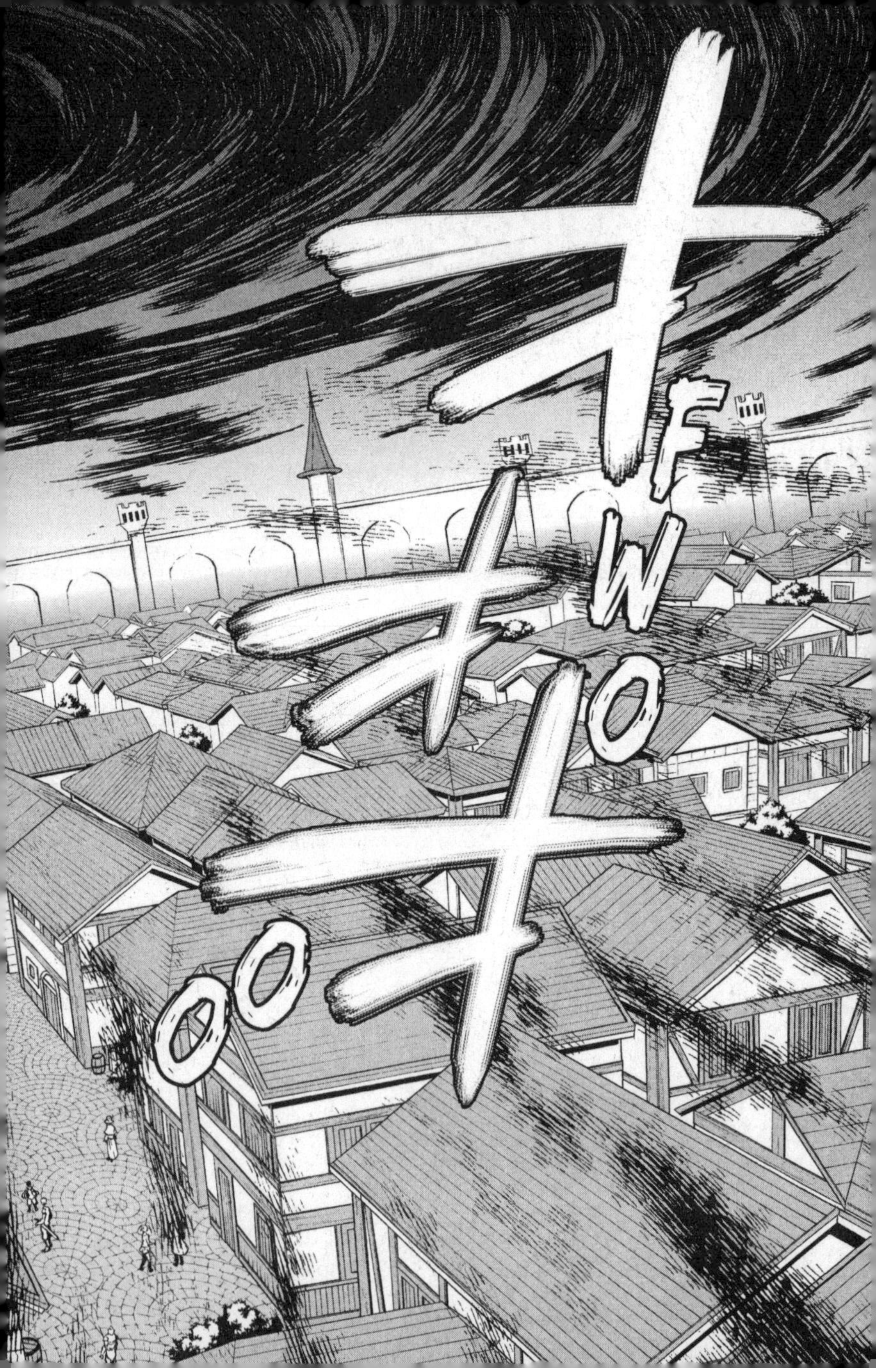
FWOOO

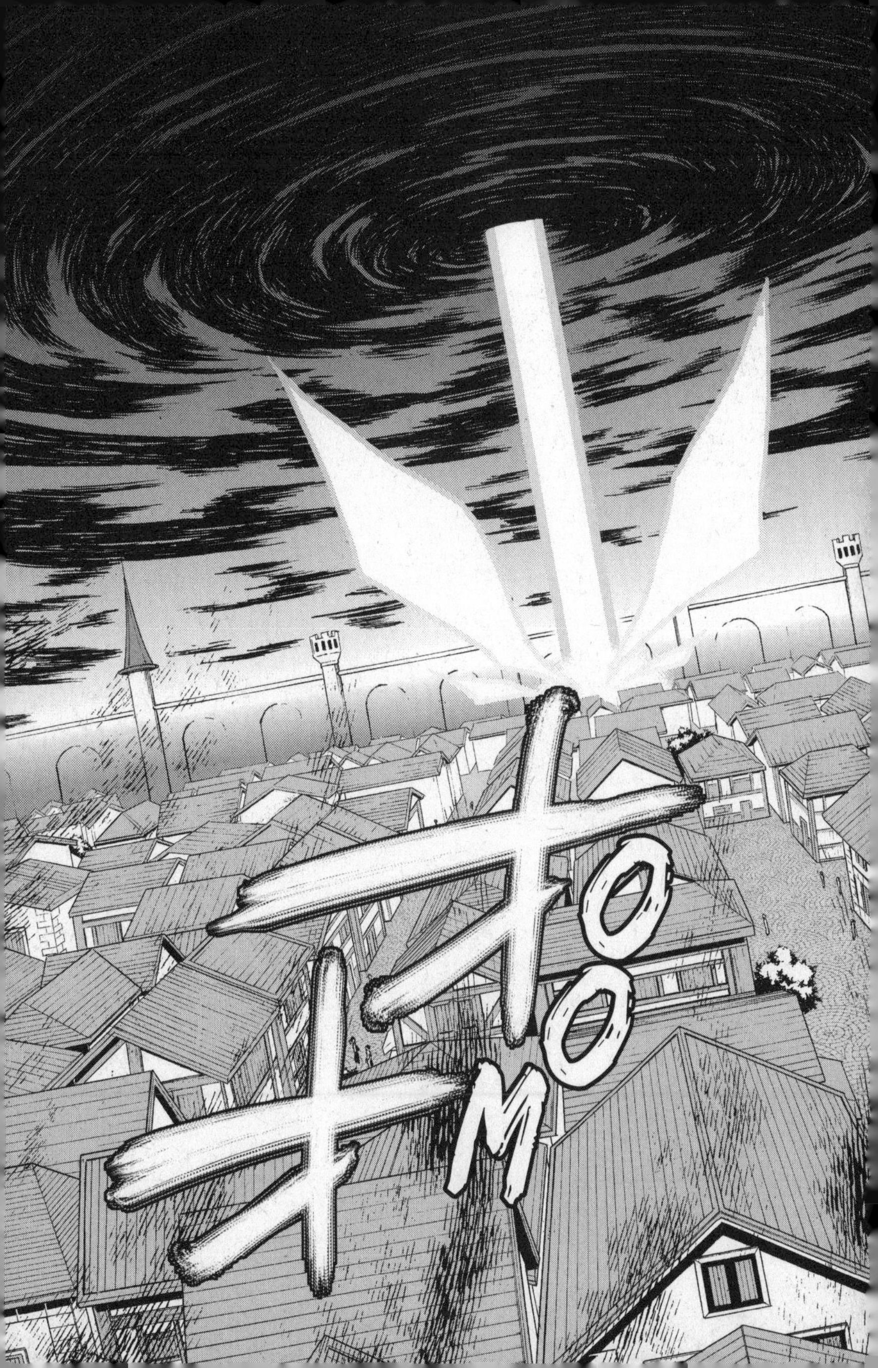
OOM

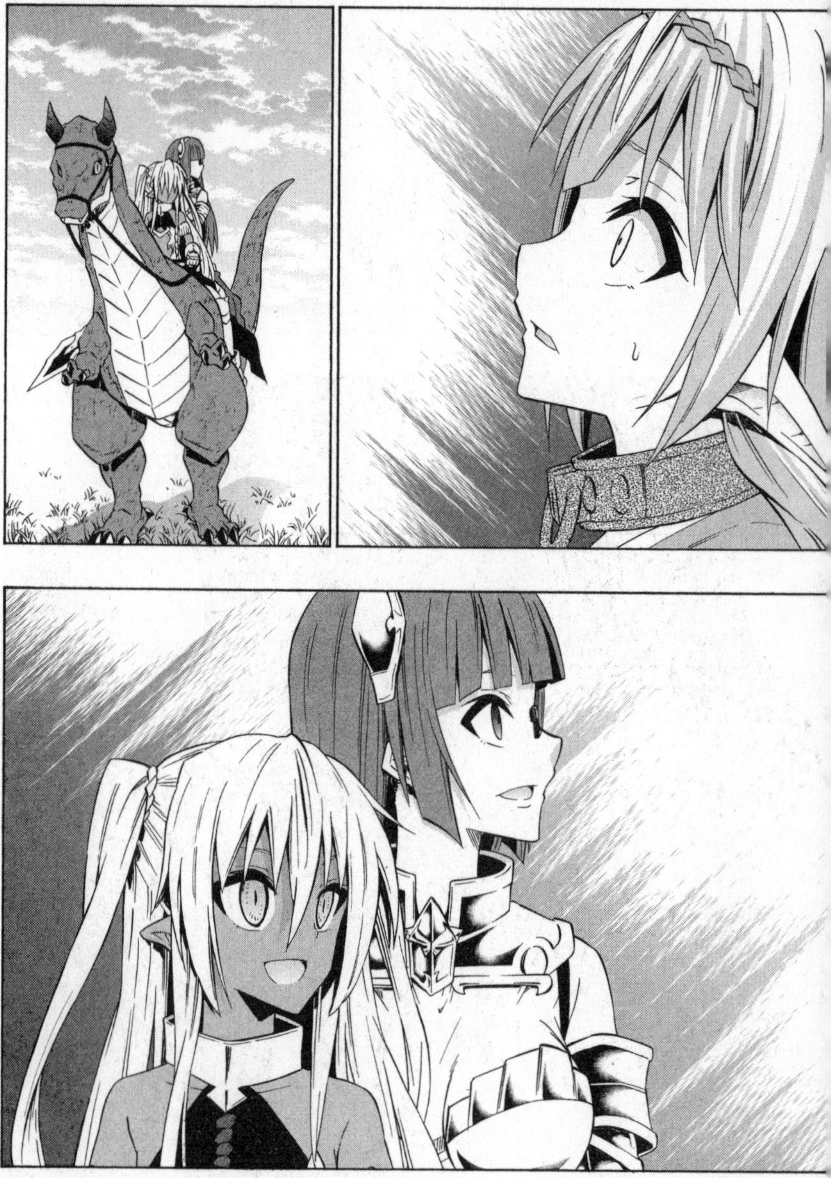

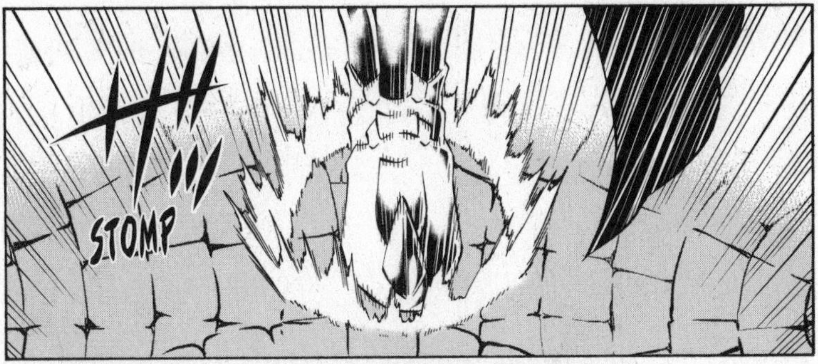
STOMP

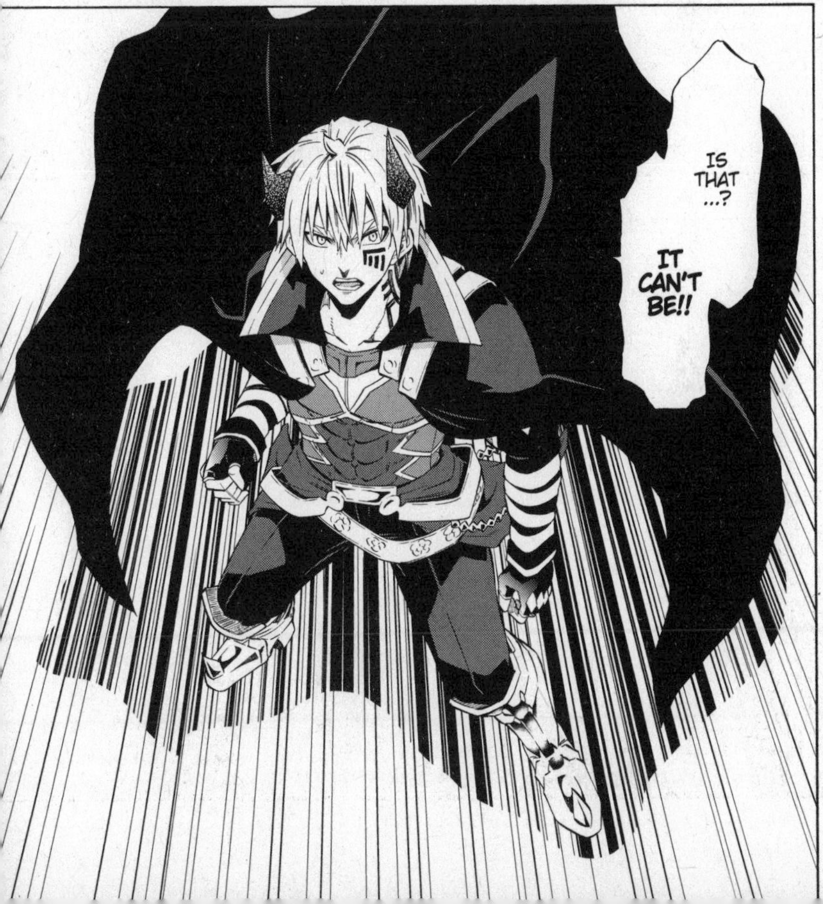
IS THAT ...?
IT CAN'T BE!!

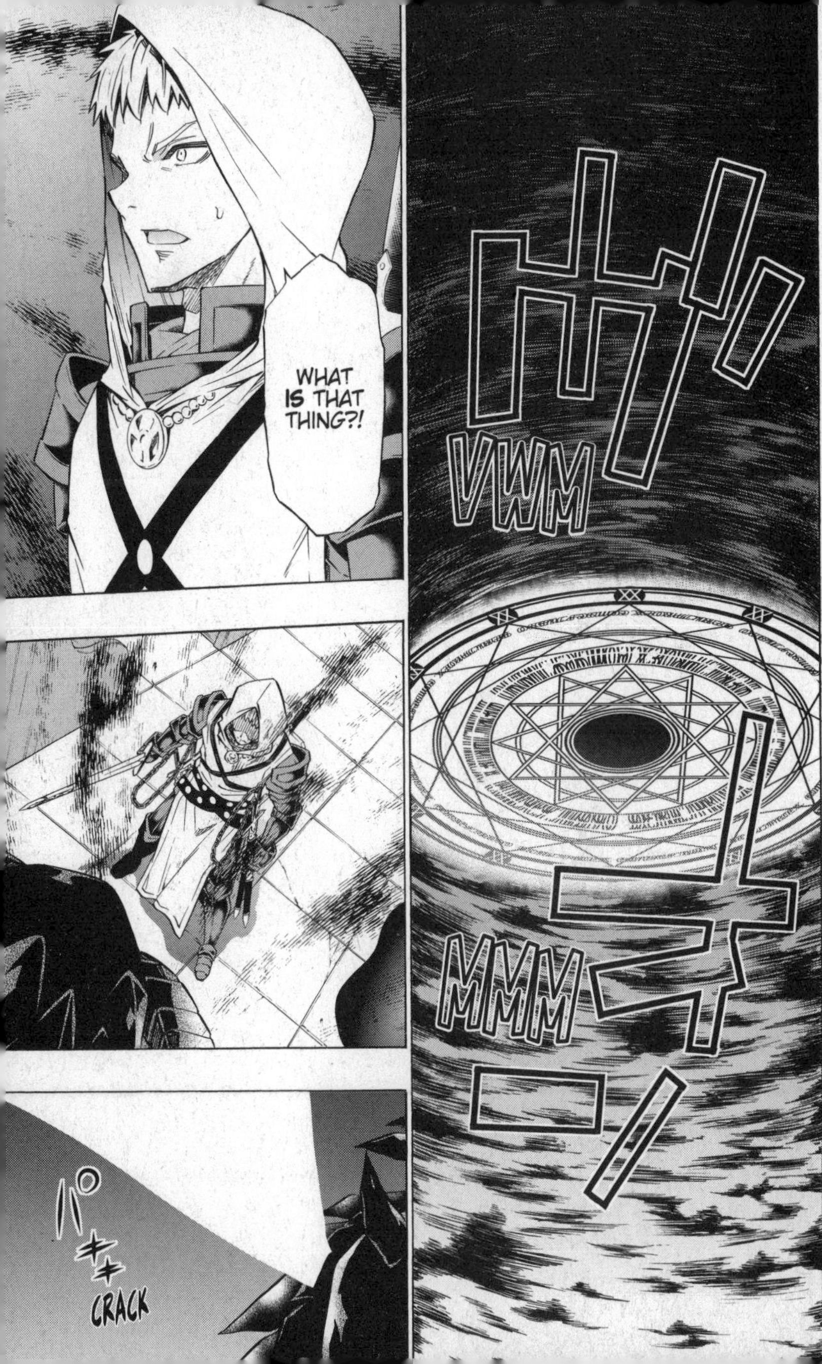
VWM
MMMM
WHAT IS THAT THING?!
CRACK

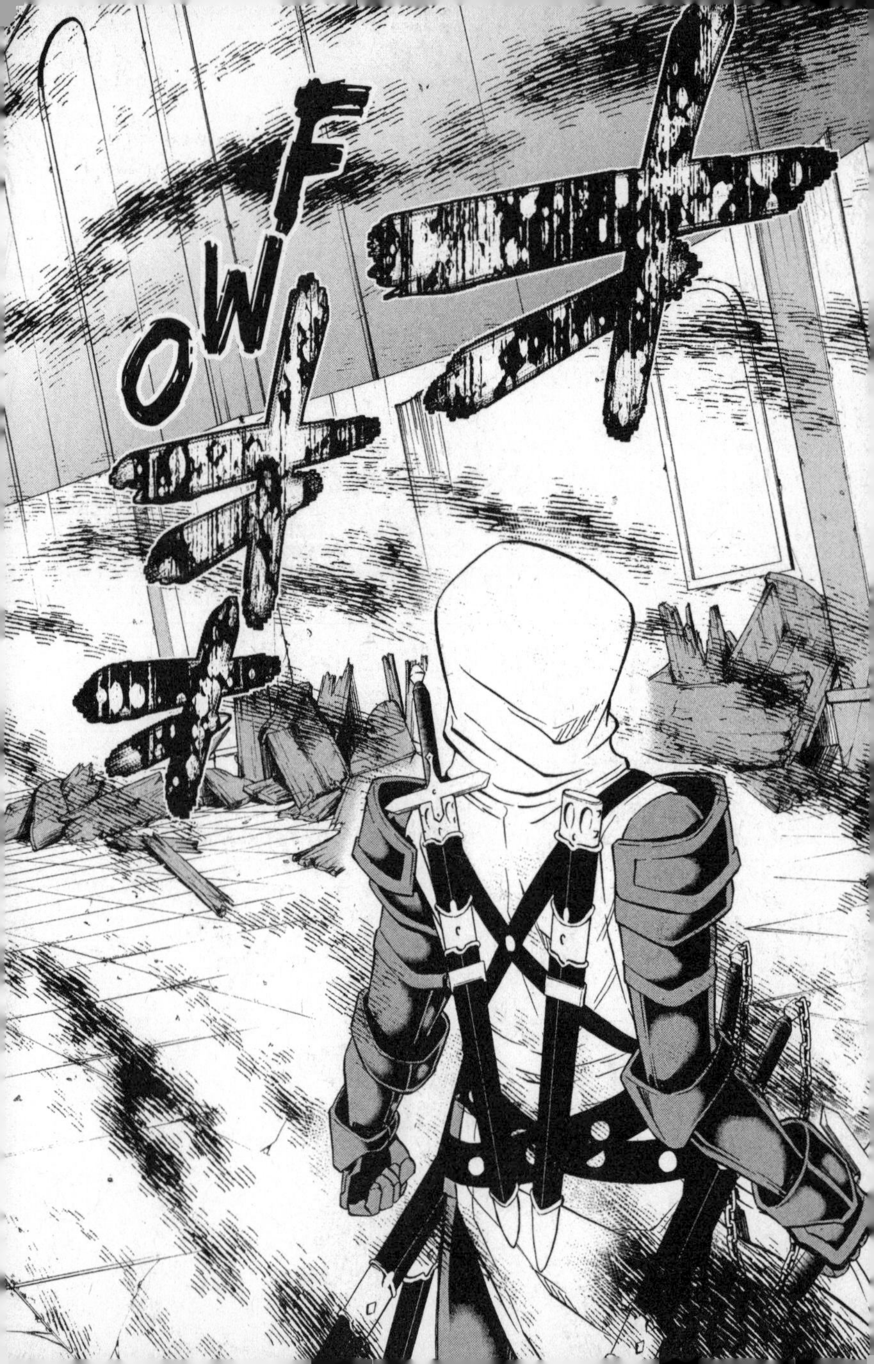
FWO

34 REM'S STORY III

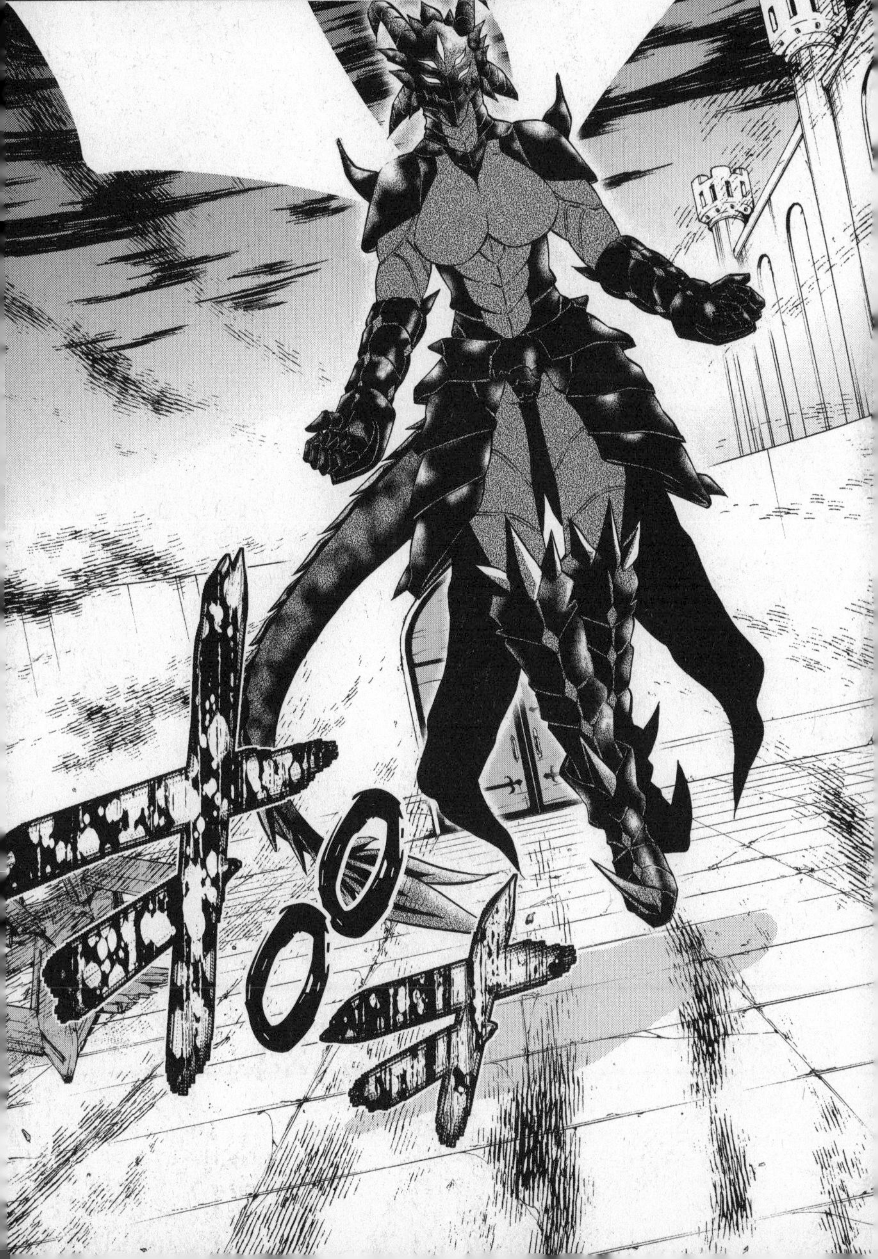

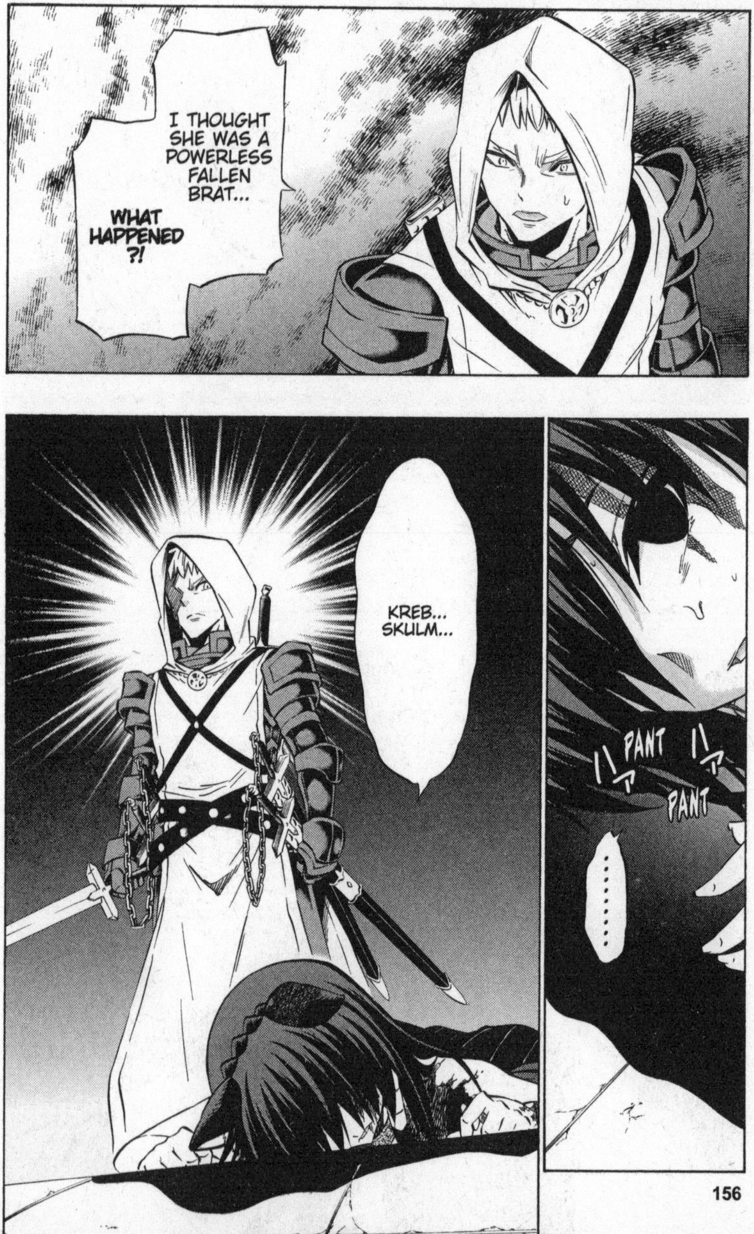
I THOUGHT SHE WAS A POWERLESS FALLEN BRAT...
WHAT HAPPENED?!
PANT
PANT
......
KREB... SKULM...

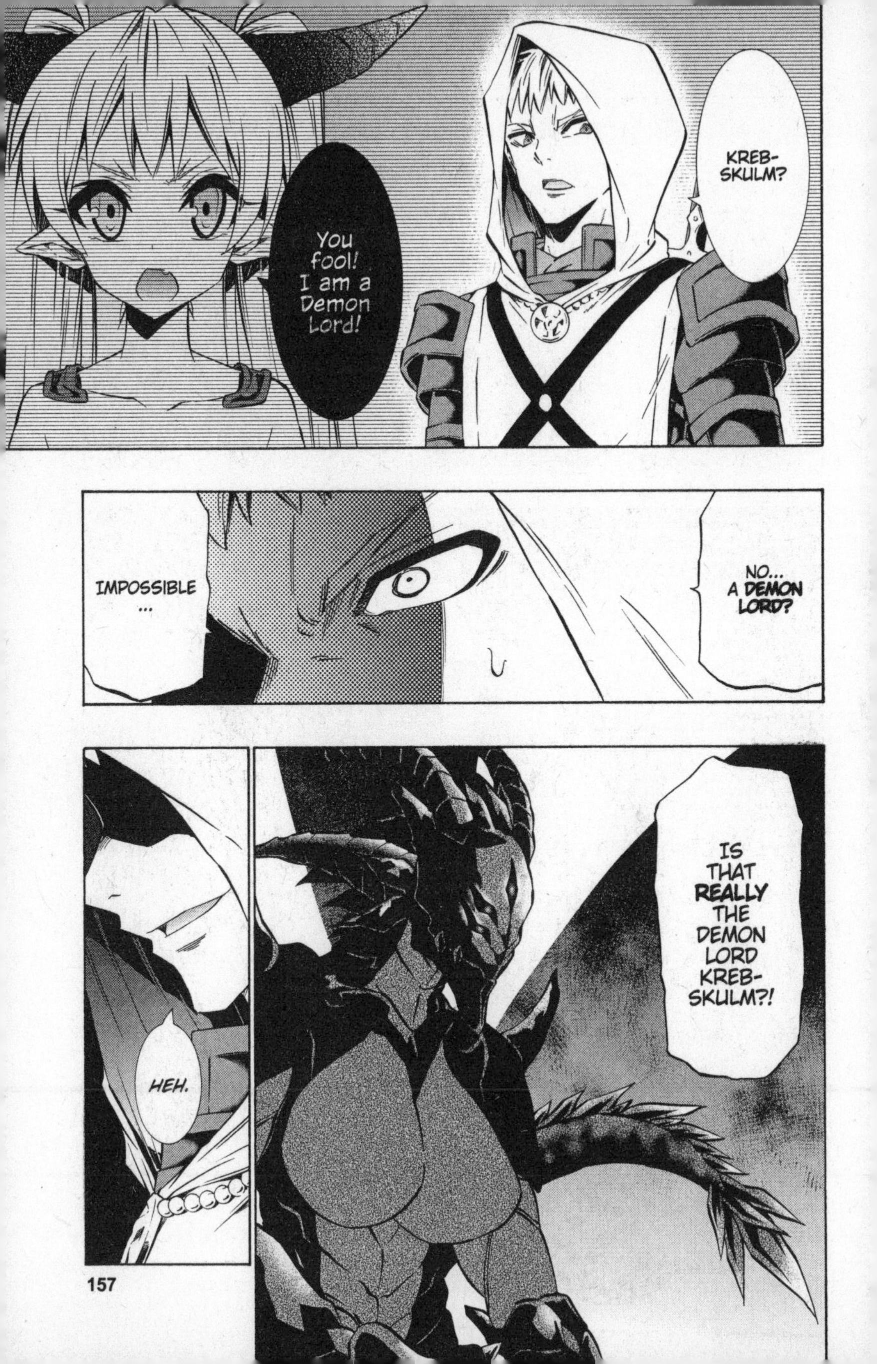
KREB-SKULM?
You fool! I am a Demon Lord!
NO... A DEMON LORD?
IMPOSSIBLE ...
IS THAT REALLY THE DEMON LORD KREB-SKULM?!
HEH.

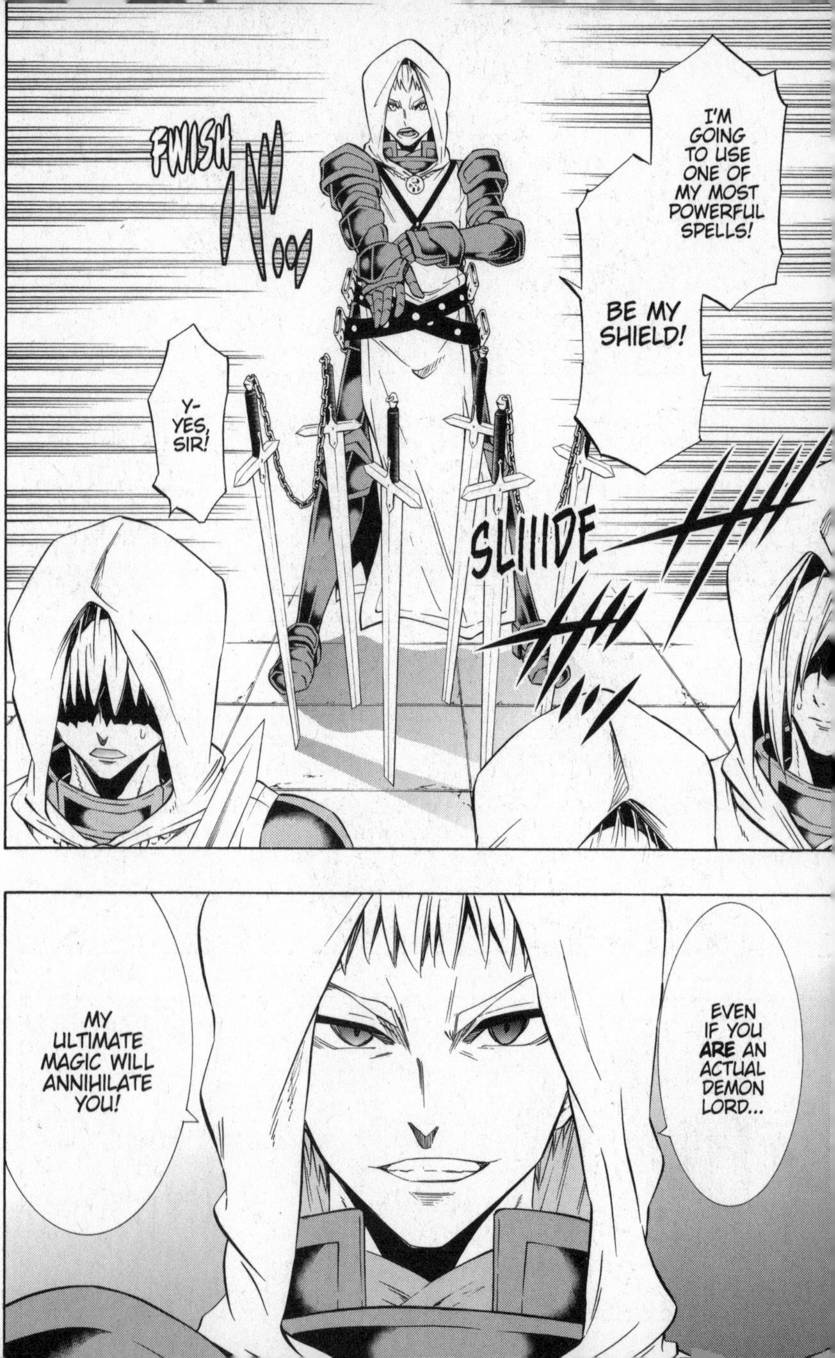
I'M GOING TO USE ONE OF MY MOST POWERFUL SPELLS!
BE MY SHIELD!
FWISH
Y-YES, SIR!
SLIIIDE
EVEN IF YOU **ARE** AN ACTUAL DEMON LORD...
MY ULTIMATE MAGIC WILL ANNIHILATE YOU!

SO, YOU'VE FINALLY NOTICED MY **POWER**, HAVE YOU?!

IT'S TOO LATE!

RO OO

RRGH!

OO

AAA

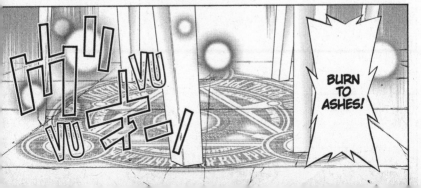

BURN TO ASHES!

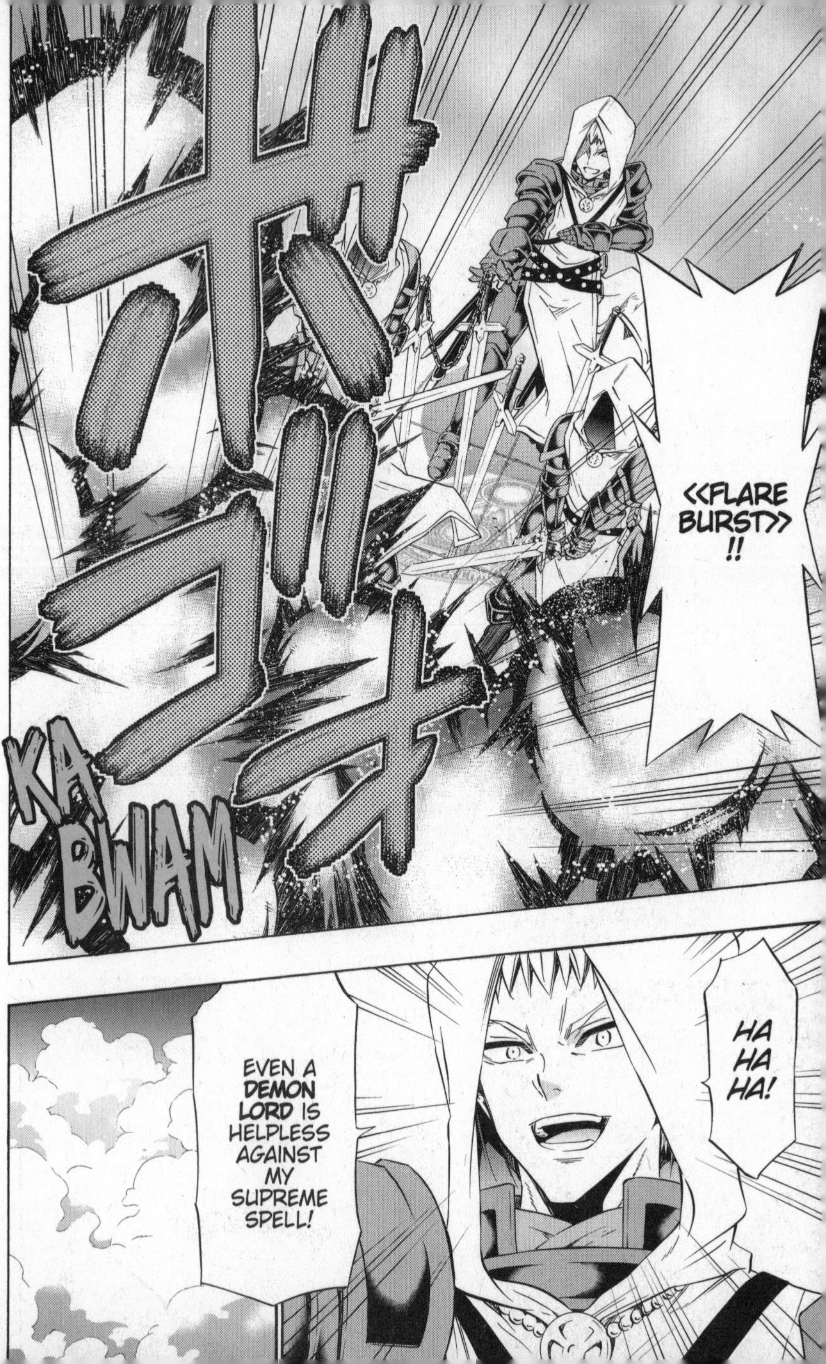
<<FLARE BURST>>!!
KA BWAM
HA HA HA!
EVEN A DEMON LORD IS HELPLESS AGAINST MY SUPREME SPELL!

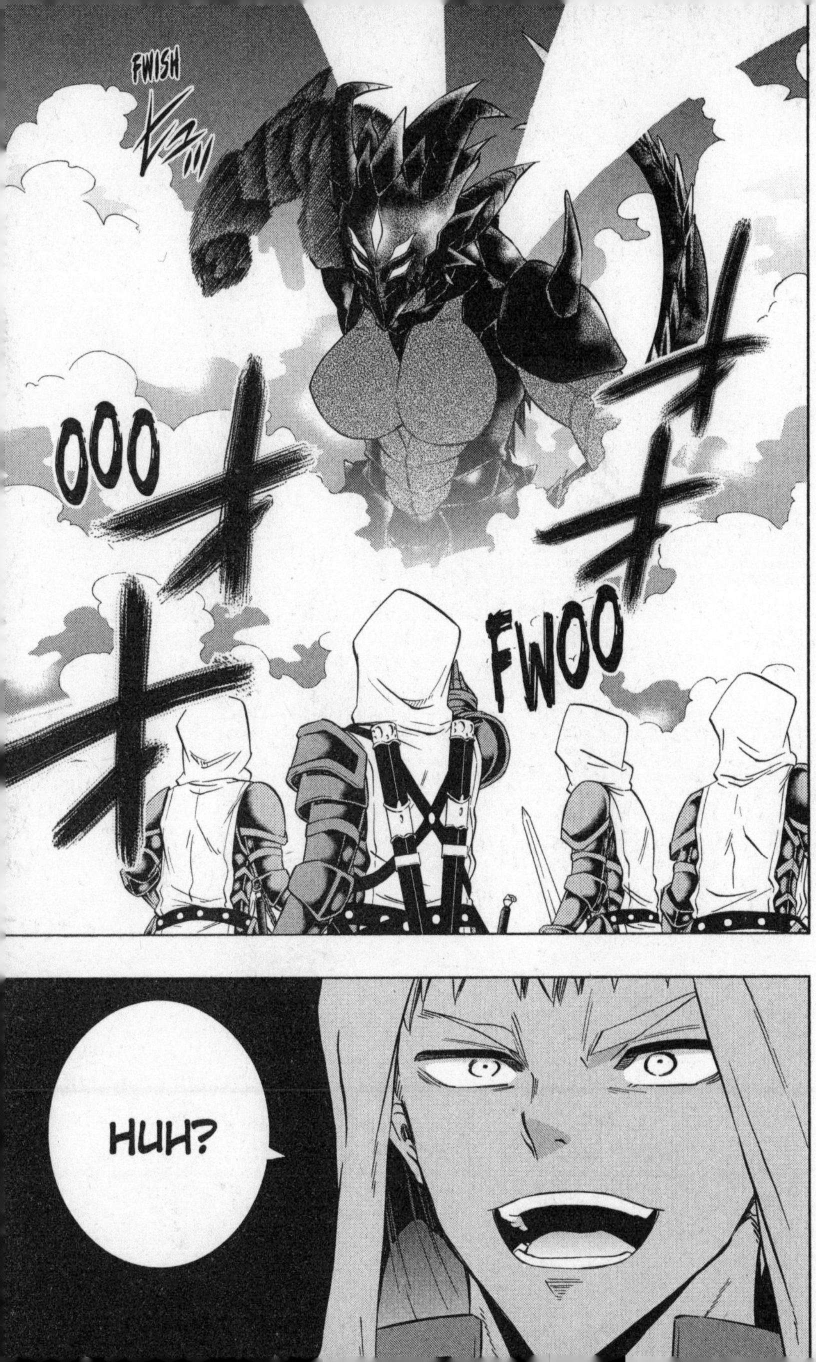
FWISH
FWOO
OOO
HUH?

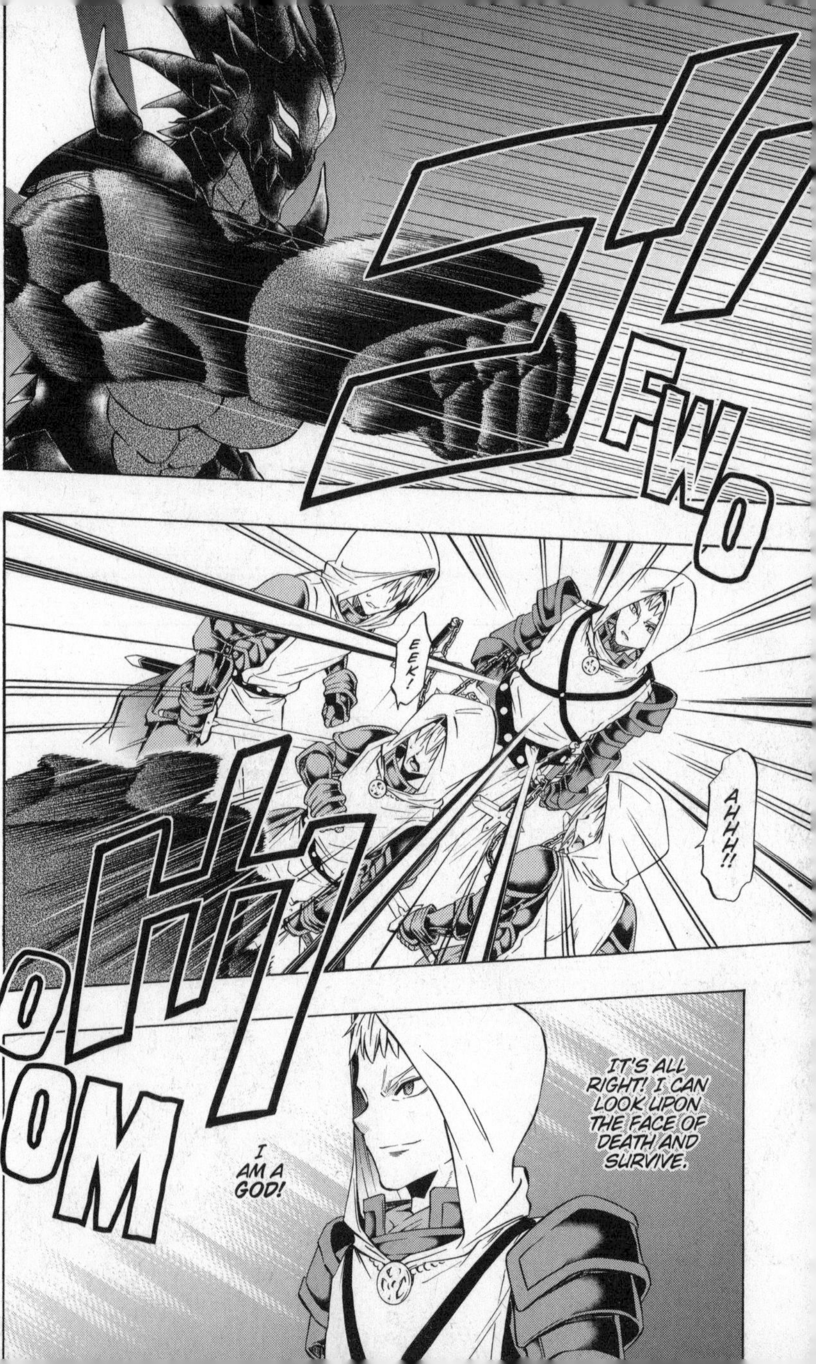
FWOO
HH
OOOM
AHHH!!
EEK!
IT'S ALL RIGHT! I CAN LOOK UPON THE FACE OF DEATH AND SURVIVE.
I AM A GOD!

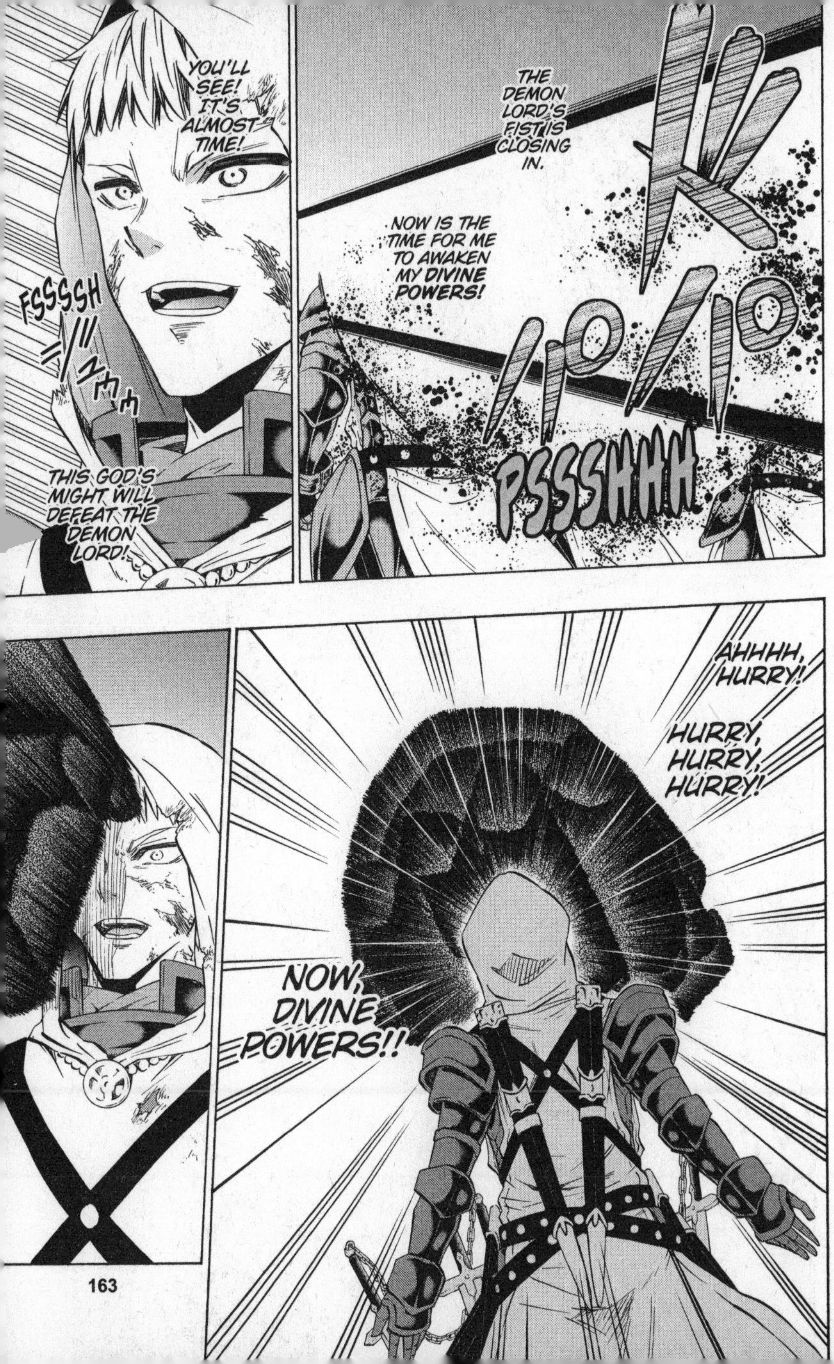
THE DEMON LORD'S FIST IS CLOSING IN.
NOW IS THE TIME FOR ME TO AWAKEN MY DIVINE POWERS!
PSSSHHH
YOU'LL SEE! IT'S ALMOST TIME!
FSSSSH
THIS GOD'S MIGHT WILL DEFEAT THE DEMON LORD!
AHHHH, HURRY!
HURRY, HURRY, HURRY!
NOW, DIVINE POWERS!!

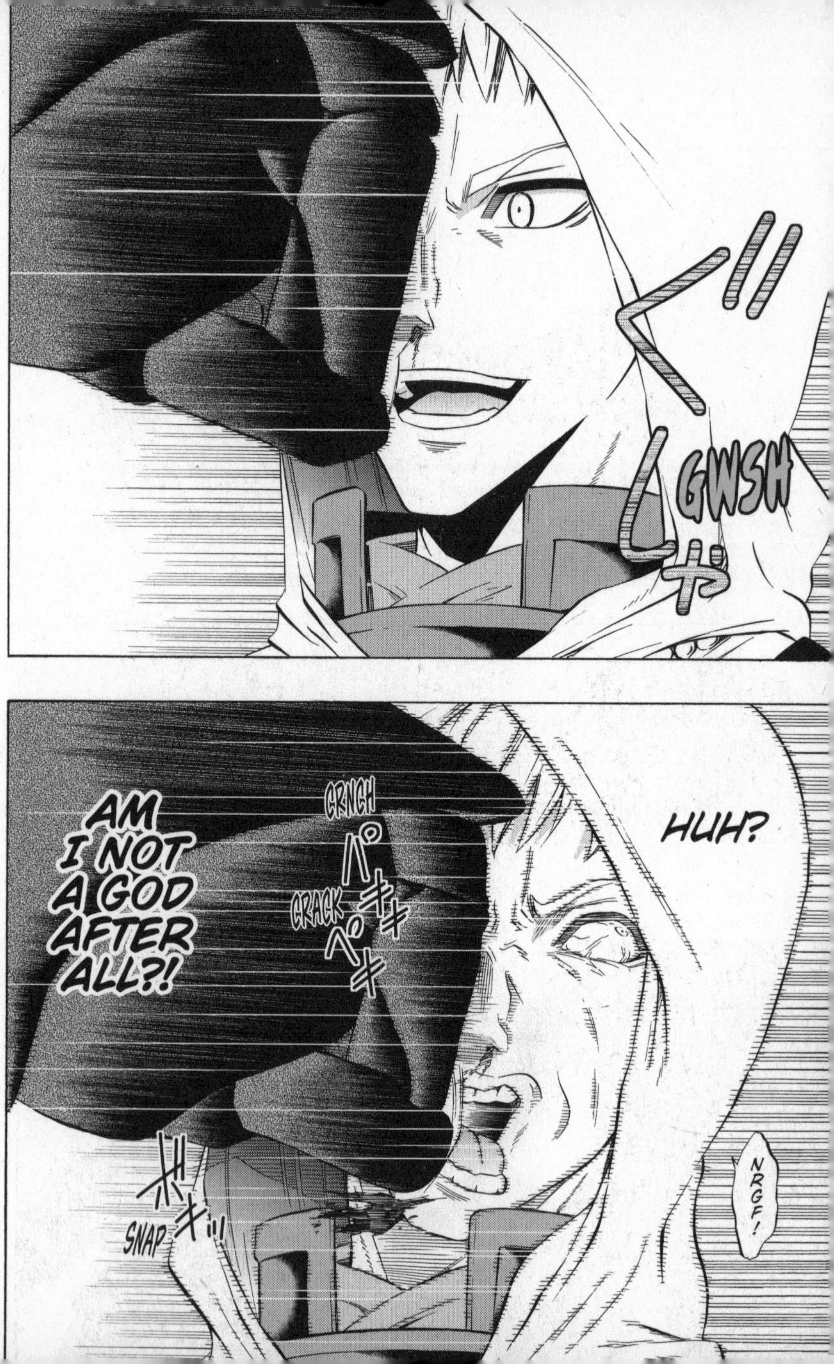
GWSH
HUH?
NRGF!
CRNCH
CRACK
AM I NOT A GOD AFTER ALL?!
SNAP

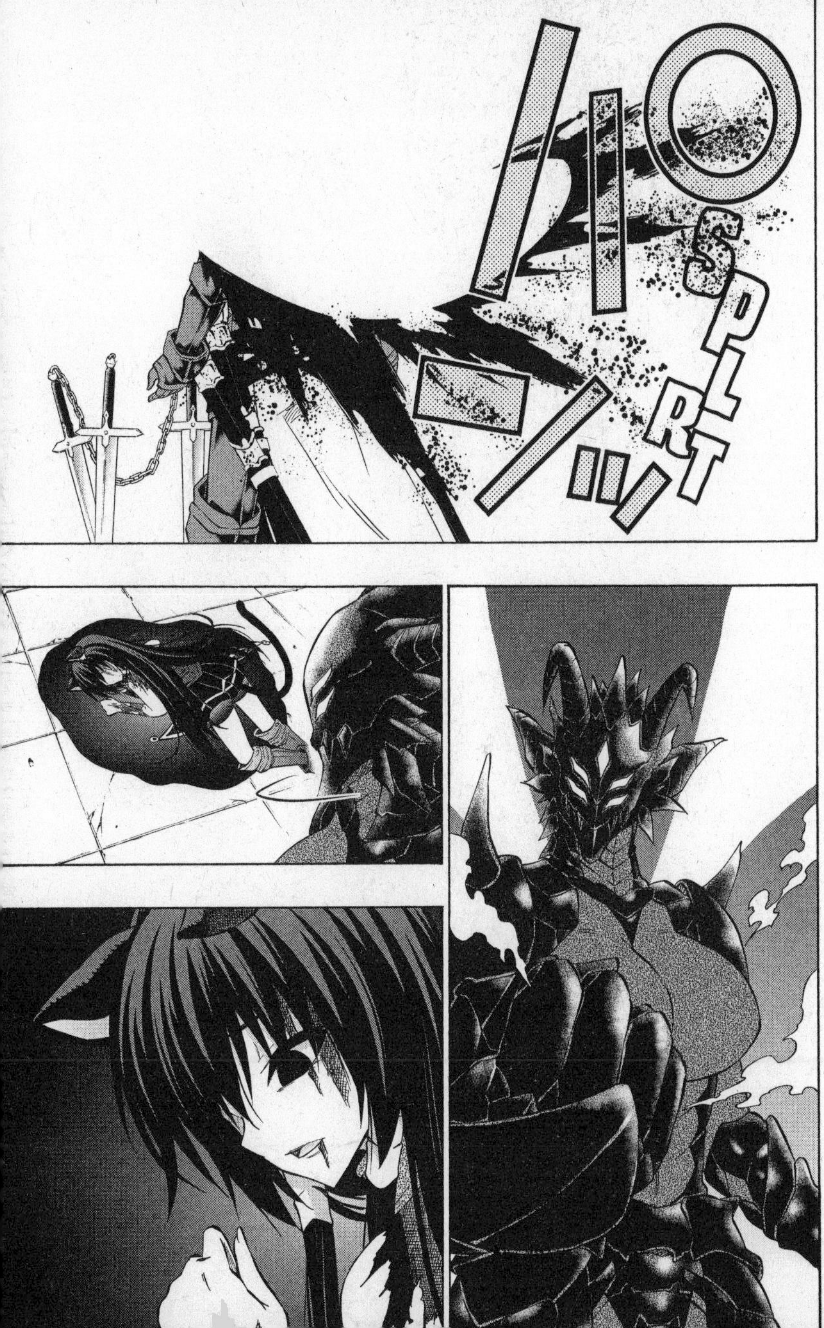
SPLRT!!

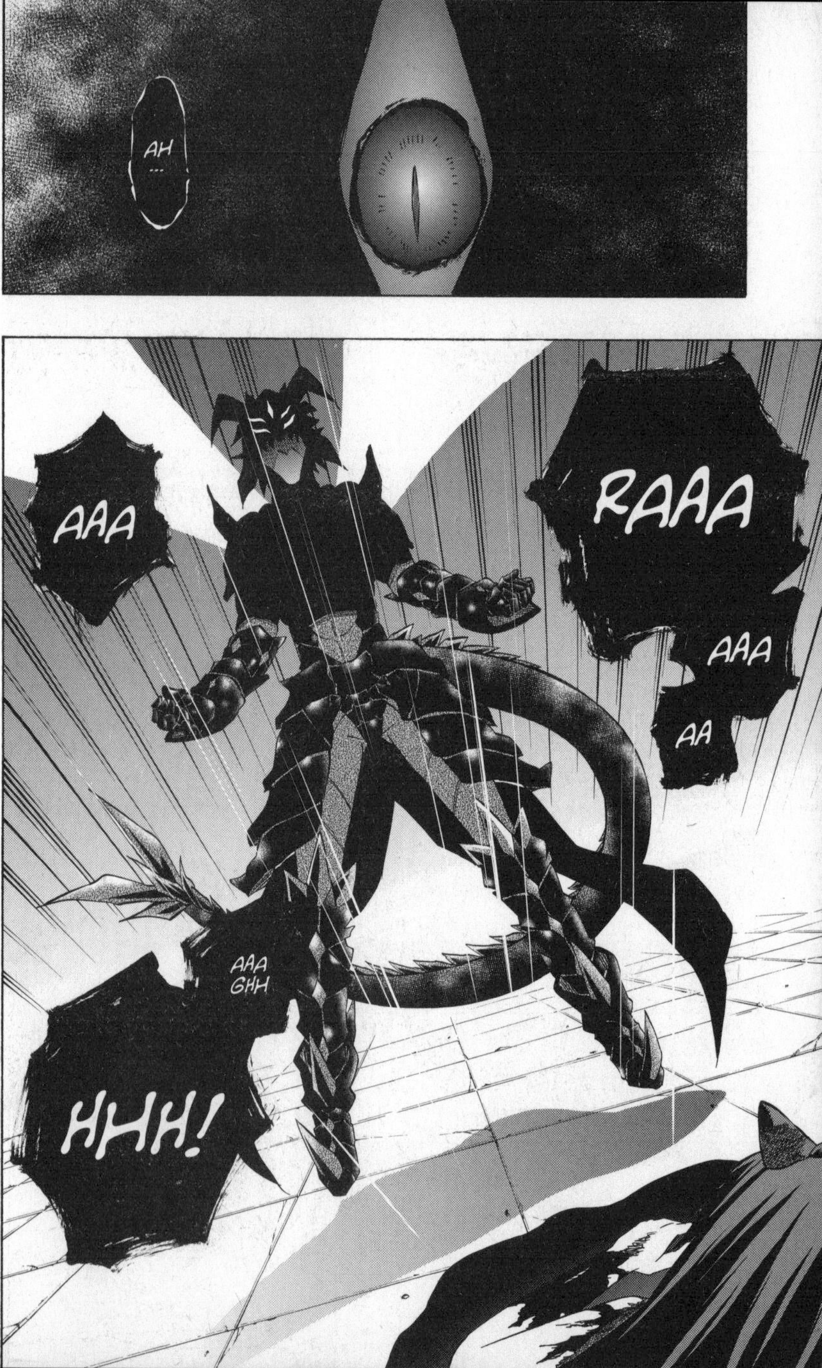
AH ...
RAAA
AAA
AA
AAA
AAA GHH
HHH!

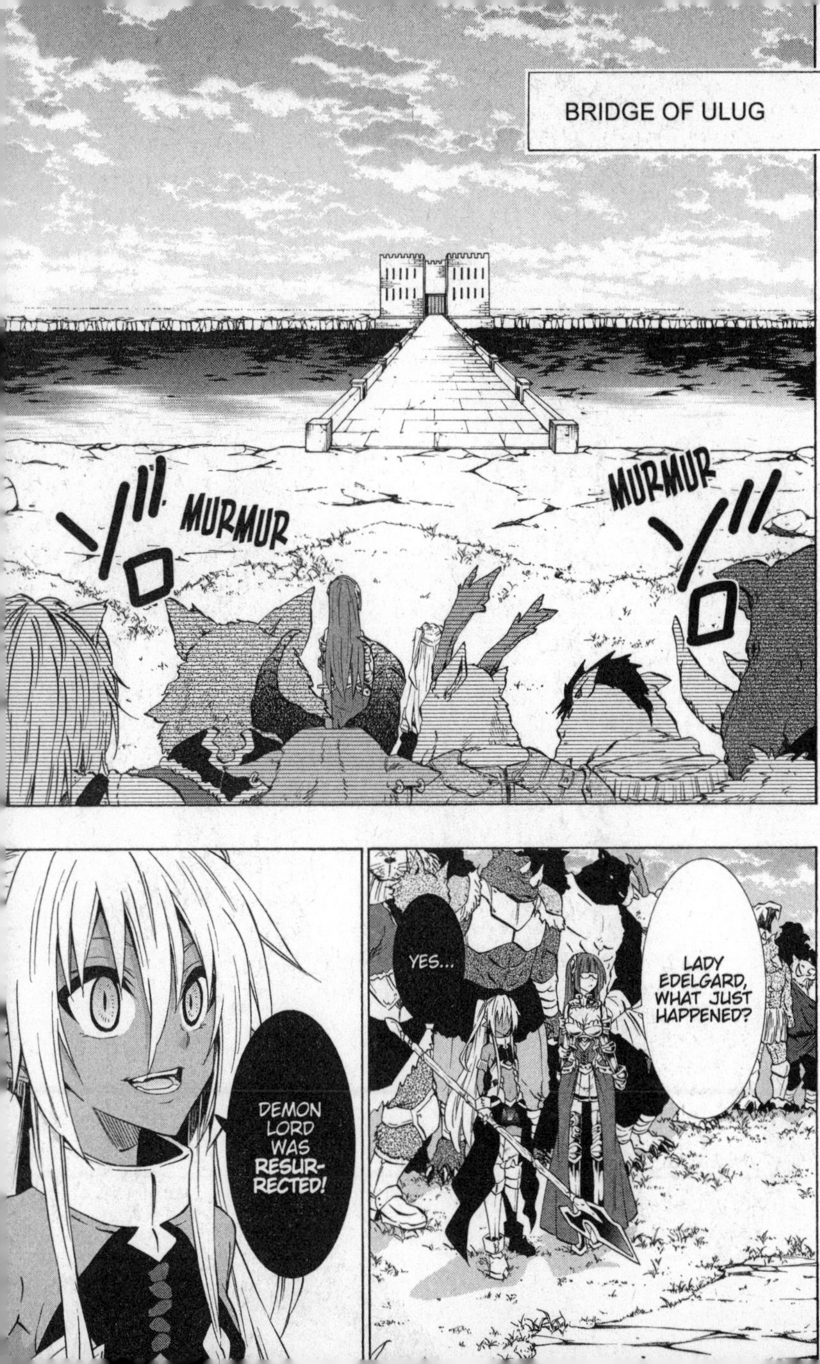
BRIDGE OF ULUG
ゾロ
MURMUR
ゾロ
MURMUR
LADY EDELGARD, WHAT JUST HAPPENED?
YES...
DEMON LORD WAS RESURRECTED!

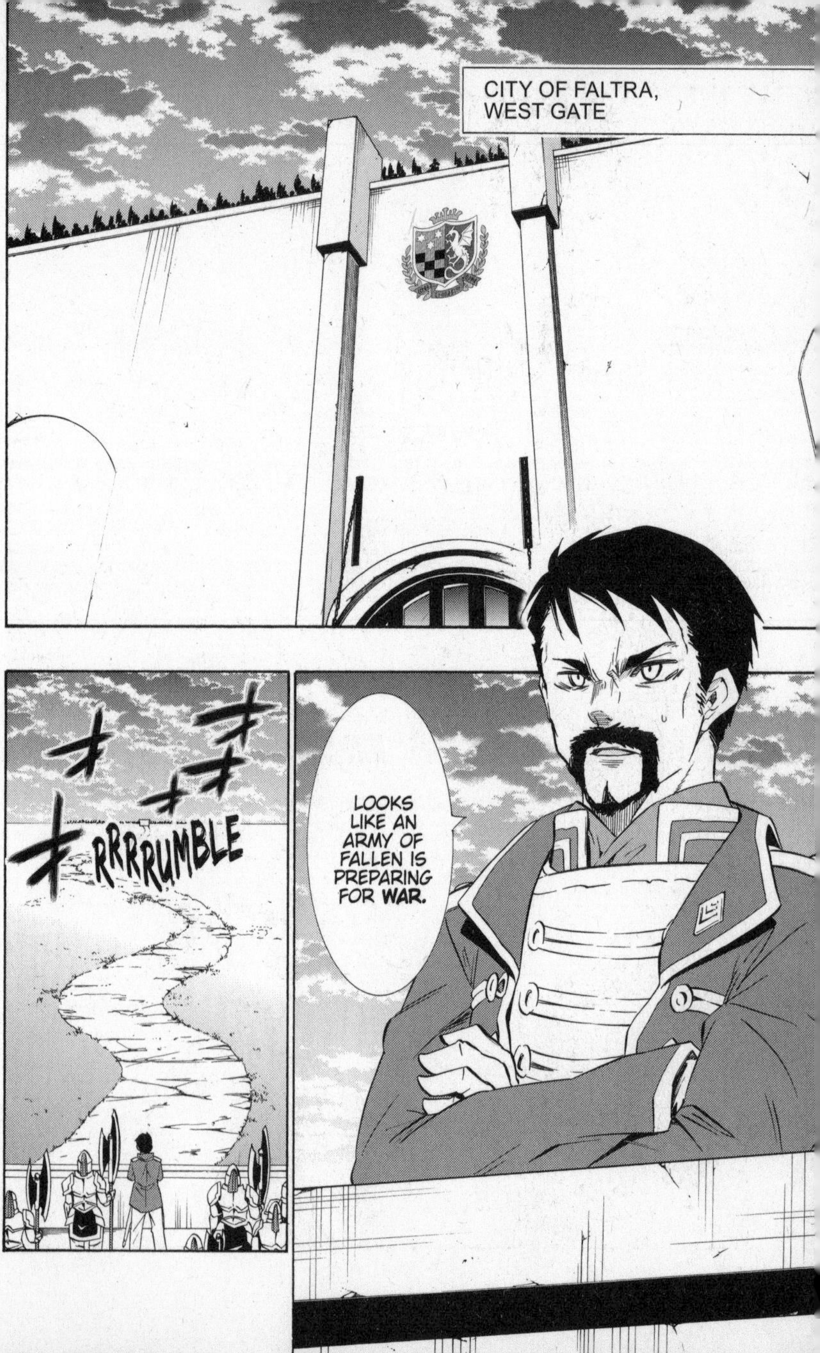
CITY OF FALTRA, WEST GATE
LOOKS LIKE AN ARMY OF FALLEN IS PREPARING FOR WAR.
RRRRUMBLE

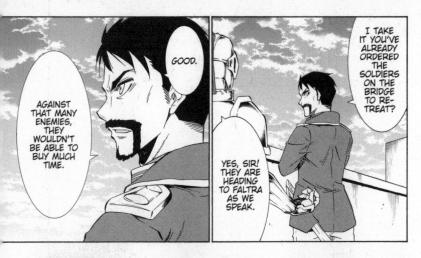

I TAKE IT YOU'VE ALREADY ORDERED THE SOLDIERS ON THE BRIDGE TO RE-TREAT?
YES, SIR! THEY ARE HEADING TO FALTRA AS WE SPEAK.
GOOD.
AGAINST THAT MANY ENEMIES, THEY WOULDN'T BE ABLE TO BUY MUCH TIME.
MURMUR
MURMUR
THIS MANY FALLEN IS UNPREC-EDENTED.
OF COURSE THE SOLDIERS ARE ON EDGE.
HAAH...

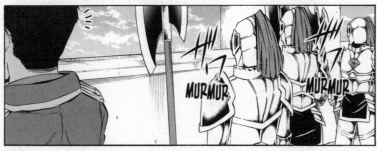

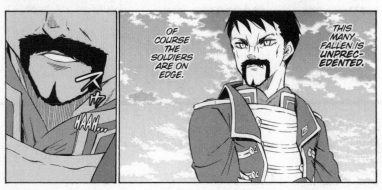

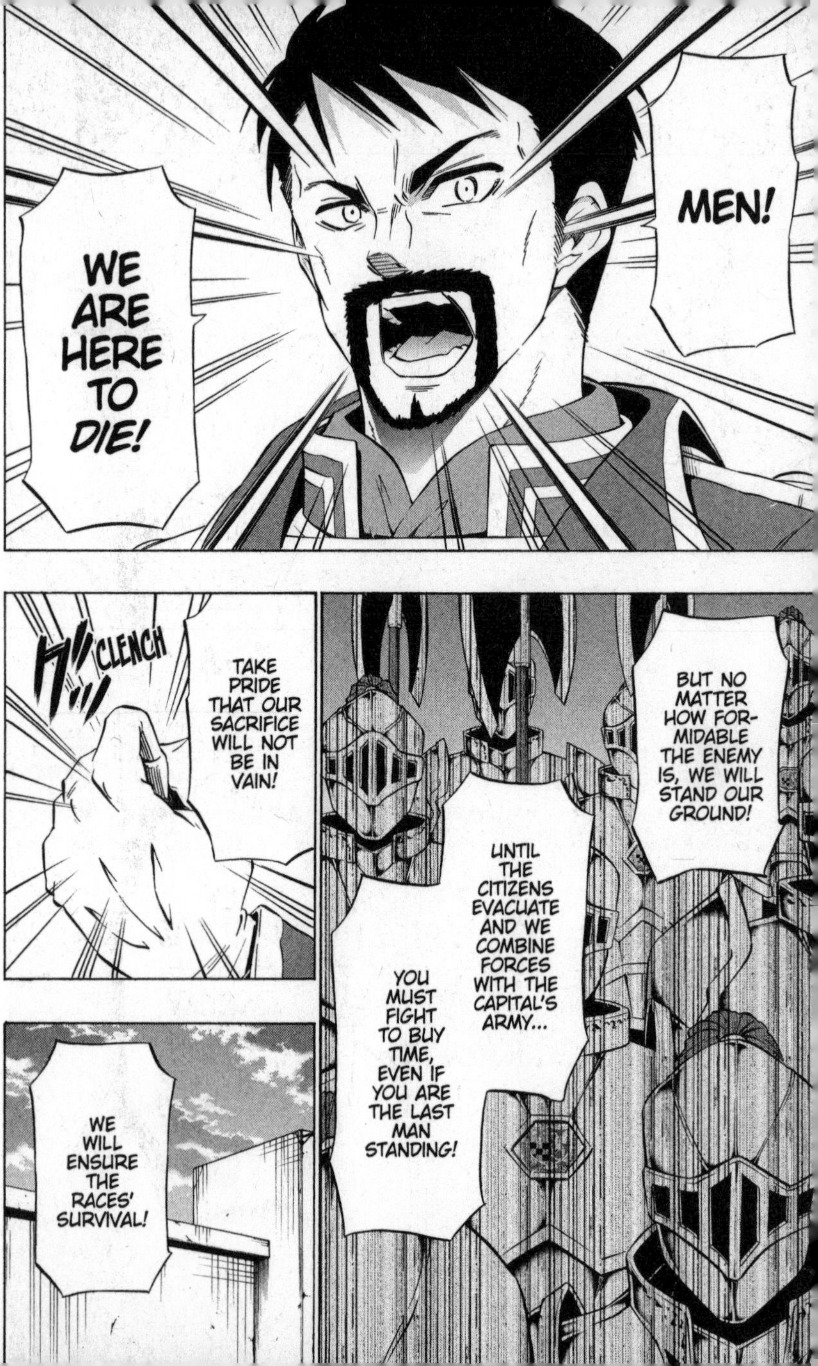
MEN!
WE ARE HERE TO DIE!
BUT NO MATTER HOW FOR-MIDABLE THE ENEMY IS, WE WILL STAND OUR GROUND!
UNTIL THE CITIZENS EVACUATE AND WE COMBINE FORCES WITH THE CAPITAL'S ARMY...
YOU MUST FIGHT TO BUY TIME, EVEN IF YOU ARE THE LAST MAN STANDING!
CLENCH
TAKE PRIDE THAT OUR SACRIFICE WILL NOT BE IN VAIN!
WE WILL ENSURE THE RACES' SURVIVAL!

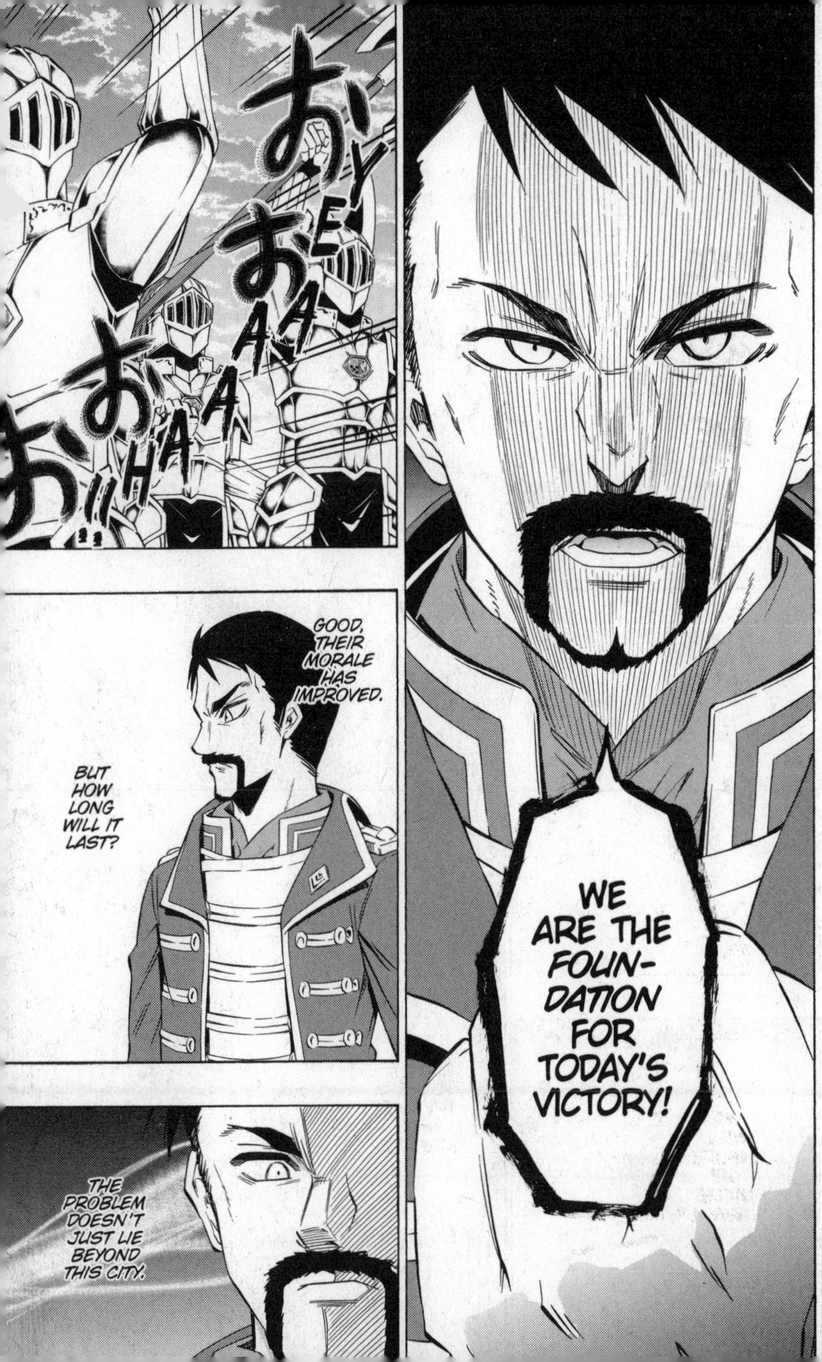
WE ARE THE FOUNDATION FOR TODAY'S VICTORY!
おおおお
YEAAAAHH!!
GOOD, THEIR MORALE HAS IMPROVED.
BUT HOW LONG WILL IT LAST?
THE PROBLEM DOESN'T JUST LIE BEYOND THIS CITY.

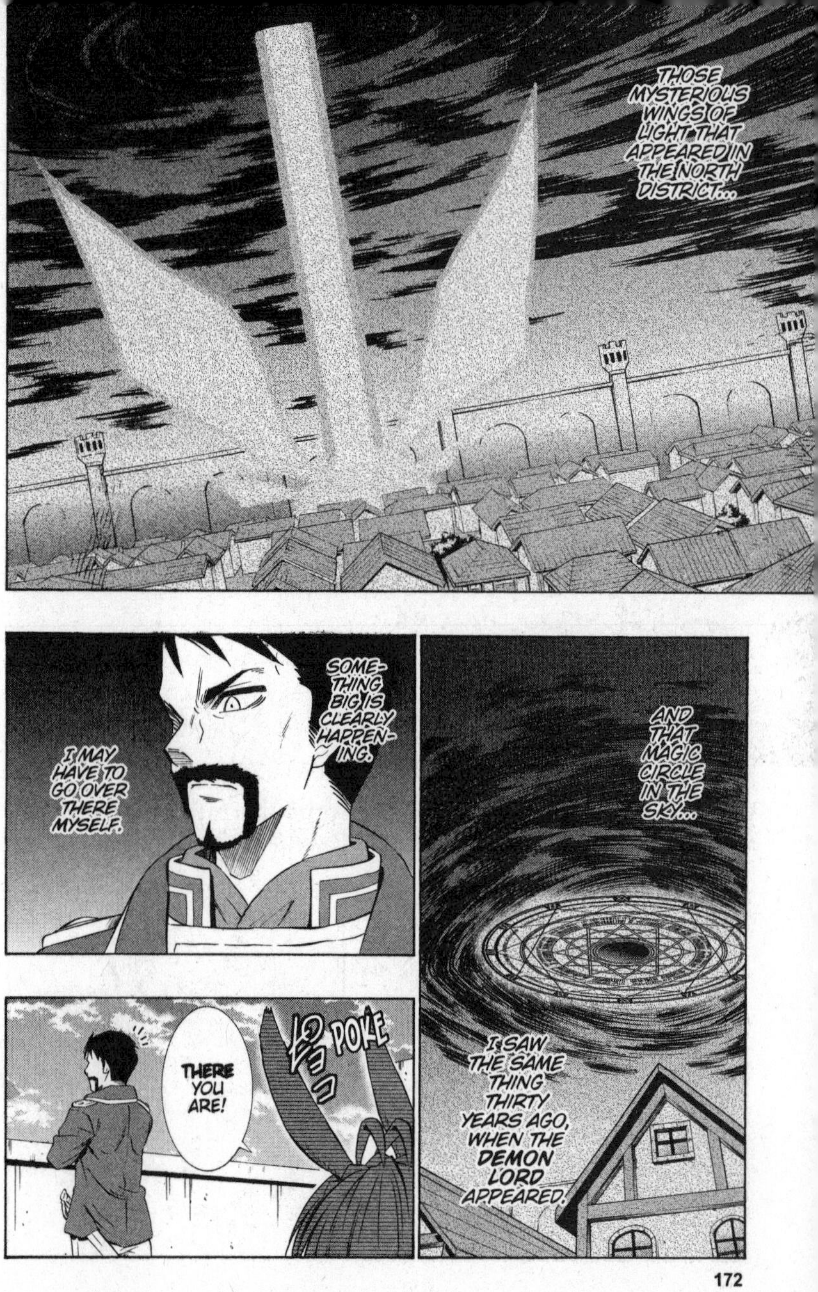
THOSE MYSTERIOUS WINGS OF LIGHT THAT APPEARED IN THE NORTH DISTRICT...
AND THAT MAGIC CIRCLE IN THE SKY...
I SAW THE SAME THING THIRTY YEARS AGO, WHEN THE DEMON LORD APPEARED.
SOME-THING BIG IS CLEARLY HAPPEN-ING.
I MAY HAVE TO GO OVER THERE MYSELF.
POKE
THERE YOU ARE!

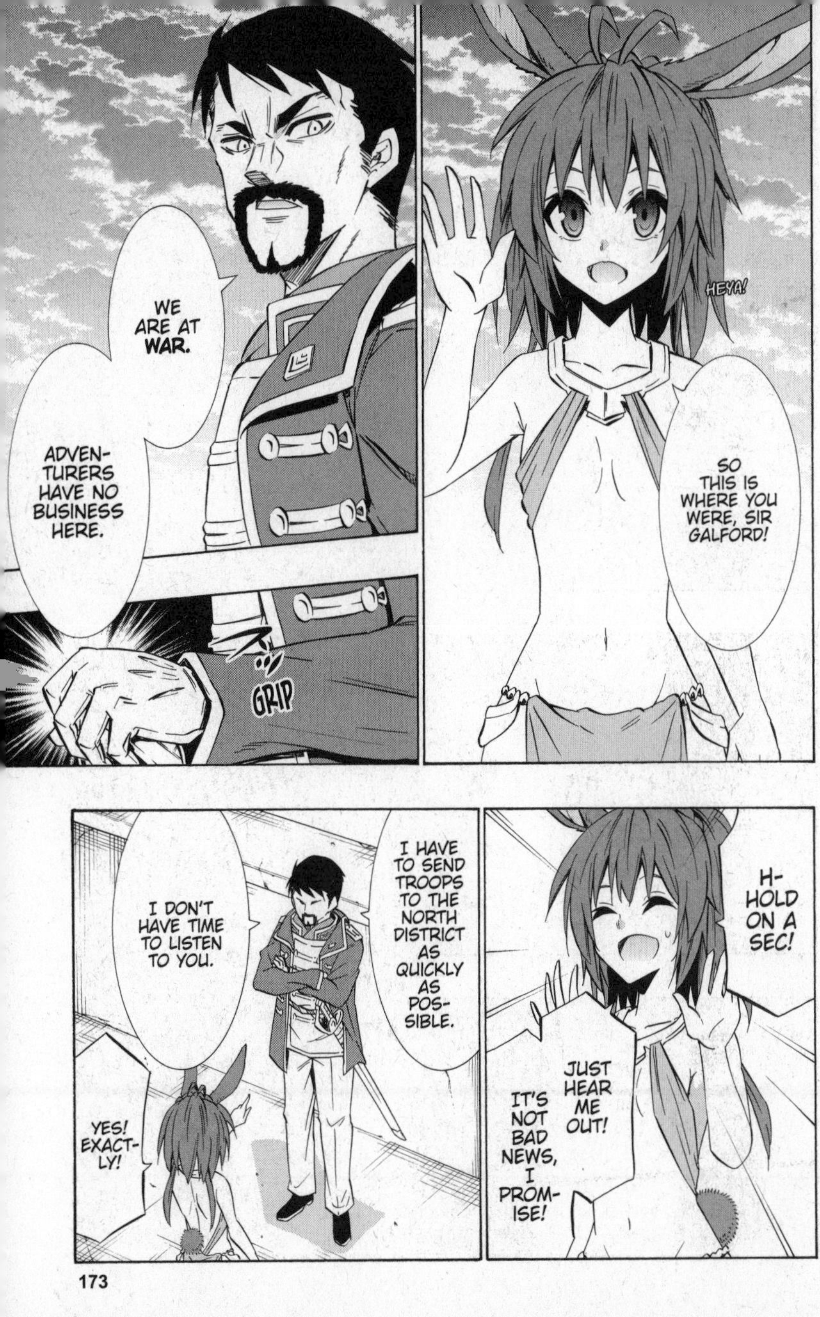
HEYA!
SO THIS IS WHERE YOU WERE, SIR GALFORD!
WE ARE AT WAR.
ADVEN-TURERS HAVE NO BUSINESS HERE.
GRIP
H-HOLD ON A SEC!
JUST HEAR ME OUT!
IT'S NOT BAD NEWS, I PROM-ISE!
I HAVE TO SEND TROOPS TO THE NORTH DISTRICT AS QUICKLY AS POS-SIBLE.
I DON'T HAVE TIME TO LISTEN TO YOU.
YES! EXACT-LY!

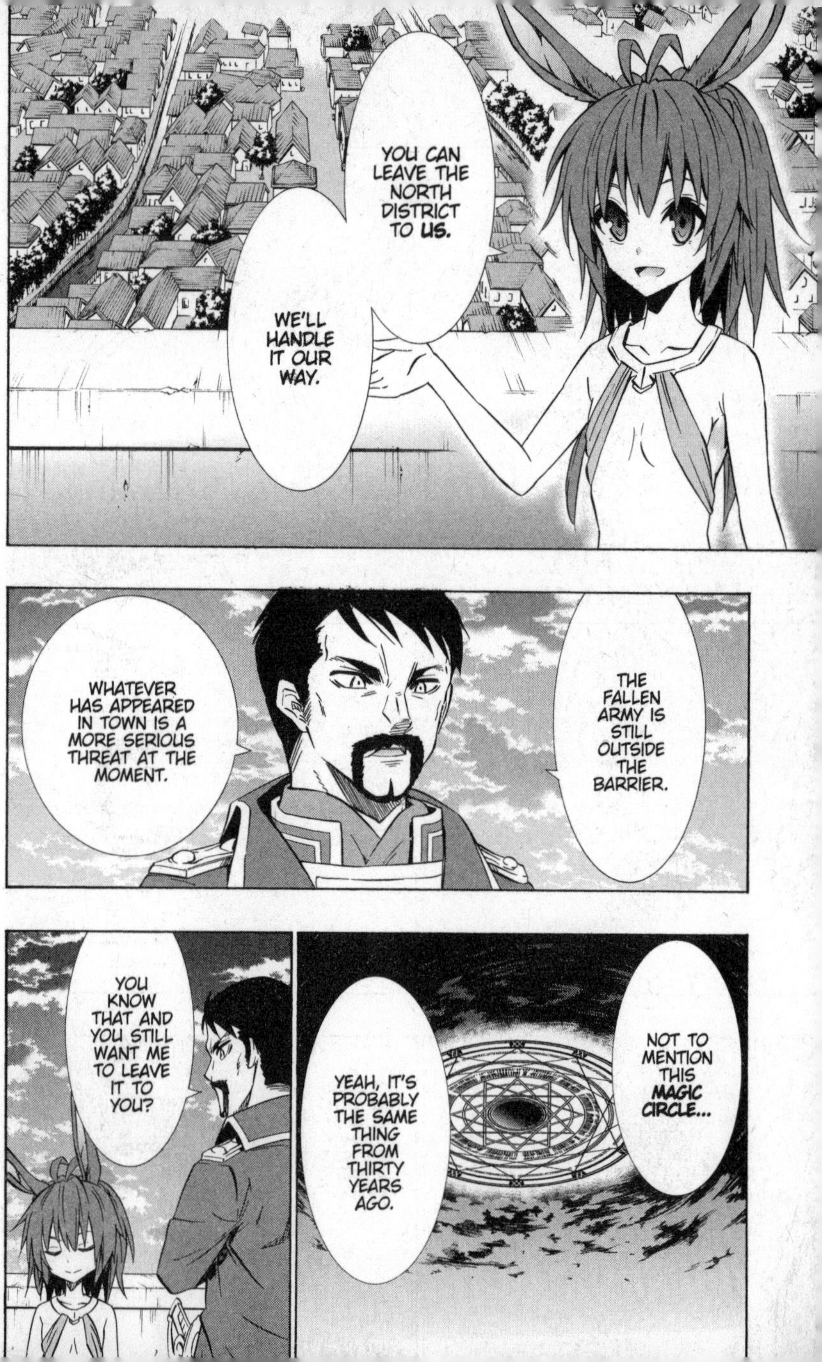
YOU CAN LEAVE THE NORTH DISTRICT TO **US.**
WE'LL HANDLE IT OUR WAY.
THE FALLEN ARMY IS STILL OUTSIDE THE BARRIER.
WHATEVER HAS APPEARED IN TOWN IS A MORE SERIOUS THREAT AT THE MOMENT.
NOT TO MENTION THIS ***MAGIC CIRCLE...***
YEAH, IT'S PROBABLY THE SAME THING FROM THIRTY YEARS AGO.
YOU KNOW THAT AND YOU STILL WANT ME TO LEAVE IT TO YOU?

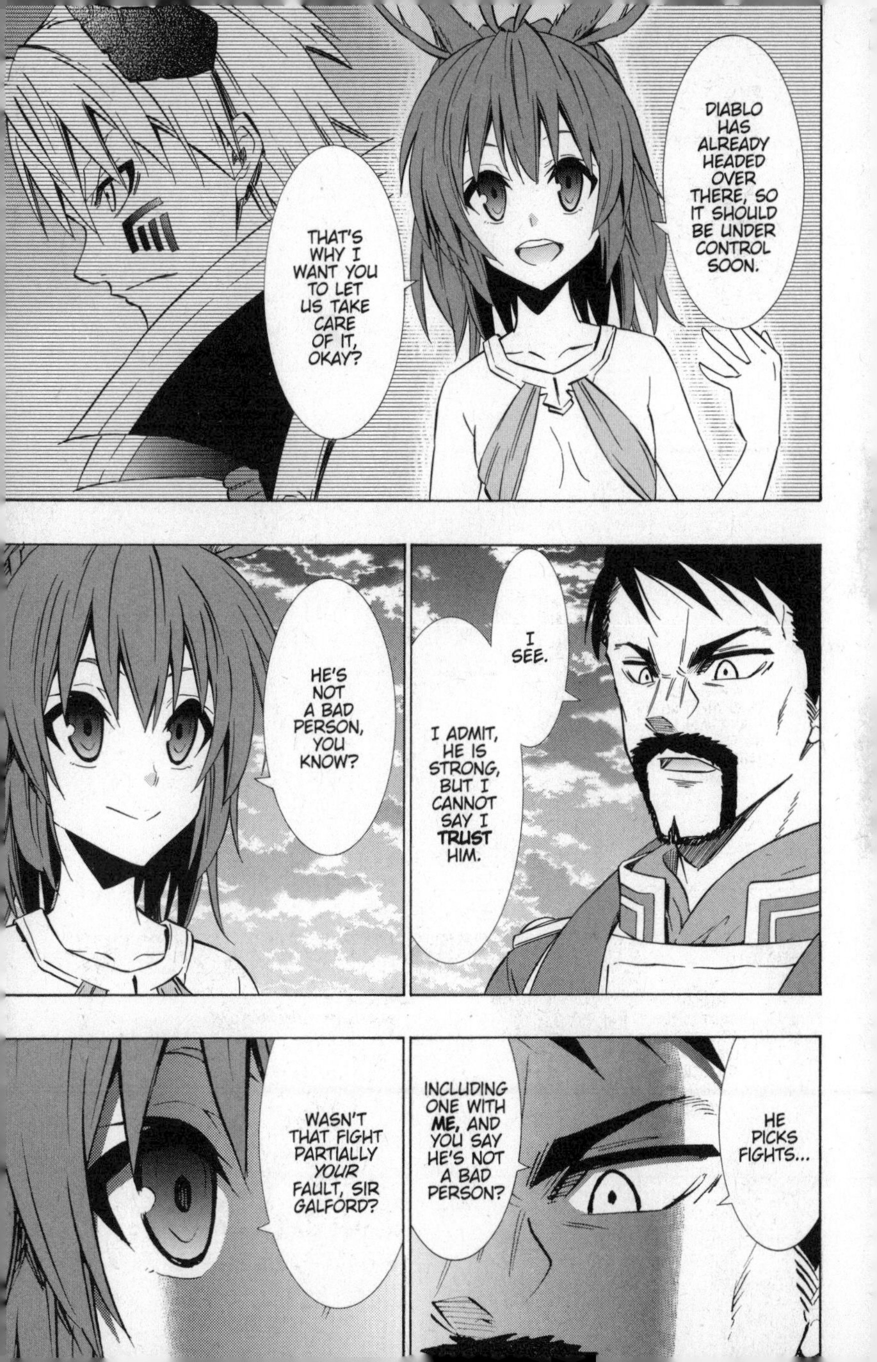
DIABLO HAS ALREADY HEADED OVER THERE, SO IT SHOULD BE UNDER CONTROL SOON.
THAT'S WHY I WANT YOU TO LET US TAKE CARE OF IT, OKAY?
I SEE.
I ADMIT, HE IS STRONG, BUT I CANNOT SAY I **TRUST** HIM.
HE'S NOT A BAD PERSON, YOU KNOW?
HE PICKS FIGHTS...
INCLUDING ONE WITH **ME,** AND YOU SAY HE'S NOT A BAD PERSON?
WASN'T THAT FIGHT PARTIALLY *YOUR* FAULT, SIR GALFORD?

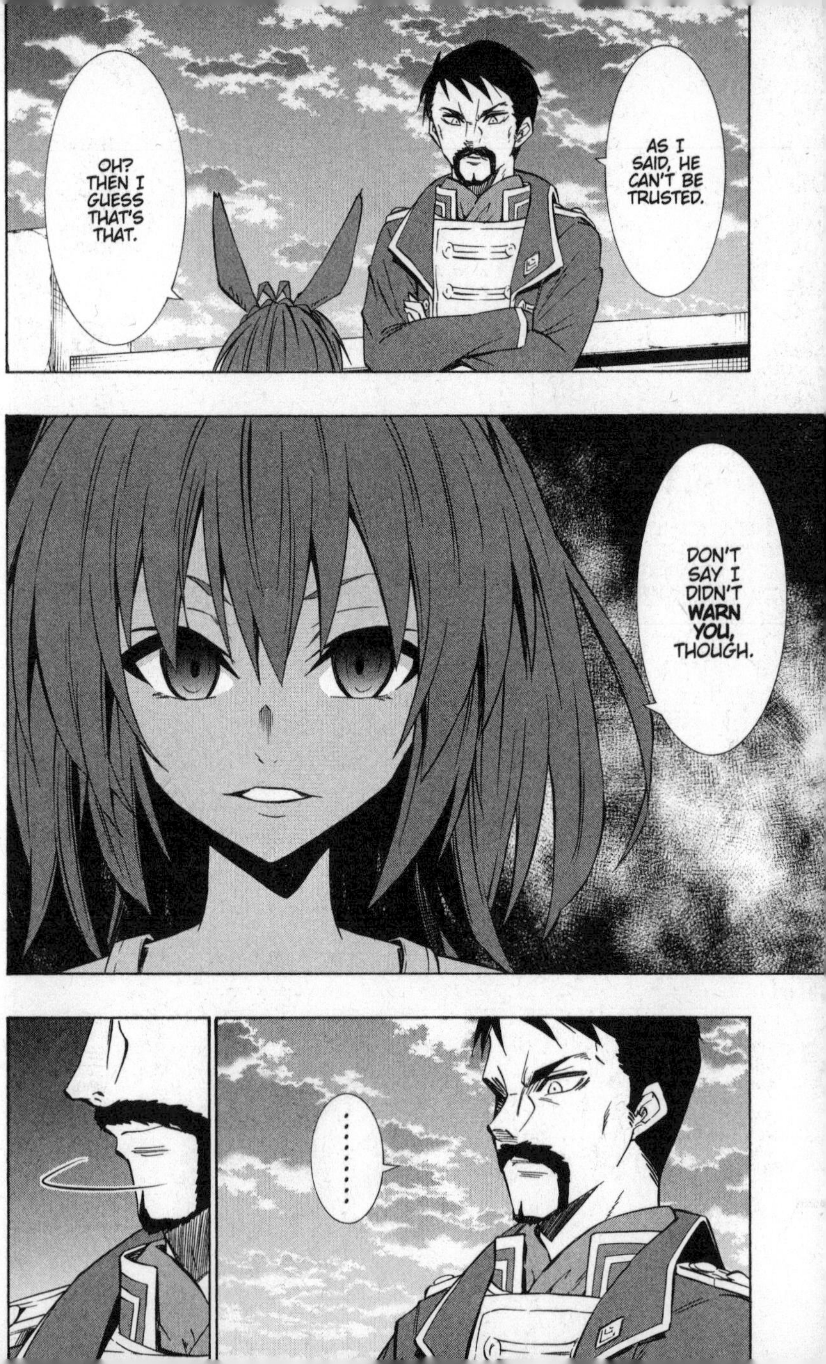
AS I SAID, HE CAN'T BE TRUSTED.
OH? THEN I GUESS THAT'S THAT.
DON'T SAY I DIDN'T **WARN YOU,** THOUGH.
......

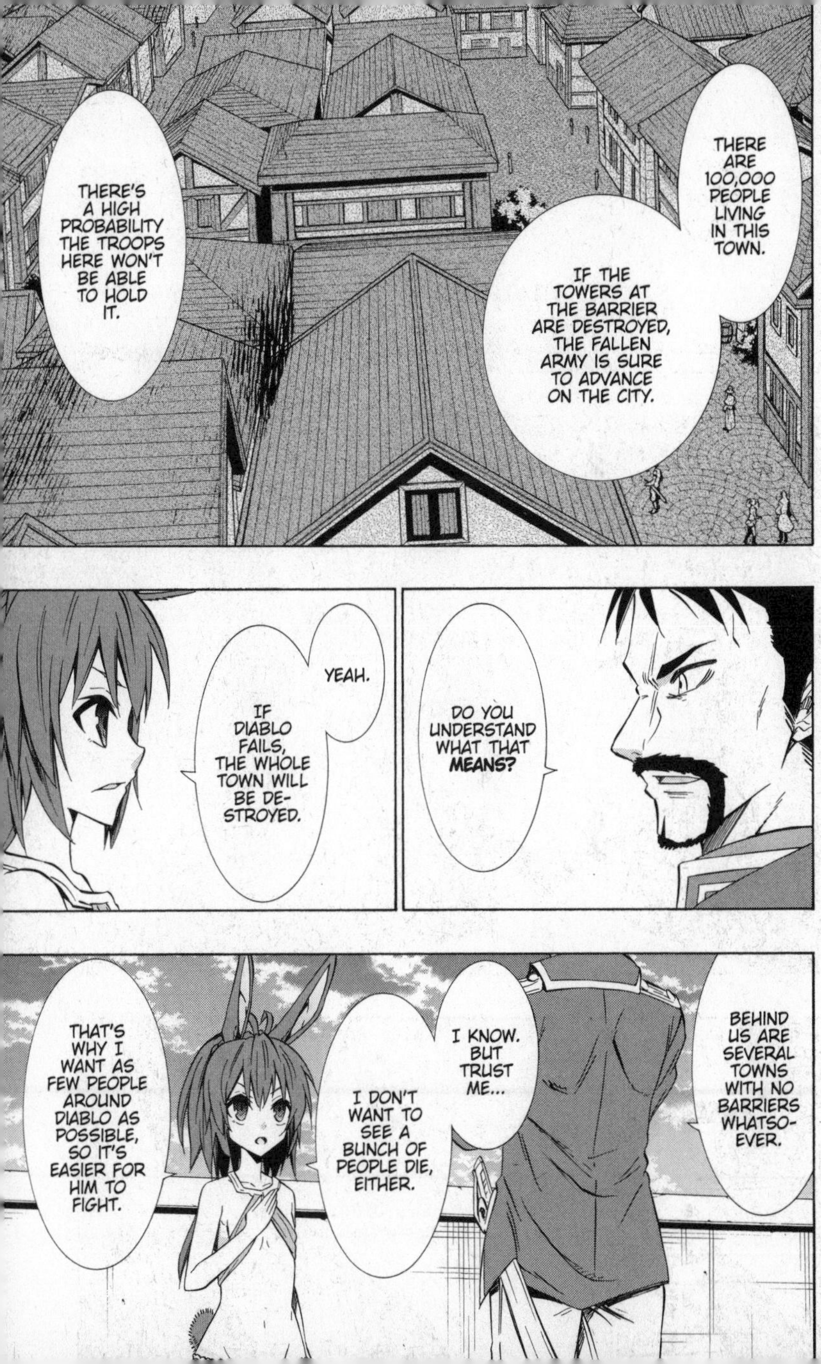
THERE ARE 100,000 PEOPLE LIVING IN THIS TOWN.
IF THE TOWERS AT THE BARRIER ARE DESTROYED, THE FALLEN ARMY IS SURE TO ADVANCE ON THE CITY.
THERE'S A HIGH PROBABILITY THE TROOPS HERE WON'T BE ABLE TO HOLD IT.
DO YOU UNDERSTAND WHAT THAT **MEANS?**
YEAH.
IF DIABLO FAILS, THE WHOLE TOWN WILL BE DE-STROYED.
BEHIND US ARE SEVERAL TOWNS WITH NO BARRIERS WHATSO-EVER.
I KNOW. BUT TRUST ME...
I DON'T WANT TO SEE A BUNCH OF PEOPLE DIE, EITHER.
THAT'S WHY I WANT AS FEW PEOPLE AROUND DIABLO AS POSSIBLE, SO IT'S EASIER FOR HIM TO FIGHT.

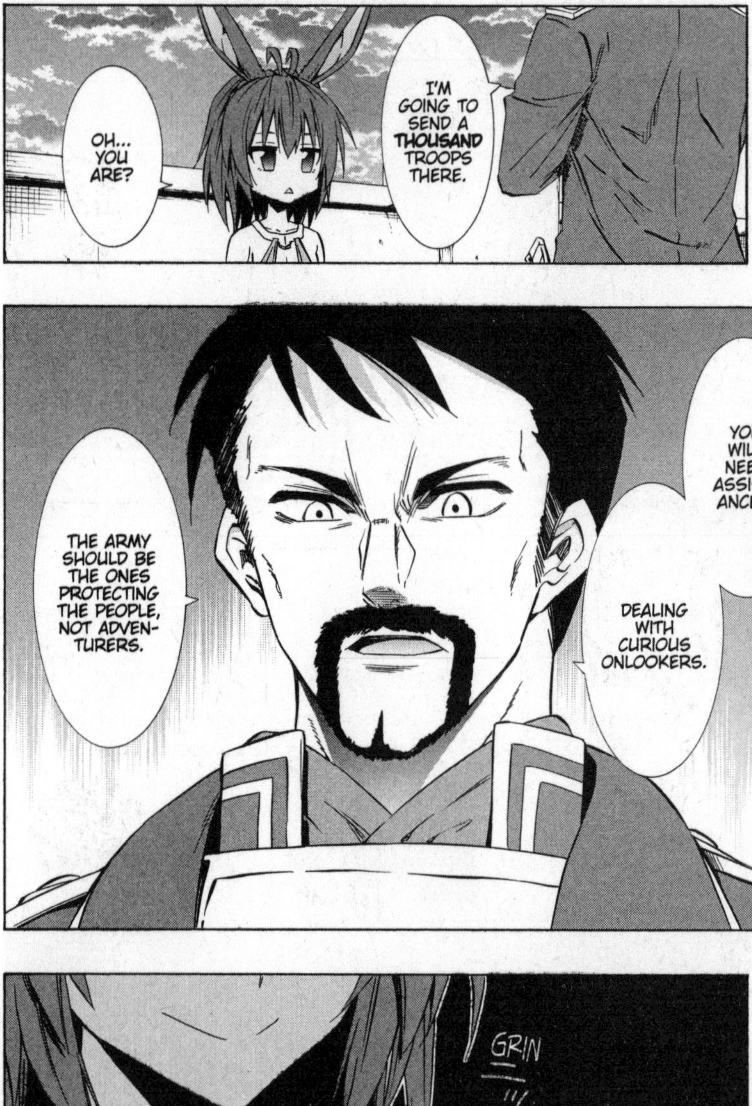
I'M GOING TO SEND A THOUSAND TROOPS THERE.
OH... YOU ARE?
YOU WILL NEED ASSISTANCE...
DEALING WITH CURIOUS ONLOOKERS.
THE ARMY SHOULD BE THE ONES PROTECTING THE PEOPLE, NOT ADVENTURERS.
GRIN

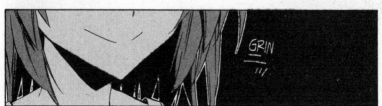

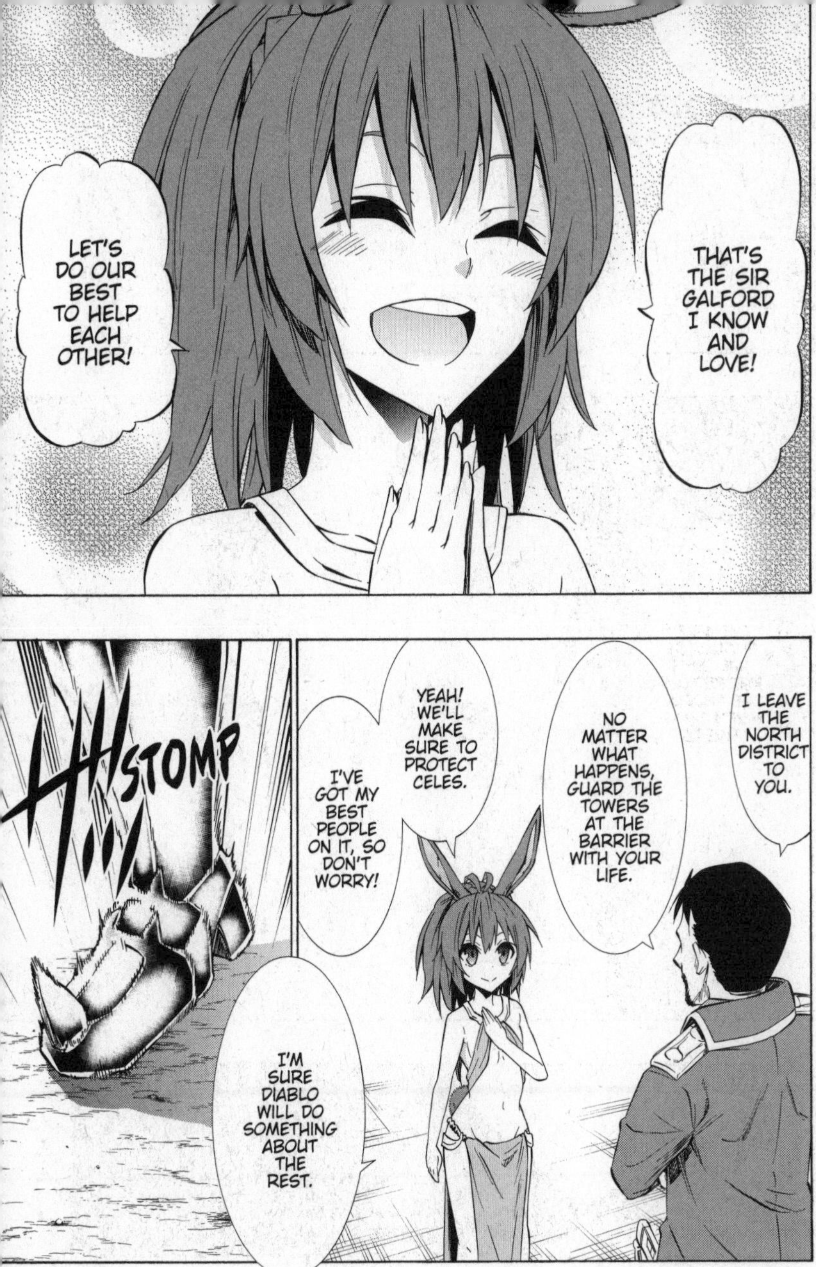
THAT'S THE SIR GALFORD I KNOW AND LOVE!
LET'S DO OUR BEST TO HELP EACH OTHER!
I LEAVE THE NORTH DISTRICT TO YOU.
NO MATTER WHAT HAPPENS, GUARD THE TOWERS AT THE BARRIER WITH YOUR LIFE.
YEAH! WE'LL MAKE SURE TO PROTECT CELES.
I'VE GOT MY BEST PEOPLE ON IT, SO DON'T WORRY!
I'M SURE DIABLO WILL DO SOMETHING ABOUT THE REST.
STOMP!!!

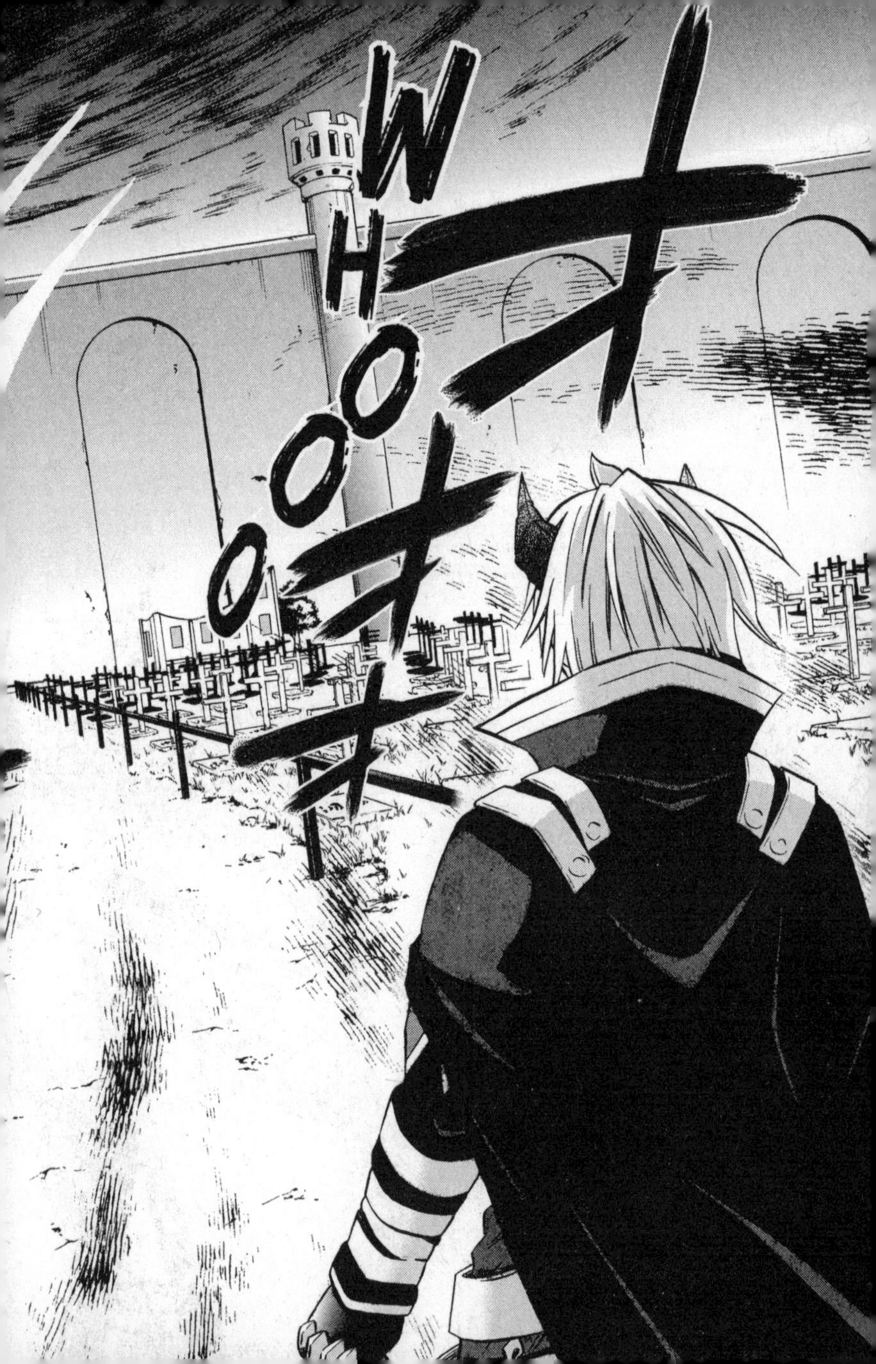
WHOOO

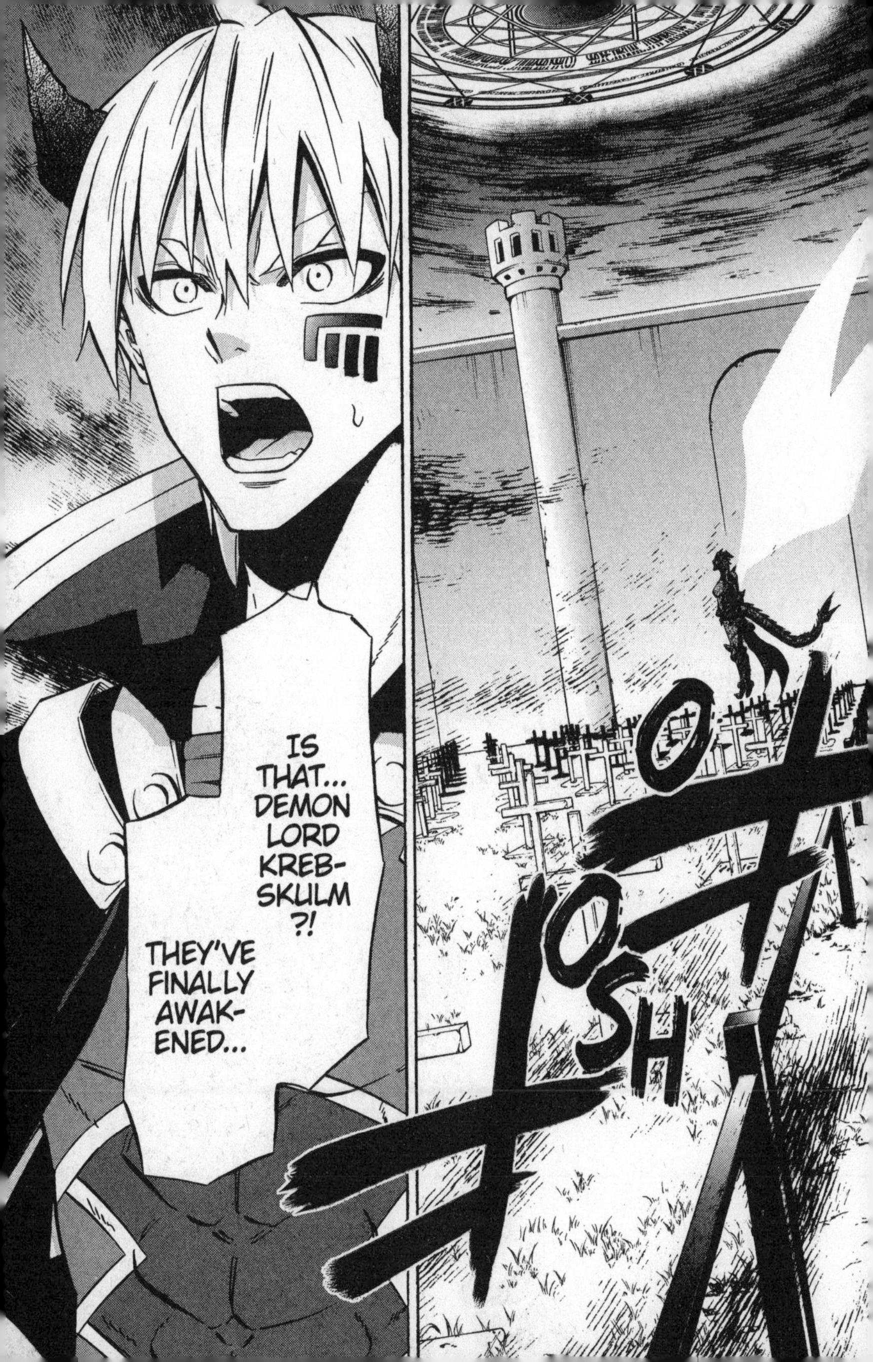
OOSH
IS THAT... DEMON LORD KREB-SKULM ?!
THEY'VE FINALLY AWAK-ENED...

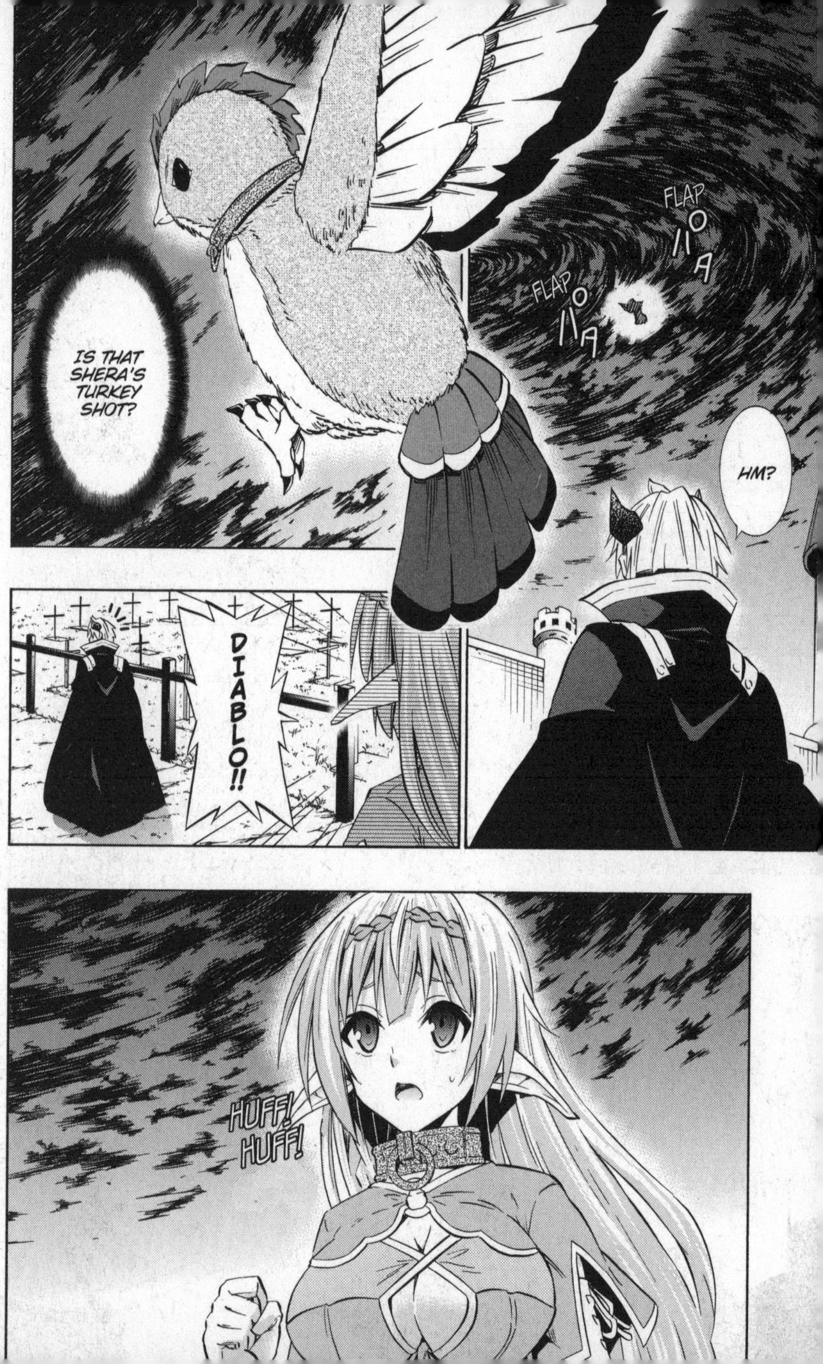
FLAP
FLAP
HM?
IS THAT SHERA'S TURKEY SHOT?
DIABLO!!
HUFF! HUFF!

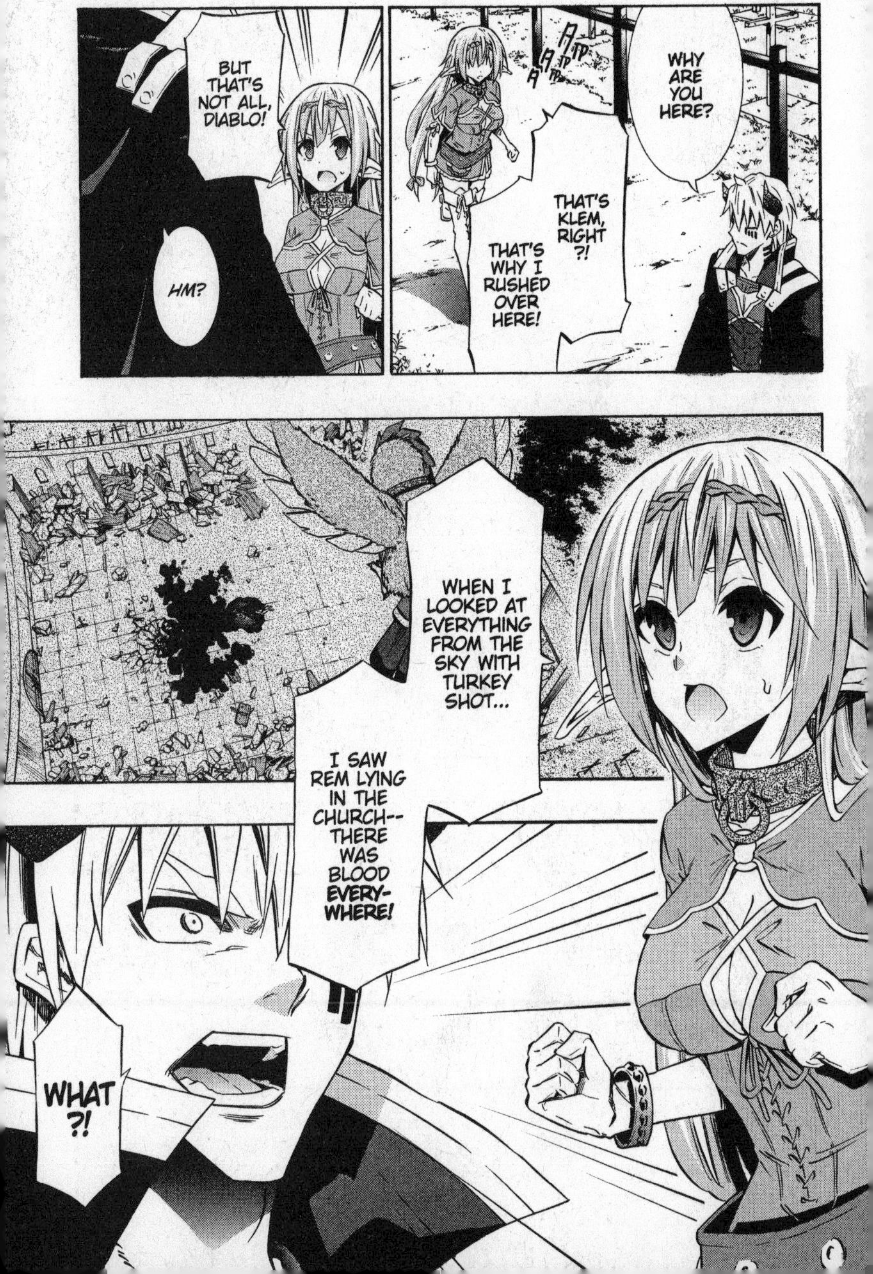
WHY ARE YOU HERE?
TAP TAP TAP TAP
THAT'S KLEM, RIGHT?!
THAT'S WHY I RUSHED OVER HERE!
BUT THAT'S NOT ALL, DIABLO!
HM?
WHEN I LOOKED AT EVERYTHING FROM THE SKY WITH TURKEY SHOT...
I SAW REM LYING IN THE CHURCH-- THERE WAS BLOOD EVERY-WHERE!
WHAT?!

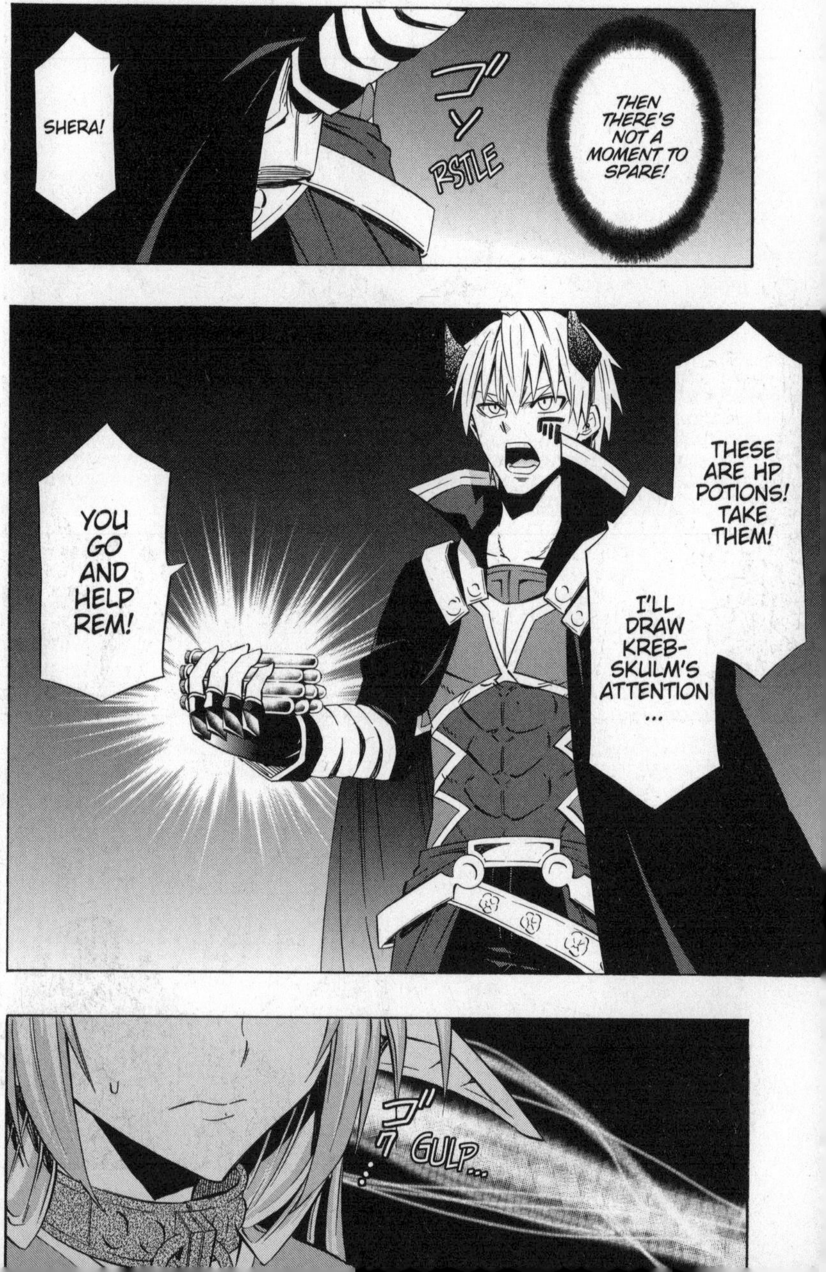
THEN THERE'S NOT A MOMENT TO SPARE!
ゴソ
RSTLE
SHERA!
THESE ARE HP POTIONS! TAKE THEM!
I'LL DRAW KREB-SKULM'S ATTENTION...
YOU GO AND HELP REM!
ゴク
GULP...

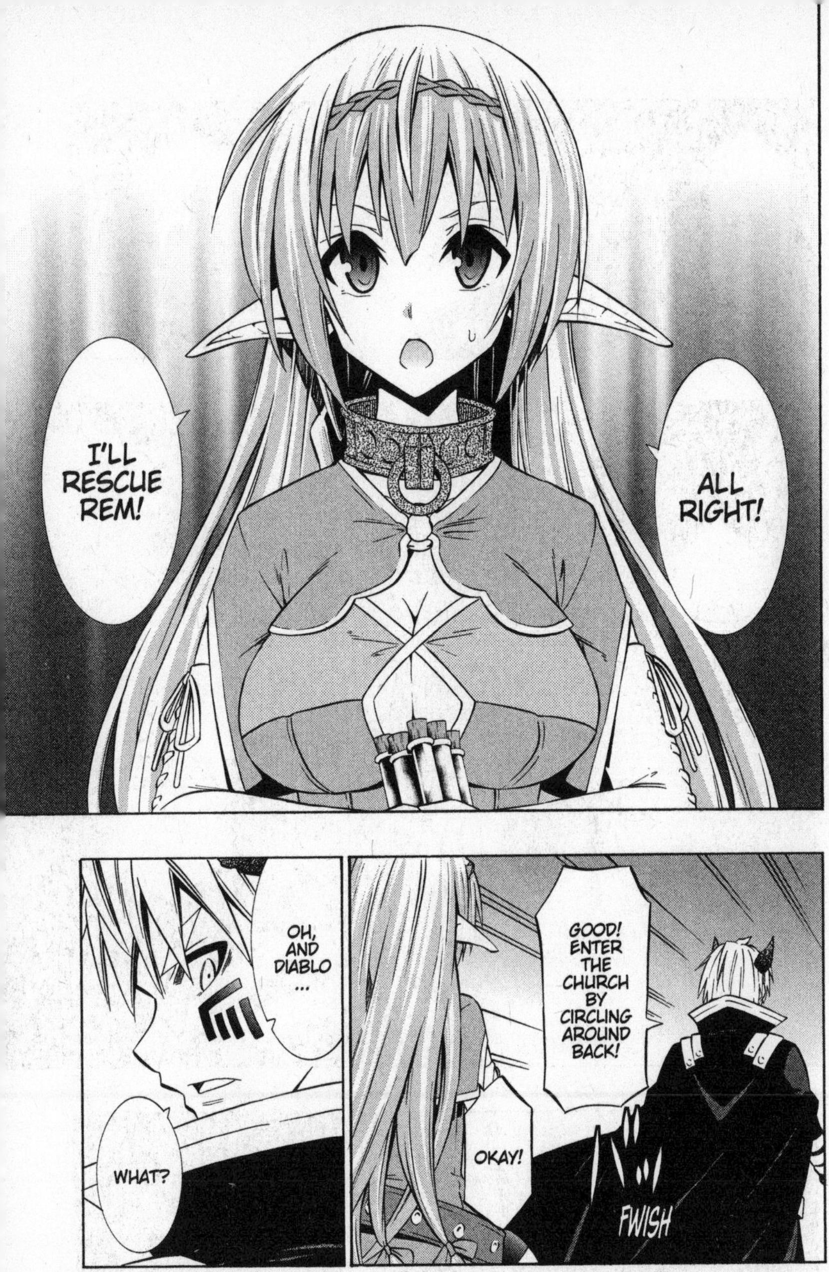
ALL RIGHT!
I'LL RESCUE REM!
GOOD! ENTER THE CHURCH BY CIRCLING AROUND BACK!
OKAY!
FWISH
OH, AND DIABLO ...
WHAT?

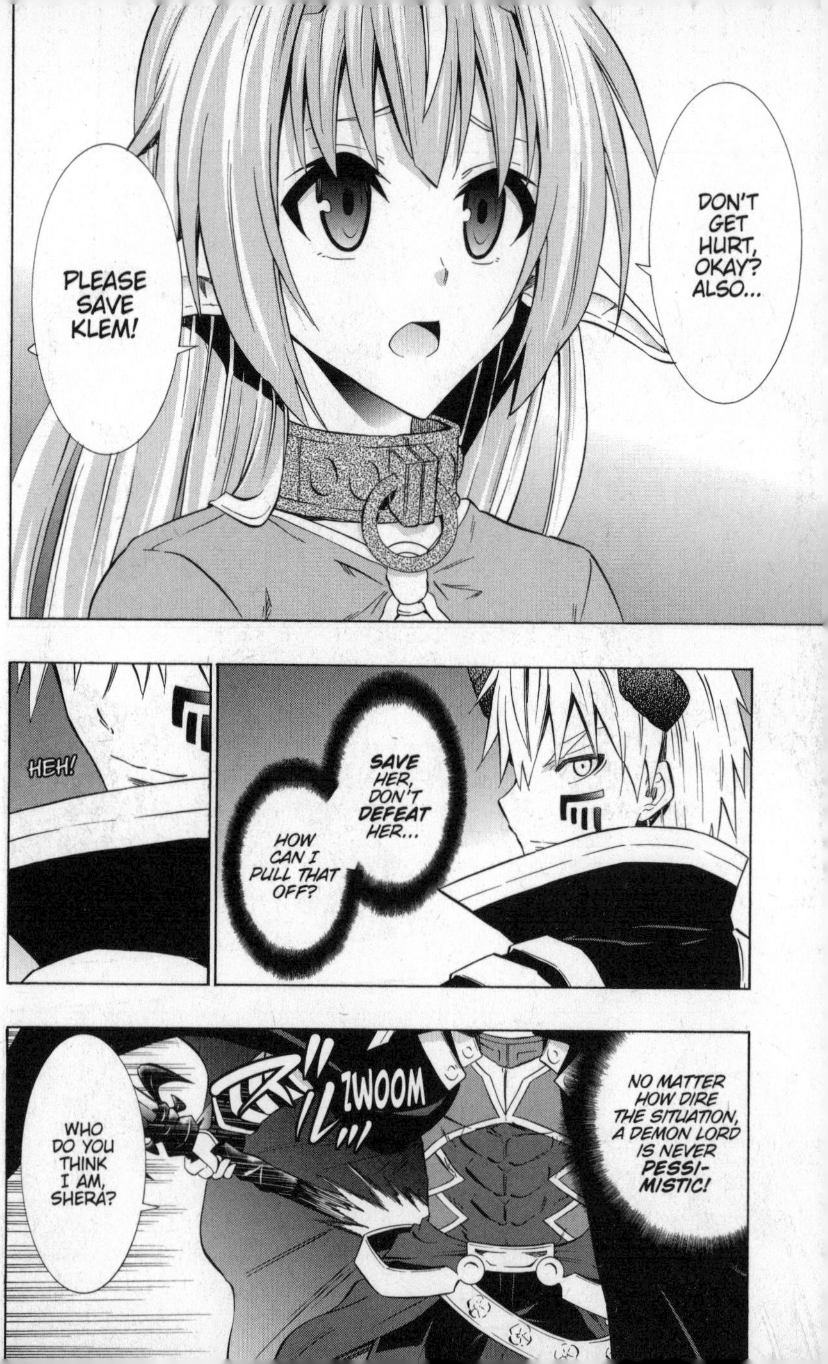
DON'T GET HURT, OKAY? ALSO...
PLEASE SAVE KLEM!
SAVE HER, DON'T DEFEAT HER...
HOW CAN I PULL THAT OFF?
HEH!
NO MATTER HOW DIRE THE SITUATION, A DEMON LORD IS NEVER PESSI-MISTIC!
ZWOOM
WHO DO YOU THINK I AM, SHERA?

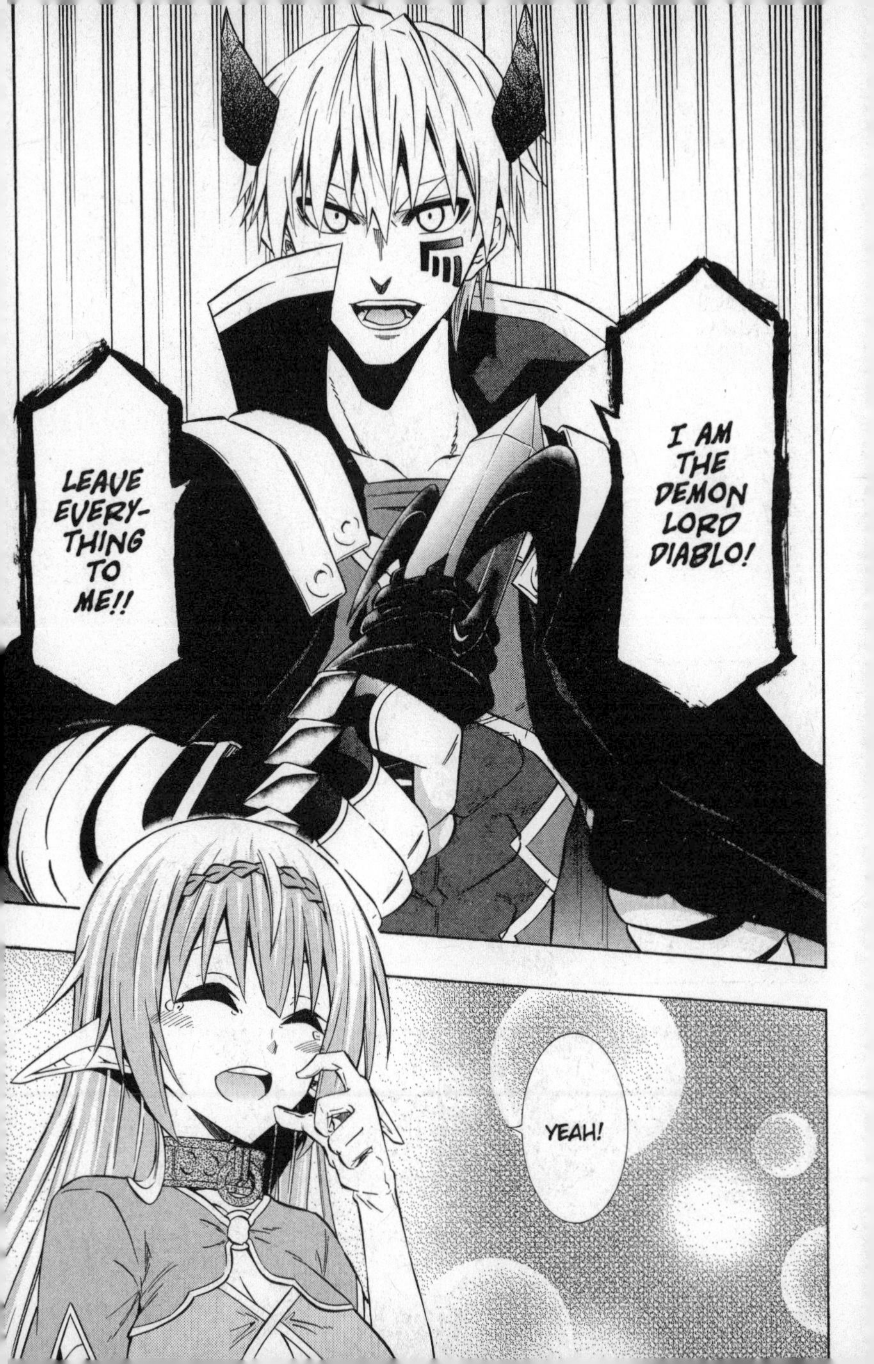
I AM THE DEMON LORD DIABLO!
LEAVE EVERY-THING TO ME!!
YEAH!

HOW NOT
TO SUMMON A
DEMON LORD

to be continued...

SPECIAL THANKS FOR VOLUME 7

YUKIYA MURASAKI
TAKAHIRO TSURUSAKI

《ASSISTANTS》

DAIKI HARAGUCHI

NAGISA

YUU TAKIGAWA

CHITOSE SAKURA

MURAICHI

MINATO SAITO

THANK YOU FOR READING!

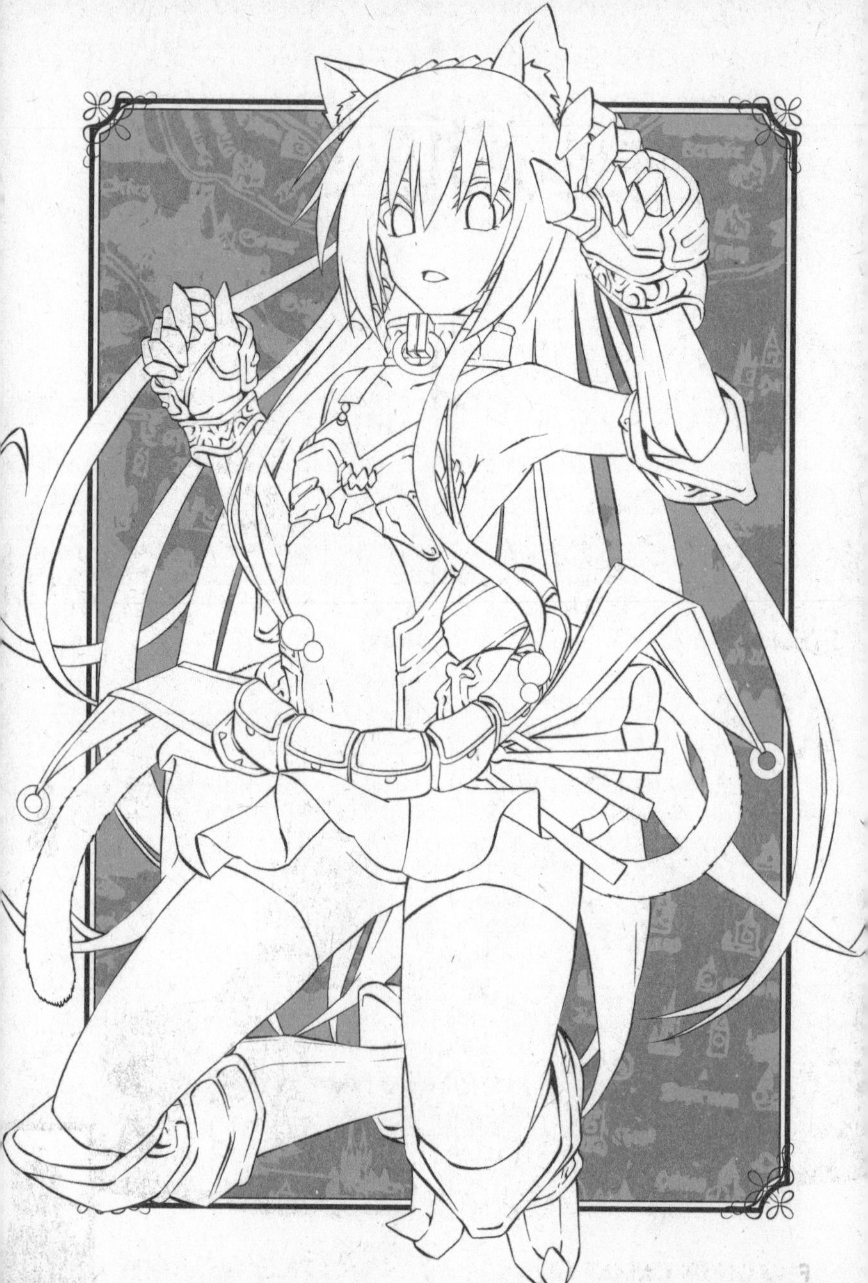